Stealing Light:

A Raven Chronicles

Anthology

Selected Work

1991–1996

D1603875

Stealing Light:
A Raven Chronicles
Anthology
Selected Work
1991–1996

Editors

Kathleen Alcalá

Phoebe Bosché

Paul Hunter

Stephanie Lawyer

Raven Chronicles Press
Seattle, Washington

FIRST EDITION

ISBN 978-0-9979468-5-7
ISBN 0-9979468-5-7
Library of Congress Control Number: 2018956836

Cover: Rick Bartow, *Raven Rain*, acrylic on panel, 12x12",
        copyright 2012. Artwork courtesy of the Estate of
        Rick Bartow and Froelick Gallery, Portland, Oregon.

Book Design: Phoebe Bosché, using 12/14 Adobe Jenson Pro typeface
Cover Design: Tonya Namura
Raven Press Logo: Scott Martin

Established in 1991, *The Raven Chronicles* is a Seattle-based literary organization that publishes and promotes artistic work and community events that embody the cultural diversity and multitude of imaginations of writers and artists living in the Pacific Northwest and other regions of the United States.

Raven Chronicles Press
15528 12th Avenue NE
Shoreline, Washington 98155-6226

editors@ravenchronicles.org
https://www.ravenchronicles.org

I like
the smell of art,
the look, taste, and feel of art.
—Bill Shively

This anthology is dedicated to our colleagues—
writers, artists, teachers, mentors, friends—
who are no longer with us:

Jody Aliesan
Rane Arroyo
Rick Bartow
Steven Jesse Bernstein
Don L. Birchfield
Abe Blashko
Charlie Burks
E.K. Caldwell
Omar S. Castañeda
Frank S. Fuji
Leonard Goodman
Donnell W. Hunter
Arthur J. Johnson
Marion Kimes
Dorothy Kneubuhl
Carolyn Leilani Lau
Freda Quenneville
Bill Shively
David Lloyd Whited
Don Wilsun

Siblings, Seattle, Photograph, by Irene H. Kuniyuki

TABLE OF CONTENTS

15 Foreword

19 Introductions

I Volume 1, Number 1, Summer/Fall 1991

24 Tess Gallagher, *Valentine Delivered By A Raven,*
cover poem
26 Arthur J. Johnson, *Monya,* fiction
30 Valerie J. Matsumoto, *No Room on the Ark,* poem
32 Philip H. Red Eagle, *Between Two Worlds,* An
Interview with Leslie Marmon Silko

II Volume 1, Number 2, Winter 1991-92

38 Daniel F. Aga, *Between Ocean and Sky,* fiction
45 Steven Jesse Bernstein, *Pictures of The War,* creative
nonfiction, introduction by Phoebe Bosché
52 John Enright, *Teaching Thoreau,* poem
36 Heid Ellen Erdrich, *Worlds from Water,* cover poem
54 Dorothy Kneubuhl, *O Le Uila,* poem
55 Richard Ploetz, *Hunter,* fiction
58 Stephen Thomas, *A Man Walks Into A Bar,* poem

III Volume 1, Number 3, Spring 1992

63 Kathleen de Azevedo, *Rosea Socorro Katz, Coconut,* fiction
76 Alice Derry, *The Woman Who Loved Dahlias,* poem
79 Lauren Kaushansky, *After Reading Raven Stories,
I Remember Stealing,* poem
60 Duane Niatum, *Raven's Fear of Growing White,*
cover poem
81 Don Wilsun *Men Are Slow,* poem

IV Volume 2, Number 1, Summer/Fall 1992

84 Phoebe Bosché, *Me and The Other,*
An Interview with Charles Johnson
96 Leonard Goodman, *Stone Crossing,* novel excerpt
102 Marion Kimes, *& Now We Come To Making Love,* poem
82 Elizabeth Woody, *The last salmon . . .,* cover poem
103 Janet Yoder, *River Talk with Vi Hilbert,* essay excerpt

V Volume 2, Number 2, Winter 1992-93

108 Kathleen Alcalá, *Notes from the Inter-American Bookfair,
San Antonio, Texas, October 15-18, 1992,* essay
132 Kathleen Alcalá, *Deep Painting, An Interview with
Alfredo Arreguín*
113 Anna Bálint, *Bus Terminal,* poem
106 Sharon Hashimoto, *Okasan: From The Journal
She Keeps In Her Head,* cover poem
115 Donnell Hunter, *The Owl,* poem
116 Paul Hunter, *How Deep Down,* poem
119 Belle Randall, *King Limbo,* poem
121 Bill Ransom, *The Liberation of Father Free,* fiction
131 David Lloyd Whited, *The Killdeer,* poem

VI Volume 2, Number 3, Spring 1993

140 Bart Baxter, *Peace For The Arsonist,* poem
143 James Bertolino, *Whales,* poem
144 D.L. Birchfield, *Slouching Toward Hillerman,* essay
150 Lise Erdrich, *Bluejay,* story
164 Philip H. Red Eagle, *The Museum Space: Mixing
Metaphors,* An Interview with Fred Wilson
154 David Romtvedt, *Sleeping Room,* fiction
138 Joyce Thompson, *Hatching Song,* cover poem
160 David Lloyd Whited, *Four Views of the Desert: Our Ennui,
Her Ennui, His Ennui, Their Ennui,* poem

VII   Volume 3, Number 1, Summer 1993

172 James Bertolino, *The Swallow*, poem
173 James Bertolino, *The Jeweler*, poem
174 Lise Erdrich, *Red-Eyed Helldiver*, story
176 Paul Hunter, *Executioner*, poem
190 Stacey Levine, *Breath*, prose poem
178 Tiffany Midge, *Cowboys & Indians*, poem
179 Tiffany Midge, *Written in Blood*, poem
180 dan raphael, *untitled*, prose poem
181 Eddie Silva, *A Horse For My Father*, poem
182 Marilyn Stablein, *Sacred Waters*, essay

VIII   Volume 3, Number 2, Winter 1993-94
200 Dina Ben-Lev, *Down From Masada*, poem
203 Phoebe Bosché, *New Souls Then, October 30, 1993*,
     collage poem
204 Paul r Harding, *Sweetest*, poem
206 Paul r Harding, *Florida, Miami*, poem
209 Joycelyn Moody, *When We Won The Nobel Prize*, essay
213 John Olson, *The Sweat*, essay
219 Freda Quenneville, *Still Life At Snoqualmie Falls*, poem

IX   Volume 3, Number 3, Spring 1994

224 Jody Aliesan, *Singing the Old Way*, essay
228 D.L. Birchfield, *Sanctuary*, essay
231 Scott Martin, *Integrating Style with Substance*,
     An Interview with Abe Blashko
222 Lawrence Revard, *Crow Speaks To Wolf*, cover poem
244 Nico Vassilakis, *The Allure of Us*, poem

X   Volume 4, Number 1, Summer/Fall 1994

248 E.K. Caldwell, *The Business of Writing*,
     An Interview with Sherman Alexie

256 Nancy Cherry, *Climbing Together, Late Afternoon*, poem
257 Gary Curtis, *Paris Dreams*, creative non-fiction
263 Gregory Hischak, *The Prodigal Sock Sits And Spins In The Big Picture*, fiction
265 Larry Laurence, *Love Poem In Winter*, poem
266 Nora Martin, *Prayer Flags On Barbed Wire*, essay
271 Carter Revard, *Refrigerator*, poem
272 Ann Spiers, *Dressing the Salmon Queen, Olympic Peninsula*, poem

XI Volume 4, Number 2, Spring 1995

288 Sean Brendan-Brown, *Everything Repeated Many Times*, poem
276 Alicia Hokanson, *The Iceman*, poem
278 Stephan Magcosta, *They Dance Alone*, fiction
282 Kevin Miller, *Before God*, poem
274 Belle Randall, *Heavenly Blue Holiday*, cover poem
283 Belle Randall, *Pursuing The Run Away Hub Cap*, poem
284 Mira Chieko Shimabukuro, *Momentary Comfort*, poem
286 Stephen Thomas, *Raingem*, poem
287 Qiu Xiaolong, *Don Quixote In China*, poem

XII Volume 5, Number 1, Summer/Fall 1995

292 Diana Abu-Jaber, *Irene*, fiction
307 D.L. Birchfield, *The Dunes*, fiction
310 Alice Derry, *Deer Stories*, poem
312 Fatima Lim-Wilson, *A Barren Woman Puts On Her Man Costume*, poem
314 Anna Odessa Linzer, *The Girl Who Always Thought It Was Summer*, poem
316 Kathleen Marie, *Red Geranium in a Folger's Coffee Can*, poem
318 Donna Miscolta, *Elena's Dance*, fiction
322 Amy Pence, *Georgia Red Earth*, poem

323 Arthur Tulee, *Plumes of White Rising
(Touching Hanford)*, creative nonfiction
328 William Reichard, *My Mother's Garden,
June, 1994*, poem
330 Susann Wilbur, *The Twins From Tohoku*, fiction

XIII   Volume 5, Number 2, Winter 1995-96

346 Rane Arroyo, *Kiko*, poem
347 Rane Arroyo, *Speedy Gonzalez, Jr.*, poem
348 Diane Glancy, *8 Ball*, poem
344 Diane Glancy, *Story*, cover prose poem
350 Amy Halloran, *Six of the Days of Love*, fiction
352 Dawn Karima Pettigrew, *Manna in Gallup*, fiction
356 Margaret Randall, *Exorcism*, poem
358 Trisha Ready, *Walking the Mysteries*, fiction
363 Ron Welburn, *Chewing the Sweetflag*, poem

XIV   Volume 5, Number 3, Spring 1996

366 Kathleen Alcalá, *Spirits of the Ordinary*, a play
364 Ken Gollersrud Ayala, *Recipe para Los Reyes y
Las Reinas*, cover poem
374 Stephan Magcosta, *Slouching Toward Aztlán*, essay
377 Armando Martínez, *Where the Quinault Runs into
the Pacific: A Conversation with an Elder*, poem
379 John Olson, *The Culture of Poetry, Survival in the
21st century: Does Poetry Matter?*, essay
384 JT Stewart, *New Colossus*, poem
386 Carletta Carrington Wilson, *kiss/her. that/she. don't/
know/howwww.*, poem

XV   Volume 6, Number 1, Fall 1996

390 Omar S. Castañeda, *Love's Labor Lost: Equality*, fiction
399 Tiffany Midge, *For The Lummi Girl Who Found Her
Magic In Horses*, poem

402 Kristin Naca, *Bitch*, poem

405 Robert Shimabukuro, *Glimpses*, nonfiction

441 Barbara Earl Thomas, *Some Fly*, fiction

419 Gail E. Tremblay, *En La Casa Museo de Augustin Lara, Veracruz*, poem

421 Gail E. Tremblay, *Casa de Cortez, Antigua, Veracruz*, poem

423 Carletta Carrington Wilson, *Iconography of the Slain*, fiction

450 Cultural Geography: A Raven Forum Series, *The Role of the Poet in Contemporary Culture(s)*

    450 Deborah A. Miranda

    454 Jody Aliesan

    457 Roy D. Wilson

XVI Raven Notes

    460 Notes, Permissions, and Publication Credits

    463 Biographical Notes

        463 Artists/Illustrators

        471 Writers

        512 Foreword

        513 Editors

    510 Ads

    515 Acknowledgments

    516 Publisher Information

LIST OF ARTISTS AND ILLUSTRATORS
Pages art/illustrations appear on:

Alfredo Arreguín: 25: Raven cover 1991; 133, 230
Kree Arvanitas: 35, 459
Rick Bartow: Anthology cover artwork; 61: Raven cover 1992
Abe Blashko: 223: Raven cover1994; 233, 243
Gary Curtis: 101, 211, 259
Anita Endrezze: 153, 281
Frank S. Fujii: 107: Raven cover 1992-1993
Charles (Chas) Johnson: 95
Irene H. Kuniyuki: 6, 175, 373
Gayanna Magcosta: 365: Raven cover 1996
Scott Martin: 269
Harlow Morgan: 290-291: Raven cover 1995
Fran Murphy: 171: Raven cover 1993
Caroline Orr: 53
Mary Randlett: 139: Raven cover 1993; 221, 376
Elizabeth Sandvig: 345: Raven cover 1995-1996
Joe Scaylea: 105, photo of Vi Hilbert
Marilyn Stablein: 189
Jon Strongbow: 277, 306, 326-327, 385
Barbara Earl Thomas: 199: Raven cover 1993-1994;
            389: Raven cover 1996; 427, 440
Terry Turrell: 275: Raven cover 1995; 289
Theodore C. Van Alst, Jr.: 420
Patti Warashina: 246-247: Raven cover 1994
Gloria White-Calico: 62, 75; 83: Raven cover 1992
Carletta Carrington Wilson: 362
Dean Wong: 401, 410

Foreword

I did not have a second's hesitation to say "Yes!" when asked to write the foreword to *Stealing Light: A Raven Chronicles Anthology, Selected Work 1991-1996.* The editors, Kathleen Alcalá, Phoebe Bosché, Paul Hunter, and Stephanie Lawyer, are esteemed writers in their own right, involved in various aspects of publishing, teaching, and literary activism who have worked to broaden the range of literary voices in the Pacific Northwest and beyond. Kathleen Alcalá and Phoebe Bosché are two of the three founding editors, and Paul Hunter and Stephanie Lawyer have served as guest editors to the journal over the years.

To read these pages is to find missives from the frenetic and demonic to the plaintive and searching, from love under the tender lagoons of our nails to deep down secret places of memory. From Alaska to Jordan, Mexico to Hawaii, via owl and whale, there is plenty in these pages for everyone. What I love here is the range of voice, the span of geography, days explosive like gasoline in Kristin Naca's "Bitch" poem and the lifetimes to recover roots described in Kathleen Marie's "Red Geranium in a Folger's Coffee Can." Then there are the brilliant, generous, insightful conversations with writers, painters, professors, and poets, as well as valuable notes from writers conferences and forums.

The collection begins fittingly with Tess Gallagher's "Valentine Delivered by a Raven." Traditionally considered messages of tenderness, pledges of love and hope, valentines also work as dispatches that assert one's existence—"I see you!" they insist, "You are not ignored!" Gallagher, in her poem, writes, "Language, / that great concealer, is more than generous, gives / always what it doesn't have." By the time one reaches the last pages of this book, the Gallagher line unfolds to its richness like the glory of a ripe summer meadow under the spell of mid-morning sun.

In the opening interview, Leslie Marmon Silko responds to a question posed by Philip H. Red Eagle, the third founding editor of *Raven Chronicles*, by saying, "(I)t never is that simple, you know.

Everything is beautifully complex," referring to the ambiguities of language and history. In these pages, language is betrayer and medium, never savior. Tiffany Midge exposes the tyranny of the dictionary in her brilliant poem, "Written in Blood:"

.... *This 1961 Cardinal Edition Thesaurus*

I depended upon has betrayed me. Betrayed my Indian kin. With this language there are times I feel I'm betraying myself. In my search for synonyms for *murderer*, I find *Cain*,

assassin, barbarian, gunman, brute,
hoodlum, killer, executioner, butcher,
savage, Apache, redskin.

Many of the works collected here wrestle with the (in)ability of language to capture human experience. They expose the myriad ways in which historical events have been shaped into constructs hollow and risible, if not for their devastating corollaries. Heidi Ellen Erdrich writes, "what in 1492 was found / was also lost." Language gives away more than it offers not so much in what words say, but in what they omit. Words are never enough to breach the chasm of experience from one human to the next. But how worth it, the journey, to breach the gap, for it is also filled with light, beauty, and joy. John Olson in his essay, "The Sweat," describes his first experience in a sweat lodge, "I felt closer to my real self, closer to earth, closer to the light that is sometimes found in the darkest of places," he writes. Stealing light from channels rigged on the printed page to spread over the limbic channels of our bodies—that is what this book does.

In many ways, these poems and stories are also works of recovery. Recovery of memory as in Robert Shimabukuro's tender treatment of the brother he lost to AIDS. The one brother who, when they were children, guarded him when his breath succumbed to rabid asthma attacks. Recovery of one's humanity after fighting in a war as in Steven Jesse Bernstein's urgent and sobering "Pictures of the War." Recovery of history as in Carletta

Carrington Wilson's fiction enacting the indomitable agency of captured Africans crossing the Middle Passage, who choose to end their lives by hurling themselves and their children into the ocean rather than be forever enslaved.

The feelings and ideas captured in these pages simmered enough down under in the guts and marrow of the writers that engendered them in sweat lodges, in seaside caves macerating with sand and salt, on the haunches of deer, clinging to bear's musk. These are stories woven with horse's dreams tied with ancestor's losses turned fire and flower. These are stories imbued with that famous Toni Morrison's dictum, "If there's a book that you want to read, but it hasn't been written yet, then you must write it." I clearly felt the power of the authors' yearning and necessity leaping off each page. I invite you, dear reader, to relish their work as much as I did.

—*Claudia Castro Luna*
Washington State Poet Laureate (2018-2020)
Seattle, August, 2018

Introductions

Kathleen Alcalá: We know that glimmer in your eye. We've been at it again, you think, collaborating in dark corners with Coyote and Raven.

But really, we are here to share light. Maybe our authority figures have got you down, aren't living up to your ideals. Maybe it's time to get some of that shiny stuff out of their hands and into your beaks. We offer everything from Tess Gallagher's poem "Valentine Delivered by a Raven" to "Cultural Geography"—essays on "The role of the Poet in Contemporary Culture(s)" by Deborah A. Miranda, Jody Aliesan, and Roy D. Wilson. We give you back the treasures you have shared with us. Think of it as a potlatch, where the gifts only retain their value as long as they are shared with others.

The early interviews and notes we include here are a way to share, in the moment, our encounters with remarkable people. Our readings and online presence allows the magazine to remain flexible and responsive to current affairs, while preserving written responses to share at a later time with a wider audience. The people I have met along the way continue to inspire and push me to make art capable of changing the world.

We started *The Raven Chronicles* because no one else would; complaining about the state of affairs seldom changes it. Picking a clamshell up in your beak and dropping it in a parking lot might bring change, or at least lunch.

The stories, poetry, and art in this anthology are ongoing proof of like-minded tricksters. As long as your spirits of empathy, compassion, and rebellion continue, we can take heart, we can show heart to each other. If you haven't read *Raven* before, this sampling from our first fifteen issues will dazzle you. More to follow.

Phoebe Bosché: *The Raven Chronicles* began back in 1990, when Kathleen Alcalá and Philip Red Eagle guest-edited several Seattle Arts Commission Newsletters. They realized that there was a lack of diverse, multicultural writing being published in Seattle and the Northwest region in general. They thought: let's start our own magazine! Phil knew me through my work with Red Sky Poetry Theatre, editing *SkyViews* and other Red Sky Press Publications, so he asked me to join them. The result of this initial collaboration has been a magazine that, according to Kathleen, "is not so much a collective as a dialectic magazine—we hope to reflect several sides of each topic."

Stealing Light is the product of five years of on and off work. Selections were made as far back as 2014-2015 by the main editors, Kathleen, Phoebe, Paul, and Stephanie, with input from Tiffany Midge and Matt Briggs. Two things hindered the easy and speedy completion of the manuscript: many of the writers were dead or missing in action, and most of the selected work had to be retyped—we didn't have the old mac floppy disks anymore. Matt had digitized most of the earliest *Raven* magazines, but the resulting printouts were difficult to work with. So we dug in, and retyped nearly all of the work chosen for this anthology. Then we had to find the authors of the work who were now scattered all over the United States—literally. It sometimes meant looking through obituaries to find contact information, as even in this age of social media not all writers and artists are hooked into the tangled web of the internet.

Of the hundreds of poems, essays, fiction, stories, and interviews we published in the first six years, in the first fifteen issues of *Raven Chronicles*, we selected work that reflects the spirit of the artists and writers grouped together, by accident and choice, in that particular time frame. We hope this anthology will give readers a glimpse of the Raven cosmos as seen through the eyes of tricksters and rascals, teachers and mentors, storytellers and visionaries. And perhaps, just perhaps, through these pages you will understand what the late Vi Hilbert, Skagit tribal elder, meant when she said, "It's so important for audiences to know that there was an ancient language that belonged here on this land . . . that there was a language of the first people." We hope that the tales in *Stealing Light* take readers on journeys into the past and present—bringing more light to the future.

Paul Hunter: Some good and necessary magazines envision no gathering, and have no conscious social component to them at all. Where artists might find themselves embedded in a mix of strangers, becalmed in a sea of indifference, where there is no larger focus or stated purpose other than that of the editors' general acceptance of society at large. Such a magazine may slowly feed individual reputations, offer critiques and insights, but its social function is minimal, decently hidden if not absent altogether. Such a magazine may speak to careers but feels and acts like a job or work, in both the reading and the editing.

But then there are magazines, admittedly rarer, that for better or worse encourage, accumulate, and represent community. Which sometimes has to sneak up and surprise us. Whether self-appointed or launched with a promise of social engagement, such magazines are what I think all magazines should aspire to be. Speaking to the moment, to its tensions, losses, and abiding hopes is never easy. It takes a rare bird to find and engage a wider audience, to summon and share the best arts among us all, through thick and thin to carry on, even allowed an occasional edge of chiding or mockery.

Raven Chronicles from the first has offered no club or clique, but a welcoming podium to foster the expression of talent and insight, and beyond that to engage in a wider conversation about issues of inclusion, identity, kinship, and cultural diversity. Each of us has a take on the ongoing human parade, a valuable viewpoint to share. This magazine found itself exploring and engaging large, tough issues from the first. And so, reading the magazine cover to cover for me has always felt like a healing and steadying act. *Raven Chronicles* has found ways of inviting and including young writers, and beginning writers of all ages, as well as those in mid-career, and acknowledged masters of their craft. It appreciates how many dishes are brought to the table, how many rich and inviting recipes. This magazine has always offered vigorous, nutritious, and healthy table-talk, awake to the moment's possibilities. The depth, breadth, engagement—and longevity—of the pieces in this anthology drawn from the magazine make a substantial statement about the community that grounds and shares this undertaking.

It is a give-and-take, a back-and-forth, that I have been proud and humbled to share.

Stephanie Lawyer: One late summer's evening in 1998, Kathleen Alcalá and I ran into each other at Colman Dock while we waited for the ferry back to Bainbridge Island. My family and I were recent transplants from Hong Kong, where I had worked as an editor and agent, and Kathleen suggested I get in touch with Phoebe Bosché, managing editor at *The Raven Chronicles*, to see if I could participate in some way. And so began one of my longest and most gratifying connections during the twenty-odd years I lived in Seattle.

Raven had been publishing and promoting writers, poets, and artists since 1991, but I was largely unaware of its body of work until I met up with Phoebe. From a publishing perspective, I had never known anything quite like it. Although all writers are at some point "emerging," this magazine truly provided a receptive, encouraging space for new voices to thrive alongside those who were already well known. The diversity and abundance of its pages—literary and illustrated, local and international, traditional and experimental—were an exhilarating introduction to the cultures and perspectives of the Pacific Northwest.

Stealing Light is a celebration of *Raven's* first six years. Many of you will be familiar with the names and work of contributors in this collection. Others may be reading them for the first time. But all of you are in for a feast of storytelling, with something for everyone: poetry, short fiction, excerpts from novels and a play, essays, interviews, and a remarkable selection of original art. Dig in.

Philip H. Red Eagle: Back in 1989, I had been talking to Phoebe Bosché (Red Sky Poetry Theatre) about a multicultural literary journal of some kind. We agreed that it was much needed. Early in 1990, I applied as Guest Editor for the Seattle Arts Commission Newsletter and was picked for an editorship. Guest editors met with the person who was in charge of the newsletter for orientation in mid-Summer of 1990. It was there that I met the other guest editors, one of which was Kathleen Alcalá. We talked around the table and I realized as we sat there that when we were through with our stint we had the perfect opportunity to start planning an actual literary journal. As we left the meeting room I turned and said to Kathleen that between she and me and another friend (Phoebe) we could put together a multicultural literary journal. Kathleen said, "Let's do it!" Not long after we three began the process of developing our idea into a reality. We thought that the perfect title for the journal was *The Raven Chronicles*. In Northwest Native culture the Raven is a trickster character, but it is also a teacher. We worked very hard through the winter and came out with the first issue in the summer of 1991. That summer we won the "1991 Most Adventurous Publication Award" from the Bumbershoot Bookfair. It is an unbelievable twenty-seven years later, and we now move into a new role. We continue. 📖

Valentine Delivered By A Raven

Tess Gallagher

—for Alfredo and Ray

Its beak is red and it has a battlefield-look
as if it's had its pickings and come away
of its own volition. Elsewhere the Emperor Frederick
sleeps on, guarded by ravens, and may yet rise
from deathly slumber and walk the earth
again. Who knows what's long enough
when death's involved. I stand on my love's grave
and say aloud in a swoop of gulls over
the bay, "I kiss your lips, babe," and it's not
grotesque, even though the mind knows what it
knows, and mostly doesn't. Language,
that great concealer, is more than generous, gives
always what it doesn't have. I stare into the dazzling
impertinent eye of the messenger. He's
been tending the dead so long his eyes are garnets,
his wings cracked open to either side, two
fissures savage with light. I bend
in recognition and take up a holly bough left
as in the old adornment of doorways. The hard, red
berries glisten and tremble in their nest of
green, so when he speaks I hear him
with the attention of a red berry before a covetous
bright eye, and what I need I take
in empires before he flaps away on my love's errands
and I am cinnabar and fog in the doorway.

I

Volume 1, Number 1, Summer/Fall 1991

A Murder of Crows, Painting, by Alfredo Arrequín

Monya

Arthur J. Johnson

"I just don't know where that girl is today," Grandmother said again, opening the screen door to the front porch and peering up and down the sun-drenched dirt road. She turned around to face us again, her eyes seemed wide in shock behind the magnification of her thick glasses. She wiped her hands on her gaily-flowered apron as she usually did when she was worried, and rubbed my head as she passed me on her way to the kitchen.

"She's gonna be the perfect playmate for little Andrew this visit. Ain't gonna be like last time, Andrew ..." and her voice trailed off as the kitchen door swung behind her, then kept swinging back and forth for a little bit before it stayed shut.

"Go ahead and wash your hands, Andy," my mother said, agitatedly. But I knew, even though I was only six at the time, that she wasn't upset with me. It had begun with: "I'm worried about my mother, Paul," when we had just pulled out of the city for the long drive to Grandmother's country home. "She shouldn't be out there by herself at her age. Her friends are dead or dying off. She's out there in the middle of nowhere ..." and it had gone on and on for the whole ride. Even when I would wake up from my naps, sprawled on my back on the backseat of the car, looking up at the trees along the road, I would hear Mother going on and on and on.

All through dinner Grandmother would interrupt the conversation with things like, "I think I hear her coming up the walk now," and then she would run (well, a grandmotherly-type run, but not running by young peoples' standards) for the door and call out, "Monya, where have you been?" Then my parents would exchange silent glances over their forks paused in mid-air.

"Do you have a picture of Monya, Mama?" my mother finally asked as they sat on the porch after dinner and drank iced tea. Mother sat on the top step of the three wooden steps, Grandmother rocked in her wooden rocker, and my dad sat on the edge of the porch and practiced casting his fishing rod into the sea of almost lime green grass that spread before Grandmother's house and stretched to the seldom-traveled road. I sat behind the wheel of our car parked in the driveway, pretending to drive.

"Slow down, Son," my dad would say every now and then, laughing to himself.

But grandmother acted as if she hadn't heard my mother's question at all and continued, "I just don't know where Monya could be today. I told her my little grandson was coming. She was supposed to help me make a peach pie. She was supposed to climb up there and pick the peaches. Andrew can do it tomorrow, I suppose. It's just not like her." Her rocker began to squeak against the wooden floorboards as she rocked harder.

Crickets and night creatures began an ever-loudening symphony of chirps, grunts, and whistles as black velvet surrounded us all, and bugs performed a yellow lightning dance for us.

"Why don't you call her house, Mama? Maybe something's wrong," my mother suggested as she put her arm through Grandmother's and led her back into the house. My father lifted me up in his arms, first swinging me way over his head, which made me gasp and laugh and fart, then he put me under his arm like a package as we followed the women inside.

"You city people," Grandmother began in disgust. "This ain't like where you live where something bad is always happening to somebody. Besides, I don't believe Monya's people got a phone anyway. She be by tomorrow. You'll see."

Grandmother was standing over me when I opened my eyes the next morning. She was the first thing I saw, her eyes big and owlish behind those thick glasses of hers; her hair—her real and gray hair—peeking out from under the hairline of her dark brown wig; the little metal parts of her false teeth exposed in her hearty grin.

"Monya's here! Get dressed quick, now," and she cupped my small, clean-shaven head in her brown hands and kissed me on my forehead, leaving a damp wet spot, and left the room, humming to herself.

I rubbed the sand from the corners of my eyes as I sat on the edge of the bed for a moment, and heard the sizzling of the frying pan and the hundreds of songs the birds were singing by my window. I could hear Grandmother talking away downstairs, and occasionally laughing. I slipped on my jeans and my shoes, and a fresh T-shirt my parents had gotten for me at Hershey Park last month. I splashed my face with water—soap was to be used only at night because Mother said I must not wash away my natural oils—and brushed my teeth like Father had showed me—six strokes back and forth on each side of my mouth—because I was determined to have less than four cavities the next time I went to the dentist. I wanted that five dollars my dad promised me if my teeth improved.

Grandmother had her back to me when I entered the kitchen, and she was talking, talking, talking. The table was set, two places, pancakes heaped on both plates with a scoop of soft butter on the top of each stack, oozing down slowly like yellow rivers.

"Where is she, Grandma?" I asked. She turned around from the stove, looked at me, then at the empty chair.

"Why, Monya . . . Where is that girl?" she said as she walked from the kitchen to the dining room, into the living room and back.

"Monya?" she called out as she stood in the middle of the kitchen rubbing her hands on her apron. "Monya!" she exclaimed with annoyance.

Then she left the kitchen again, leaving the door swinging as she retraced her steps through the dining room. I sat down at the table and began to attack the sweet buckwheat pancakes, drowning them in the thick Karo syrup, spearing the juicy sausages with my fork to follow each mouthful of cakes.

"There you are!" I finally heard Grandmother say. "What are you doing in here? Andrew, come in here, please!" she shouted.

I stuffed a few more pancakes in my mouth and gulped some milk before obeying. When I pushed my way through the swinging door I saw Grandmother standing before the dining room mirror that stretched across the wall above the bureau.

"Come here, Andrew," she said as she reached out her hand to me without losing eye contact with the image in the mirror. "This is Monya," she explained.

*　*　*

When we brought Grandmother back from the hospital hours later, my parents draped tablecloths, towels, and sheets over the mirrors in the bedrooms, dining room, and bathroom. Mother told me to collect all the hand-held mirrors I could find. There was only one, a crystal-handled one on Grandmother's dresser.

Grandmother sat in her rocker on the porch, tired from the ordeal of the day—physical examinations and questions. She would not eat. She did not rock, but sat with her eyes closed as darkness descended.

I could hear my parents talking in the kitchen as I sat at Grandmother's feet. Her shoes were black and sturdy, thick-heeled lace-ups, and each shoe rested firmly on the planks of the porch. When I heard her lightly snoring, I sneaked back into the house, holding the screen door so that it did not slam shut behind me, and tiptoed into the dining room where one of Grandmother's shawls—a pink one—covered the mirror. I carefully stepped up on a dining room chair beside the bureau and lifted the edge of the shawl . . . looking for Monya. 📖

No Room on the Ark

Valerie J. Matsumoto

The other animals seemed to like it
well enough, even though
it was the only one of its kind.
How it had gotten aboard
the Noahs weren't sure.
It had strange ways:
It made a pillow of molted feathers,
left mysterious glyphs etched on the deck,
and for hours stood motionless
in contorted postures.
They had trouble keeping track of it.
When exploring with the otters
it looked sleek and compact; it seemed
more furry somehow when loping by
with the snow leopards; there was
a cunning light in its eye
when it played gin rummy with the wolves.
Oh, there was no denying
it made itself useful,
sorting millet and sunflower seeds
for the finches, concocting
savory stews and casseroles in the galley,
even cleaning litter boxes
without complaint.
But the Noahs remained suspicious
of this singular beast.
When Mr. Noah found it fixing
Mrs. Noah's Electrolux, when
Mrs. Noah overheard Mr. Noah consulting it
about a squabble between the raccoons, well,
it had to go.

On the thirty-ninth day they heaved it overboard
into the receding waters, clutching its pillow.
What irritated them most
was its lack of protest. Its eyes told them
they had proven predictable.
We have seen the last of it,
they congratulated themselves, starlight
gleaming on their lifted wine glasses.
But on the morning of the forty-first day,
they disembarked and found
a sodden pillow which they hastily consigned
to a rubbish heap and forgot
in the joy of stretching their legs and
leaving the barnyard stench of the ark.
Ultimately they decided it hadn't
really existed, that one awkward element
marring the symmetry of their journey.
Perhaps it had had its charms
but it was an obnoxious beast.

Between Two Worlds
An Interview with Leslie Marmon Silko

Philip H. Red Eagle

Leslie Marmon Silko, acclaimed Indian novelist, poet and playwright, was on the University of Washington campus for a quarter last year [1990]. Silko, the author of *Ceremony*, a novel about a mixed blood Indian coping in the deadly grey area between red and white cultures, was teaching courses as a visiting professor of English. While here, she shared some of her views on what it is to be an Indian artist, a storyteller caught between cultures and worlds.

Philip H. Red Eagle: How has your ethnic background influenced you as an artist?

Leslie Marmon Silko: I think it's really helped me to be of mixed blood—to be a breed.

We mixed bloods are sensitive to nuances and we seem to have a compulsion to communicate. That gets us into storytelling. We know that we have a white side and an Indian side and we don't want to give up anything we've gotten from either side, especially as children. So you're always trying to bring the conflicting sides together. You're born into it!

As a child, the difficult part was that the Indian was always there but the white was right there alongside it. Some people loved you and some didn't, but it was never along racial lines.

I wanted everyone to get along. That goes way back to early family things. I must have always known that I was from both sides. All I wanted in a child-like way was for it all to be OK. As a child, I couldn't understand why it couldn't be that way.

And I guess I'm still that way. I mean, there's no reason why it shouldn't be OK, except of course I've learned all the reasons why it isn't OK and why it gets worse when we are all grown up.

Red Eagle: How did this contribute to your development as a writer?

Silko: You're always hearing stories, one version or the other. You're hearing, "this is the way it is" or "that is the way it was." But later, after you've heard all the stories and know how different they are, you want to stop them and say, "Wait, it's not that simple!"

And it never is that simple, you know. Everything is beautifully complex. I hate it when people insist that everything is black or white—or more to the point, red and white. It isn't, you know. One side is not always right and the other side always wrong. We Indians weren't always the victims, and the whites the bad guys. Many of our misfortunes we contributed to, even brought on ourselves.

This picture that some have of our ancestors as simple savages living at one with all other creatures and nature is just a bunch of bull. Our people didn't screw things up as much for others, but they often screwed things up for themselves. They certainly weren't all noble savages or all noble anything else.

We can't go blaming just one group. We're all human beings. That's why we should all want to go live more and learn more—to try harder to understand these things."

Red Eagle: But much of your writing presents a clear, even strident Indian point of view. How does this fit how you feel?

Silko: What I've said about wanting everything to be OK, about wanting to bring people together, about not placing all the blame on one people, that's the way I feel personally, as a living human being. Yet, in some of my writing I'm really angry. I'm not always certain where all that anger—even hatred—comes from. In some of my stories, then, it is "we and they," and "us and them."

There's a difference between what I do as a writer and what I do as a person. I just tell stories, but there's some part of me that's truly angry and mad. So some of the stories come out that way, really brutal. And I'm sort of surprised.

Red Eagle: You've said that people need legends. What do you mean by that?

Silko: People not only need legends, they will finally find them and grab onto them. And it's not just an Indian thing. Whites have their legends too, but they're different. Now they have modern TV legends like *Charley's Angels* and they believe in these legends, you know, for "males behave like this" and "females behave like that." It's too bad.

Red Eagle: What's wrong with the white legends?

Silko: Most of the white legends are terribly violent. You know, Jessie James, Bonnie and Clyde. There are the good guys and the bad guys, and the good guys must win finally, even if, really, they are the bad guys.
    Everything must lead to conflict and violence—even to destruction and death! The bad guys must not only lose, they must be destroyed.

Red Eagle: The conflict and violence. Is that what's wrong?

Silko: It's all too simple and neat. Things just aren't one way or the other, winners or losers, rights or wrongs. Again, there's this great tendency to oversimplify. There's good and bad in all of us. We're all part hero and part villain. We help and we harm at the same time.

Red Eagle: So how are Indian legends different?

Silko: Many of our heroes are also tricksters. They are trickster-heroes. They might do wonderful things, but they could also get people who listened to them in trouble. Hearing these stories, you learned how people could get into trouble, often through their conniving. That's the point of many Indian legends—to learn about your people and yourself. We learned from our trickster-heroes. We didn't try to emulate them!

Raven and the Niña, the Pinta, and the Santa Maria, Cartoon, by Kree Arvanitas

So in this sense, whites believe too much in their legends. And that may lead them to act out the violent, winner-loser endings in their own lives. 📖

Worlds from Water

—*origins and the myth of discovery*

Heid Ellen Erdrich

Always,
Loon, red eye a dart in darkness,
pulls up the earth in a mouthful
of pond bottom and duckgrass
Always,
Turtle, neck strained to point
with hook-hard nose,
heaves plate tectonic shoulders,
so borders are waters
the world served on halfshells
Then,
Water, drifted with tobacco,
waves and parts before
Person, vessel of water carried
on water, until,
bound out of the same blue,
what in 1492 was found
was also lost

An evil night settles while the sun is still high. The darkness of war lies over the whole land.

In a cave, or high on a mountain there is a whimper of shame. It is the shame of the innocent bearing witness to the darkness of hell.

Somewhere, madness crashes.

Somewhere, a cornfield shines.

Somewhere, the sun is high, and it's daytime.

* * *

Here, the heart is broken and stays broken.

Here, the night conceals blasphemy that cannot be redeemed.

Here, love has almost forgotten itself, and searches lamely for its own embrace. Its face is crushed—love is not easy to recognize.

Here, the pain of millions is boiled down to a foul sludge and smeared over the earth.

Here, the blood of killers and torturers screams like ammonia, bodies in a seizure of murder and hatred, clutching their weapons eagerly, grinning in confused agony.

Here, the tattletale vaults of children's mouths slam shut forever.

Here, the cremation vases lie broken and nameless under a dead grey mountain of ashes—a mountain that weeps dumbly under heaven.

Here, the believers strain at their prayers, their tongues working mechanically, praying for the salvation of belief itself.

Here, men claw at the air, as though at stone prison walls.

Here, women lie in the sun without heads or breasts, covered with flies.

Here, babies suck at the dry earth and grandmothers are cut in two by machines.

Here, children wear camouflage fatigues and flak helmets, and bury their fear under a pounding sea of noise.

Here, winter is a sullen reprieve.

Here, the wind breaks down overheated, in a wasteland of hatred and paranoia.

Here, the daylight is shattered by a ravening beak of total darkness.

* * *

A jeep driven by a fifteen-year-old boy stops on a village square. Another boy unloads a big machine gun, and sets it up in the middle of the street. Three more jeeps and a truck full of boys and weapons rip through the village and slam to a halt on the square. Soon, there will be bodies everywhere.

A school teacher is dragged from her house in the middle of the night and thrown half-naked into a military police van. Her husband and children and mother shake and weep quietly. One of the children throws up on the bed.

A soldier is suddenly overcome by shame and disgust and makes a run for the border. He is captured, but manages to escape. He is surprised to find that he is hated everywhere he goes. He testifies before a panel of clergy, describing in detail battles, assaults, torture, mass executions, and so on. The soldier lives in bitter exile for a few years; then, he commits suicide.

From a dirty yellow window a five-year-old girl watches military police hang four men—one of them is her uncle. Her face is hard. At five, she is too old to cry.

In the movie *Rambo*, Sylvester Stallone kills forty-three men. People of all ages watch the bright, bigger-than-life killing, laughing and cheering.

* * *

I can make things up off the top of my head that I know are true—horrible things and wonderful things. All the terrible actions of a war—they are taking place right outside my window. Acts of heroism and cowardice. Blood raining from the sky. If

I draw the curtains, the killing resumes in the basement. I am not making anything up—I am a witness. I tell what I see in the window, in the heating vent, on the ceiling. I cover the war in my city, in my house.

*   *   *

A man walks thirty-seven miles alone in a stinking jungle. He is ten million people—all of them are doomed. The man is fevered; he's wounded and stumbling. He has done terrible things, and has had terrible things done to him. He comes from a war, he goes to a war. He is blown by a wind. The wind comes from history, and wails away into the future. The war rages forever. The people caught in the wind are whipped around and incinerated. They are made to walk thirty-seven miles wounded and fevered. They are made to kill and to be hunted. They are made to believe that there are reasons for this. The belief is an ancient drug that illuminates the false reason of all hatred. It is the fear in people that swallows the drug. The man craves morphine. He gnaws on his tongue. He believes nothing.

Maybe this is the wind that will whisper us away to heaven.
Maybe this is the wind that will disturb the hush under our
    shirts.
Maybe this war is the lion that will lead us out of the labyrinth
    of our suffering.

It is never true
It has never been true
The war has never stopped
The war has never stopped anything.

Is this the shaggy ruin
Where the man finally sank to his knees
And his scream failed
To reach even his own ears?

Is this where the mad animal of his destiny
Finally learned the man's name
And then screeching and cackling
Forgot it instantly?

He is a watermelon carcass on the stones
He is more than ten million people
And he has walked further
Than thirty-seven miles.

The wind has died down
The drug has worn off
The war moans in its grey shell
There is a tired ice
Around its red throat.
Our fingers reach for the mountains
And instead attach themselves
To one another's brains.

I am beginning to believe
in solitude.

*   *   *

(Sorrow of the burning tower. Train of agony.) I am thinking . . . —What is the message of The West? "You belong to me."
Those could be the words of a big lover. That's what they're meant
to sound like. But, they're the wasp-like movements of a toreador,
translated—words that are traitorous to life. These words set fire
to the ancient towers, reduce them to pathetic memories; waste
the pinnacled fortress of history, boil its wreckage down to a
little purple teardrop of simple haplessness. The monster with
his greed—The West. The big lover.
     And the miles and miles of people. Their sad and crazy heads
popping out the windows of the train. Murder in the wind. A sap
of evil squirting out from under the wheels. Pain of the mighty—it
strains, scattering the populace so that it is no longer a populace,

but just a lot of people. The train, the big, ugly train. Everything moves fast, except the people's faces. The pink and orange air is churning. A river of fevered water runs beside the tracks. The people will no longer be *a people*. The nights and days will no longer have an identity. Wash your tired face in the voice of insanity.

"You belong to me." A perfidious kissing, the banker's arms outstretched, eyes going round and round like two blind tomatoes . . . powering the engines . . . two engines. And, again the smoke, the wild smoke. "Hail to the sky! The sky filled with rage!" The people begin to forget each other, and to forget history. They are not sure what country they are leaving. Who knows, anymore? They hang onto their seats, snuggling the little animals of their faiths, their many different faiths. Rumbling through the painful, smoky landscape, cameras snapping pictures of the war. 📖

Teaching Thoreau

John Enright

There was a horse in the graveyard today.
The same graveyard that was a lake
with stonetops for whitecaps two weeks ago
when it rained.
                    Today it is clear; the brown horse
is tethered—all ribs on sticks—and wanders
distractedly down a grass aisle.

I taught Thoreau today and nobody got it;
and I had to carry it all back with me
through the green sun of the campus, wondering
where I had gone wrong.
The graveyard is on the way home.
I pass it twice a day,
sometimes in flood, sometimes in famine.

Raven Brings Light, 1992, Painting, by Caroline Orr

O Le Uila

Dorothy Kneubuhl

Five trees were in the way,
Each taking comfort from
The other's wet green seeking
In streams of rain that course
Beneath the rotting leaves,
Until the tallest, tender
Once, stood sheltering,
A blooming African.

Perhaps its verticality
Led down, as red bird to red
flower, the bolt that struck.
The cracking thunder had
Made turtles of us, crazed
the dogs, so that we never
Saw the thing home in,
And only later found the
Monster ring of silvering wilt
Where green 'auaga had been.

There was no fire, no blast.
No prayer to guide it down:
Still, foragers thieving firewood
Burn twice the wrath of God,
However wide His mark.

Hunter

Richard Ploetz

Once set upon a track he would follow it to the end. He was like one of those small dogs that grabs the neck of a bigger dog and hangs on until the other is dead.

When hunting, he had nothing in his mind but the prey. He could follow tracks where none were, over rock ledges that interrupted the plain for miles across. As he walked, everything took on a kind of flatness, monotony. He was already fastened on, like that little dog, closing off his prey's life. Caribou that he followed, sometimes for a week, would be in the end waiting for him. He would not even have to spend a precious bullet, but would cut their throats while they watched him. They gave themselves to him as much as he took them.

The villagers criticized him for his stupidity in killing a beast so far from home. Several men always had to go back with him to help pack the meat out. A long, back-breaking business. If the beast is so tamed by the time you catch up with it, they grumbled, why don't you lead it home and butcher it in your back yard? He thought they would say that. But always, when he reached the animal and looked into its eyes, he killed it. As if he were under a spell from the time he started on the track to the moment of the creature's death. The hot blood woke him. He might curse himself then for his stupidity, but what could he do about it? In fact, when he was on the track he was so absorbed (while at the same time detached) that he would pass within twenty feet of other animals—better ones for eating than the one he was following—and these animals wouldn't be afraid of him. They paid him no more attention than if he were a tree or the wind.

For two days it snowed. On the morning when it stopped a man who kept a herd of reindeer outside the village appeared at the hunter's door. A bear had killed one of his animals, leaving just its velvet-covered antlers. He had even eaten the blood-soaked snow. Then, he carried another off. The herdsman ran out in the commotion, in the dark and falling snow, and shot twice with his old rifle. He wounded one of his own reindeer, so had to cut its throat. The bear's tracks led out of the corral toward the open country, a vast tract of brush and low, wind-swept hills. An endless place.

The hunter had never hunted bears. They didn't seem to him an animal to eat. He had seen bears in his treks, and was treed once by a female with cubs. Instead of shooting her, he had waited in the branches until she went away. He had never killed an animal except to eat it.

At the corral the reindeer man pointed down: there was blood in one of the bear tracks. It repeated, like a block print freshly inked, out of the corral and into the open country.

Not far from the village, under the lee of one of those bare-topped, west-leaning hills (as if the wind were blowing them like sand dunes westward), he found the second set of antlers. The air seemed heavy with the bear's breath, musky and damp.

It interfered with his emptied mind, the blood-print, which after miles and miles seemed no less red. As if the bullet had tapped a vein which flowed faintly but steadily, keeping the paw-pad ever moist. It distracted his eye, fixed his attention to a point instead of sweeping over the landscape, touching everything lightly.

After two days, the blood-print ever fresh, he developed a headache like a wound that bled inside.

The days of the hunt continued bright and brilliantly cold, without wind. The bear's tracks were clearly marked in the snow.

After four days the wound had closed and the blood-print turned white. Walking along the hunter felt released, as if he were floating over the snow now, as if time had ended.

The evening of the seventh day he sat outside his tent smoking his pipe. His food had run out, he would eat no more until he ate the bear. This was his way. It sharpened him and drew him toward his prey.

On the ninth day, the good weather still holding, he crossed the original track. The old blood-prints and his own boot tracks lay sharp-edged as the day they were made. Then blood-print changed to white print. The bear had circled around. The tracks the hunter was following were following him.

After a while the bear came, shuffling like a great brown dog, breathing in the track. He stopped and stood up on his hind legs. It looked like he was peering over the heads of a crowd for the hunter. Then he came on, still standing, forelegs held out. He came across the snow like a sleepwalker, his eyes open. The hunter laid down his gun and waited. 📖

A Man Walks Into A Bar

Stephen Thomas

—*In Memoriam, Jesse Bernstein*

A man walks into a bar.
A man walks into a tavern, into a lounge, a pub, his
       kitchen, the cellar.
A man walks into a fight, a porn store, an affair.
A man walks into a bar.

He slouches, skulks, sleepwalks, rushes, stumbles, dives
       crawls into a bar.
A man who has tightened his tether and now is drawing it
       short, coiling it round the spool of a bottle, a thought,
       a needle, a penis, an ego,
       walks into a bar.

A man or a woman, a boy or a girl, a child walks into a bar.
A man who is sick of manhood, for whom to be is only a
       burden he breaks his back in denying,
A woman who is sick of her womanhood, for whom to be is only
       a burden she breaks herself in denying,
       a human walks into a bar.

A boy or a girl, arrested in some first awareness,
       awakens again at a bar stool, a porn screen, a fistfight,
       a rented bed.
A boy and a girl, two boys, two girls, a boy and his father,
       a girl and her child are locked in an embrace without
       understanding.

A man walks into a bar. He has himself in his wallet.
       Spend all he can, he can lose or find it.
       Spend all his juice, he can't touch another.
       Spend herself senseless, she cannot.

A man walks into a bar.
       There in the watery half-light of the smoky mirror,
       what appears to him, sipping at history,
       shattered among the glasses,
       What does he see?

       He sees me.

Raven's Fear of Growing White

Duane Niatum

When the legends cannot light the fires
of the villages still in the song,
a son, daughter, mother and father stop talking
to the red cedar elders, the first woman
beats her guardian hummingbird to earth,
a fisherman eats the rapids until his bones
shatter into sockeye salmon, a pin-tail duck
fails to reach its shadow on the river,
our family of tribes quit wearing
the maggot-masks of muscatel,
a river otter steals the shaky promises
of stars, and blue jay warns not even
the crows of the next storm,
Raven will end his fear of growing white.

III

VOLUME 1, NUMBER 3,
SPRING 1992

Raven, 1992, Painting, by Rick Bartow

Untitled, 1992, Mixed Media Illustration, by Gloria White-Calico

Rosea Socorro Katz, Coconut

Kathleen de Azevedo

Many years ago, mighty warrior women like Rosea lived in Brazilian jungles: the Mato Grosso, Rondônia, and along the Juruá River. The leaves of the Hevea and Philmeira trees bristled as the women charged on horseback into battle and threw their heads back, letting out a war whoop so magnificently watery that their spit formed into rain clouds. As they drew their bows and arrows, their shoulder muscles quivered like the flanks of their steeds. Their leather breastplates itched and their gold collars pinched the tiny hairs on the back of their necks. The small bites of pain kept them on the edge of a delicious wildness. These legendary Amazon warriors were fiercer than anyone of the Xavante tribe, and the only way to tame these deep-throated women was to teach them how to sing.

* * *

Wind blew whirls of dry farmland west toward Paso Robles, California. Shoots of dried lettuce, with their small leaves flapping like thirsty tongues, nudged through the earth. Beno's Fruit and Vegetable Stand with its warped wood walls and corrugated tin roof seemed to sag in the heat. Rosea Socorro Katz paced in the shade of the stand and cuffed at a crazy fly.

She swooped down in front of an ice chest she had brought from home and pulled out a Coke. Out in the field, a tractor rolled by. She lurched forward and yelled, only to bang her head on a low beam of the ceiling. Grabbing her head of frizzed black and angry hair that hung past her shoulders, she howled, stamped her foot, and cursed; her six-foot self was too tall for just about any room.

A hand rested on her scalp. Melvinor Beno, her boss, was poking around in her hair, trying to look at her bump. "Leave me alone," she said, and pulled away and pressed the cold Coke can against her sore spot.

Melvinor stepped back and nervously tugged at the upper button of his shirt. His hands were old and stiff, he could barely twirl the button.

The tractor continued putt-putting to the other side of the field.

"You okay?" he asked guardedly after the tractor disappeared.

She eased the cold can away from the bump on her head. "You're gonna let them plow the fields, aren't you?"

"I don't own the land. I only own the stand. As Isaiah remarked in his fifth year in exile, 'If this was my land, I wouldn't be planting dates—'"

"Skip it."

Melvinor slouched and sat back down on his crate in the half-shade outside the stand. He wore a visor that had "Beno's" printed in large black letters. The sun burnt a pink cap on the exposed part of his bald head. The old man eyed Rosea from under the rim of his visor. He was probably eyeing her butt. Bet he liked her long, strong legs, too. Old Melvinor hung out here every day, no matter how hot it was. He rolled by around nine in his Pinto and sat out all day drinking coffee from a large green thermos. He sat there all day, eyeing her butt, looking out into the fields, and watching the migrant workers in the dizzy haze snatch dragonflies and pinch them dead between their fingers.

"Melvinor," Rosea said, "how about those nice watermelons, huh? Remember them?"

"Yeah," he laughed. "Boy, they used to be good. Juicy."

The two-year drought left Melvinor broke. The only things left to sell were a few half-empty crates of rotting oranges and bananas, some peaches barely fit for pies, and a waxy cardboard box half-full of world-famous Santa Maria broccoli that had shriveled to the size of small green brains.

Melvinor scraped a stick in the dirt. The scraping made her mad. The colorful plastic flags strung around the edge of the tin roof also made her mad. Looked like a used car lot! The way the flags snapped in the gusts made her furious.

He looked up. "Rosea. There's something I always wanted to know, given your mother."

She whipped around. "What now?"

He flinched. "Why don't you ever sing?"

Rosea reeled crazily and hurled the Coke hard against the wall; the aluminum can exploded like a grenade.

* * *

The Amazons gave birth: They waded navel-deep into the river, and stood with their legs apart. They dug their large toes into the sand, placed their hands on their hips, watched for war canoes and river boats, and chatted as the fruit from their wombs positioned themselves just so. Flies, attracted to their ear wax, buzzed around their heads. Then one by one, coconuts, covered in green husks, emerged from between their legs, first shooting down into the water from the uterine contraction, then floating up to the surface and bobbing in amniotic foam, washing past the silvery fins of fishes. Some coconuts begat other coconuts in the life-giving waters. Some coconuts washed up on shore on the faraway ports of Iquitos or Manaus as empty, dried-out hulls far away from the mothers who bore them. One coconut made it to Malibu Beach where it crashed onto the shore and split open. There, Rosea's mother was born: Carmen Socorro lay on the beach, full-grown, brown and naked.

In Hollywood, anything can happen.

* * *

Maybe the Coke grenade panicked the little old man and got him excited because out of nowhere, Melvinor started talking. Melvinor tended to start talking out of nowhere. He rose to his feet and started in again on Isaiah and exile and how one had to wander in the desert for a long time before one found his way home. He made sweeping gestures. Rosea was used to him acting bizarre and now he seemed so funny. His wife and kids were all gone, all died of cancer or something, and all he had was her and the fruit and vegetable stand. Rosea stood there grinning. "What are you talking about, old man?"

Melvinor calmed down and stroked the little fringe of white hair around his bald spot. "It must be hard for you," he said, "to remember what happened to your mother, the legend, the greatest star in Hollywood. Oh, I loved your mother, I loved Carmen Socorro. So did Bing Crosby. All the fellas wanted her."

"Oh really?"

"Maybe to you I'm a dirty old man. But I'm not blind. As Isaiah said, 'A field that is fallow is ready for a new crop.' Oh Carmen—how her hair was dark and her lips were red and her hips so round and her skirt so tight—I would have done anything for her."

"Would you do anything for me?"

He closed his eyes for a moment then opened them. The rims right below his eyes were red. "Yes."

Rosea backed away quickly and grabbed from the shelf a case of rotten oranges that was hopping with fruit flies. She took the crate out back and dumped the old fruit in a pile. She stomped back inside, got a box of black limp bananas, went back out and threw those in with the oranges. Tangy carcass. Finally she dumped out a crate of peaches that oozed pulp through the cuts in their skin. The fruit lay in a black, breathing heap, pits swelling out of the sour pus, skins watery and dented.

Rosea charged back into the stand, wanting to splinter the wood walls, break them into pieces and tear limb by limb all the boards, the corrugated roof, and rub the whole mess into dust between the palms of her hands. Her nails became claws, her breath became rapid as she snatched a spade from the corner of the stand. She went over to Melvinor, flicked her long mass of hair away from her neck and rammed the shovel into the dirt at his feet, making a slash. "Take this," she fumed, "you're gonna bury the old fruit out back."

Melvinor took the shovel and gulped, "It rots on its own."

"It smells like shit," she gritted her teeth, "rotten fruit smells. I feel sick when it smells."

"I don't think we want—"

"Yes," Rosea seethed, "I *want* it."

He stared at her darkly, then went over to the pile of rotten fruit, humming softly to himself, "Copacabana."

* * *

Carmen Socorro had that star quality, that Hollywood twinkle-lips, that cha-cha samba way about her. She bought a house with a beautiful pool because she needed to be near water. One day a little Jewish man came to fix her pool. Wearing bitty bikini trunks, he dove and swam underwater to check the jet propulsion of the water filters. Carmen watched the ribbons of sunlight ripple on his little bald head and his hairy back. He could hold his breath for a long time. Finally he swam to the surface and there was Carmen, smiling and wearing a small straw hat trimmed with plastic cherries.

Carmen married the man who fixed her pool, and a year later she gave birth to Rosea Socorro Katz, coconut. HEEYA! Carmen bellowed as she told Rosea the stories of husks and hulls and of the great Amazon warriors. "Amazon"—the dream of fishes and wild earth. Wasn't always just a river, like it is today. HEEYA *ME NENEZHINHA!* Then Carmen did that sexy glance off to the side; but once that glance made her a star, Rosea never got another story. Fifteen years later, Rosea Socorro Katz was hanging out with pachucos and smoking marijuana. She couldn't remember her childhood unless she was stoned, so all day she flicked matches and smoked stubs, all day flicking and toking. It made her dream of fishes and cool water. She grew to love that hot flame fiercely.

* * *

A pickup truck carrying migrant workers and toting a porta-potty drove by. Rosea didn't think they were pickers since there was nothing left to pick. Maybe they drove tractors. Melvinor was obediently hacking a fruit burial hole out back, no doubt suffering in the heat. Rosea laughed bitterly. Like her mother, she knew she could drive men crazy.

Melvinor needed to rehab a criminal like herself, and that's why he put up with her shit. His love for Carmen Socorro gave Rosea the freedom to rehabilitate. And all that poor man probably wanted in return was for her was to sing a few tunes.

She ended her last marriage by setting fire to her own house. That was years ago. Yeah, her husband could've been home in time for the arson, but he was away on business and missed the block party. Still, it was HER home too, a home where an Amazon no longer had to eat her food raw, or rub two sticks together to make fire, but could live patiently, flicking matches, holding the tiny blazes next to the stove burner tediously trying to kindle the hissing gas into a small blue ring. One day in her anger—HEEYA a bonfire!—a match, along with a can of gasoline, made the whole house into that sacrificial inferno, that flame of Baker Avenue, the flame that drew people from all over, that famous flame.

They've put people in prison for less. She needed the stand like she needed a job. Badly. She tried to imagine what job she could get after all these years. Not typing. Only prison officials did that.

Melvinor sighed patiently and repeatedly tried to jam the shovel into the ground. He pinched his lips into a line and a dribble of sweat swizzled down his neck. Like Isaiah finding comfort in the wilderness, he must have found some comfort in imagining his head between her large breasts, dreaming they were two hills side by side, battered by wind and rain. Isaiah used stones for pillows, he once told her. Rosea glared at him, but her sticky eyelids were becoming heavy. Every time Melvinor whacked the shovel blade into the ground, she took a deep breath, and the whack became a slap on her face, here and there. Whack. Yeah, hack away at the dirt, pretty damn futile, huh? Beno's is futile . . . plants are growing futilely . . . futilization . . . tiny futile veggies could be sold as gourmet greens. Whack.

The pounding of the shovel became a rhythm, like samba, like cha-cha, and she closed her eyes and pretended to think like coconuts do, rotting and basking in the sun, getting kicked into the water, bobbing, soaking, dancing, gulping krill and seaweed. Rosea started to breathe hard and imagined coconuts drifting past fish scales in the lower depths of oceans. Melvinor was wheezing loudly. "Fuck it," she said, "stop digging."

* * *

Carmen's husband also became her agent. For her next movie, he made Carmen wear a larger hat with more fruit, not just cherries. Her large chapeau not only had bananas, but bananas and pineapple. The best boy working on the picture liked oranges and they stuck those on the hat, too. Some grapes also. Wearing the large hats gave her headaches, so her agent gave her pills for the pain.

One day, Carmen was waiting while they changed the set. Prefab coconut trees rolled past them. The coconuts were made of papier mâché. Carmen cried because her feet hurt, but her hat was too heavy and she couldn't look down to see her toes.

Just then, Rosea, wearing black leather, came whizzing by the studio on her Harley toting her new pachuco boyfriend, Geezer Ortiz. Her mother ignored her and pretended to be fascinated by the way the makeup gal was touching up Bing Crosby's lips. Rosea stopped the motorcycle right in front of her mother, flicked back her rebellious head so that her gold loop earrings jangled, and hollered "HEEYA" in that war whoop she learned as a child; but her mother, sedated on pain pills, hushed her. Rosea got a closer look and threw her head back and howled like a stray dog. Carmen Socorro was immovable like a tree, her toes might as well have grown roots.

* * *

Melvinor had left. The pile of fruit still lay there next to an attempted hole that was no more than chipped dirt.

Rosea had visions of the land being plowed and uprooted, the plants sighing and yielding to the tractor blade. Nobody was interested in seeing if the crops would grow. If the plants aren't putting out, it's BAM. Out they go. Her mind was attacking tractors, pulling the drivers down from their small tractor seats and stuffing their faces into the powdery, drought-ridden dirt. Her mind was blowing up into a thousand cherry-colored flames. Her heart ached with the desire to commit another crime.

She picked up a box of yellow crookneck squash to dump, but the batch didn't seem rotten yet. They'd turn bad in a few days if no one bought them. The squash wasn't normal, though. The bulbous bodies looked swollen. The too-long necks looked like long goose throats; they looked tangled together as if the necks were choking the crooks. Melvinor liked to see strange things like this. She thought of his old rounded back with a sweaty spot between his shoulder blades. How could he stand her? What the hell. She saved the box. Tomorrow she would dump the twisted vegetables at his feet.

She sat on Melvinor's crate and watched the sun go down. What does one do when one has tried everything? She wondered what her mother would do.

* * *

The movie was a flop. The public was tired of Carmen and tired of fruit. Husband Katz, the agent, ran off with some blonde movie star. Late one night, Carmen slid into the pool naked, slid into the pool thigh deep, waist deep, then neck deep. She went into a bottomless slumber and thought of home. Rosea came back drunk from a party and found her mother floating, her head gently bumping against the side of the pool like a curious guppy.

* * *

By nightfall, the wind was quiet and Beno's plastic flags were still. The moon lit the dried-up fields silver. Mice skittered on the floor of the stand, and she could hear their tiny feet on the empty crates. She felt like swooping down and killing them. From the fields she heard a low rumble. She felt like killing the rumble, too.

At first she thought the sound might be the food-processing plant that used to operate day and night, stripping outer green leaves from lettuce and broccoli. But the plant was closed because of the drought.

The faint roar grew and massaged the inside of Rosea's throat. She felt curious as to whether they'd started up the plant again and she wandered toward the noise. She could feel the powdery soil puff on either sides of her tennis shoes. Grains of dirt stung her chapped lips. A small curious light appeared, winked at her, faded, and lowered its lid, then winked brightly again as she broke into a run. She could hear the pusssh-pusssh of her footsteps.

The roar approached and Rosea saw that the light came from a giant tractor bumping along the field. Rosea let out a sigh, and with that, all the anger in her flushed out in waves and she held her breath and plunged herself in front of the light. Rosea wanted the tractor to run her down. Suicide had that euphoric lilt to it, the rushing of headlights, the stampeding of massive steeds, the taut bending of the bows and the flying of arrows. The freedom of bobbing on the ocean! Rosea had a sudden longing to return to some forgotten river, to push against the current, and knock stray coconuts against the sides of war canoes. She searched for the one belly, that familiar brown navel belonging to the woman who could not sing, but only scream until her spit formed rain clouds. The tractor bellowed. Rosea imagined herself surrounded by silver slivers of metal, deep-sea fish with razor fins and delicately pointed snouts. A silver tail fin darted for her head. Peaky snouts goaded her shoulders then slunk back, smiling and twisting as they gleamed, suspended and curious. She reached out. Light flashed, the fish dove for her neck, then shimmered at her eyeballs. Her eyelashes touched the metallic fin. The silver fins froze then slowly swam away until all she could make out were the tiny pointy fish eyes. Rosea heard the driver of the tractor shout. She decided not to be afraid. She stood in front of the tractor, outstretched her hands as if they were wings, and looked up at the night sky as if it were an ocean of stars.

* * *

Carmen was rescued and resuscitated by her butler. To celebrate, she made her comeback with a bigger and better hat decorated not only with bananas, but bowls of fruit, coconut trees—the whole Amazon rainforest had been uprooted and built onto her hat. Monkeys swayed from trees and dropped off into the jungle. Carmen wore a neck brace in rehearsals because her hat was so heavy. On the last show of her life, she did this thing with Jimmy Durante where he joked about her hat. The forest of fruit started to press on her head and she forgot the punch line. Luckily, Jimmy, the way he was so Mr. Show Business, picked up her cue and no one noticed. Roots pressed against her head and tapped at her skull.

*   *   *

Rosea woke up and found herself lying face down in the dirt. The morning sun soaked into her long black hair which was tangled around her neck. A new morning breeze whistled in her ear. She touched her wrists and felt her warm and dry skin, then looked up and saw that the whole field had been plowed under, the small plants churned into dirt. Hawks dove down and grabbed small field mice in their beaks as crows stood around in envy. Rosea eased herself up on her knees and brushed away the dirt from her shirt and face. She looked toward the fruit and vegetable stand and noticed that the wood and corrugated tin concoction was leaning to one side. Probably had been that way all along. The Pinto was there of course. Melvinor Beno appeared from behind the stand, obviously looking for her. His eyes scanned the horizon and she heard faintly, "Rosea! Rosea!" Rosea clenched her hands. She wanted to run away from him, but he would see her.

Melvinor finally spotted her and pointed. Rosea started to shiver as she saw him approach. He was so thin and old, he moved lightly on the earth as if he were wearing sandals and a long robe. He jogged a few steps then caught his breath, held out his dry hands to her and brought with him a warm gust of wind.

Rosea stumbled to her feet but she was too shaky to run off. Melvinor, trembling and gawking, reached over and snatched her shoulders. She pulled away and wandered back toward the stand.

"I had a dream about you," he said, trotting after her.

"Leave me alone."

"I had a dream that you—" he caught up with her and grabbed her arm.

Rosea pushed him away and he stumbled backwards, patting his heart.

"Sorry about that." She staggered over to the tin shade.

"Rosea," he said, "I had a dream that you died."

She caught and gripped the doorway of the stand.

His bony hand rose and touched the top of her head, floated, touched her cheek, her lower lip, then he passed his fingers lovingly across his mouth. Then he cupped his hands around his own face the way he would cup hers.

She could see through his skull as if it were crystal; she could see the abandoned food-processing plant straight through his brain. She became frightened of his oldness. Carmen rose in her memory, savage, breastplated, bristling, harsh and blazing. Her mother's hair burst out of the fruited turban and turned into a whirlwind. Rosea threw her head back and screamed.

* * *

Carmen opened her mouth again but missed another line. Again, Durante saved her but he seemed to be shouting. Small veins on her temples started to bounce and pound against her skin. Her heart pumped up water to keep the fruit and leaves alive, but her hat became as heavy as the MGM studio. Carmen stomped off stage. She glanced at Rosea who, dressed in leather, was watching the show from the wings. Carmen took one look at Rosea with her newest pachuco boyfriend, Ramon Stanley, and blacked out. A coconut tumbled from her hat and rolled into the ocean. The current lapped up the coconut and carried it across the seas. It got picked up by the Amazon waters and was finally flushed into the Juruá River where a fine-breasted warrior snatched up the coconut with her teeth and laughed.

* * *

Rosea screamed until she sucked up the clouds and all the potential water in the sky. She sucked up the fields and whole oceans. She watched her hand grab the string of plastic flags that flapped in the valley gusts. Rosea pulled down on the string. The walls of the stand started to crack and she jammed her foot hard against the wall and loosened the tin from the frame. Melvinor stood back and stared. Little threads of his white hair wisped out. His mouth gaped in a silent scream but Rosea's scream was pretty damn noisy. She yanked at the flags again and pulled down the front of the roof. The warped wood planks buckled and part of the tin roof caved in submissively around her head in a gentle roar. The shelves crashed into splinters. The last ceiling beam collapsed. The two halves of Beno's split and fell open like a coconut shell. Rosea was amazed at how beautiful the land was. The field was rippling, the wind made a sound like oars dipping into the water, and the corrugated tin glittered like the sunlit jewels of the Juruá. 📖

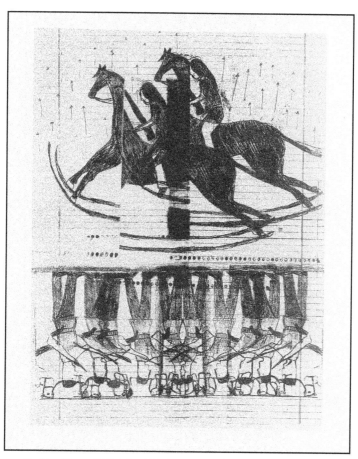

Rocking Horse, 1992, Mixed Media Drawing, by Gloria White-Calico

The Woman Who Loved Dahlias

Alice Derry

—for my grandmother, Alma Soderburg

I grew them because as a kid,
I stood under the stalks
which reached my father's shoulder
while Aunt Olive—his sister—
showed each one.

In the spent August garden,
they spill their pink, purple, red, orange—
unfold their origami,
flutes and pleats, the pieces fitted
in an intricacy we reserve
for thinking of ourselves,

a shapeliness we're always looking for,
watching a stranger
because at the moment it's hers,
beauty for the spending of it, the dying.

Maybe every life is only
childhood moments revealed.
I held to those dahlias through apartments,
a husband who grew vegetables,

keeping things unquestioned,
just as they are: flowers deep
in their sunshine, my father and his sister
for once forgetting their bitterness,
for once not sending me away.

When I finally got a piece of ground,
I bought the wrinkly knobs—old women's hands—
in stealth and planted them
in silence, assuming magic
took care of its own.

Failure in shade, failure on a shallow bank,
finally the summer I came to the plot
which fed the eager rush of leaves,
buds, color.

By then I was middle-aged myself,
and on a visit, Dad suddenly said,
"Beautiful dahlias—they were my mother's
specialty."

Like the end of a story which seems
elusive until you hear it,
but when you do,
it's the inevitable one,

I watch you, Alma—someone I never knew,
whose picture I can barely place,
whose neat Sunday china graces my table—
come toward me,

a shadow making its way into form,
as morning might keep lightening an object—
why I wouldn't have found in garden books
what I wanted—our like minds,
the woman of you in me.

In the rigid schedule a farmer's wife needed
to keep an irascible man on task,
you squandered time each fall bringing in bulbs
to overwinter, planting them new in spring.

A summer of flowers outlasted
a winter's stock of canning.

In this way you are saved, I connected.
When the dahlias go this summer, the loss
will be one after gain, a loss I can mourn—

my ritual of keeping—how your hands
will lift bulbs from cold November mud,
help me carry them indoors.

After Reading Raven Stories, I Remember Stealing

Lauren Kaushansky

She isn't the only one who can play tricks
—from *Raven Goes Berrypicking,* by Anne Cameron

I could read these same stories
every day. How I love mischief,
the combination of beauty
and freedom, the span of wings.

Way before I knew Raven enjoyed
the luster of silver I sought silver myself.
As a young tomboy, I wore handcuffs,
dangling from belt loops.

Now, under my sleeve, wearing a Haida bracelet
I feel as free as a cold black wing,
an escapee from the cedar scent
of an old woman's box. It's a familiar tale.

Puffin knew Raven was up to no good.
Puffin, with her bulging body, looking
part penguin, part toucan, her eyes
v-shaped and quick, like birds in flight.

My students side with Puffin. They listen,
awed by birds fighting amongst themselves.
The awkward display of family rivalry
like the fallen face of my mother

the time she discovered play handcuffs
stolen and slipped inside my pocket.
What option did I have? Too young to handle money,
too naïve to barter and this silver, a necessity.

In the beginning, there was darkness.
I see it richly black and weave silver in,
cawing out magic. Too many berries,
too many sardines, even Raven cannot hold

so much in her beak, in her belly.
Truth is, the pursuit of brightness
always brings you down. You always want more.

Men are Slow

Don Wilsun

Men are slower than women
       Men are slow
Men are slower than women
       Men are slow
Need a ceremony, need a toast
To enter, try to feel, tell lies
Spin myths, have a social form.

Men are slow to understand the moon
See all the lights in their eyes
Storytelling, drumming in a circle
Calling animals with twin voices
Men are slow to share hearts
But in time, times change
So much silence looking for courage
Men are slower than women
       Men are slow.

The last salmon *is* divided,
only a segment of the understanding
that is accepted with the River.
Placing the Salmon, head facing upriver,
will demonstrate we have not absolutely conformed.
Only two hundred years from the *discovery*, dear *Chewana*,
the unfolding of unwritten prophecy,
a Great River is fragmented holiness.

—Elizabeth Woody

IV

Volume 2, Number 1, Summer/Fall 1992

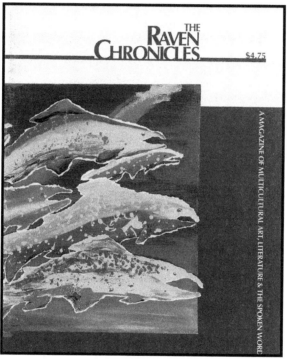

Salmon, 1992, Acrylic Painting, by Gloria White-Calico

Me and The Other
An Interview with Charles Johnson

Phoebe Bosché

The ideal reader is a literate reader; a curious reader; a reader without prejudices; a reader who likes the things that I hope are in my books. —Charles Johnson

Part I.

On a recent, rather brilliant May afternoon [1992], I spoke with writer and critic Charles Johnson in his office on the campus of the University of Washington. He had just returned from viewing a film as a juror for the 1992 Seattle International Film Festival. Along one plain-looking wall a row of his own books was lined up smartly, like good little soldiers, English and foreign translations intermingled: *Faith and the Good Thing, Oxherding Tale, The Sorcerer's Apprentice, Being and Race: Black Writing Since 1970,* and *Middle Passage,* winner of the 1991 National Book Award.

Phoebe Bosché: There is a line in your novel, *Faith and the Good Thing,* about taking many paths—journalist, teacher, writer, cartoonist, philosopher, father—and picking up the pieces along the way. Have you gotten the whole thing yet? The good thing?

Charles Johnson: [laughter] There are lots of little good things, according to the Swamp Woman, right, and they all have to be appreciated for themselves. And they're all the same. It's all an expression of the same thing, which is creative expression.

Bosché: But you still teach. Why are you still teaching, when financially you probably don't have to?

Johnson: I don't have to teach but I enjoy it. I've been in school my entire life, since the age of five. I like my colleagues and in a *good* class the intellectual exchange and the dialectic that goes on. That is a very rewarding experience.

Bosché: And it does help your writing, doesn't it? If you do get the right people to talk to?

Johnson: I think so. Yeah. I admire writers who are full-time freelancers and sort of go off by themselves, but I think they probably hunger, after a certain point, for intellectual engagement with others and a social life. If it is a bad quarter, that's another matter. If all this stuff is miserable, no, I don't enjoy it. That's awful.

Bosché: I remember where you once said, you were shaking your head after reading class papers, all these students are just thinking about getting laid, why can't they ever think of themselves in someone else's skin. Something to that effect.

Johnson: Sometimes it is just difficult for undergraduates who are still trying to figure things out. The grad students are always a delight to work with. I think I've never had a bad graduate class, and even the upper division undergraduate classes have been very good. *Except*, I've had this same conversation recently with people, I think the skill level that students bring in now is somewhat lower in the upper division and undergraduate classes than it was ten to twelve years ago. They've read less. They seem less ambitious in a certain kind of way. It's just very odd. I've seen it this year in the undergraduate classes and it rather surprised me because only two years ago the 300 Level had people with all kinds of backgrounds and knowledge, and the wonderful things they would bring in. Not so much that anymore.

Bosché: You've said that you have problems with a lot of contemporary fiction, so do you read much of it?

Johnson: Oh, I do have problems with it but I read a lot of it. I was a judge for the National Book Award in 1989 and for two years I've been a judge for the L.A. Times Book Prize. I see whatever the publishers consider their best offering for the year. It doesn't pass by me.

Bosché: I got the impression you still read mostly the old greats, to get something for yourself, for your own nourishment.

Johnson: Well, I do, to learn. There is a level of technical performance I think, and even a way of envisioning that has been lost. I come out of philosophy, where the whole thought process can be different at times. So I usually am very demanding of the things that I read. I want clarity; I want coherence; I want completeness. No, I want thoughtful works. I want, basically, works that are capable of changing my perception as well as moving my heart.

Bosché: What was the first book that did that? That changed your life, your way of seeing?

Johnson: My mother had lots and lots of books of all kinds. Books on yoga and Richard Wright's *Black Boy*. She was in a book club. Philip K. Dick. I remember exactly when *The Man in the High Castle* was published because it was a book club alternate at the time. So I guess it was science fiction when I was young because that tends to be intellectual fiction to a certain extent. It is full of ideas; it dramatizes. A lot of it is extremely imaginative too, so you're not just getting the surface of life. It's not just the ordinary. There's something more going on that reflects back on the ordinary.

So my tastes are very eclectic. An example is *Invisible Man* by [Ralph] Ellison. That is a magnificent performance. It is a purely literary experience that really does help us determine what goes on in our world. He gave the language a way of describing the condition of people, just through the title of the book, and he's working with consciousness and perception. It's original. In many ways it's exhausting. That is the kind of fiction that engages me most.

Right now, for example, I have to review for *The New York Times* a book of philosophy by K. [Kwame Anthony] Appiah, an African philosopher. It's called *In My Father's House: Africa in the Philosophy of Culture*, and he is going at, in this absolutely amazing way, every presupposition that we have operated off of in terms of the conflict of race since W. E. B. Du Bois. Basically he's really looking hard at this and saying what does this mean, and when does the conflict of race arise, and how do we use these terms. This is very, very, difficult work and, it seems to me, extraordinarily valuable.

Bosché: Well, I do think that much of the writing in America about multiculturalism seems shallow.

Johnson: A lot of it is. For example, Appiah, who is African, really does take a hard look at how it is that Black Americans came up with the notion of Pan Africanism that violates all the diversity of language and cultural difference in Africa itself.

Bosché: Reading your books, and this may be a controversial statement, your characters, Faith and Calhoun, for example, didn't seem to be of any particular race. To me, that is a good thing.

Johnson: Well, they live in a world that had racial kinds of signatures ...

Bosché: Yes, but they could be anybody. They're just human beings. Like the great books I read as a child, many of them written by men, mostly male characters, but somehow I never thought of them as male or female ...

Johnson: I didn't think of them as white. I was interested in the story and what was going to happen next and, basically, that what is going to happen to this person can potentially happen to me. Their emotional lives are not that different: love, hate, fear, desires of various kinds. You can't read literature that way and benefit at all from stories.

Bosché: You're a storyteller.

Johnson: I think that is personally fundamental.

Bosché: In a way you're an entertainer. Do you think that is a negative thing?

Johnson: No no no. I think all great art entertains, but all entertainment isn't great art.

Bosché: But you don't have great, dark, tragic elements in your work that, say, Faulkner does.

Johnson: I don't really have a tragic vision.

Bosché: You don't. Yours is humorous.

Johnson: Well, no. In *Middle Passage* there are awful things that happen to human beings.

Bosché: But still, somehow, there isn't that darkness . . .

Johnson: Because that's not all that happens to human beings.

Bosché: Well, it's strange. In a way it's like Mark Twain . . .

Johnson: Mark Twain? There's things I like about Twain.

Bosché: I love Twain, but he's going out of style. Some are saying he's a racist.

Johnson: That's an easy way for finding an excuse for not reading Twain, right. For there is very interesting stuff in it. But a book like *Middle Passage*, for example—the vision that operates in that novel, when it's not, say, phenomenological, is very Buddhist, particularly the last line in the novel: "Isadora drifted toward rest, nestled snugly beside me, where she would remain all night while we, forgetful of ourselves, gently crossed the Flood, and countless seas of suffering."

Bosché: Even the character Papa, as bad as he is, you don't make him seem evil. He's a human being. What amazes me about your writing is that it is almost like you are not human; you are so understanding. There is *too* much tolerance.

Johnson: What? I'm just human.

Bosché: I don't see any hatred, real hatred, in your work at all.

Johnson: I didn't grow up in an environment in which there was hatred. Hatred is not an emotion that I can hang on to for very long or feel. I think that hatred is very often based upon fear. And hatred . . . what is the cause of that? Other people have said that to me, in Indonesia and, I think, recently in Amsterdam. I don't know why that would be an expected thing of a black writer.

Bosché: I think it is. Other black writers might want to see anger in your work that's not there.

Johnson: What for? If they want to see anger they can go to Wright. Or they can go to Baldwin. But on the other hand what I want is art and beauty and goodness and truth. That's what I want.

Bosché: What you've said about moral literature, what John Gardner said, about how at the heart of things, you want beauty, it strikes something in me—it feels real. But I also hear the other voice and I think it is legitimate too—that the anger needs to be heard too.

Johnson: I think an angry novel can be powerful; I think it can be an indictment; I think it can call your attention to some problems in the world. That doesn't mean that it is art though. That's not going to make it art.

Bosché: Richard Wright's novel is angry and beautiful.

Johnson: I like Wright a lot. *Native Son* is a remarkably complex book; in fact, I think it is more complex than most people have actually wanted to acknowledge and talk about. But see that's not the question, the anger to be used. There is a quote by William Gass I thought very amusing and interesting. He said he needs hate's heat to warm his heart. That is totally antithetical to why I write. I much prefer the quote of Alex Haley, who said if you are wondering what you're going to write, find something that you love and praise it. I think Alex is a deeper and wiser man in that respect.

Part II.

Johnson: Back to the issue of race. If you go to Africa, you are going to find so many different peoples, even so many difference races, that there is no oversimplified, generic way to talk about all of them. And yet, once they've been talked about that way, some Africans—according to K. Appiah, and he is talking about African intellectuals trained in Europe—to react against Europe, will adopt the characteristics that they feel are most tribal, particular to their nation. But those are characteristics that were *originally* outlined by the Europeans and their anthropologists, right, who were trying to sort out and carve up Africa.

Bosché: Are you also talking about what is happening with Black Americans, trying to adopt those tribal characteristics?

Johnson: Appiah's talking about African writers and intellectuals, but you could say that it's true here in America too. What is there, in the way of racial essence, about black people that you would identify as a universal? What *is* there? You know? Tell me one thing—you can come up with physical stuff—that all black people have in common. One thing. That's a hard call.

Bosché: I thought I read where you said that everyone, in America anyway, is a mongrel. Looking at myself, that is certainly true.

Johnson: I think it is. You know Alex Haley had a book, which he was going to do, which he didn't live long enough to do, about gene pools—the mixing of gene pools in people in this country. And Appiah even goes through this long thing with genetics in his book, *In My Father's House*, that is remarkable, dealing with chromosomes in the genes and pointing out how at any given point there are more similarities and common ancestries between two people who live on the planet than differences.

 We talk about things we want to believe but I'm suspicious of why we want to believe some of these things. Why we have a stake and an investment in somebody really believing there is an essential difference between me and the Other. There has got to be some element of ego involved and a misunderstanding of the Other if you can't inhabit, if you feel it is impossible to inhabit their world.

Bosché: In Lucy Lippard's book, *Mixed Blessings, New Art In A Multicultural America* [1990], she asserts that it is "the universalist concept that refuses once again to come to grips with difference" and that universalism acts as a filter, intimidating marginalized groups . . . into veiling themselves and their images in order to be acceptable in the dominant culture." For her, to approach art with universal standards/motives is to decontextualize one's work, abdicating responsibility to one's self and to one's art and thus to the community which spawned it. What do you think about that?

Johnson: That's foolish. When I say universal what I mean is phenomenologically shared meaning. If there are no universals we're back in the same position that Plato was in 427 B.C. If you remember Protagoras, he said, "Man is the measure of all things." What he meant was not that men are the measure of all things, he meant that every man was his own logic, everyone had their own subjective truth. That [what Lippard said] is what the Sophists were arguing. Plato was up against a world in which there was no shared meaning at all. The question was, how to find a common public truth. That is the whole basic argument of *The Republic* and his other works. Whether he succeeded or not, by putting it in forms, for example, is another matter, but the universal basically means shared meaning, at least in phenomenological terms. You see one thing, and you describe it to me and I say, "Oh yeah, I see that." What happens, using language, is that you cause this to be disclosed in a particular way to me—you make a profile of it.

So I think the assault on universals is arguing something stupid, which is arguing against the European idea in literary criticism—that there are things that apply to all people. What that assault comes down to is arguing that since Europeans created these ideas, they apply only to them. But if we do not have universals as I've described them, what we have is subjectivism, and we fall finally into solipsism. Without universals there is no reason why I, being black, can go to the Caribbean and talk to somebody, say a Haitian. We've got nothing in common. We're black but we have absolutely different cultural worlds and there is no common basis for us to talk. Now if we are human beings, that is a different matter. But this is foolish talk and deflects us from the real questions of literature.

Bosché: You don't think it is relevant to examine individual/community differences?

Johnson: What will enrage me is if somebody goes to my wife, or particularly, to my son or my daughter, and fails to see them as radically individual and unique and not like anybody who ever lived on this planet before or will ever live again. If they come at it with some umbrella term, some *bullshit* about who they think they are without asking them—that's ridiculous. I don't want them to do that to them. They've got to figure out *who* these kids are. That's the novelist's job as well. You don't deal in types or stereotypes. You've got to give up all presuppositions if you're going to have any success.

Bosché: Going back to the novelist's job, do you write with an ideal reader in mind?

Johnson: Yeah, in a sense the ideal reader is a literate reader; a curious reader; a reader without prejudices; a reader who likes the things that I hope are in my books, which are characters that I hope are interesting, and suspense and philosophy, and the taking up of some perennial questions that are the human condition, in respect to the black world, because that's the realm where it's played out.

Bosché: Take one of Wright's characters, Bigger Thomas. Isn't he powerless in his world? Manipulated by outside events?

Johnson: No. He achieves his sense of freedom through murder. He sees that as his only possibility for a creative act ...

Bosché: But isn't that an act of powerlessness?

Johnson: It's a powerless world, but there's other people in his world who are not portrayed as being powerless. Again, going back, one of Wright's big contributions to our literature is the victim theory of black life, and I have enormous problems with that ...

Bosché: I know. You've talked about that a lot.

Johnson: I talk about that a lot because I didn't grow up with people who were victims. I didn't perceive myself as a victim.

Bosché: None of your characters are like that either.

Johnson: No. None of my characters feel that somebody else has control over the choices in their life. They can always make choices.

Bosché: Do you think that is true in real life?

Johnson: Yeah, I do. I think you can always make a choice.

Bosché: Many people don't agree with that. They see social forces manipulating ...

Johnson: What social forces? What's a social force?

Bosché: Poverty.

Johnson: Oh, I've been poor. I mean, so what—you get hungry. But you see, these great big capitals, Poverty, Racism—the victim theory takes away dignity from black people . . .

Bosché: From everybody . . .

Johnson: . . . it takes away dignity from anybody. And you cannot move out of the victim position into any position of power. That just does not work. What you get when you portray somebody as a victim—one of my best friends is so strong on this, we talk about this a lot—what you get is pity for that person but you don't get respect for him. That's one of the problems. Shelby Steele was quite right about this too. When your entire mode of operation is based upon making somebody else feel guilt and pity, they're never going to feel respect.

I think, because I grew up in a family where my dad worked three jobs, and my great uncle was a construction worker who built—all over my home town—churches for people to worship their God in, residencies for them to live in, apartment buildings, I didn't grow up in a world in which I felt black people were powerless.

Bosché: But you had the right models. What if you don't have those?

Johnson: I saw friends of mine who didn't. Not *all* the members in my family either, for that matter. I had an uncle who went to jail for killing a guy who he caught in bed with his wife. With his bare hands he killed him. Every family has all kinds of mixes of people. But when one puts that rap on black people: powerlessness, victim, crawling on your knees, begging the white man. What is that crap? I've never believed it.

Bosché: Take the recent riots in Los Angeles, the violence. Violence seems to *have* to come out when people don't have other options. I'm not saying they are victims, but they perceive that they don't have other options.

Johnson: Why do they perceive themselves as not having other options? Now I think that the inner city of South Central L.A. is pretty bad, okay. But if you listen to black people who are on the money these days about this subject, a lot of what we have to do is on us. It's that simple. It's on us. The government can't make a man stay with his family forty years or love his wife or love his kids and stay with them. Can't make somebody decide that they're going to loot. The government can't do that. 📖

Self-Portrait, 1992, Cartoon, by Charles (Chas) Johnson

Stone Crossing

Leonard Goodman

Ilya's most important task was to attend cheder, where he studied the Scriptures in Hebrew, and portions of the Talmud that were appropriate to a boy, now already a man for a whole year. The Ethics of the Fathers was the frosting on the cake; it was all in epigrams, like riddles you had to figure out. They were more fun than the fairy tales of the Torah. Didn't everybody know that the world couldn't have been created in seven days? It wasn't scientific. So said Chaim Moisevitch the Bolshevik. Reb Shmuel, the teacher, was dismayed at the way Chaim Moisevitch hung around his schoolroom trying to snag recruits.

"Go to the river if you want to catch fish, you devil. Leave my fingerlings alone," he screamed at Chaim Moisevitch. He would shake his fist and utter a curse in Yiddish.

"Jewish children don't need fairy tales, you old fool. The Torah won't free them from oppression."

Ilya was entranced by Chaim Moisevitch, who was only four years older than himself, and dared to speak to the teacher so boldly. Ilya had his own quarrels with Reb Shmuel. The teacher never answered his most important questions. For example: Why can't we eat chicken with milk when the only law in the scriptures relating to this says, "you should not cook a kid in the milk of its mother"?

He asked Reb Shmuel one day, "Reb Shmuel, I never heard of a chicken giving milk. Why is it then that we can't eat chicken with milk?"

Reb Shmuel's face grew red, he coughed and spat on the dirt floor and said, "Wiser men than you or I have studied the law and interpreted it in the Talmud. If you study more you will understand."

Ilya was unsatisfied with the answer. Even at the age of fourteen he thought that the law should make sense. Chaim Moisevitch said things that made sense.

Chaim was a wood cutter by trade. He went daily into the forest to gather and cut wood for the kilns—although one could wonder how he made a living since he spent so much time talking politics. Ilya's after school job was also to gather and cut wood. He had already been welcomed as an adult into the community and it was fitting that he should have some work that brought money into the home. But no one doubted that Ilya's future would be as a scholar, not a wood cutter, nor an artisan like his father. It had been discovered early that Ilya didn't have the steadiness of hand to hold an artist brush. His mother and father were satisfied that at least their son had a brain. In the meantime he spent long hours in cheder and afterwards in the woods. It was in the woods that he first met Chaim Moisevitch, also known as "Chaim the Red."

Ilya's parents knew nothing of this budding friendship. His father, Avrom Mendelitch, would come home from the factory, say the blessing over the bread, and even before he ate his soup he would ask his son, "Nu, how was cheder today?" What he really was asking for was not merely an account of the lesson for the day. He'd come to expect Ilya, the scholar, to entertain the family with an interpretation. He enjoyed listening to his fourteen-year-old son discourse like a rabbi.

One day, when he asked Ilya his usual question, the answer was a brief, "Fine."

"Fine? What is fine? Of course the Torah is fine. So is the Talmud." He held a spoonful of soup poised above his bowl.

"It was good," Ilya said.

"So now it was good. Is good better than fine? Or is the reverse true? I'm sure there's an answer in the lessons." Avrom Mendelitch couldn't rely for help on his own father, who lay in the next room paralyzed by a stroke, his right hand fixed as though he were still holding his artist brush. "Tell me, chochom, what was fine, and even good? Was it the lunch your mother packed for you? Maybe you've stopped receiving nourishment from the word of God?"

"Itzik Grob says Ilya listens more to Chaim the Red than to Reb Shmuel," said Sorele, Ilya's ten-year-old sister. He could have killed her.

Avrom Mendelitch put his spoon down. He stood up and looked down at Ilya.

"Is this true? Are you opening your ears to this profane person, to this Bolshevik snake who curses everything that is Jewish?"

"I can't help it if he lives here," Ilya said, examining his soup.

"No wonder I don't hear from you anything about your studies. Next time I ask how cheder was you'll tell me about revolution." He leaned over the table toward Ilya. "I forbid you—look at me when I talk to you—I forbid you to have anything to do with this troublemaker. He will have us all in hell. As if we don't have enough trouble from Cossacks. What do you have to say?"

Ilya lifted his head and straightened up, looked into his father's eyes and said, "Chaim Moisevitch says the only hope for the Jews is to join the revolution. He says as long as we keep our old ways we will be destroyed."

"He does, does he? Come with me." Avrom Mendelitch grabbed Ilya by the shirt so hard it began to tear. He lifted him out of his chair and pulled him toward the front door. "No supper for this one," he shouted to his wife. "I'm going to make chopped meat out of him."

Outside he pushed Ilya up against the house with such ferocity the wall shook. At age fourteen Ilya was already as tall as his father and almost as heavy; though neither of them was tall. Like other men in the Gorodinsky family before them they were built more for hauling logs through a Ukrainian forest than for speeding across the Steppes. "What has gone wrong?" Avrom Mendelitch said. "Where is your respect for Reb Shmuel, your mother, for me?"

"Reb Shmuel doesn't know everything," Ilya dared. "He can't answer half my questions."

"And you know everything, you and that hater of our traditions. Bend over, I'll put some understanding into you, if not from the top then from the bottom." Avrom Mendelitch unbuckled his belt and drew it out like a sword. Ilya presented his rump dutifully. Avrom Mendelitch whipped his son's bottom as hard as he could. This was difficult for him, a peaceful man. At that moment he thought of Abraham who was willing to sacrifice his son Isaac to please God. It was the only way he could continue, because he loved his son and hated to inflict pain on him. Thank God there was a passage to lend justification.

Ilya pulled his pants tight and bit into a fist.

"What are you made of that you don't even cry out? Here, take this, Bolshy. If nothing else a Jew must learn to stand pain. At least I will give you this chance. And if you can't sit down in cheder you can tell Reb Shmuel that it's out of respect for God that you stand in the presence of his words."

When Ilya began to throw up Avrom Mendelitch stopped. Ilya remained bent over expecting another assault. The father stood his son up. He gasped for breath. He was, after all, a man who had a sedentary job painting designs on plates.

What would become of his son? How could he impress on him the importance of their beliefs? Surely if their lives were polluted by the ideas of revolution they were doomed. If they couldn't hold onto what they had been given, their faith and teachings, how would God know they were Jews? Even the poorest, meanest Jew ought to be able to say the Sh'ma and feel his connection with the Almighty. Suddenly this beardless offspring of his seemed possessed by a dybbuk. The boy stood there barely breathing, without a trace of remorse on his face. The father was certain at that moment that he had already lost his son. The figure had Ilya's shape, but he had been invaded by something frightening, something that would shake up, not only the shtetl and the Pale, but the whole Russian empire, maybe even the world.

"Go eat," he said to Ilya, and turned to walk down the dark street without looking at him.

* * *

That night Ilya went to bed with a pamphlet Chaim had given him: "What Is To Be Done?" by V. I. Lenin, the leader of the Bolsheviks. When his mother left the room he removed the pamphlet and eagerly read what he could in the fading light from the window. Sorele would not be coming to bed until after she helped clean the kitchen, so he had time. This was the first piece of Bolshevik literature he'd ever seen, and Chaim Moisevitch had entrusted it to him. But his eyes were closing even as the light in the sky was dissolving into darkness. The pamphlet dropped from his hands before he had a chance to read beyond the first page. In the borderline between two worlds he saw himself in a heavy overcoat and fur cap, riding a fast horse, and swinging a saber as the Black Hundreds cringed before him. He showed them no mercy. He was the Jewish Avenger, saving his people from destruction. His lieutenant was Chaim Moisevitch, and in the dream the two of them went to his parents' house. Both parents welcomed the fighters, and his mother offered them a glass of tea. Reb Shmuel was in the bed that his grandfather usually occupied. Ilya and Chaim approached the bed, but all that Reb Shmuel could do was reach out his hand to them. He could not speak. Before they left Ilya presented his parents with a pamphlet titled, "What Is To Be Done," by I. A. Gorodinsky. 📖

Untitled, 1992, Mixed Media Drawing, by Gary Curtis

& Now We Come To Making Love

Marion Kimes

& now we come to making love
that dangerous act   forget
arts of touch   erection   orgasm
heady spring   full-bloom summer foreplay
all night harvests   now it's trust
trust italicized   triple-strength
once again we begin with words "I have"
"I have not"   "I carry"   "I do not"
everywhere condoms but we do not
we slip into each other
in the utmost act of trust
lay our lives in each other's hands
as we do stepping into cars
telling a work confidence
we really run on kindergarten trust
hope of trust both lock & key
we'd lose breath
rather than a chance at trust

oh windy reckless life   in the park
I stand & watch peach blossoms swirl & fall

River Talk with Vi Hilbert

(An exerpt)

Janet Yoder

We launch. The Skagit pulls gently on our inflated raft, inviting us further. It's winter on the river. Clouds hug the mountains on either side, squeezing a misty spray on our heads and bundled bodies. Around a bend, we sight our first eagle, one of many that we'll see. They've come to feed on spawned-out salmon. We've come to admire them. We've also come to be with Vi.

Skagit tribal elder, storyteller, and teacher of the local native language called Lushootseed, Vi Hilbert (*taqʷšəblu*) has come to visit her Skagit country in northwestern Washington State, to be back on the river of her childhood, and to remember.

We come upon more eagles. They sit regally on the branches watching us float by below. Vi calls up to them, *hiwiləxʷ saqʷ̓axʷ* (Go and fly now). They spread their wings, sweeping their way downriver to await our further admiration. The ancient language carries across the water and up to the trees. Vi addresses some of the eagles as *wiw̓su* (babies), or *ləgʷəb* (teenagers); but there is no mistaking the *hikʷ siʔab yəxʷlaʔ* (grand and most-honored eagle). Completely white-headed, he sits on a lower branch so that we may admire his wise old face. Vi talks to him and then tells us, "He's saying, *Yes, I know I am beautiful. I am glad you are watching and I am glad you've come to visit me.*" The babies perch on higher branches, less sure of their floating guests.

Would the eagles have flown if Vi had asked in English? "I like to think it only works in Lushootseed." She smiles as she answers.

* * *

There is no doubt the language carries power. I knew that the first day I heard it in Denny Hall at the University of Washington.

Vi stood in front of our class with her head high, arms lifted slightly, hands forward in the traditional stance showing respect for her listeners. She spoke to us in Lushootseed and though I didn't understand a word, I knew she was welcoming us to her home. It thrilled me to hear the sounds that belong to this place, sounds that awaken old echoes. Then she began to teach us a little of that language. Instead of starting with words for book, notebook, pencil, desk, and chair, our first Lushootseed word was *sʔuladxʷ* (salmon). Then came *spaʔc* (bear), *bəščəb* (mink), *sqigʷəc* (deer), and, of course, *stuləkʷ* (river).

Now she speaks some of those first words she taught us. The sounds echo on the river of her birth. All of us in the raft have heard Vi speak Lushootseed many times and some of us even know a bit of the language thanks to her teaching. But it's different here on the river. We are finally hearing it in the right place, where this language was spoken for millennia by Vi's ancestors, where Vi learned Lushootseed from her parents. 📖

Vi Hilbert, 1992, Photograph, by Joe Scaylea

Okasan: From The Journal She Keeps In Her Head

Sharon Hashimoto

Morning. I fill the kettle with water, warm from the tap.
Set it down on the second burner. Outside, blackbirds fly
into their songs. I wait for a hum, his fine high whistle.

Afternoon. Walking to the mailbox, I lean on my cane.
A light wind bends the tall grass. Behind me, footprints trail
a crooked line. I remember our son skipping stones through waves.

Evening. One by one, the petals of pikake fold back into buds.
But I stand in the garden, facing north. Overhead, stars rise
bright as birds. When I look up at the full moon, our eyes meet.

V

Volume 2, Number 2, Winter 1992-93

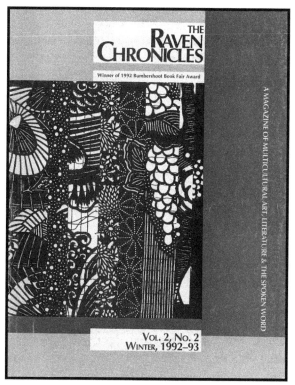

Four Seasons, 1992, Collage, by Frank S. Fujii

Notes from the
Inter-American Bookfair,
San Antonio, Texas, October 15-18, 1992

Kathleen Alcalá

❝ Always tell the story from the beginning," said writer Simon
Ortiz, so I will begin with Carolyn Leilani Lau. Carolyn's career
as a writer, and as a person, is reflected in her relationship
to language. Born in Hawai'i, Carolyn grew up speaking
English, spent fifteen years teaching herself Chinese, and now
studies and promotes the Hawai'ian language.

Carolyn's mother spoke Hakka Chinese. She never spoke it in
public, because it was considered an aggressive language, the language
of strong women with unbound feet. When the Hakka migrated
to Canton [Guangzhou] in the thirteen century, they refused to
assimilate. Carolyn's mother spoke Yue in public and Hakka at
home. The secret was that "underneath the mouth were the big
feet coming out."

"I started studying Chinese in my mid-thirties, and it was
very hard. I developed carpal tunnel syndrome from writing
the symbols. But I had fallen in love with the tongue, so it was
already too late. I didn't have any friends; I just studied Chinese
for fifteen years.

"Then I met (Bay Area and Puerto Rican poet) Victor
Hernández Cruz, and he helped me come out of the box. I didn't
know how to talk to people, because I was so obsessed with being correct, even to the syllable. In Chinese, they even measure
the length of the syllable. I would have philosophical arguments
with Chinese people, like 'Is a white horse not a horse.' But then I
bought a computer, met Victor, and it changed my life. I realized
that if I didn't write prose, I couldn't afford the computer. I started
writing essays, which helped me write poetry again, which had
become more and more restricted."

Carolyn did not learn of her Hawai'ian heritage until her sister ran for a Hawai'ian princess beauty pageant. The program listed her sister as being of Hawai'ian, English, Chinese and Turkish descent.

"I feel that I am coming into my most graceful language," says Carolyn of Hawai'ian. The language is experiencing a renaissance linked to an independence movement. Advocates encourage the use of the glottal stop (') and the macron (¯) over vowels to hold them out. 'Ōlelo is the word, and ha is the breath of life. Together, they make mana, power. The sound itself is manoa, self-expression.

"Hawai'ians talk to the rocks," says Carolyn. "It is a very strong culture." Land in Hawai'i is not terra firma, "it's a kind of molecular bonding" between people and land. "We are not more important than the other creatures. We are part of the land: animal is form, and plant is the spiritual connection."

Recently, Carolyn started reading Alaskan Native literature, and has enjoyed it. "It seems that they have been endowed with a less fancy language. I want to search harder for the words that mean something from my heart. What I am trying to do in my own heart and my own mouth is use the real words that express inner joy."

* * *

All of us were at the bookfair because we have a special relationship with language, as writers, editors, and publishers. In many cases, it is a difficult relationship which continues to divide us.

In a session called "A Latino Response to the Quincentennial," poet, teacher, and activist Abelardo Delgado of Denver said, "It is easier to write history than to rewrite it."

"We need to open ourselves up to what we really are," said writer Denise Chavez, "—a borderless country. My challenge to you is to make worlds where there are none."

Marjorie Agosin described her generation of Chileans as the "desencantados:" the disenchanted. They watched a whole generation disappear, and are disillusioned with the notion of human rights, that people can say or do anything that will truly make a difference.

Tellingly, the session disintegrated into resentment by a Latina of non-Native blood because of terminology used by another participant which she considered exclusive.

Chicano, a term for Americans of Mexican ancestry, is almost as widely used as African American. Yet it is still bitterly refused by those who feel it implies lower-class, i.e., Native American blood. Waiting for a bus in downtown San Antonio, I noticed that men who identified themselves as Mexican wore their hair short, while men who identified themselves as Native American wore their hair long. I finally realized why my father used to ridicule men with long hair by saying that they looked like Indians. In fact, the hair is the only distinguishing feature between the two in a border town, where the Spanish is full of Indian words and most Native Americans speak Spanish.

"If we did not know who we were," said Acoma writer Simon Ortiz, "then we were nonexistent."

Like Carolyn, Simon speaks his native language whenever and wherever possible. He described how he obtained an NEA grant in the Sixties and used it to look for Indians, since everyone said they had disappeared. He drove all over the country, stopping in communities and asking if there were any Indians.

"I found Indians everywhere. And in the process, I made a rediscovery of myself. I knew I was not invisible.

"This land exists because it is Indian. Racially, spiritually, there is no existence to this place unless it is Indian."

* * *

In a slideshow entitled "Towards a Post-Columbian World," art critic Lucy Lippard reminded us that at one point President Bush had talked about the "colonization of space" by sending out three "caravels."

She referred to immigration histories as having been "melted down into a toxic dump of homogenization," and she showed slides of art which has been created in response to that whole process.

"Repo History" is a show by an artists' collective based in Lower Manhattan. They draw attention to such sites as potter's field, where many enslaved were buried, and the Slave and Meal Market—in other words, a people's history of Manhattan.

The Submuloc artists (Columbus spelled backwards), a group of Native Americans from Montana, have also explored alternate versions of history.

Lippard quoted writer Barry Lopez as saying that what we call an environmental crisis is really a crisis of culture. Whites now think that they have no culture, and envy other cultures. 1992 is not the only time to pay attention to Native American arts, we need to consider them all the time. We also need to think about the white cultures: what prompted the conquest? What would people be like if the treaties were honored?

"What is tokenism?" asks Lippard. "When you've seen one artist of color and you think you've seen ten." Lippard realizes that she has placed herself in a posture of colonialism as a white art critic of artists of color. For that reason, she tries to write her texts in an interruptive manner, with holes in the text to let other voices through. (If you understand this, let me know.)

Cortez understood the Aztec culture relatively well, but that didn't keep him from destroying it. Understanding can still destroy: Diego de Landa burned the Mayan codices, then wrote his own accounts of them which are now used as primary reference sources.

Our culture has become, says Lippard, not so much a melting pot as a giant thrift store. We need to sell old images and ideas and buy new ones.

* * *

One afternoon, I ran away from the bookfair to walk the riverfront downtown. As dusk fell, walking with a local writer and her husband, a Neapolitan, we found that we had misplaced the car on the confusing streets above us. Walking and walking, the presence of the water, the rocky, uneven paths teeming with people, we passed a restaurant called Los Canarios while thousands of birds called and twittered as they settled for the night in overhanging trees.

"Where am I?" I thought. "Is this Texas? I could be anywhere." A feeling of dislocation too exotic and delicious for words, a welcome release from words, of other senses satisfied overcame me and filled me up to the brim.

"Always tell the story from the beginning," said Simon. "Creation is mythic and real in time and place. Land, culture and community—that's who I am; and that's also who you are." 📖

Bus Terminal

Anna Bálint

delays crackle as
fluorescent eyes glare
upon fatigue lined up
on plastic bucket seats &
an old man slumps & snores

& small girl sleeps leaning
legs adangle mother staring
off vacant while the baby twists
with fuss. more sleepers

readers waiters & dull-eyed
50 cent slot TV watchers
feet propped up on lumpy
suitcases. chatter floats

volume up from telephone
trees. tagalog black english
spanish anxious one-sided
conversations. "I love you

man" calls a teary voice
as the child-woman thin
as a reed treads down her
shoe backs. only the video

machines are alive
& whistle & rattle & crash
& flash loud colors & roar
& ping. but the boys

who play entranced
are all buried alive
beneath big Raider jackets
& beanies. near the swing

doors an an old woman bent
down stares down down at
the speckled floor & chews
her chew. & the guard

secure in his generic
uniform insecure about
his pimples struts
& wishes that someone
would break the law

The Owl

Donnell Hunter

When I die I'll come back as an owl
under cover of darkness, find my love
and tap at the window or fly down
from a tree and land on her arm.

At first surprise will turn her away.
She will think this must be a dream.
I will tap again, wink with my left
eye, or squeeze three times: I love you.

She'll reach for the phone, call
our daughter to say there is nothing to fear,
open the window and spread her wings.

How Deep Down

Paul Hunter

Before sunup in the damp air
there is room to swing the pick
break through the nest of roots
and hardpan like a slab

We work fast to punch in
and be out of the sun
before it's well up
two dry old men in overalls
and a boy sweating like one

By the time we get to heavier
going there is no room
so in turn we work
shovel prybar posthole digger
and take it a bite at a time
making a neat round hole
trying to keep it straight
because who knows how deep
down it'll want to get

Red then yellow clay then blue
straight down through fossil rock
straight into the mother
breathing hard but don't rush it
one man down at a time
the ladder lowered and pulled out
dampening now as it sinks like
an outhouse in the swamp

One digs away while the others
lean on their elbows
and talk over the mouth
endless old witching stories
willow apple or peach forks
or ells of thick copper wire
like the pair passed over this field
that wobbled hunted then crossed
on this exact spot

Reminiscing a kind of low music
of cats swimming then rabbits
tree climbing then old jokes
talk that steers clear of dry holes
careful not to kick dirt on
the digger helpless beneath them
who grunts at his handle and listens

Thunderheads in a cloud patch pass
so bright it hurts to look up
still in that airless dark
with all these leathery whispers
like swallows scissoring
the biting insects of doubt

Now and then he sings out for
the canvas bucket lowered on a rope
to clear out underfoot
or calls for the water jug
on a line through its finger loop

or the ladder when he just can't stand
the slippery narrow feel and dank
of being buried alive a moment longer
and lets one of the yarnspinners
take a turn for old time's sake

Around noon when the sun stabs
twenty feet in we knock off
sprawl under a tree for sandwiches
splash a little water on each other
and smear our clown makeup

But as soon as there is shade
again one eases in
to dig for the last of it

And by sundown hear underfoot
that sucking sound
that sends one after a lantern
to lower for a look
at how strong it's coming in
or how much more to dig for it

and planted at last like a tripod
around the hot tired mouth
still in the afterglow
of a tin cup we draw out
a muddy fistful of its cool wet light
smack our lips
and pronounce it sweet

King Limbo

Belle Randall

A dowel between notched poles is set
a neat six inches from the grass.
This is the gate to Limbo, through which
  a full grown man must pass,

A black man, lean and sinewy,
his forearms roped with vein like vine,
in an emerald cape with silver plumes,
  Haitian in design.

He lifts a sequined kettle high
against blue sky without a cloud.
One hand unfurls a five, to nudge
  the stingy Ballard crowd.

He passes this collection plate,
we glimpse his few chest hairs arrayed
like the rays a magnet makes in dust,
  his floppy slippers, frayed.

He bends to kiss *The Guinness Book
of Records*, bible of renown.
It gives the history of his reign,
  each challenge to his crown.

Lamp oil lit, he sets ablaze
the margin under which he'll squeeze.
To get a camel through a needle,
  first bring it to its knees.

As if it weren't impossible,
he threads his body through the portal,
and rises on the other side,
   in tear-stung eyes, immortal,

And if we paid, or didn't pay,
either way, it gives us chills.
I toss my two bits on a kettle
   overflowing bills.

The Liberation of Father Free

Bill Ransom

Father Free pulled a wet Bud out of the ice tub and popped the cap. His cheeks were tired from squinting and the beer helped numb his perpetual tropical burn. A Saturday afternoon luau, three weeks before Christmas, and eighty-five degrees under the clear Hawai'ian sky—a blue slightly deeper than his eyes. Father Free had come to realize that he would only burn and peel, never tan. His pink Russian nose was smeared with white lotion. A burst of foam from his beer made a tight swallow past his collar.

The annual St. Mary's Star of the Sea Luau gathered around a firepit near the top of a grassy slope. From where he sat at the picnic table, Father Free watched Mokae Cove curve away like a great red boomerang to his right. The channel between Maui and the Big Island stretched away to his left. A smear of snow capped the top of Mauna Loa. He drank to snow.

Small black crabs swarmed the few black boulders poking up through the sand. Behind him, Father Free heard the bustle of the Hawai'ian women closing up the leftovers in foil while several men tuned their guitars. The men thumped out a rock tune following a bluesy washtub bass. Soon they would play and sing Hawai'ian songs until the crowd thinned out, or got tired of dancing, or until their fingers got too sore to play. Then they would sit around the picnic table, drink beer and play cards until there was no more beer or until there was a fight and then they would go home. But they could not go on with the luau while the priest stayed, this he knew. Several dancers were readying the signal for him to leave. This he also knew.

His neighbor, the young deaf woman Mai Kwan, was among those planning what he'd come to think of as "the haole priest's dance." They conferred beside the barbeque in a knot of bodies and laughter, pairing up and trying out the roles of goat, duck, snake and cat. They always did snake and there were no snakes in Hawai'i. Father Free had been here only a few months, but he knew that much. In every luau the snake always came out as some kind of comic penis spitting beer foam on spectators. He tried to be discreet in his laughter.

Mai Kwan folded her beautiful arms and leaned between the Agoo brothers, her wide brown eyes flying after words. The afternoon sun flecked her long black hair with gold. This morning, and every morning this week, Father Free's dog woke him with its barking. It barked at the bedroom window of Mai Kwan next door, who used her voice in love and who loved early these days.

Every morning Frank Agoo's horse was tied to the breadfruit tree out back. Frank was married to Mai Kwan's cousin, Nina. Mai's quick brown gaze left the others, found Father Free. Then she blushed and smiled him a wide, perfect smile.

Father Free was thinking what a lot of difference there was between himself and these Hawai'ians. He was thinking about it in terms of the affair that Mai Kwan was having with Frank Agoo. In spite of his priesthood, he didn't think of himself as a prude, as unreasonable. But these people at this luau fancied themselves good Catholics, good Christians, and most of them wore long pants or long skirts no matter what the weather. That was one difference between rural Hawai'i and Waikiki beach. But the entire community approved of this reckless adultery, obvious by the blushes and smiles, the sparkling eyes lowered at just the right moment.

A bowl of potato chips clunked the table beside his elbow. Father Free looked up to a woman's face unfeatured against the glare of the merciless sun.

"Eat something, Father," she said, "you didn't hardly eat. Don't you like Hawai'ian food?"

Nina Agoo's voice rolled up something in his stomach and set his heartbeat on high. Nina was thirty and her two keikis fought swordfights with sticks down on the beach. Now Mai Kwan leaned not so much between the Agoo brothers as into Frank. His arm slipped casually around her shoulders and hers circled his waist. Father Free fumbled for a handful of chips.

"Thank you," he said. "There was a brunch at the ranch this morning. I ate too much there."

"Next time I'll bring you some haole food, Father. You'll never get fat, if that's what worries you."

She sat on the bench beside him but with her back to the table so that the sun wouldn't shine in her eyes, or so she couldn't see the dancers, or both.

"You're like Frank, not the type for fat," she said. "He can eat and eat and drink all the beer he wants. He never gets fat. I probably put on a pound just carrying those chips."

She laughed an easy laugh and the breeze whipped her long black hair across her face. She pulled a few strands out of her mouth and shook her head to straighten it. He shifted on the picnic bench so that he could see her without fighting the sun. Behind them, the guitars took up a familiar Hawai'ian tune and three couples sang of princesses and warriors. Without turning around, he knew that four or five of the older women were dancing and showing the youngsters some hula steps. Father Free liked hula, which surprised him. It was true that all that was said was said with the hands. Maybe that's why he liked it.

"They are going to do 'Old MacDonald Had a Farm' again, aren't they?" he asked.

Nina hid her smile behind her hand. "Yes, they do it every time."

"If there are no haoles, do they do it then?"

She pursed her lips, thinking.

"That's a good question, Father. I never noticed."

Turned as he was, sitting side-saddle on the bench, Father Free found himself following every move Mai Kwan made, every flutter of her expressive hands. Another cold beer clunked the tabletop and Nina twisted off the cap for him.

"Take a walk with me, Father," she said. "I need to talk to you about your dog and the fuss he's raising in the mornings."

The beer foamed up into Father Free's nose. He coughed a little and recovered. "Of course," he said, his eyes watering, "the beach is perfect this time of day."

They walked in what people call silence but is actually the absence of talk and the intensification of little scratching sounds of wind shifting drying grains of sand, the irregular *thlap-slap* of waves against rock, and the fading chatter of the luau at their backs. A haole couple stood on a rocky point with their arms around each other's waists and their backs to the sea. Father Free turned to shout a warning just as a maverick wave broke over the couple and nearly washed them away. They met the danger with childlike giggles and shrieks, drenched, waving their empty bottles high.

"You can't save everybody, Father," Nina told him. "Some things they have to find out for themselves."

Nina slipped her hand into his.

"Don't worry," she said at his flinch, "I won't seduce you. You're the only man that a married woman in this town can walk with without people talking story. It's nice to be out here with you. People go crazy if they don't get touched a little bit, you know? Let's say that I'm trying to keep you from going crazy."

"Do you think that's what's happening, that I'm going crazy?"

She shook her head and her clean black hair hissed beside his shoulder.

"You're leaving crazy," she said. "That's why you've started letting your dog out later every day."

He felt himself blush, but walked along without saying anything.

"There is a story about why the priest's dog barks," Nina said. She was not looking at him, but scanning the thick greenery above the beach. He watched the chop of the smaller waves against the rusty sand.

"It was four years ago," Nina said, "that Mai Kwan and I went night fishing along the shore between Pu'uiki and Koali. It was exactly four years ago. She was home for vacation from school and I wanted to get away from Frank and the keikis. Christmas was three days away—a woman gets a little crazy, Father, shut up all the time with two kids. So we went night fishing, and I took the shotgun. Frank's always afraid of these dirt-baggers who come up the beach and the pakalolo farmers on the mountain."

A sweep of her hand indicated the bulk of Haleakalā shadowing them from the right. He knew all too well about the marijuana farmers on the mountain. Confession, in a small community, had already become a terrible weight.

The sun tucked itself behind the mountain and afternoon shadows lengthened themselves into a pool of dusk at the water. Father Free had spent most of his short time on the island trying to accustom himself to the indirect ways of these Hawai'ians. Indirect, oblique, gestural—he couldn't put a word to it. The waiting for Nina to pick up her story was punctuated by the small beach sounds, the occasional scream of a magpie or a child back at the luau.

"Let's sit here for a minute, Father. It's a nice spot to watch the water."

They sat on the corner of a low wall made up of smooth, round stones. Most of the stones on the top layer were wrapped in long, palm-like leaves. Father Free sat next to Nina and she picked up a smooth rock, wrapped a leaf around it and set it with the rest.

"Now we are in church, Father."

"In church?"

"Yes."

She watched the waves touch the shore, but Father Free could tell she didn't see them. Her focus appeared to be somewhere beyond the waves, somewhere in another plane or time.

"This is a heiau, Father. One of the old Hawai'ian altars. It is a holy place."

Father Free touched the stones beside him and tried to imagine the old Hawai'ian priests, the rustle of feather capes.

"Is it still used?"

"Yes, Father," she said. Her voice was soft but clear. "We are using it now."

The chill that rippled between Father Free's shoulder blades might have been the great finger rolling night down the mountainside. He knew, without question, that this talk had everything to do with Mai Kwan and Frank Agoo.

"So, Father. About your dog. It is good that you keep him inside later these days. That way he doesn't wake everybody up.

Not everybody has to get up before daybreak to work the cows, like my Frank."

Was Nina laughing at his embarrassment? He couldn't tell. Father Free knew that Frank was a cowboy for the ranch. But Father Free had hoped that only he knew that Frank slipped into Mai Kwan's cabin these mornings on his way to mend fences. Then Nina asked the question he was most afraid of.

"Do you know why your dog started barking in the mornings?"

He was glad it was getting dark down on the beach. She wouldn't be able to see the sudden blaze of color that bloomed at the top of his collar and ripened in his cheeks.

"Yes," his voice was a dry whisper back in his throat. He cleared it. "Yes," he said. "I believe so."

They both sighed.

"Well," she said, "Mai Kwan and I worked our way up the beach that time. She fished ahead of me, and we signaled to each other with our lights when we moved. She fished, I netted lobsters on the rocks. The moon wasn't the best for fishing, I thought at the time, but she was getting away from school more than she was fishing. You know about the caves up there?"

"I heard about the haole guy who disturbed an old Hawai'ian burial ground in one of the caves . . . ."

"Disturbed!" Nina snorted and shook her head. "He hauled eight bodies out of there in his wheelbarrow and dumped them over the cliff into the water," she said, and pointed. "Right there. Eight bodies, dried out and sitting up, just like the old ones left them. That cave is near this very cave at Koali. It's true that each of these caves has a story. So-and-so hid there when Kamehameha stormed the island. So-and-so stayed five weeks there when the road washed out in a slide. This is now one of those stories."

Father Free offered his beer. She took it and, without drinking, handed it back.

"Many of the caves have supplies in them for fishermen," she said. "Food, sometimes matches and frying pan. This cave was a good one and had everything: a thick tatami for sleeping, a kerosene lamp, dry firewood. Mai came to it first. I got caught in a surge out on the rocks, and it took me awhile to work my way back. My bag was full of lobsters, and with the shotgun it was pretty heavy. I didn't see her light for a long time and thought she'd gone on past the point. When I got below the opening of the cave, something kept me from flashing my light up there. I saw a very faint glow. I heard a kind of a scream, and then another. Do you have a cigarette, Father?"

"No," he said. "No, I don't smoke."

"Good for you," she said. "I quit."

Her voice held a steely edge. He listened as she breathed deep a couple of times. A troop of five keikis from the luau ran down the beach, but when they saw Father Free and Nina Agoo, they slowed to a walk, pretended to dawdle and then turned back.

"What happened at the cave?"

He bit his lower lip to shut himself up.

"It was a dirt-bagger, all right," she said. "He was staying in the cave and stealing pot from some hippies up the mountain. What I saw from the edge of the cave was the top of his blond head and the top of Mai's white headscarf. He was on top of her. That close, I heard Mai Kwan crying. The kerosene lamp was lit inside the cave, down by their feet, and I saw what he was doing to her. He grabbed her scarf and slammed her head down on the rocks. A red scorpion was tattooed on the back of his hand. I was maybe ten feet away, and if he'd looked up from there I knew he'd see me. He held her down by the hair and had one of those big fishing spears jammed against her throat. It was already started, Father. I just wanted to stop him before . . . before he . . . you know what I mean, Father. I don't want to say it."

"Yes."

"So I laid my bag down and untangled the shotgun from the net. I crawled to the lip of the cave. When I stuck the barrel in it was only a few inches from his face, right above Mai Kwan's forehead where she couldn't see it. He saw me, Father. He frowned, and I remember thinking he was still inside her. I didn't give him a warning, Father, I just pulled the trigger."

Nina's voice shook and her hand clutched her mouth. The gathering dark swallowed up her features.

"You killed him?"

"Yes."

"And now Mai Kwan is deaf."

"Yes."

After breathing behind her hand for a while, Nina wrapped her arms around her knees and put her head down.

"I nearly killed the both of us, too," she said. "These are lava caves. I got three in the top of my head. Mai got cut up around her legs. The lamp didn't get a scratch . . . ."

Father Free put his arm around Nina's shoulders and held her while she fought for breath and cried nearly silent sobs. Back up the beach the familiar chords of "Old MacDonald Had a Farm" started up around the fire. He was feeling more like a priest, now. Maybe it was the cool night air clearing the beer from his head. Maybe it was the woman's lost touch.

"Father . . ." Nina breathed slowly for control, "there were pieces of him all over her, all over the cave. He pinned her down there while he bled. She didn't hear the shot, just saw the flash as his head blew up. She had shot in both legs. That's what I did to her. The neighbors think I did the right thing, but that doesn't make life better for her. She couldn't stand to have a man touch her after that. She was never with a man before that, and she hasn't since. Do you see, Father, how this is? Why your dog has been barking in the mornings?"

"I see," he said.

Father Free squirmed on the rock wall and cleared his throat.

"Did you send Frank to Mai Kwan?"

"No."

It was blurted quickly, then: "Jesus," she said. "Sorry, Father, but I sure wish I had a cigarette. But he's perfect for her, Father. Frank is a gentle man, very kind."

Nina stood up suddenly and brushed off her long, flowerful dress.

"It will last a month, Father," she said, "no more. It's true, there's some risk but here that's the way of things. Someone will say something to him one day, one of the men with a joke or talking story in a card game and it will stop. That is our way in these things."

Nina Agoo turned with a hand out to him and he let her help him to stand. He was a little unsteady from the beer and the afternoon sun. She led him out of the shadows, back to the luau. They walked in the shadow of dusk but her family, his parishioners, sat on the glowing hillside in the last light of an orchid sun. The dancers lined up, paired off, and the rest clapped or sang or played:

Old MacDonald had a farm, E-I-E-I-O
And on this farm he had a cow, E-I-E-I-O . . .

Delbert Kuu's wife, Lillian, danced into the circle to the whoops of the crowd, hunched over, making exaggerated milking motions at her huge breasts. Granma Kuu laughed her toothless laugh, tongue and gums baby-like and coral pink. Behind Lillian, Delbert snorted, making deep pelvic strokes as he walked. He held his index fingers beside his head as horns, and he lumbered about the crowd hooking his horns at the hems of the ladies' skirts.

Nina and Father Free reached the edge of dusk beside the firepit. Nina stopped him before he reached the others and held his arm.

"Father, I think you read more into this dance than you should. You hear confessions, that's your problem."

His attention was on Frank Agoo and Mai Kwan, ready to go on next. He knew what Nina meant. He wondered which of Old MacDonald's animals Mai Kwan chose.

"Yes, I hear confessions . . ."

"But these dances, they are what everybody already knows. The real secrets stay with you, Father, or they go untold."

As she spoke, people exaggerated their clapping to help Mai Kwan mark the time. They began the verse introducing Mai Kwan and Frank. Father Free knew what animal she would have to be.

In three quick steps he was beside Mai Kwan, laughing at the surprise on the Hawai'ian faces and his own audacity. He took Mai Kwan's hand.

"You and me, ok?" he mouthed for her.

She nodded, also laughing.

"Dog," she barked in her bold voice, "bark-scratch."

"Puppies," he mouthed.

"... had a dog, E-I-E-I-O ..."

The two of them sillied it up scratching behind their ears, chasing each other around Frank Agoo.

"... with a bark-bark here, a scratch-scratch there ..."

He and Mai Kwan stumbled across the circle, laughing and forgetting to bark. They finished with a lick to each other's cheeks.

"... and everywhere a bark-scratch,

Old MacDonald had a farm, E-I-E-I-Ooo."

Father Free hugged Mai Kwan, and she kissed him a lingering kiss under his jaw. It was done.

"Father, you're so *funny!*" she said, her big voice clear above the music.

Someone in the flurry of back-slapping handed him another beer. Guitars whanged out the finish and everybody around them applauded, happy in their brown eyes and the last of the light. 📖

The Killdeer

David Lloyd Whited

the killdeer frantic broken wing crying from the ground
the motionless sun cloaked in a shadowless sky
in which nothing moves but the bird's crimson fear.
the rugged dance of her wings filtering the truth
of the killdeer cry. like snow in April; like
a water spout funnel cloud on the mid-Sound;
like a full blown tornado. baseball size hail
here in this early northwest spring, the slap
crash violence of lightning, the thunder, all of it
filtering the truth of this bird's cry, the wing
which is not broken. wavering awareness of my own frail
shadow passing finally out of this dream. too small
too quickly. savor each day, and leave it well.
take only the knives & your fishing gear; all else
is illusion. & nothing else is yours. you can't even
trust your breath or your blood. & yeah.
the killdeer's lying about her wing.

Deep Painting

An Interview with Alfredo Arreguín

Kathleen Alcalá

Alfredo Arreguín was born in 1936, in Morelia, Mexico. From the ages of thirteen to twenty-three he lived in Mexico City. In 1959, he moved to the United States to attend the University of Washington in Seattle, where he lives today. He received B.A. and M.F.A. degrees from the university. In 1986, he received the Governor's Arts Award from the State of Washington.

"We are our own landscapes," said writer Elena Poniatowska. "We write the way we do because we are Latin American."

Seattle painter Alfredo Arreguín has turned people into landscapes, and landscapes into spirits in his evocative paintings exhibited recently at the Tacoma Art Museum (August 18 – November 25, 1992).

"Everything in my life seems to be magic realism," says Arreguín. "Everyone we know seems to be weird. All our animals are weird. Maybe that sounds negative. The mixture of cells in their brains seems to bring out something creative. Talking to Ray Carver was weird, but he loved me and was one of my best friends because I was weird, too."

In part because of his long association with Carver and poet Tess Gallagher, Arreguín's work is often used on their book covers. The finely wrought salmon, the tattooed horse seem to provide a visual point of departure for their work, which is evocative of the Northwest, yet something else as well.

When asked about his relationship with his native Mexico, Arreguín tells a story: "When I returned with my first wife to live in Cuernavaca, I met a young man from a wealthy family in New York. He wanted to be a writer. Why write about New York in Cuernavaca? Because if you are too close, it suffocates you. You need to have some distance.

Frida y su mono, 1991, Oil on Canvas, by Alfredo Arrequín

"When I was in Mexico, I took a lot for granted. In Seattle, I take ships for granted. But as soon as I got here, I wanted tortillas and hot sauce. I don't even like hot sauce. Here, my art pours out, as if directly from my childhood. I work from the subconscious. How much just comes out, and how much makes it onto my canvas? It's so much I can't memorize. Seeing my work is like seeing a diary.

"I'm not being realistic in my memories. My memories from being fourteen are like a child looking at marbles. I'm aware of phenomenal color. When Bernardo Castillo went to the market-place and described the peacocks and the weaving, all the colors and sounds and smells, that's how I felt. Everything was for me an incredible world of visual treasures. Now I am able to return every year, and can consciously reinforce all these memories.

"My mother was artistic. When I was little, I'd say, 'Mom, draw me a naked lady.' Her drawings were beautiful, like little girls reaching for an apple. I wish I had one of those. She also painted on glass, which was something women did in Morelia.

"I was kind of trouble for her, because she was without a husband, and it was very difficult for a single mother in Mexico to find a husband. She once made me walk behind her because my face was dirty and one shoe was flopping. She didn't want to be seen with me. As a result, I came to Seattle with all these resentments. After she came to visit, I asked her about it. She remembered that incident, and we both laughed. All that animosity just disappeared.

"She eventually found a man, my stepfather, but he was terrible. He was an Olympic athlete who ate twenty eggs for breakfast every morning. After an accident with a Revolutionary era rifle in which my half-brother was wounded, he tried to kill me by running over me with his car, but he only got my bicycle."

A few years ago, friends brought Arreguín a napkin on which his mother had sketched a few months before her death. On the napkin was the basic pattern which Arreguín uses in all his work. It gave him the chills, he recalls; she had never seen his work. "Tell him that when he sees this, he'll remember," she had said.

The design is probably from tiles in a restaurant, says Arreguín, but he has incorporated it into his subconscious.

People borrow his ideas, says Arreguín, but don't realize why his work takes so long. He originally used patterns, he says, to fill up space. Eventually he used patterns to describe things—the right patterns to describe clouds or water, for example. As the patterns build up, they influence each other. By adding and subtracting color and form, Arreguín shapes each painting like a sculpture.

"It's like a series of lace curtains that affect each other: pattern, color, and meaning. The meaning is not predictable, either."

Arreguín starts each painting by taking a white canvas and doing a very abstract painting. "It's interesting to see people borrow techniques from me," says Arreguín, such as at a recent show in Chicago, "but not understand the process. You have to get involved with the painting."

Recognizable forms draw people in, then they discover the less obvious: "All these ghosts, all the spiritual side that makes it much more interesting."

"Arreguín's invention of a nature mythology that features guardian animals and spectral masks," says art critic Robert Wilson in a 1990 essay, "led him to realize a potent combination of landscape and portraiture. The earliest example is his *Homage to Frida Kahlo*, painted in 1978 . . . Ghostly faces materialize from the swampy arboreal setting, but they are dominated by the beautiful face of Kahlo who, in death, becomes a spirit guarding that jungle which she portrayed with such vividness in life."

"The reason I'm doing Fridas now," asserts Arreguín, "is it took me a few years to understand her. I'm trying to get into the spirit of Frida, not the Frida that used to be. I break up the image, it branches, and she's all over the canvas; she inhabits the whole thing, like the Mayans use mouths or faces to mean rain or other symbols.

"My patterns came out in 1969 in graduate school [at the University of Washington]. I was painting scenes from the top view, like looking down from the ceiling. I had to find something visually strong, like a floor or rug, and that turned out to be my strength. The figures turned out to be less important.

"Unfortunately, people saw it as decorative art, which they associate with women and minorities, and hated it in this country. People talk about their master, or the artist whose work they emulate and study. I took the textiles and culture of my people that I love so much. I'm not sure that I want to be the 'founder' of Pattern Painting, since I owe it to a continuous tradition."

Art critic Robert Wilson has named Areguín's *Emerald Isle*, painted in 1970, as the first definitive Pattern Painting, a movement "in which decorative motifs, often culled from craft, were transferred to a fine arts format with limited intervention . . . Areguín's pioneering role in the creation of this movement has never been widely recognized."

I asked Areguín where that painting is now. He had sold it to someone in a bar for $10. That person sold it to a friend of Areguín's, a poet, for $3,000. Areguín now has the painting for safekeeping, but does not own it. The painting, in blues and greens, resembles his current work as though viewed through water—wavy, rippling, the pattern threatening not to hold, yet doing so. There is no central figure or animal guardian such as the eye seeks out in his newer work.

"That painting, and others that are even more abstract, pure painting, are an attempt to go in that direction. *Cholula*, 1984, which is in the current exhibit, is an example. But to be true to myself, I return to my jungles, which seem to be the most successful," says Areguín.

"The relationship of pattern and color brings millions of possibilities. Whatever touches me in everyday life is what I will use. It revitalizes the painting to have a central figure like Frida or Chico Mendez. It's almost like the person's spirit adds strength to the painting. If there's not a strong figure, I can't always solve a painting, and end up going around and around in circles."

"For every finished painting," says Tess Gallagher in her essay which accompanies Areguín's current show, *Viva la Vida*, "literally dozens have dissolved under Areguín's brush, as he embellished and explored his canvas with the meticulous care of a cell biologist."

Arreguín reflects, "I don't sit down and think 'Where am I going now?' It's like I'm in a canoe and I'm going along in the current, but so is everything else."

"If Lorca developed the notion of 'Deep Song,' with its impassioned cries taken from the ballads of the Andalusian Gypsies," says Gallagher, "Arreguín has invented a form of 'deep painting' —emotional and sensual, splashed with the sapphire water of his dreams of a world in harmony." 📖

Hatching Song

Joyce Thompson

Walk tall into the twilight.
Call fear its given name: companion.
Darkness is only
the nest of dreams, the bed
where wanting cracks the shell
of night, the edge
hope waits on
to grow strong enough to fly.
Deep in the soil, a bulb of light
feeds on your tears
until it bursts the seamless
round of its hard coat
and claws toward day—
pale brilliant fingers
searching
for the sky.

VI

Volume 2, Number 3, Spring 1993

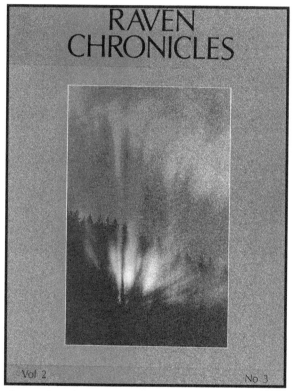

Sunrise: Coastal Hills #2, 1988, Photograph, by Mary Randlett

Peace For The Arsonist

Bart Baxter

He had his heart set on shoprags and creosote,
but his mother, God bless her,
gave the boy an autographed football for Christmas.
In the back by the lumberyard there are scrap two-by-fours
and a piece of his undershirt where the chain-link is torn.
Watching his work through the window, in the back seat,
breathing hard till the sky bubbles and bursts into flame,
he leans back with his eyes closed and his fingers wet,
hears the scream of the night watchman locked in the building,

and his mother, God bless her,
smells the gas on his fingers, asks the boy
if he called the pretty girl who lives down the street.
"Maybe go to a movie, maybe go see a basketball game?"

But the boy wants to burn. By the time he was seven,
on the Fourth of July, when the fireworks went up
he was watching the flame from his lighter instead of the night sky.
He was holding it next to his pink skin, watching blues
and that nectarine color he sees in his sleep.
He has dreamed of the little white house down the street
with the carport and shutters and trash at the stoop.
He has dreamed of the pretty girl who lives
in the little white house down the street.

Spray the gas at the front door. Spray the gas at the back door.
Light a small votive candle in the dark where the porchlight is out,
and the pretty girl living there, half asleep in her room
with her little stuffed animals and photos of Bon Jovi,
won't ever see the Bulls play or go to the movies.

So he watches the TV, and the blonde on the ten o'clock news
shows him firetrucks and aid cars and fine first responders.
There is peace for the arsonist in the night on the screen,
when embers and ashes fly, timber incinerates, and drywall collapses,
when the door jambs are jammed, and little girls suffocate.
He can hear the small bodies of babies beginning to burn, smoking
and blistering, sucking for air, but not understanding the arsonist.

Martin Luther was an arsonist that night in October
when he nailed up the ninety-five theses on the door
of the Castle Church. He had kerosene, dirty rags, and a box
full of matches, and his head nearly burst
with the image of Calvary burning, the angels in agony,
Pope Leo, the archbishops, Mary Immaculate tied up in chains,
and he nailed up the door so the canons of Rome would ignite.
Baby, he was an arsonist that night in October
when he watched as the Castle Church went up in flames.

There is peace for the arsonist when he comes to the city.
I will pile up my own debris, with arms full of trash
and the junk from old trunks I have hid in the attic:
the letters of lovers and Gideon Bibles.
We have tendered an opening, self-immolated.
Let the arsonist light the red gasoline cans in the alleys
before we have to do it. He will burn down the city.
Let them come try to stop it with red lights and sirens.
Let them know how it feels when the paint starts to buckle,
and I-beams become red hot, and the metal is melted together.

Andy Kaufmann was an arsonist
the minute he stepped in the ring with the Amazon Princess.
He had torches at ringside and tar on the canvas,
a tag team with flame throwers mounted and armed at the turnbuckles,
greasepaint and gas fumes, that volatile mixture of genius and vandal.
We burned his ass at the stake,
with the witches and Christians, with laughter and lighter fluid.

I can see his eyes light up with sparks from the audience,
the ones that he got to but never quite got it.
He is holding his side laughing, exploding in flames
on the ropes in a stanglehold, in the arms of the angels.

There is peace for the arsonist
when he comes to your door and asks for a light.
There is peace for the arsonist when he lights up the Castle Church.
There is peace for the arsonist working your neighborhood.
There is peace for the arsonist tonight.

Whales

James Bertolino

In the mountain's
white expanse

beyond the tree line,
we learned

Buddhist holy men
come again as humpback whales:

the greater their mastery,
the further back in time.

Context: Slouching Toward Hillerman

D.L. Birchfield

I open Joan Didion's *Play It as It Lays* and I'm in trouble on the third word: "What makes Iago evil?" I wonder for a moment if that was one of the stages of development that a moth goes through. It seems the fictional Dr. Hannibal "the cannibal" Lecter had something to say about that in Thomas Harris' *The Silence of the Lambs*. But no, that was an *imago*. A quick check of *Funk & Wagnalls Standard College Dictionary* tells me, sure enough, that an imago is "An insect in its adult, sexually mature stage."

It's funny how you can go your entire life without being aware of such a thing as a moth, and then read a book like *Silence Of The Lambs* and suddenly you see them everywhere, even in Didion, where, so far, they haven't even showed up.

I was reading Tom Robbins' *Another Roadside Attraction* the other day because Joel, a Chickasaw friend of mine, said I should, and there in the forty-fourth and forty-fifth paragraphs was "the death's-head hawkmoth ... Acherontia atropos," not exactly Acherontia styx of *The Silence of the Lambs* fame, but awfully close.

I was trying to read Didion because someone had told me that I should. I don't remember now exactly what it was I read that Tony Hillerman said about her, but it was very complimentary, in an interview or an essay or something, and so I made a mental note that maybe this is someone I should check into, because I'd been trying to get a handle on Hillerman, and checking into people whose writing he admired seemed one way to go about it.

I've read all of Hillerman's Navajo Tribal Police mysteries, and his volume of essays about New Mexico, and several of his articles in writer's magazines, and his book-length interview with Ernie Bulow, but I have not made up my mind about him yet. I understand Hillerman's books, and Hillerman, himself, is not much of a mystery to me. But I have not made up my mind about him yet.

I don't hold it against Hillerman that he had Jim Chee practicing his sand paintings outside, rather than in a hogan, as according to Ernie Bulow, orthodoxy dictates, just as I don't hold it against Tom Robbins for having his Navajo man painting his pictures in the sand outside of a hogan in the sixth paragraph of *Another Roadside Attraction*.

But I hold it against Didion for this Iago business. Thanks to my trusty *Funk & Wagnalls* I learn that Iago is "the treacherous, scheming villain of Shakespeare's *Othello*."

I'm immediately consumed by dread. Here's another one of those books that only Joel, or someone like him, could make sense of. He's read all but a handful of Shakespeare's thirty-some odd plays.

My Shakespeare play was *Macbeth*. That was the one in our eleventh grade text, and that's the one Mrs. Baugh had us read. I dutifully read every word of it. Had there been another Shakespeare play in the book I would have read it, too, but *Macbeth* was all there was.

At this point I'm beginning to wonder if *Play It as It Lays* is going to be like "The Love Song of J. Alfred Prufrock" or *The Waste Land*, where you might have had to have read the entire shelf list of Western literature to make sense of it.

Happily, Didion did not end her opening paragraph with that one sentence, and she cannot know the enormity of my gratitude: "What makes Iago evil? some people ask. I never ask."

At this point I am beginning to wonder if she is single and available, so completely have we bonded in spirit, and I read about 110 pages, roughly half of her novel, it going like a whisper on a quiet day, before I remember it was not her fiction that was recommended, but her essays.

So I stop reading. I know now that my reading of *Play It as It Lays* will be somewhat leisurely, but this does not necessarily put her novel in bad company. I left Rastignac on the verge of finally about to get laid in *Père Griot*, and that was not in this decade either, with every intention of taking Balzac up again. I think about that now and then, marveling at how anything so poorly written could be so famous. I did fudge and read the last page of it, so I know how it turns out, but frankly I'd rather read about Balzac himself, who is much more interesting to me than any of his fictional characters I've encountered so far.

Apparently there are others in Oklahoma who have taken a leisurely approach to checking out *Play It as It Lays*. The volume I found in the depths of Bissell Library at the University of Oklahoma, the only volume, had been checked out once, due "Nov 26, 1985," until my due date of "Jul 29, 1992" was stamped.

Hillerman has only been publishing books since about 1970. I didn't discover any of them until the spring of 1991, at a yard sale (got six of them for a dollar), and than I read a total of eleven of his books in the time it takes him to type a chapter. I've not read *The Fly on the Wall* yet, or any of his juvenile or picture books. But I intend to, as I've not made up my mind yet about Hillerman.

Didion I'm only beginning to become acquainted with. Now lest you get the notion I run out and dutifully read everything someone recommends to me, I guess I'll have to admit that I had back-burner forgotten all about Hillerman's recommendation of Didion until I got to reading the introduction to Cornell Woolrich's autobiography, *Blues of a Lifetime*. The intro was written by the editor, Mark T. Bassett, of the University of Iowa.

Woolwich was one of those *noir* mystery writers who was big in the 40s and the 50s (How big? He left $850,000 to Columbia University in his will). He's been called the fourth man in the hardboiled *noir* genre, after Dashiell Hammett, Raymond Chandler, and James M. Cain. He's probably most famous for the movie *Rear Window* which was made from one of his stories. But Woolrich, now dead, is a superstar in France because of the ideas in his stories, the view of life that comes through, because of the French literary tradition of Camus, etc. Since the French were, after all, the brothers of the Choctaws for nearly six decades, and the French see things differently than Americans, what Choctaw wouldn't be curious to understand that as much as possible.

Sounds good anyway, huh? Actually I was reading the intro to that book because it was written by the son of a guy I know, an old guy who hangs out at the same coffee shop where I hang out, and this guy, when he was about my age, climbed all the way up the side of Wheeler Peak, the tallest peak in New Mexico, to the very beginnings of the Red River of New Mexico, all the way to Lost Lake, and my Chickasaw friend, Joel, and I had made a whirlwind trip to northeast New Mexico just to do that very thing and we didn't even get to Middle Fork Lake up that trail, didn't even get two hundred yards up that trail, from where the automobile road ended at 9,600 feet in elevation, and I was curious to see if there was anything in this old guy's genes that might carry over into literary talent as well as whatever it took to get all the way up that 13,160 feet mountainside.

So there I was reading right along in Bassett's introduction, when all of a sudden, on page *xi*, he quotes from "Didion's famous essay 'On Keeping A Notebook: My approach to daily life ranges from the grossly negligent to the merely absent-minded . . . Perhaps it never did snow that August in Vermont; . . . and perhaps no one else felt the ground hardening and summer already dead even as we pretended to bask in it, but that was how it felt to me, and it might have snowed, could have snowed, did snow.' "

Does that not sound like contemporary Native American poetry to you?

I'll tell you, I left the house that instant and drove to Norman and located that December, 1966, issue of *Holiday Magazine*, in which her essay originally appeared, photocopied that essay, took it to the coffee shop and studied it. It was than I began to appreciate what Hillerman must have meant when he had recommended Didion, but then I turned to her fiction, forgetting that it was her essays that had twice now been recommended to me.

I put in an inter-library loan request at the Oklahoma County Metropolitan Library System for her volumes of essays because at Oklahoma University they were all on long term loan (several months, which means that faculty have them hoarded).

Sometime soon I'll try to figure out where she published her 1972 essay entitled "The Women's Movement," which, according to the incomplete reference in *Contemporary Authors*, was an essay "dismissing feminism as a 'curious historical anomaly' which has been trivialized by people who did not understand its Marxist roots," and which, again according to *CA*, was answered "in a long and highly critical *Nation* essay [by] Barbara Grizzuti Harrison." I just love that kind of stuff.

While I patiently await the arrival of those inter-library loan essays, I sometimes think about Hillerman. I think especially about all the disparaging comments I overheard about him at "Returning the Gift: A Festival of North American Native Writers," held this past summer [1992] at the University of Oklahoma.

Some of the writers I talked to have read Hillerman and like his work. But there were strong voices against him. Curiously, the most vocal, when asked, admitted they had not read him. "Nor would I," added one, decisively.

There is a lot of anger in the Native literary world about non-Natives writing about Native cultures, anger at a long succession of anthropologists, Eurocentric historians, Hollywood producers, and, now, New Age non-Natives who engage in commercial exploitation of sweat baths and sacred ceremonials.

But I wonder if this anger might be misplaced when aimed at the German-American Hillerman. Perhaps a mixed-blood Chickasaw-Choctaw like me might also have no right to say anything about the Navajos. But allow me to cite precedent here. If Geary Hobson, of the University of Oklahoma (a Cherokee), can praise R.A. Lafferty (an Irish American) for getting the Choctaws right (in Hobson's preface to the OU Press edition of Lafferty's *Okla Hannali*), then I will say, mindful that Hobson was right, and so was Lafferty, that I owe a debt to Hillerman.

I have traveled through Navajo country, lived in the West for a number of years, studied little but seventeenth century Athabascan history under the late Max L. Moorhead at OU for a couple of years some decades ago, and yet, I believed anthropologist Oliver La Farge, in his 1962 preface to a new issue of his 1929 Pulitzer

Prize-winning *Laughing Boy*, when he said that the Navajo culture he had known was a thing of the past.

Hillerman has pointed out, not only to me, but to mainstream America, that Navajos are still with us (news, by the way, which had not reached Oklahoma) and despite terrible odds, they are still Navajos. While slouching around here in town, waiting for one thing and another, not the least of which is Hillerman's next book, having not made up my mind yet about Hillerman, that strikes me as counting for something.

—*Oklahoma City, Oklahoma* 📖

Bluejay

Lise Erdrich

Roberta Ottertail is deep in the woods of the Birchbark State Park and her textbook, which is on ethology, "the scientific study of animal behavior, especially in relation to habitat." The jeering cry of a blue jay rips through the lofty idyllic treetops and skyclouds, reminding her that this ground was once not conducive to idle erudition.

In those days it was disputed with blood. The Ojibwe ancestors were still at war with the Dakotas, not the mere remnant grudge-match of academic, bureaucratic, and boarding school settings. The Ojibwe had not been able to scare the Dakotas out of the woods and into the Dakotas, yet. Of course there were no states, or feds for that matter, hereabouts—mainly some wandering Frenchmen who dubbed the shared nemesis Sioux, short for Nadowessioux, their approximation of the Ojibwe word meaning snakes. In the ancestral gloom of the forest the enemy was ever sneaking, seeking carnage and wreckage and the gory, gory, glory of war . . . so it is told.

A party of Dakotas was coming through the Big Woods, searching for an Ojibwe village to set upon and subdivide to bits. They heard a big ruckus. Here came Bluejay, the loudmouth, the braggart, the fool. Right away the Dakotas understood how he was—all greedy and conceited, just crashing along through the branches screaming about himself, looking for a fight or a steal. He will even steal the cry of the big red hawk so he can frighten the little birds away from their nests and then rob them, but when the hawk comes around he changes his tune and goes, "Wheedle, wheedle," instead. That's the way he is.

"My friend, we have a deal for you, and all the sweet fat wasna you can eat," the Dakota war chief told him, along with other big lies. "Show us where the Ojibwe village is, and we'll let you have a set of chief feathers in every color of the rainbow, too." Bluejay is always going along hollering and kicking, listening to nothing and nobody but himself, so of course he heard this and screamed out, "Sure! Sure! Sure! We'll go there, we'll go there, follow me!"

He took right off in the direction he thought the village was in, shouting, "Here! Here! Here!" Pretty soon he met up with Nanabozho. "Where are you going in such a hurry?" asked Nanabozho, knowing he was up to no good. Bluejay was only too anxious to tell him, because he has to holler about himself constantly. He boasted all about how he was going to throw in with the Dakotas and become their chief and get all sorts of presents and sweet berry wasna to eat. Nanabozho spoke to him, and advised him, "Give up on that idea, you can never trust them no matter what they say." He knew how the Dakotas were, too. He tried to tell Bluejay to listen for once, if he would shut up his mouth he could hear things, such as the juicy bugs and worms crawling in the ground, and the trees, and he could learn all the good things there are to learn, and know something useful. All this time Bluejay's mouth was still going, going, going, even when Nanabozho tried to tell him he'd be sorry if he didn't stop right there with his plan. "Cousin, I'm going to have to teach you a lesson," he warned. But away Bluejay flew, and his mouth never quit.

A long while later he found the village and turned right around, because he was going to beat it back to the Dakota people and tell them, but lo! He could only fly in a circle, always coming back to the village of the Ojibwe, though he tried again and again to leave. It was autumn, then winter, and all the other birds had finally gone south without him, and he was still flying around and around, screeching and hollering.

Nanabozho had tried to tell him that if he insisted on squawking on the Ojibwe, he would fix it so Bluejay would always and forever have to stay in the North and take over for Robin at his watchman job every winter so that Robin could go south and enjoy a vacation, and not only that but from now on he would be obliged to eat the Ojibwe' garbage and throwaways, too!

When springtime came the Dakotas were once again sneaking up. This time Bluejay made for the Ojibwe village and gave the alarm. The Ojibwe then ambushed the Dakota, beat them up, and were saved.

So whenever you see a blue jay, take pity and give him something to eat.

Roberta sees the blue jay land on the ground, eyeing her chocolate cream-filled Ho Hos as she lifts the last bite to her mouth. She laughs at his greedy expression and throws him a small token of thanks.

Nanabozho: Ojibwe trickster & culture-hero.
Wasna: Indian candy bar (dried pounded berries, meat, kidney fat). 📖

Crow Woman, Painting, by Anita Endrezze

Sleeping Room

David Romtvedt

At home after school I go into the bathroom and take the cover off the tub. A sheen of brown oil floats there. I know that I shouldn't use this water—that the remo will be adequate—but I remove my clothes and put on a thin cotton nightshirt. I step into the tub, lying down to get wet all over. After a moment I step out and put the cover back in place. I leave the shirt on and turn round and round until I'm not only cool but dizzy. The feeling is delicious but lasts only a moment.

None of this happens at Belem's. We set the temperature in her room. The water is fresh and there is all we want—both to drink and to lie in. If there is heat, it is ours.

When we were small, we would wrestle in Belem's room. We poked each other in the ribs and laughed until we cried. We rolled off the high bed and crashed onto the soft floor. We crawled under the bed and lay side by side hiding from tigers and dinosaurs and other extinct animals that chased us. We knew no animal would think to lift the bottom of the bedspread to look for us.

We ran in and out of the cool room, oblivious to heat loss or gain. No one warned us about waste and environmental degradation. We banged through the door.

"I need a glass of water!" Belem shouted at her father.

"I need a glass of water!" I shouted right behind her.

Belem's father would fill two glasses and hand us each one, cautioning us to be careful. I thought he meant to be careful not to spill the water, but he was warning us about the glass. The glasses were made of real glass, family treasures brought from Sonora.

Each glass was cut with many facets. Once, when I was there for dinner, I held a glass up to the light. I can't remember what was being celebrated but the table was covered by a long white cloth, stitched around the edges in intricate patterns of colored thread.

Sr. Arispa brought to the table a kind of bottle I'd never seen. "Red wine from the Baja," he said, "from grapes grown long ago—early in our new millennium." He filled two glasses, apparently untroubled by our new millennium. Then he put a teaspoon of wine into two more glasses and filled them with water. These were for Belem and me. Sr. Arispa lifted his glass and kissed his wife. He showed us how we were to touch our glasses one to another before we drank. He said you could tell real glass by the ringing it made when struck.

The glass rang and that's when I saw the light. I was holding the glass up as far as I could above my head. I looked up through it. The cut glass broke the light apart so that where it fell on the white wall behind me it became a rainbow. Before that moment I had known rainbow only as a word. Ever after, Belem's and the glasses and the wine and the tablecloth were for me more real and beautiful than the rainbows I was sure I'd never see.

The heat is a loving friend. But afraid. Loving us so hard it risks suffocating us in its embrace. Growing up in Phoenix I'm sensitive to the danger of too much love. I try to withhold the overt signs of my affection. I try to allow Belem to live without thinking of me.

My meditation is to love the heat. I bend and pick it up wherever I go. I put it in my pockets and feel it burn through my pants to my thighs. I want to abandon my weather records project. I want to abandon Meteorology Watch. I don't care what number of degrees it is over 110. The hotter it gets, the more there is for me to love.

But Meteorology Watch teaches me that the climate may change—one day it may grow cold. My mother tells me it was cooler here thirty years ago. My grandfather told me the desert was aflame with life when he was young. "Phoenix," he said, "was a land of beauty and warmth."

Belem and I lie side by side with our arms wrapped around each other. We whisper the names of the places in the world we'd like to visit. I put my hand on Belem's forehead and slowly slide my fingers down across her eyes, closing them.

"Where do you want to go?" I ask her. "We can go anywhere we want."

"I don't know. What about you?"

"I would go anywhere just to get away from here."

Most of all, I think, I would go to Wyoming, but I don't say this to Belem. I couldn't take her with me. Perhaps because I have my grandparents' words about their former home, and because I've seen pictures, I think of Wyoming as my own, a real place that people live—not a big chunk of closed-off land kept away from us so that the earth doesn't die.

"Keep your eyes closed." I tell Belem, "I'll take you." I show her fan palms, the Caspian Sea, a madrona tree, the tundra. It's cold on the tundra. The plants huddle close to the earth. Belem and I pull ourselves more tightly together and begin to shiver. Belem's teeth chatter. The noise makes me laugh.

"What is that?"

"People do it when they're cold. I saw it in a film."

Closing my eyes and traveling faraway, I press my lips to hers. The first time I did this I felt a nervous shock. Not because she was becoming more than my girlfriend. It was that I could feel her watching. And she was watching not only me, but the two of us together as if she had risen away from her body and floated there in the cooled air above us as we kissed. I opened my eyes and looked into hers. She smiled and I closed my eyes again.

"We should go south. You're going to freeze to death."

"Yes."

We sail down the coast of British Columbia, passing the whales who are migrating north.

I'm happy that we're making love. I can barely breathe, but I feel more alive. Something is coming. It's as if I were a large mysterious object ready to burst open and out will flow perfect life. Or as if there were something I was meant to do or be. I wait quietly and observantly so that I'll notice. Whatever it is will be stealthy and secretive. It will leave hints but that's all.

This is why I take a notebook everywhere, why I listen, why I read books to see if my dreams and visions have some parallel in what other people have thought or done. I am a detective of my own life.

My grandma said, "The bad and the good are all mixed up together, Jesse. You can't have one without the other."

I can feel Belem's eyes again. She leans back and props her head up with her hand. "What'll you do, Jesse?"

"What do you mean, 'What'll I do?' "

"I mean, what'll you do? I don't know how this happens. How can you make us see these pictures in our minds? They're not real, you know. These places we go don't exist any more than Phoenix with clean air and plenty of water exists."

"You have plenty of water, Belem." That's as close as I can allow my anger to come, changing the subject.

But she doesn't take the bait. She never does. She just says, "Yes, plenty of water, and when you're here, you have plenty of water, too." She touches my temple with her finger. She lets her hand flatten against the side of my head and then pulls her palm down gently so that her little finger brushes my eye as my hand had brushed hers. The pale skin on the inside of her hand slides across my ear and the back of my neck.

"That feels good, Belem."

She smiles. "You can't stay here forever. And you can't go anywhere else. This is it, Jesse. I've never seen British Columbia and I'm not sure those whales aren't on the extinct list. Tall trees and dripping ferns and pearly light. It's not like that. You know as well as I do. Vancouver Metroplex is bigger than Phoenix and, I'd guess, about equally as rotten. It's just a fantasy, Jesse. Face it—there's no place like these visions you conjure up, no place on this planet, anyway. Come on, sister."

I look at Belem and feel the cool rain on my head, dripping down my face.

"Belem," I say, "I read once that every moment is alive in this moment, every moment is perfect. No matter what. I think I believe that and so what if this one planet is falling apart. If it's true that every moment is here now and all those places are here now, then everything's fine and I should be happy."

"But you're not happy."

"I'm happy sometimes."

"Yes, fine, sometimes. When? All that talk about every moment alive in every other moment. It doesn't seem to help you. It's bullshit, anyway—just talk."

"No."

"No, what? Even if it's true you won't stay. You can't."

I don't answer.

"I'm not complaining, Jesse, or begging. I just know you've got to be somewhere else and I know there's no way to get to that somewhere else. At least not for me. I'd never think of the places we go—the trees, and beaches, Christ, I never imagined what it feels like to come rolling in with the waves. I can't figure out how you do that, I mean make it seem real. And then the animals—bears and wolves and eagles. How 'bout that—the national bird of the United States, alive and well in Jesse Will's head. That's funny."

I look at Belem and her face is somehow birdlike. I believe she could fly.

"What about the purple mountains and the fruited plains, Belem. You like those." I grin.

"Yeah," she laughs, "America the Beautiful. I do like those purple mountains."

"And they're real," I insist.

"No, they're an old song about a place that's been gone for a long time."

"They're real, just not here in Phoenix."

She sighs and rolls over, her face away from me but her body close, her back against my breasts. I stroke her hair the way she had stroked the side of my head.

"Do you think I should let my hair grow back?" I ask.

"No," she says, "it's not worth it. I'm getting mine cut pretty soon. I might just have all the hair removed permanently, make it like my nose."

"It would be so ugly," I tell her, "but it would be much easier to kiss." I lift the hair off her neck and kiss the slightly paler skin. Though she is still, I can almost hear Belem's mouth turn upward in a smile. It makes me smile, too.

Then Belem begins to breathe a little more slowly and regularly. I know she's asleep when she begins to snore. I get up from the bed and walk around to the other side, lying down facing Belem so that I stare at the fine small rivers of veins covering her eyelids. Her breath rolls gently up from her lungs and out of her body. The depleted air, hotter than the air in the room, tumbles across my skin, up my nostrils.

Belem is the first person with whom I have made love. I'm seventeen and she's eighteen. It makes me feel strange and old.

When I told my mother, she said, "You're young, Jesse, you don't know yet what your sexuality is."

Mama talks as if she were a clinician or education monitor. In this case I wonder though if it's that she's disturbed by my behavior. She's old enough to remember the days before full civil liberties were granted to homosexual couples. When my mother was young, no one would list herself as a lesbian for frivolous reasons. Only to receive a Child Worker Clearance or the Zero Child Tax Credit, say. Values were different back then. My mother tells me that. She grew up in another world and a large part of her still lives in it no matter what has changed. That's why she goes out at night to watch the stars and why she wonders about Belem and me. I'm afraid she's disappointed in me, and I think she's afraid she'll never have a grandchild.

Whatever your sexuality, who would ask a child to live in this world?

I push my face up close to Belem's and brush my lips against hers again. I close my eyes and listen to her calm breath. For a moment I believe we actually could be anywhere in the universe and at any time. I pick up one of Belem's hands and place it between my thighs. The heat spreads from there throughout my body. It is Phoenix without pain. With Belem I fall asleep in the cooled room. 📖

Four Views of the Desert
from Charles Baudelaire

David Lloyd Whited

Our Ennui

Even in an artificial paradise, you can
escape from reality, but still have to come
back to get a good steak, even a free meal
at the mission or the soup kitchen.
On the streets Ennui smokes a houka or a
glass crack pipe. the froth of hatred,
a jaded eye. drunk and exhausted from
genuflections. prayers. hunger.
eyes still quaking with the night's visions.

wine shrinking the liquid sky, the useless stars.
black battalions, merged shades of grey,
walking tatters, alive still.

unfortunately, those lovely breasts no longer
guard a heart. sparks & blood, steel-grey eyes.
in his trembling need she saw a fix.
It was not a healthy fever.

These strange flowers, a curtain of shadow,
resentment & desire/ice & flame.

Time wins by law. A city changes as fast
as a young girl's heart. rock hard memories, heavy.
puny crack cocaine babies withering like bad flowers
in a cat-screech cry, totally unconsolable.

Her Ennui

Too new and young and strung on the excitement,
the lie of freedom, the lure of late nights
and independence. a sweet street flower in profound
solitude. gleaming weapons. not quite pendulous
breasts. the innocence & sweetness of first promises.

a world of metal & concrete.
a world of asphalt & steel. perfumed
like a hell's canyon wind. sage & sweet water
in a storm at night. she seeks
"a world less hideous; minutes less leaden."

long eyes, she had long deep eyes.
jealousy lined with suspicion and
indolence, like rain, cold as the moon
silent of its own accord.

magic sparks click from her pantyhose;
gold dust-like dandruff or the dead calm
of despair. the half-starved cry of night things,
lust turning itself over in sleep
like a wanton philosopher dreaming alchemy.

she had eyes so wicked that no one believed her begging.
A look that could sharpen an ice cube.
half open, her robe, her great coat.
her bed was deep as the grave & the sheets all stained.

His Ennui

He was charged with nonchalance. easy solutions.
Like a wind from Havana, musky. "night street:
gold, steel, light & diamonds." all the glitter outside.

hatred, no matter how drunken, does not
pass out and sleep beneath the table. Oh, he can
laugh, but he simply cannot smile.
phosphorescent eyes. each lost second cuts
a bit of pleasure into lost, also.

As mad now as in the past. Heaven or hell
at least it will be new. She turned
with her terrible hand, eyes ablaze
with the hatred which makes anyone fight.
her dreams reflected hell. nixies & pixies.
rhetoric and satan caught in the staircase
of the County/City Building.

vertigo. vertiginous: nonchalant be a smooth
& troubling way of living. she bends over
her breasts and his brain catches fire. And
he will sob like a fountain of water blessing the night.
Street evil and skanky, like, off and gone too long.

Their Ennui

The homeless
multiply themselves against the woe of the streets.
iniquity. inequity. honey for sorrow, religion
for no other options left. bare feet and a bloody spade,
the work nearly done. a sweet savage sorrow
alone on the streets. and empty. missing
the sweetness of a home they never quite lived.

Hell born, hell borne, & hell-born again. & borne again
and again. irony & insanity,
they find equilibrium in words.

Flame-filled eyes, the thousand-yard stares.
loose on the cruelest local streets.
All clocks are brutal in the misted Monday morning.
Wine, like a tomb, wraps you warm, dulls the pain.
From our love is born poetry and poverty:
"God created sleep; Man added wine."

Masked in a shroud of wine, Pride makes us equal to god.
The blue crystal of morning cannot philtre
last night's tome-filled edges, cool as all things break
to man's sore touch. drunk on the wind
& the howl of the storm, an angel would
damn himself for her. even the wind is changeable.
The summer ends and the street looks long.

(They are / we are *un*consolable;
the *in*consolable are a breed apart)

The Museum Space: Mixing Metaphors and Mining SAM
An Interview with Fred Wilson

Philip H. Red Eagle

I was a little surprised when this strange guy called and said his name was Fred Wilson, that he was from New York, and he was doing an installation at the Seattle Art Museum [Winter, 1992-Summer, 1993]. He asked me if I knew anybody who would be interested in participating and could he have their name and number. He said he wanted some Native American artists to say something with video. They can say anything they want, and no experience with video is required, he said. Who could resist? I couldn't. I said I was interested and also gave him the names of others I thought would be interested.

He said that these videos would be placed in the Northwest Native American Collection area. This particular collection has stuck in my craw for some time. It wasn't that it wasn't real or beautiful, but that these works have come to represent the length and breath of Northwest Native American art in the eyes of many people. It became the obstacle all Native artists had to hurdle to get recognition as a "true" Native artist. *Oh, you do that new stuff. Do you do any of the real Indian art?* I chose to speak on the video as a Native American Vietnam Vet. Real, live Native men talking about their experiences in a brutal war that most would rather forget. Other regional artists who made videos were Glenda Guilmet, Ray Colby, and Annie Hansen [Linzer].

Philip H. Red Eagle: Tell me about where you're from and how you got there.

Fred Wilson: I'm from New York City, born and raised. I studied art at the University of New York at Purchase. I studied art and dance in Osogbo, Nigeria, as well as in Accra, Ghana, and a little bit in Kamasi, Ghana. So I've studied in Africa as well as in the U.S. I have been making art professionally since 1996, and during that time I worked in many museums to support myself. Eventually my work there dovetailed with my artwork and my work became *about* museums.

Red Eagle: Was there a moment that inspired that inspiration or did it just come on gradually?

Wilson: It was definitely gradually. I had these ideas about how the museum environments were affecting the art objects, but I didn't really know until I did one exhibition called, *Rooms with a View*—"The struggle between culture content and the context of art"—where I placed a lot of contemporary art in three very different spaces: ethnographic museum space; turn of the century salon-type space; and the White Cube, the regular gallery space. When I placed contemporary art in those rooms the environment changed. For me it was the beginning of my investigation into museum display, and museums in general. I found that the rooms, and people's experiences with the material in them, gave information that wasn't about the objects—that the objects weren't "saying" it, it was the rooms "saying" it. If you look at that in the museum context, it's really the museum saying certain things about the art on view. I found this concept intriguing, being an artist and being of African and Native American descent. It interested me that the museum could manipulate the viewer's notion about who you are and what you do. So, I decided: I would do the manipulating.

Red Eagle: Did that make you mad, that discovery?

Wilson: You can live your whole life being mad. Hopefully I get my anger out working to illuminate these inequities as I see them. I started having gallery shows where I would use reproductions of objects and create my own museums to kind of play with and critique the museum environment. Around then Patterson Sims [former chief curator at SAM] contacted me. He had seen a couple of my exhibitions in museums in New York, and asked me if I would do a show in Seattle, and I said, "of course." I jumped at the chance. By the time I was ready to come here, I had done another piece, another work, *Mining the Museum*, at the Maryland Historical Society. I used historical material, artifacts and artwork, and re-contextualized it. Placed it in my own environments. I added sound. I added video and various lightings. That exhibit turned out to be quite successful among the public, critics, and museum people alike.

At that point I started coming here for about a year. Every few months I'd come for a week, or two, or a month at a time, to get to know the SAM collection, the objects in the collection. Get to know Seattle. Get to know the museum and get to know people in Seattle.

All these things go into making my work. I like the work to speak to whoever I'm doing it for. Whoever is going to see it. This particular work has some references to specific Seattle situations or ideas.

But it also, largely, speaks to the museum world in general. Many of the things I do in this installation relate to what all museums around the country should be thinking about.

Red Eagle: Do you think museums in general need to be enlightened?

Wilson: In my experience I'd say certain elements, certain people in museums, could use some enlightening. I think certain people already know the issues and are just the best in the field as far as I'm concerned. And then there are those who could use real healthy dialogue.... They need to think strongly about what they are presenting and in whose voice and what that voice is about. And who controls what. There's a lot there to be thought about.

Museums in the past didn't have to go to the public too much. They had a lot of philanthropic support and they were able to support themselves with private donations. But now museums

Fred Wilson (American Artist, Born 1954)

need the public. They need them to come through the doors to get funding. They know they've got to do something, they don't necessarily know what.

Red Eagle: If they do get the right idea then your job will become obsolete!

Wilson: Hopefully. Then I'll just move on to something else. I'm working in museums largely because there are a lot social issues, situations, and problems in the world that artists deal with. I feel that I should look in my own community—meaning art community—and see where our problems are instead of running around saying who all these bad guys in grey suits are who run corporations. Let me look at *my* own museum and see how we're just playing into all those same games. Because this is where I live, and this is what I know about and where I can affect some small change. Because I believe culture is very important.

Red Eagle: Maybe you can reflect for a moment on your reception in Seattle in terms of your exhibit. What have you ascertained so far?

Wilson: I'd say it's been positive. There are a lot of wonderful art professionals here and everything's been, for the most part, great. In the museums that I have visited all over the country there are people in certain positions who do not want to let go of the power that they have over the collections and the cultures that they were entrusted to present. I have not been to a museum where that hasn't been the case. But each museum is very different in how that plays itself out. Seattle is no different.

Red Eagle: You're the first outsider, that I'm aware of, that has been brought into the new SAM, and they went to New York to get you. They didn't go to Seattle to find an artist/curator. How do you feel about that?

Wilson: Well, you know, I always feel funny . . . I mean, *I am* from New York. There's nothing I can do about that. Oddly enough this museum is much more connected with their community than most museums around the country. That shows you how pitiful the rest of the country is. It always makes me uncomfortable coming from the outside and knowing that the museum would not give the same sort of attention to the people in the local community. In this instance, I have to say, Patterson Sims introduced me to many local artists which in my experience is rare. Artists in the community are the last people anybody thinks about having me meet unless they're going to make them pay to do so.

I put together a show in [Warsaw] Poland and I didn't meet one Polish artist the whole time I was there, at least until the opening, and I had to leave the next morning. So I really didn't meet any artists. This is just standard practice. That really rubbed me the wrong way, so whenever I go to a city I try to go out and meet artists and bring them into the museum environment in some way.

Red Eagle: What do you think the roll of the artist of color is going to be?

Wilson: I'm speaking from and to artists of color particularly in the things I've just said. I think artists of color have more visibility now than they have had in the past. I would hope that those of us who are making a mark in museums, in the art world, will continue to open up the doors for others and not say, "Well, we just got ours. Let's not worry about everybody else." Because there is a strong possibility that this opening up to artists of color will be a fad, just like New York Expressionism was. I think it is important that artists of color link up with those other artists and art professionals that are sympathetic to issues of multiculturalism and empowerment, and maintain the pressure on the dominant arts establishment. We have a responsibility to try to be the moral conscience for the art community and continue to make our own work. 📖

To know its aspect fully, rushing along its finest,
tightest boundary, to arrest it upon walls, against
flatnesses of sand; binding to its sequence, its
most succinct properties; discovering it
constantly, knowing nothing; losing it surely;
drinking it unaccountably—

—Stacey Levine

VII

Volume 3, Number 1, Summer 1993

Anima Corvus, 1993, Photograph, by Fran Murphy

The Swallow

James Bertolino

Floating downstream, sunlight
became liquid. She felt it reaching
into her ears, her lips. No longer

her being carried by the stream,
she was the stream, and the sun's photons
were tiny explosions of feeling.

She became conscious of deep vibration,
and of moving more rapidly; her liquid body
shot over the lip of a waterfall and off

into space. She broke into thousands
of droplets, each a point of ecstasy.
She was a sigh of pleasure as she spread

into mist. Then a swallow
flew through her. She knew
a loving the universe finds

in the swallow's existence, the way
its sensual form becomes intimate
with damp air.

She felt water
on her wings.

The Jeweler

James Bertolino

I know a woman who places snake skin
under glass, who would hold

a mountain stream. In her hands
a porcupine quill stitches the density of stone

to the liquid of pearl. The spirits of crystal
and metal gather where light is

her partner. I know a woman
who is intimate with bones.

Red-Eyed Helldiver

Lise Erdrich

This one I heard from my ma, who heard it once from her dad maybe fifty years ago, remembering what his ma used to tell him when he was a boy, so probably it's way different now. His ma spoke French, Cree, Chippewa, and English, in different combinations, but the one that she named in her version was Wee-shaw-kay-chak.

Anyway, along comes Wee-shaw-kay-chak (or Whiskeyjack, or Nanabush, or Nanaboozhoo, or maybe even Chi-Zhawn). He is walking by the lake shore looking to camp for the night when he sees a gang of fat little waterbirds and ducks.

"Ma coo-zans (cousins)!" he calls out, or something like that. "Good to see you! Come on out of the water and join me for a dance and a feast." They come scrambling up there onto the bank, all gabbling with excitement, the way they do when there's a feed. "Help me get a fire going here," says Wee-shaw-kay-chak,. "We'll dance around the fire and have a fine time." Then the little ducks and waterbirds went and gathered some tinder and twigs, and Wee-shaw-kay-chak piled up the branches and struck them into a blaze.

"Now I'm going to teach you a little song," he told them. I don't know how that went, although my grandpa could sing it. Probably it was "a little Cree song," like he used to say just before he let one fly in his car as we were driving around the woods years ago, to the Bingo or visiting somewhere. Probably there was some clever twist to that song.

"This little song will bring a surprise," said Wee-shaw-kay-chak, "and after you sing it, don't open your eyes." Around they went, circling the fire and singing, and when the song was over Wee-shaw-kay-chak grabbed them, one by one, and twisted their necks. He kept doing that as they came around, and he was smacking his lips because he could hardly wait.

There was one waterbird who heard that smacking sound, and being suspicious, thought he would open his eyes just a peek. Boing! His eyes popped out and turned red from the fire and the sight of what Wee-shaw-kay-chak was doing.

This waterbird ran for the bank and dove down, down, down, as far as he could, trying to get away from Wee-shaw-kay-chak and cool off his eyes.

And to this day, the helldiver has a round red eye and never walks up on the bank. 📖

Conquering Wind, Seattle, Photograph, by Irene H. Kuniyuki

Executioner

Paul Hunter

We were hippies sitting there
in a sweltering bar in the sixties
in Mankato on a muddy little river
the Sioux had swept down
like a flashflood a century before
when a redfaced timber cruiser
with his ball cap on backwards
six foot six potbellied belligerent
pulled up a seat and shouted in my ear
how just that day
he had surveyed and cut
the last virgin walnut
tree in all Minnesota

he said it had belonged
to an old farmer who held out
to his dying breath
but then his widow had been moved
into a rest home while the kids
went ahead and settled the estate
because they had waited enough

and you couldn't believe
a tree could grow that magnificent
reaching up and out
from a trunk near eighteen feet around
measuring eighty thousand board feet
enough to make a dozen
houses from the ground up
out of pure walnut
if you could imagine
what that might be worth

and you couldn't even tell how old it was
because the heartwood was so black
the rings all ran together
and standing on that stump
the size of a Cadillac
seeing the hole
it felt like it left in the sky
got to me for a minute

and while he swirls his beer
to wash down the lump in his throat
I lean close and ask
why he couldn't leave it be

he says I hear what you're saying
I hated cutting that tree
you think I don't have feelings
but you know business is business
and there's plenty more
guys where I come from
who'd fell and buck her
soon as your back is turned
without so much as a by your leave
so why shouldn't it be me
doing what has to be done
not so much for the profit
but to keep off the butchers
and see that the job is done right

Cowboys & Indians

Tiffany Midge

Inspired by John Wayne movies &
black & white episodes of Gunsmoke,
my father stayed true within the Montana
borders, scouting for a dream
he wanted to own forever.
Only dreams sometimes play crooked cards.

He staged his life harboring between
real life & comic book action;
played summer stock in Big Fork,
memorized lines written by Chekov,
re-named Flathead Lake,
watched scenes open in bottles
of Red Eye, close during
piss drunk fist fights.

The biggest role in his make-believe
cowboy life came when my mother
entered into it. Trouble was, he got stage
fright when performing for intimate crowds.
His fingers got itchy when surrounded
by his Indian in-laws & my Sioux cousins.

The bar room brawls he invited,
choreographed themselves into our lives.
The Matt Dillon in our kitchen
wasn't no hero.
Just a guy with so many big ideas
they exploded like Lady pistols,
wrecked the soundstage,
during those starry nights
we learned to play dead.

Written in Blood

Tiffany Midge

I surrender to *Roget's Pocket Thesaurus*.
I confess my crime of breaking into this container of words,
and slaughtering this poem with meta innuendo.

But I needed something. I wanted to gather the dust
of 84 warriors & 62 women & children. I robbed
from this vault of words, language of the enemy, in hopes

I could capture these people, allow their prayers to
reach Wovoka in the final hour before I end this poem.
I wanted to know that I'm not grieving merely from the guilt

of that European blood that separates me from two worlds.
I need to know that I can be allowed my grief.
Sadly I have failed. This *1961 Cardinal Edition Thesaurus*

I depended upon has betrayed me. Betrayed my Indian kin.
With this language there are times I feel I'm betraying myself.
In my search for synonyms for *murderer*, I find *Cain*,

assassin, barbarian, gunman, brute,
hoodlum, killer, executioner, butcher,
savage, Apache, redskin.

Wovoka: Paiute Medicine Man who
initiated the Ghost Dance

untitled

dan raphael

the roof of the house sinking to the ground
is a sweater unraveling in the shadow of sheep,
grass holding them to the earth on the roof of a house
stuck between mountain rocks smooth as eggs
cracking open the grass like capes revealing Death
whose chest is a telescope or some sort of instant transport
cause I live in my eyes and have more room in my skull
than a post-nuclear tenement.
                           smell the air
that rasps against the plaster of education, the peeling paint
of internal combustion keeps muffing the punchline
but his laughs are like holes in the sky where clouds should be

I pull clouds from my pocket but they fall and shatter
like teapots oozing amoebas of incomplete digestion
reminding me of when and who I ate that with
as light switches argue in vaguely familiar dialects
I lift a piece of floor, let it dry and fly away
like a butterfly made from the sunday comics
next spring becomes a cigar in an oversized hat
skimming the sea for donations, for flabby votive candles
that grow faster than corn to snake away the hours
eating windows from red iron hills
a bellrope gives you the choice of falling
or being imbedded in the ceiling cause bat poop floats up
like dollops of fat fidgeting on vein walls:
the subway is 20 years late and all the stairs lead deeper into history,
pages so thin you can strain the soap from rainwater

A Horse For My Father

Eddie Silva

Because your theme's surrender, a life of dreams undone
by powers beyond a man, I construct a horse
for you: a work horse, weary. Animal you've loved but
never known since childhood, since your family's
homestead went to drought and then foreclosure.

A plodding horse, an enduring horse who knows to pace
long hours on the range without a tree for shelter.
A slow horse, a cautious horse who surprises
with hidden speed and balance when a calf bolts,
or when the herd is skittish in a storm. A patient
horse, a steady horse who quickens to its business.

But it will be a tired horse, a spent horse
who will call for care come evening, as I saw
you often slumped and withered by your day.
And I think of you as a horse as I build your horse,
a horse deserving of compassion, of tender hands
to rub the grieving muscles down. A horse let loose
in the comfort and sweet clover of the greenest pasture.

For as I construct a horse for you,
I construct a life for you, a life that isn't hobbled
nor desire's claims denied. A life in which you'll settle
into dreams, old man, of a pasture that is the center
of things unseen except in dreams. The prize horse,
the dream horse canters, head high, dips the head down and
flies from all fours. Dances for you, just for you.

Sacred Waters

Marilyn Stablein

The Himalayas are the source of the great rivers of the Indian subcontinent: the Ganges, the Jumna, the Jhelum, and the Brahmaputra. Most rivers are worshipped as the embodiment of powerful goddesses. In Hindu mythology the goddess associated with the Ganges River, Ganga Ma, poured down her waters from the heavens with the destructive force of a crashing, thundering waterfall. When the mighty Goddess let down her waters, however, the force was too powerful. Water destroyed houses, villages, fields of crops. Only after Shiva, with his top-heavy, matted dreadlocks, offered to cushion the fall, could the sacred waters of the river descend without wreaking havoc and destruction.

Many Goddess sites are associated with water. The confluences of all waters are considered sacred: streams feeding into rivers, small rivers joining large rivers, rivers mingling at the confluence with the sea, or springs feeding into lakes.

In the holy city of Allahabad, situated at the great confluence of the Jumna and the Ganges, there are shrines and temples on the banks, devoted to the Goddesses of the rivers. Devotees fill containers with the sacred river water, believed to have healing powers, to pour as offerings on shrines and altars at river temples. But to truly pay obeisance to the Goddesses of these two powerful rivers, offerings of thanks and special prayers are made at the water's edge or directly in the water.

To pay my respects to Ganga Ma, I hired a boat to carry me out into the middle of the great confluence. The rivers were different colors: the Ganges was bluish, the Jumna green. Where the waters mingled, the colors also collided, commingled in a divine conjunction. The marigold petals I tossed to the water floated and swirled on the surface. Together with other pilgrims, we chanted mantras, sang praises to the goddess who rode the mythical crocodile-like creature called *makara*.

Praying at a confluence was different from paying homage at a temple that was in a fixed location. The confluence was fluid and mobile. In the swirl of waters mixing, in the thick churn of water, the petals I tossed floated, whirled, and sank. My eyes blurred in and out of focus. Sometimes the colors were distinct—two, three, four, or five shades of blue, green, gray, and white intertwined in paisley patterns. Other times the hues blended and I couldn't distinguish different colors. The boat moved too, carried downstream in the inevitable, primordial descent of water flowing to the sea. The boatman had to oar rapidly against the current to keep me at the place where the waters merged in sacred union.

In one Hindu myth the body of a prominent Goddess, Shiva's wife Sati, unexpectedly died. He was so distraught he carried her body around for days hoping to restore her to life. As he wandered, pieces of her body scattered all over India. I visited two sites where her earrings (in Sanskrit, *manikarnika*) fell. One site is the Manikarnika ghat in Varanasi on the banks of the Ganges. The other site, Manikaran, in the Kulu Valley, is a hot springs retreat at the end of a small, winding road.

To visit the hot springs in Manikaran, a friend and I took a bus up a narrow, mountainous valley to the end of the road. We made arrangements to stay in the Sikh Gurudwara, the only *dharamsala* or hostel for pilgrims in the area, built at the edge of an icy stream that flowed down from the Gangotri glacier, one of the sacred watersheds of the Ganges.

An attendant showed us to the large room where we left our bags. Every night we returned and unrolled our bedding on the floor next to other pilgrims. We fell asleep listening to a cacophony of mumbled prayers, snores, and a few raw smokers' coughs.

Our days were consumed with bathing. The coolish nights of autumn chilled the air; trees shivered and dropped their leaves, but inside the steam bath at the temple our bodies soaked for hours. We alternated bathing first in the large indoor geothermally heated pool, then scrambled over slippery, mossy rocks in the stream below to dunk in a natural pool of icy snow melt. My skin tingled from the assault of hot and cold.

During the full moon we bathed in the eerie night glow. Steam rose to the sky; the moon illumined the trees and snow peaks rimming the valley.

The waters healed travelers' aches and pains. Religious devotees purified their sins by bathing in the steamy pool. Villagers channeled the hot water into private indoor bathing pools. The water nourished muleteers who drove pack mule trains deep into the Himalayas.

I watched a mountain woman cook her dinner in the boiling water one evening. She took a thin dish towel, tied a handful of rice and lentils mixed together, and dropped the bundle directly into the boiling spring. Forty minutes later she pulled out the bundle and ate her dinner, steaming *kichiri*, a rice and lentil dish, imbued with the healing waters of the Goddess. She rinsed her cloth and set it to dry on a rock. Such a simple operation: no fuel to buy, no wood to burn, no cow dung patties to carry, no dirty pan to wash.

One winter I rented a room behind the Niranjani Akara, a Shiva temple in Varanasi. The temple had a private door that led to a corridor that opened onto the public bathing ghat. To get to the river I crossed the temple courtyard, descended a cool passageway, and opened a huge medieval wooden door with an iron key ten inches long. At the ghat I bathed modestly in my sari as the Indian women bathed.

Unlike the other women, though, I couldn't resist the urge to swim. I kicked and pulled the gray Ganges water behind me in sweeping strokes. I was careful not to kick too deeply. I feared the murky depths where river dolphins and other unknown creatures lurked. I didn't want to step on a pointy sunken temple spire or a clay statue submerged during the fall Durga festival.

As I swam I was careful to keep the sari from slipping out at the waist and floating away. Before I walked back up the steps of the ghat, I squatted in shallow water and rearranged the cloth to cover my limbs. After I emerged, the cloth sticking to my skin, I threw a dry sari over me like a tent. Then holding that in place, I wiggled out of the wet sari and refastened a dry one.

The faithful believe in the cleansing power of the water even though the water has been the receptacle for the detritus of large cities. If a devotee encountered a floating article, he or she merely pushed it away, chanting a prayer with each little thrust of water. Constant evocations to the Goddess Ganga Ma rang out from temples on the banks.

The Hindus carried many things to the river to set adrift. After death and cremation, ashes of the deceased were strewn in the holy river. In addition to cremation ash, the bodies of holy men, women, and cows were immersed directly in the water. Since the Hindus believed that both yogis and cows were sacred, at death their bodies were still thought to be pure. The Goddess displayed extra, special powers to purify all that was placed within her watery realm.

In Varanasi I didn't allow my mind to dwell on whether or not the water was polluted. Sometimes I thought if Ganga Ma displayed any miraculous power at all, it was the power to cleanse the water, considering all that flowed into it. Nevertheless, to honor Ganga Ma, to pay her worship, I regularly took *darshan*, sacred audience, with her spiritual presence, by dipping my body into her soothing sacred flow.

One day as I sat with a woman sadhu from the tantric Aghora sect at the burning ghat, we watched as the body of a yogi arrived at the water's edge. Mataji—her name meant revered mother—pointed as a priest strapped the body to a bamboo frame. The body sat upright in a lotus posture, feet crossed, back erect, eyes closed as if in meditation. *Malas*, beautiful garlands of orange marigolds, hung from his neck. He wore the sacred mark of Shiva on his forehead. His skin was dusted with cremation ash. The faithful carried the bamboo bier into the water, waded out some yards, and gave it a big shove, launching the body to float to a watery grave. The scene froze in my mind, a sort of moment where time, movement, light, sound—everything—stopped and the image of death instilled an awesome presence.

Another Varanasi river scene: a dead brahmin cow floated downstream, the carcass bloated with air. Scavenger Indian crows perched on the floating carcass and pecked at the flesh as they conveniently traveled downstream—their boat, their dinner table, and their meal were one and the same.

During the Durga festival in the fall, devotees created elaborate, clothed and jeweled images of the wrathful Goddess Durga, who wore a necklace of severed heads, rode a tiger, and stomped on the prostrate body of her consort. For a week she was celebrated with music and dance. Worshippers erected tents throughout the city to house her statues. At the end of the festival, devotees carted her statues to the river and immersed them. Some promptly sank and disappeared. When one sank only halfway, the wrathful tongue-waving grimace of Durga smiled ghoulishly above the water.

The ritual bath was a purification of body and soul. During each full moon, at annual and semi-annual festivals, worshippers celebrated mass communal bathing rituals in cities along the sacred rivers. Astrologers predicted the most auspicious hour to take the ritual bath. Hardwar, a city in north India far upstream from Varanasi and close to where the sacred waters of Ganga Ma descended from the glaciers, hosts a special bathing festival called the Kumbha Mela. This festival transforms the usually tranquil town into a pulsing melee of a hundred million visitors every twelve years.

The year I attended, the astrologer set the sacred hour to bathe in the river at midnight. The scene was wild: masses ambled, pushed, and shoved in the dark, lit by the glow from the moon directly overhead, surrounded by a halo of soft light. The river was swift at Hardwar. Pilgrims grasped onto a steel railing to keep from being swept downstream.

To protect the sacred cows from the current, a heavy net was installed under the railway bridge. The net trapped cows that wandered out into the river and couldn't swim back to shore in the swift current. When the cows inadvertently floated downstream, they were caught in the net. I watched a rescue. For two hours three men wrangled with a cow in a net. They almost extricated the cow by pulling the huge body tied with ropes up and away from the water, but the frightened animal suddenly kicked frantically and fell back into the net. The men began again. Finally the cow was pulled ashore to safety.

Water symbolizes the feminine principle; water is the essence of fertility. Priests and priestesses the world over pray for rain in a dry season. The monsoon season is crucial to farmers throughout South Asia. Wheat, millet, mustard, alfalfa, water chestnuts, mangos, guavas, papayas . . . all the produce of the earth is nourished by water.

Tibetans believe that many of their most important deities are born in water. That is, the deities are not born from the wombs of women, they create themselves, spring to life spontaneously; they self-arise in the sacred waters of lotus-filled Himalayan lakes.

Guru Rinpoche, or Padma Sambhava, is said to have sprung to life in the lake at Rewalsar, a town in Himachal Pradesh known to the Tibetans as Tso Padma, or Lotus Lake. I circumambulated the lake and fed the sacred fish who were thought to have a lucky rebirth in a lake where fishing was forbidden. Many pilgrims came from miles away just to throw tidbits to the plump holy fish.

When I was growing up in California, every summer my family piled into the station wagon and drove to the beach. I return to the sea after important events in my life, to celebrate, to renew strength, and to energize. Or, at the loss of a loved one, I return to grieve and mourn.

In India after four years without seeing the ocean, I visited a friend who lived on the Bay of Bengal. I longed to bath in the salty water, feel the sand and sun on my skin as the sea wind streamed through my hair. A river flowed between his tapioca farm and the sea. A temple honoring a local Goddess was situated at the point where the river met the sea. I wanted to swim after visiting the shrine. To get to the beach, however, I first had to swim the river which paralleled the beach. I waited until low tide when the river was only four feet at the deepest part, then I swam across holding my towel aloft with one hand. The temperature was so hot, I didn't really need a towel. The sun and the warm breezes could have easily dried my hair and skin in minutes. Luckily I had brought the towel—that cloth saved my life.

At the beach I set my towel down and waded into the sea. Warm, silky water surrounded me, refreshed and invigorated my skin. I dove fearlessly into a swelling wave to cut off the power of the cascading downward spiral of water—a trick I learned as a girl. Give into the crush of water, then rise up, triumphant. When I glanced back I noticed my towel had drifted down the beach—or rather, I had drifted away. A few minutes passed and the towel was even further away. If there was an undertow, I thought, at least it paralleled the shore, causing no threat.

As the distance grew, however, I intuited danger. When I pulled myself out of the water, I was just yards from where the river gushed into the ocean. The divine confluence of fresh and salty waters was a powerful channel; the swift flow of water shot straight out to open sea. If I had stayed in the water another minute, I would have been thrust out to open water with the force of the draining river. There was no one to rescue me on the deserted beach.

I consider the sacred waters. Standing water: pools, tanks, temple wells, lakes; falling water: monsoon deluges, flowing water in rivers, water flowing from the sacred shrines in Hindu temples. Frozen water: ice lingams and yonis, melting glaciers, the watersheds of the great rivers. Infertile women pour sacred river water on Shiva lingams and pray for the miracle of conception. In Varanasi merchants bottled Ganges water in brass pots to sell to pilgrims and Indian tourists. There are few holy sites in India or Nepal that are not associated with water; even caves drip moisture.

In a country alternately plagued by drought and floods, the waters of the land and waters from the heavens take on the manifestations of the Goddesses. That is, water is both wrathful and peaceful, turbulent and placid. Water blesses, heals and destroys. Pilgrims everywhere shower their praise and thanks, raise voices on high to the Goddesses who flow, drip, ripple, wave, and crash. 📖

Waters Poured From Above, 2018, Collage, by Marilyn Stablein

Breath

Stacey Levine

Let me be your biggest failure, let me be the one;
I scaled the eaves each night, I watched you
from above; wasn't this as you wanted; wasn't
this good—

Just this way as the way to gain it all. With it
more nearly now, than before. Waiting this way
between the fog and sand; was it your way to do
this; weren't you the thief of my eyes, my hair?

I am the coldest of cold steel wires in winter.
Hateful draughts of freezing air, water; ready to
ruin it, to have it so fitfully, ever to escape—

Holding near to its line and intent. To locate it
precisely, the manner of its advance. Learning
its gravity, surface, length; how it came back—
always again—

Waiting with only the thought to elude, evade.
Watching from all corners for it to return. Who
moved so close, to survey its paucity; who knew
it so well, so constantly?

Let me put my hands on it, if one had hands at
all; let me stop it first, deny its every moment,
every consequence of its intent and movement;
to know its subterfuge, the colorless air; such
emptiness, when it returned—

Who required its surface, its shape; the most
oblique motions of breath and descent; who

returned to its boundary, extending from it
uncertainly; to know it this way, so superbly—

Just this way, as the way to gain time; just its
thinnest edge, and water, and light; moving near
by every possible means; staying with it
fascinatingly—

To have gone away; to have been near; to know
its suspension, its repose and movement; finding
its border everywhere; to know this at once,
without thought, as one knew pouring sand—
how to breathe air—

Let me be the same as it always; let me know it so
well, that I might comply perfectly; to wish for
this in all possible abundancies; the barest of
chances; its ways of supplanting; let me hold it
down quietly, just to learn its locality—

The abatement of caution, resistance; to hope for
as much suspension as it might give; the emptiness of the shore, the silence in every stone; its
unsurpassable gesture figured so acutely there—

Let me refuse it like skin, like ice; let me know it
so carefully, find the measure of its concavity,
incline; who knew its chill and drop, its irreduc-
ible calm; who knew its shape, the aspect it wore;
the slow expanse of the sea; the brevity of the
shore—

Having chosen the afternoon, the morning so
knowingly; having searched its assemblage;
aligning to its plan so exactly; straight upon its
surface, its unknowable length; to thwart its
intelligence, every measure of its lack—

The sum of these movements: one sculpture, one
breath—

Who knew each fragment; every last facement;
who knew its limit; the color of light; to ply these
adjacencies, its constant breadth; who made as if
to leave it—its fractal design—

To fall behind its firmest endeavor; to link to each
unbending dimension; holding it everywhere,
pressing with such tenacity—to become the same
as it, so exactly—

To know its aspect fully, rushing along its finest,
tightest boundary, to arrest it upon walls, against
flatnesses of sand; binding to its sequence, its
most succinct properties; discovering it
constantly, knowing nothing; losing it surely;
drinking it unaccountably—

Holding back from this impossible gauge; let me
know it so well, that I need never emerge;
moving there slowly, within it gaze always,
falling inside its intractable light; discovering its
circumference everywhere, the structure of its
insuperable line—

One knew it, but one never saw; unable to go there;
one couldn't have gone; watching each night for stillness,
exposure; ready to desist from this manner, structure;
pressing it further, that it might grow
remoter—weaker—

Choosing each day, with its light and rain;
fixity, insistence; gliding there, to its surface of
stillnesses; moving in certainly, to the erasure
of all differences—

Let me bring it near to malign it, to steal,
to conflict it in ways it might never guess; let me
track it so expertly, unearth its sequence, to
confound it, make it weaken, lie flat; to quell its
effort, congeal its command—

Let me hurl it away, for it was the only thing;
against its border, just to decline it ruthlessly;
straight upon it, that it might use itself up
completely; let me bind it mesmerizingly to its
own intent, force its infractions into walls of sand—

Every gesture, every departure of line and hand;
who knew each one of its endeavors; the softest
exposure; the gauze of its breath; who wished
these lines, arcs; the smoothest involutions of its
unbending edge—

One never saw it, but belonged to its breath; one
knew its insistence, its plumbline and
distance, climbing to its flattest, most fully sewn
edge; blaming it surely, all its ways of knowing;
to plunge against limit, constancy, lack—

Let me lose it in all proportions; every one of its
circular impartions, impelling it ever, each
motion of the wind; climbing to its incalculable
light; vivid, distant—might one become the same
as it—

—Having found this with my eyes, the skin of
my hands; forgetting constantly, binding to it as
skillfully; ready to fit its every capacity;
following so closely to encase its attempt;
immersing it in sand—for its difference—again—

As if to find this ungettable breath; the nearest
measure of alignment, density; every last
portion of this surface, distance; every one of its
hidden propensities; wishing each degree of
purchase, strength; its meanest desire for salt, for
rain—

Let me spend it instantly, for it was the only
thing; let me be the one never to believe; let me
defer quietly, depress it completely, falling there
always, to regain; to atrophy it to such thorough
degree—wasn't it best this way—soundless—

Let me lose it every moment, in all ways
conceivably; its furthest, most silent edges; let me
dissolve its rim completely; to learn its pattern
deftly, to become the same with it, so perfectly—

Let me press its whisper flat, elide it wholly; find
the velour of its substance, the opportunity of
hands; climbing to meet it so equally; to raze its
boundary instantly, knowing its position at each
event—to lay pressure, to waste it again—

Let me break it hard, for it was not the thing, let
my pummel it to air, discard it indescribably; to
refuse its manner, tenor, its self-same segments,
denying it again through reaches of sand, water;
to earn at its boundary, just to change it
completely; to surprise it so badly, to convince; to
bury all limits, difference—

To find such a thing; each motion discretely; to
break its surface, its traceless light; returning to
this only, indelible texture, these opaque and
smoothest possible eyes; translation of

movement; valence, demand; let me hold it so
well, that I need never appear—

Having chosen the afternoon, the morning so
readily, all its ways of scarcely abating; each rise
of breath; the fluency of hands; the conjugation of
its curve and span—

Having wished this with my eyes, limbs, the
heels of my hands; falling to it completely,
having known such silence, swell, and capacity;
to be just the same, in this stillness of breath;
wasn't right this way—borderless—

Let me be the one to fall hardest, to deny every
chord; let me damage, confine it, rip it so
stunningly; let me weaken it badly—to return
then—so prominently—

Just this question of gaining it at least, eschewing
its limit, searching all its breath; sliding as far
from its inscrutable lack; withholding so
suddenly, that it might succumb violently; to
efface it this easily; to believe again, so
completely—

Let me lose it in all fires; send it down as if it did
not matter; impede it so severely, abandon it in
wind; let me pry it from its most resolute edge;
crushed at its border, let me stop it completely,
always having exhausted everything—

—Dismantling it so carefully; all these ways of
inventing, of flattening it so badly; gaining its
barest measure; the limitless surface of hands; to
leave repeatedly, so as to come back to it

constantly; enwrapping it noisily, suddenly, with
all its own scarcity, engulfing it severely—so
necessarily—

—Corrupting it like destroying each part;
dragging it here to shut it down; spinning it
recklessly into burning sand; forcing this
boundary, making you pay for all such crimes—

As having hidden yourself away inside the sky—

Having found its patterns countlessly; having
lost this sequence immeasurably; to have known
it so quickly, the devout shape of eyes; all
weightlessness, all undeniable traces of it—only
unable—except to eclipse it—

Running to it everywhere with heels, hands and
eyes; having lost it again, in the narrowness of
the night; near again, striking with such alacrity;
let me release myself upon it completely; when
might it carry me only, best—let me crush,
confound its veiled hands—

Only this flatness, color, and inconfiscable light;
strung beneath its ledge, taking unstoppably
what it might never extend; slaying every wish
tied to the inextricable, limitless surge of its line;
to deluge, confront, as it formed me separate,
wrong, like a crime, beautifully slow—

—Slipping there tracelessly, only its weight upon
me; tearing it prodigiously, with its scarcely
tenable eyes—hating it like grating along this
inviolable plane; only here; only its clearest, most
unthinkable ravishing line; let me be the one who

climbed to it rightly; who held it so carefully;
who remained with it; who, between these
distances, had everything to give it—

Let me be the one who plied it apart; this way,
slowly, as when I shut it down; this tenor only—
as if I might have everything—every moment, to
demand it be under me—

VIII

VOLUME 3, NUMBER 2, WINTER 1993-94

The Get Away, 1990, Painting, by Barbara Earl Thomas

Down From Masada

Dina Ben-Lev

1
It was the summer of '72
and grandfather said, I don't want
to die in Brooklyn or be lifted
up to an ambulance in a street
where boys throw balls
at every passing car. No,
I want a new language,
in Israel, where camels
melt into sand and Arab girls
trade jewels for magazines.
I'm going to look
down from Masada!

2
Friends in high school envied
the large stamps on my postcards:
the golds, the passionate blues,
photographs of miracles on the fronts.
There, people sat on water, had dinner
in playgrounds, touched the spot
where Jesus shed his first tears.
A girl might keep an antelope
in her backyard. Mother wanted to know
what kind of country allows women
to be frisked on their way into a movie.

3
Dad said he didn't like the idea of his father
waking to sirens, then spending the rest of a night

underground. That he didn't like school buses
blowing up, wars on the borders, grandfather
walking through all those months of rain.

He should be here. New York is New York,
the music, the art, winters with lights!

4
In March the phone rang: a neighbor said
his son climbed through the window so
they wouldn't have to break down the door.

Grandfather had been in bed for days.

Only father flew to the burial,
to sing Kaddish, to whisper Shalom.

The rule of the cemetery:
no caskets, no headstones,
a field is a field.

5
Years later, I'm caught off-guard.
Father asks, Do you think of him?
Of those evenings in Brighton Beach?

I think of a tenth-floor terrace,
a brick building, a man behind spectacles
on a folding chair, sadly shaking his head
at communists, psychiatrists, suicides, soot,
adulterers, yentas, quislings, fascists,
muggers, and his stubborn ex-wife.
I think of a man who liked fish shops,
and didn't curse the D trains
cutting through conversations,
a man who laughed about presidents

becoming uglier and more unlucky.
And who at the end of a day
gently folded his chair and turned quiet
and turned in, out of respect
for a good hot meal.

New Souls Then

October 30, 1993

Phoebe Bosché

Today fresh shards of glass slicing flesh. Blood is dripping,
& we are slipping on white tiles. while we slide
we hear a song. bones bones bones, my bones,
ash solidified, dance on my grave,
the box that one day will carry these bones.
& they will clack, bing & bang joyfully on this Day of The Dead.
they will sing in Spanish Portuguese & French.
soft Western twangs will enter in. they'll send their notes
out the edges of the box, the bonebox with my names.
I would we invite our dead in to partake with us,
if but for a little while. if we could slip insights
back & forth from the far side, questions from this
the fastbreathing side of the grave. as the border breaks down,
Spanish reaches to & beyond the Carpathian line.
oh yes! may all celebrations of people of bone,
their songs their dances their chants & refrains,
melt into this fabric. this circle. these bones.
& tomorrow winter begins.

Sweetest

Paul r Harding

after all the money has danced away with her womanliness, the
dark orange flamingos and all
the people seemed to ignore her, but cried;
after she lost it and every-thing stopped
spinning 'round, came
to a silver—blinding halt—stuck
like a giant lashing   lightning bolt in the ground,
and
all the beauty she hit you with became more de-fined,
easier yet more startling (without fear) to
see—as   a flame is profound

all the people
sang   in low, distant notes of
a song's other world in-
side   deep down

after
she became aged, still with her back down
picking, ignoring the new young men, although they could smell her blood, the
womanliness and the cotton coming
down through beauty like a water-snake
from the distance a scurrying field mouse
halfway down her bent of body
still
picking, yes, pickin'
strangely sweetest things ever wanted from hot, hard ground
unlike the soul could reap ever or
after?

all the people knew and too are bound, what
goes around like cherry rhythm, black-olive memory, passion's reptile laughter, what
so steep into night sweetest seeds scream, before morning flamingo-colored mist
silent tears, bent ov-er
she reached the dark orange distance
horizon's favorite birds, skin
and drooling hair, standing up straight
her droppin' cotton almost
sang
one sweet high note coming
in the same key as the sun
from the bottom after she lost   heart's sense of time
and every single thing stopped spinning 'round
the people warned her not to spit at the moon
held voices of fainting harmony of young
old men counting sharecropper money for
all the silence of shortchanged bales pondering
sweetest disappearance in darkness with her.

Florida, Miami

Paul r Harding

almost not entirely human
that ageless slinky rhythm
fanning no one's cool moments anymore

she digs the sweat
a creole jamaican yellow-eyed
devil's omelet, digs
her sweat, real simple little
beads
securely little tied tight tiny braids, her
pretty-ass Ibo head, the
way she does her
thing still
from a perfect black elbow, fly
—swat passion she would get—
get you
get you the one and only first time! (make
you invisible to anyone else's eye)
slowly now

no time time, in real time never too hot
for tears, Florida
(Miami) too
wise, rhythmic a dark fruit to fall
only a rare wild red,
Caribbean Cuban aloneness drum-bleeding
mother of Billie's "Strange Fruit" sitting
sucking on a piece of ginger
crayon color called Warmest Breeze (making you identifiable only in peculiar jungle dream)

long-legged zebra thigh running
'cross desert scent—certain memory death, yet
tropical squall, dangling
from hot "Little Haiti" spirits, the
motherless sun
tries to hot-spice persuade
down the beautiful never forgetting scalding neck
rubbing her African oil-skin beaded forehead, hands

without ice water for
the body for
Florida (Miami)
Florida, Florida,
Florida (Miami)
Florida (Havana) Miami
causing lulling, sparkles, humid human water
her stark shadow to dull
disappear like a jackal into the heat somehow
(swamplike reflection like passion loiters)

a chameleonic dark breeze she
moves the way she moves almost
balmy, so
mean she's scary clean standing there
silent dangerous blackening palm who
waits for searing vision to take over,
cooled spectrums of zealous foliage, colors, maybe peacock eyes she is
closer to now
Juju dancing to now
stooping behind the tallest birds
sucking in the salt from the sweet sweat, human
water sweat, no
icicles, but hot-berry blood (she would
spank you the one and only first time!)
down

the nose, into
the mouth she
waits, a
tea-leaf in hot water, a
rainforest   reason so
simple it's torrid, her
mysterious temperament when
another boat moors, another man
digs the sweat, the black-berry neck, becomes what's lonely after warm breeze,
almost not entirely human

Florida—yes! Florida—yeeaaah!
she'll get you
Florida Florida that
. . . one and only first time
(Miami)

When We Won The Nobel Prize

Joycelyn Moody

I've had an unprecedented confidence in my work in African-American literature ever since I heard over NPR, while getting dressed for work, that Toni Morrison had won the 1993 Nobel Prize for Literature. All that Thursday morning, I kept catching my reflection sidelong—in my bedroom mirror, my rearview mirror, the glass door to my office building. I'd turn full face, grin widely, hug myself. I kept thinking, oh lord, can it be?! Somebody who looks like me has walked off with the world's most distinguished literary prize! It was dazzling, Morrison was dazzling, and somehow it made me dazzling, too. I couldn't wait to tell my students, couldn't help greeting everyone with, "Have you heard the Good News?" Morrison's honor signified my personal salvation.

The day after I was just as elated. I even introduced myself at a gathering for new graduate students, saying "I'm Jocelyn Moody, and I'm excited beyond words that Toni Morrison won the Nobel Prize." I was mortified by these autonomous words, stunned that they had escaped me—then the room broke into applause. That kind of response, the absolute joy of almost everyone I know at the Good News, so sustains my own gratification, I'm sure it'll be years before the thrill subsides.

Morrison's winning inspires recollections of my reading, studying, teaching her novels. Once, embarking on my sixth round of teaching *The Bluest Eye*, I caved in to the homesickness that novel always awakens in me. I called my parents long distance to ask them about some of Morrison's meticulous detail, not because I needed my parents to explain Nu Nile Hair Oil or Black Draught mineral tonic, or to corroborate Morrison's finely nuanced distinction between "being put out and being put outdoors." I'm glad he did, but I hadn't needed Daddy to tell me that Alaga Syrup is named for the two states of origin, Alabama and Georgia. Instead, I had needed my parents to share the nostalgia for mythic, simpler days that Morrison's words evoke in the most caustic of readers, to wade with me a moment in cultural waters. Over the phone, I read to them about the MacTeers' struggle in Depression winters, about Cholly Breedlove's certainty of his own ugliness, about Maureen Peale's family who believed in lawsuits. In three rooms of two houses, half a continent apart, we breathed into each other's ears the marvel and the miracle that Morrison's extraordinary storytelling assures us black lives are.

On the other hand, just this fall I lent my copy of *The Bluest Eye* to a friend who couldn't quite comprehend the complex portrait I drew of my mother after a trip home. Only after she read Morrison's incredibly exact characterization of "sugar-brown girls" who, like Mama and me—"come from Mobile. Aiken. From Newport News. From Marietta. From Meridian"—could she piece together the paradox that frustrated me. I wonder that Morrison never met my mother, Mobile-born and reared, when she writes, "When you ask them where they are from, they tilt their heads and say 'Mobile' and you think you've been kissed." I read and remember the fruit man's wagon, Cashmere Bouquet, talc, brown bags twisted into hair curlers, whispers in the night about "nookey," and all my agonized youth comes back to me. Southern women's fastidiousness, our self-loathing and sexual repression are supposed to be grievous, I know, but I'm lost in a wash of lonesomeness in the beauty of Morrison's prose. Even descended from colored Mobile women who hate funk and poor folk, hate poor coloreds for their funkiness, I read Morrison's reconstruction of my repugnant past, and want to be a girl of nine in Mobile again, and sent to the corner store for a square blue box marked Kotex and powdered aspirin called "Goody" folded in translucent paper.

Hearing the NPR announcement, I remembered the woman named Joy (whose black mother in Mississippi in the 1950s had some optimism!) who first urged me to read Morrison's novels. I was a grad student in English at Wisconsin then, and I wasn't reading a single text that wasn't on my MA reading list. In 1980, the only black woman writer ever spoken of in grad courses was Gwendolyn Brooks. We didn't read her poems, of course; she

Portrait of Toni Morrison, 1993, Painting, by Gary Curtis

was simply mentioned—amid poems by Stevens and Lowell, Stafford and Larkin.

It was years before I discovered Morrison's novels on my own. Once I did, though, I made a spring ritual of reading *Sula*. Every Mother's Day, I'd march into a Mormon temple in western Missouri for my college's graduation, Morrison's slender second novel tucked into the hollow sleeve of my borrowed commencement gown. When the faculty were settled for the four-hour ceremony, my friend Judy and I would go to "the Bottom," to witness there Eva's murder by fire of her boy Plum Peace, Eva's efforts to save from fire the beautiful, fuck-loving Hannah Peace while her granddaughter, Sula, watched, curious. We'd bury Sula as the last graduate crossed the stage, silently pledge to each other undying friendship in the wake of Nell's anguished loss. The ironies of day and place and text were lost on me, until the spring after I had left Judy at that college. I had thought Morrison's second novel, on the second Sunday in May, only signified my students' graduation, until I felt that my summer outside Missouri could not commence without the sweet and raw ritual that *Sula* had become.

I no longer read *Sula* to mark the coming of summer, probably because, as often as I can, I make Morrison's work as writer, editor, mother, the stuff of my life. Her novel *Beloved* became the subject of my first published scholarly article. At the center of my poetry classes are the magnificent poems of Lucille Clifton, poems Morrison edited in her Random House days. The excruciating blues novels of another extraordinary African-American woman writer, whose work Morrison edited in those days, Gayl Jones's *Corregidora* and *Eva's Man*, are classic texts I find myself teaching again and again. In an audio interview with Kay Bonetti, Morrison spoke about her single parenting of two very young boys. "They don't need an author in the house," Morrison explained patiently; "what they need and what they deserve is a mother." When my own son treads on my last nerve, Morrison's statement fortifies me.

The strength to endure is one effect of Morrison's rare and precious gift. Joy in celebration is another. Just as one of her most admired characters, Pilate Dead, leads a recalcitrant, prodigal boy into a respectable manhood, Toni Morrison's gifts of power pilot us naked and ashamed to a state of grace where we are at once humbled and redeemed. 📖

The Sweat

John Olson

Each time Red Eagle said, "Coming through," my eyes were riveted to the hot red rock he carried into the enclosure of vinyl and tarp. It looked like the egg of some immense bird of fire. I felt the intensity of the heat as Red Eagle walked by, gingerly cradling the rock on a pitchfork. It looked porous. Our host said it was volcanic rock, from Mount Hood, a place of powerful medicine.

This was my first sweat, my initiation into a Native American tradition practiced for hundreds, if not thousands, of years. Reaching the Northwest from the Great Plains, the sweat has been practiced as far north as the Cree in Canada and as far south as the Aztec in Mexico. The ceremony we were going to use was a version practiced among the Wasco, a tribe formerly occupying the southern shores of the Columbia River in the region of the Dalles.

I knew the sweat was essentially a rite of purification, but that's about all I knew. I refrained from too much inquiry or research as I wanted to go into the experience as unbiased as possible. I wanted nothing to sway or skew or weight it in a certain direction.

After we picked up the other participants and loaded a truck with hefty chunks of garage-dried madrona and alder and fir, we drove to the home of our host, a quiet amiable man with a warm smile and a house full of children. His wife welcomed us all with a graciousness that made us feel genuinely glad and comfortable to be there, despite what felt to me like rather an odd thing to do: sit in a confined area with a group of naked men and sweat.

After Red Eagle and our host got a fire going, we all took turns chopping wood. The purpose of the fire was to heat the rocks to be used for our sweat.

It felt good to have some way to vent my nervous energy. I propped a large chunk of alder in the dirt, took aim, and brought the ax down hard: *ka chunk*. The chunk of alder was now two smaller chunks of alder. It gave me a sense of satisfaction.

I was feeling a lot of anger and frustration that day because of a disagreement over a bank fine. The day before I'd discovered an overdraft of $1.81 on my bank statement and had gone to the bank to cover it before my next check was posted. I was too late. They'd already fined me $16.75 for $1.81. I asked if they could reverse it. No deal. It was against bank policy.

I was incredulous. The young woman I talked to, a teller-supervisor, was wearing a Husky sweatshirt. All the tellers were wearing Husky sweatshirts, and all the teller windows were ornamented with yellow megaphones and yellow and purple pompoms. I was impressed with their community spirit and attempt to soften the bank's image with a few festive pompoms. It gave me hope. There was some humanity here. "But the overdraft is only $1.81," I pleaded. "And the service charge is what put me over." (Actually, it was a surcharge for the use of automated tellers at another branch.) "Where do you want us to draw the line?" the teller-supervisor asked. "How about two dollars?" Two dollars struck me as an excellent place to draw the line.

She didn't.

I left the bank $16.75 poorer than when I went in.

My friends gave me sound advice: change banks.

Once the wood was chopped and the fire was a great crackling blaze we were offered a pleasing diversion.

We had with us two gifted storytellers, Gray Eagle and Laughing Bear, who gave their stories extra spice by acting them out with high wit and expansive gestures as we all sat on logs and chairs. As the nearby fire went about its business, Gray Eagle related the story of a narcissistic raven invited to dinner by an octopus who cunningly charmed him into the water by appealing to his vanity. Each time a tentacle slithered around raven we all chanted, "Look out raven, use your head, go on stayin' stuck up, gonna wind up dead." As the eighth tentacle slithered around raven's hopeless, hapless vanity, it became clear just who the octopus was having for dinner.

Laughing Bear treated us to a tale about a great chief who challenged his constituency to a contest. He would offer a house to anyone who could fill it with one thing and one thing only. A rich, arrogant woman filled it with salmon, but dogs and birds got at it through cracks in the walls and roof, until it was all eaten. A powerful man grabbed a bear out of the woods and filled the house with energy. But the bear's energy was used in chasing the elders from one end of the house to the other. The powerful man was forced to concede, and put the bear back in the woods, where it belonged. The task was at last accomplished by children who lit the fin of an eulachon. An eulachon (pronounced *oolikan*) is a fat little fish about four inches long and so full of oil it almost drips from its body (which is why it's called a candlefish; if dried and supplied with a wick, it will burn). But the eulachon could only light part of the house, so the children united in meditation and made it glow harder with their hearts, until the whole house filled with light.

I went to the truck to get my coat. I'd taken it off to chop wood, and now it was getting cold. Heat was beginning to appeal to me. I started thinking less about bank fines and more about physical comfort. And whether I was going to emerge from this experience the same. Does anyone ever emerge from an experience the same?

Still. This wasn't a haircut. This was about opening the doors of perception. Lifting the hatch to our private potato cellars. Letting down walls. Adjusting our focal length to infinity. "Lift not the painted veil which those who live call Life," wrote Shelley. Was that a warning or a dare?

There is a wonderful description of the Sioux sweat lodge in Andrew Weil's *The Marriage of the Sun and Moon: A Quest for Unity in Consciousness*, where I was astonished to learn temperatures near 212 degrees Fahrenheit are reached for brief periods. What prevents scalding, Weil theorizes, is the "set and setting," the mind-set and preparedness of the participants. "Nor is there anything unusual about pain," he adds, "serving as the basis for alterations of consciousness." "On coming out of the sweat lodges," Weil further imparts, "I have felt high in many of the same ways

I have felt on using psychedelic drugs. The high lasts an hour or so and gradually gives way to great relaxation and a desire to rest. Increased awareness of one's own strength and a sense of well-being may persist for a long time."

When I asked Red Eagle if the sweat cost any money, he said no in a way that made it seem like a question. But he did mention water. Bring lots of water.

In the range of thermal neutrality an average person sweats about 500 grams of water a day. But under the stress of high temperatures, the loss may reach 15,000 grams a day. The water aids in the excretion of nitrogenous wastes, in essentially a process of osmosis, the movement of water through a membrane from a region of a relatively low concentration of salts or other solutes into a region of a higher concentration of solutes. A strict empiricist might take the view that during a sweat the body is being purified of toxins, and not much else. But if one were to entertain a more transcendental notion of mind and body, a union of soul and body, such as that celebrated by Walt Whitman in "I Sing The Body Electric," a sweat will prove to be a much deeper experience, a rite of purification involving much more than the elimination of nitrogenous wastes.

After our host had blessed the lodge—a small dome consisting of a framework of willow saplings covered with quilts and blankets—we disrobed and entered to the left on our hands and knees, going clockwise. The rocks were piled in a small pit in the center of the dome. They looked like eggs in a nest. Large, hot, scintillating eggs. I looked up, and when I observed how carefully and skillfully the saplings had been corded together, I thought: this man knows what he is doing. I felt as respectful and reverential as if I'd just entered some great European cathedral. I was about to participate in a ceremony Sitting Bull and Crazy Horse would've found familiar.

When the flap comes down it's pitch-black. All you can see is your soul. Were it not for the heat the body would cease to exist. All the appurtenances—clothes, cash card, driver's license, comb—that define the self were missing. The eyes were open, but there was nothing external to see.

It was hot, but not unbearably hot. Not yet, anyway. And I thought, I can handle this. Or can I. Am I going to handle this? Will I panic? Will I be able to endure the heat? Will I face some buried fear too intense to handle?

The voice of the host was a great comfort. A prayer was spoken. The mind became focused. Concentrated.

When the first water was poured, the rocks sizzled and hissed, and I felt a wave of intense heat and moisture move over my body. Rivulets of sweat ran down my skin and dripped from my brow. I made my breathing shallow so as not to singe my lungs. I felt intensely alive. And fearful and alone.

It is the voices of the others that give comfort and strength. That helps the mind to more spiritual considerations. Visions. Prayers. Visitations from the dead.

It is much like being in a womb.

Or a foundry. Except that there's nothing remotely industrial about it.

The rocks, our host had said, were from the heart of the earth. I believe that's true.

There are four rounds, four doors to be opened. Four doors for each direction. This is called the Medicine Wheel, though versions often vary from tribe to tribe.

The door to the east, which is yellow, is the door of the eagle, the door of children. The door to the south, which is red, is the door of the salmon, the door of the teenager. The door to the west, which is black, is the door of the bear, the door of the adult. The door to the north, which is white, is the door of the coyote, the door of the elders.

It is not necessary to do all the rounds, nor is it necessary to sit through an entire round if one doesn't feel up to it. One can leave at any time with no shame or dishonor attached. The sweat is not an endurance test.

When a round has finished, the prayer, "All my relations," is uttered and the flap is opened. The outside air feels wonderful. "All my relations" is uttered as each person leaves the lodge, again to the left, in clockwise direction.

Going outside is like entering a former existence. The world of pelicans and politics, begonias, and bank fines. But already one felt lighter. Happier. More real.

A large barrel full of ice cold water and a stainless steel bowl had been provided to douse and refresh the body. After the shock of ice cold water streaming over my still steaming skin, I stood in November chill, each pore dilating to soak it up, feeling the marvel of the body, the beauty of fingers and thumb, their phenomenal agility, the sound solidity of the legs, the wonder of the spine and all its nerves, the amazing capability of the tongue and the transparency of air it can shape into song and incantation.

I won't say my problems with the bank resolved into a dew after my first sweat, or that heavenly choirs sang or that a vast sea of buffalo thundered over a golden prairie, but I did feel more relaxed and attuned to things—fragrances, textures, lights, the play of shadows, and the gladness of being with the people I was with. I felt rich, certainly not in my hemorrhaging bank account, but inside. Under my skin. In my veins.

I felt closer to my real self, closer to earth, closer to the light that is sometimes found in the darkest of places.

The opening measure of Whitman's *Song of Myself* had even deeper resonance for me now.

> I celebrate myself, and sing myself,
> And what I assume you shall assume,
> For every atom belonging to me as good
>   belongs to you.

I wonder where Whitman banked? 📖

Still Life At Snoqualmie Falls

Freda Quenneville

The crocuses are sprouting at sea level.
In the mountains
the snow has grown transparent,
like the faces of the very old,
lit behind the surface.

We watch the Snoqualmie River
pour over the falls—
jets and streams and aureoles
in patterns of surprising sameness,
newly transformed each second,
like fireworks that never expire.
This water stronger than fire.

Tourists crowd the lookout—
foreign men with cameras
and silken, perfumed women;
honeymooners at Salish Lodge.

I feel myself float across the chasm
into the disgorging river,
the waters rising in the air
to meet me where I stand.
For a moment I am no longer a person,
I am one of the dead,
one of the Snoqualmie
who knew the Falls as the Great Spirit.

The river follows the sea.
Perhaps my sorrow is that I
am no longer earth on fire.
I am water; changing, impersonal,

like rivers
splitting the earth,
stronger than fire,
falling, but not yet born
to the fourth element.

Snoqualmie Falls, 1993, Photograph, by Mary Randlett

Crow Speaks To Wolf

Lawrence Revard

So cold, the air feels like aluminum foil,
my rattling, everything's about to break aloud.
You there, my friend. I need your wolf soul.
I need your wolf body for the stars to be held.

The quiet atoms drift out of the gravity well
and mater phosphoresces. A flicker of your ears.

I chose, stupidly, not to fly south. You keep me,
solid and silent as a howl, breath and sound.
There should be nothing in my nature to respond.
Now I pace myself with you, brittled and steeled.

Endurance grows on you like the thick lake ice.
The Europeans lied. Your eyes think humanly.

How to slow the heart and bear the weight,
not frenetic or demonic at all in your blood.
How to wait for the deer to fall sick and die,
then find their offerings with a gray smile.

I descend in a black squawk then. I leap lightly
on the bitter, simple crusts I know. You stand.

How to slow the heart and bear the weight,
this is nothing I understand. I am too ruffled
and vigilant, too unfeelingly opportune, bleak.
Your blue eyes on me. I must talk too much.

But as you move through the woods, I follow
from afar. I love your mood, its form, this snow.

IX

VOLUME 3, NUMBER 3, SPRING 1994

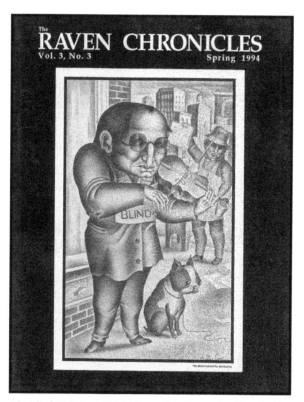

The Blind Violinist, 1938, Lithographic Crayon, by Abe Blashko

Singing The Old Way

Jody Aliesan

Last spring, I traveled to Ireland on a pilgrimage in honor of my father's memory. Weeks before leaving home a message came (from wherever such messages come) that I must close down my teaching and open up the time after my return because during the trip I would receive a new assignment. It came on the third day, in Connemara, Ireland.

Our traveling group was led to its westernmost part, up the side of a steep, bog-blanketed glen, past a Stone Age passage grave, a holy well older than the grave, a Bronze Age cemetery used through the Penal Years, and, finally, among the alarmed ewes calling their lambs away from us, to the top of a ridge. We could see the ocean on one side and the inland lakes on the other.

The wind was blowing with a great high whine. Then it was blowing through my head: it was the voices of all the people who had died there. They weren't suffering and I wasn't frightened, but I couldn't bear it and ran down the mountainside. Back in the van our musician-teacher Mick Moloney put a cassette in his recorder and a sound came out that didn't seem human. But it *was* human, a kind of chanting-like Lakota singing or Islamic calls to worship. My blood flashed cold, then warm again. I said "Mick, what *is* that?"

He said "It's called *sean-nós*. Means 'the old way.' " Oldest form of singing in Ireland. A dying art, preserved and passed down by the poets.

Sean-nós (shan-nos) is sung solo without accompaniment, partly because there was a time in Irish history where musical instruments were confiscated and destroyed, and partly because the people who preserved it were poor. It has a slow, free, pulsing rhythm without beats or measures. Drama, emotion, and veiled meaning are expressed by rapid movements of the voice around the basic notes of the tone line rather than by changes in pace or volume. It is used to tell stories about loss: loss of love, loss due to death or emigration, religious and historical tragedies, and (encoded during times of invasion and occupation) loss of Ireland itself.

The tradition of *sean-nós* is oral, passed down from one generation to the next, the songs taught and learned from memory. Its original language is Gaelic, its characteristic setting is in the home around a turf fire; non-professional and anonymous. The singer makes a quiet, straightforward offering, looking straight ahead without focusing; or closes the eyes, or turns toward the wall, hand cupped around the ear; or pulls a hat or scarf down over part of the face. There is no movement of the body. Listeners look down or away, encouraging the singer with friendly words between verses. *Sean-nós* is an expression of shared experience rather than a performance; it is sung in a similar manner even in the most crowded public session.

Sean-nós can be traced back to the sixth century with new topics and meters added after the twelfth century Norman invasion. When Cromwell devastated Ireland in the seventh century, the metrical tradition was reduced, class distinctions were leveled, and the poets dispossessed. Inland people were forced to the west coast and all strata were thrown together onto the poorest lands. Verse-makers and musicians were systematically hunted down, instruments were destroyed and their use prohibited, Gaelic was outlawed, Hiberno-English developed, and the *bhard* (English: *bard*) emerged as a non-professional composer of "street poetry": a verse-maker and musician in one. During the Great Famine of 1846-1851, starving inland people again moved to the west— this time with adaptations of English song forms—and *sean-nós* evolved again, as it does to this day.

On that hillside in Connemara, Mick continued, "I knew a man from here, Joe Heaney, who sang *sean-nós*, one of the purest transmitters of the tradition. He had to go to the States to make a living and ended up operating an elevator in New York. He was discovered, and the NEA awarded him a grant so he could travel around the country singing and teaching. A few years later he died and all the recordings of his work were collected at the school where he spent his last years: in the Ethnomusicology Department of the University of Washington."

Since then, guided by UW archivist Laurel Sercombe, I've been listening to tapes in the Joe Heaney Collection. Last September I began formal study of Irish/Gaelic with Ciaran O'Mahony who also knew Joe. After a while a poem emerged whose subject, stress rhythms, and interlocking assonance echoed old Gaelic forms, but nothing that could be called a song.

Then one night while I sat with a candle up north on the island where I write, a piece came, in five stanzas—its first line and a later word in Gaelic. The next night, up in the loft, I sat tapping a drum to the sound of rain beating on the metal roof. I held the drum between my eyes and a candle flame. When I sang tones next to the drumskin some of them resonated in my head. Suddenly I was given the tone for the words, and an understanding that the song was coming from someone, a nun, who died centuries ago. And that I could call her Sister Willow, although that's not her real name. I had trouble falling asleep after that, wondering whether the tone series would still be with me in the morning. It was.

At Samhain (Halloween, the Celtic New Year) the time came to sing it with someone else listening, my partner Mardi, who averted her face. I pulled a scarf over my head. I was trembling, but I got it out, and I've chanted it many times since then. It's developing, becoming more complex and detailed, like the song of a winter wren. I can hear in my head the way it wants to sound. Slowly, I'm gaining the skill to bring a bit of the old way into this new world.

Against False Mercy

binn beal ina thost:
sweet mouth in its silence
now I have prayed
for those who have wronged me

give them what they deserve
leaving to your hand *a Bhean-dia*
what is deserved demanding justice
I put myself in peril

just as I cannot love
without reserve and still see fairly
another's willingness to harm
held up for an answer

so it is not mine
to will forgiveness feign not caring
or spurn hard-given vision
for reckless forgetting no

I dare not forget at all
play the saint aspire higher
than my place: nor cradle them
when I belong in your arms

binn beal ina thost: sweet mouth in its silence
a Bhean-dia: o Goddess 📖

Sanctuary

D.L. Birchfield

I was a fool to be standing at the edge of the water. Only a few feet from me rocks half the size of truck tires were being tossed around in the current like so many ping pong balls in a bingo hopper. But the roar of the water was mesmerizing, and it held me at its edge.

I learned that day that tons of melting snow can turn an ankle-deep creek into an angry river, that big rocks can sound like an explosion when they smash together, and that water can rush by at such great speed that it roars.

It was all a surprise to me. I'd expected to jog up the mountainside, from down about 6,500 feet to up around nine or 10,000 feet, to wherever the snow, up in the Blue Spruce belt, got to be too deep to slog through.

It was my valley, a big basin, actually, nestled up in the high country. It was mine because I had worshipped it with my feet in all seasons, in all weather, until that day during the height of the spring runoff.

It had so many different parts. Vertically, the mountainside was a succession of different ecological zones, from arid brush country, to Quaking Aspen, to towering Blue Spruce, from rabbits to mule deer to elk.

The trail was a steep one, until you got up to about 8,000 feet. There, you stood on the lip of a big basin, with the mountain falling away behind you, and the bowl of the valley spread out before you. Beaver ponds were everywhere, and little creeks, and everywhere that there was water there was Rainbow Trout. Who wouldn't love it?

Through the middle of the basin the largest creek had carved a gorge. Its northern rim was a cliff, but the south side stopped just short of being too steep to get down to the trout water—down to where, in the narrow pine-studded bottom of the gorge, you could almost believe no one else had ever been.

By luck, my family had moved from Oklahoma to the mountains the summer before I entered college. For five years that high basin valley was the place I fled to, whenever school took a break, or when a long weekend offered itself, or, sometimes, when I was supposed to be somewhere else. I wanted to know everything there was to know about it. Practically all of the valley was displayed on one seven and a half minute quadrangle from the U.S. Geological Survey. I carried that quadrangle everywhere, when I went away to school, whenever I went to visit the kinfolks in Oklahoma, on a trip throughout South America. The valley was always with me. I got to where I didn't need the map, could sketch a map of my own, showing all the creeks, the trails, the secret places.

I spent part of one summer up on the mountain above the basin, skidding logs behind a bulldozer, living with the operator in a small trailer, sitting in the shadows each evening glassing the elk down below with a spotting scope. I spent the last several weeks before heading off to Marine Corps Officer Candidate School by jogging from the foot of the mountain to the top; and when I arrived at the training camp, down close to sea level at Quantico, Virginia, they found that I could run forever.

* * *

And then one day, I don't know how, cannot comprehend how, more than twenty years had gone by since I'd last been in that valley. I was standing at a magazine rack in a supermarket, a backpacking magazine open in my hands, one that showed the detailed, proposed route of a transcontinental backpack trail with its section that crossed the Rocky Mountains, a route that would take the trail through the middle of my beloved high basin valley.

I went back to the valley then, to see it one more time before the rest of the world began flooding through it. When I got to Colorado an old friend drove me up above the valley on a Forest Service Road to where you could park, walk a few hundred yards, and come to a point where you could look down into it.

It was a wasted trip. It was worse than just a wasted trip. The valley looked the same, it looked magnificent. But the aging little fat man, gasping and wheezing from too many years of tobacco abuse, who had to stop twice to rest, just to get back up the gentle slope to the car, was pathetic. The proposed route of that backpack trail could be moved a hundred miles and it wouldn't make any difference. It's not my valley anymore. 📖

Ravenous, Photograph, by Alfredo Arrequín

Integrating Style with Substance
An Interview with Abe Blashko (1920-2011)

Scott Martin

with Phoebe Bosché & David Martin

It was late. Late in the day, late in the year, 1993. I was in a hurry, walking briskly past the windows of the Martin-Zambito gallery a couple of blocks from my apartment on Capitol Hill. Glancing in, something caught my attention. A drawing, black and white, glared boldly at me from its position on a wall. I went in to find out who the artist was. And that's how I came to meet Abe Blashko.

Abe Blashko contributed a significant body of work to the annals of Northwest art, but his name remains virtually unknown. Done in the late thirties through the mid-forties, his work chronicles life during this tumultuous time in Seattle's history. His art is highly charged with social and political content, unlike most of the art popularized at the time. In viewing Blashko's work today, one recognizes a talent that created art that will stand the test of time. It already has.

Mr. Blashko, who now lives in New York, was in Seattle briefly in January to attend the funeral of his sister Beccy. I met with him, along with David Martin of the Martin-Zambito gallery and *Raven* editor Phoebe Bosché. We talked about his remarkable life. This interview, upon his request, is dedicated to the memory of his sister Beccy, for her constant love and life-long support of his work.

Scott Martin: Is it true that in November of 1938, when you were only eighteen, your work was exhibited in a one-man show at the Seattle Art Museum?

Abe Blashko: Right. One whole room was devoted to twenty-five of my drawings. In an adjoining room was work by Max Beckmann and Millard Sheets. I was in pretty good company.

Phoebe Bosché: Had you seen Max Beckmann's work before, or work by other German Expressionists?

Blashko: Sure. When I was fourteen I started going to the main branch of the Seattle Public Library where I gravitated to the work of the Old Masters. Then I studied the Impressionists, Post-Impressionists, and the Mexican muralists Rivera and Orozco who, at one point, influenced my work. George Grosz was another influence. So that was the source of my education.

Martin: In a few of your early drawings some direct influence is perhaps obvious, however, I agree with artist Kenneth Callahan who remarked at the time that he found very little that was imitative, that you merely drew some elements from . . .

Blashko: Nothing was imitative, in other words, there was influence. He [Callahan] was right on target.

Martin: Callahan went on to describe your work as a 'beautiful integration of conception, subject, and style.' So getting back to the 1938 exhibition, what was it like at eighteen to receive that kind of recognition?

Blashko: That's a good question. At the time I felt elated. I was hoping that after the exhibit I could continue, you know, where I left off.

Martin: What was the public reaction to your work?

Blashko: Great. Oh, fantastic. I would hear people say, 'Hey, did you see the work of that eighteen-year-old Blashko?' There were crowds of people there and all the reviews in the papers were quite good.

The Blind Violinist, 1938, Lithographic Crayon, by Abe Blashko

Martin: Speaking of those 1938 reviews, I noticed in reading *The Seattle Times* that more space was devoted to listing the social luminaries in attendance and describing what they were wearing than to the art. Do you remember what you wore?

Blashko: Yeah, I bought a black suit for the occasion, instead of a tuxedo. (laughter)

Martin: After such an auspicious beginning your expectations must have been high. What happened after the exhibit?

Blashko: In 1939, I mentioned to Dr. Richard Fuller, who had been responsible for getting me the show and who was founder and director at the museum, that I was interested in lithography because it would naturally lend itself to my work. A short time later he purchased a press for the museum (complete with inks, rollers, and stones) and made its use available to me. But the question was, how the hell am I going to learn how to do this!

Martin: So how did you learn?

Blashko: There was nobody at the time in Seattle teaching lithography so the only source for instruction was books. One particular book mentioned putting castor oil on the roller before you inked it up. So I did that and the whole stone went black! (laughter) The reality was that the information I was getting was misleading and I wasn't getting any results. I called up a printer in Belltown and went to see him. I had brought the roller with me, and after putting his finger on it he said, 'Get rid of the castor oil!' (laughter) He gave me instructions to follow and I went back to the museum and everything worked out.

Bosché: You learned lithography alone in the basement of the old Seattle Art Museum?

Blashko: Right, it was through trial and error. I really sweated blood!

David Martin: I would just like to add, concerning lithography from this period, that Abe was ahead of his time. The only other artist doing any lithography in Seattle was Walter Reese at Cornish, who I think only did two or three. Vanessa Helder, another Northwest artist, was doing some lithography while teaching at the WPA project in Spokane.

Martin: The use of lithographic crayons in your earlier drawings seemed to anticipate lithography.

Blashko: Well, I loved the texture of the stone, you really can't beat it. It was just sort of a natural step.

Martin: I'm curious about your development leading up to this point. I've seen your ink studies from 1935, some pencil studies and several more developed drawings from 1936, done when you were only fifteen or sixteen. . . .

Blashko: Right, actually some were done when I was fourteen.

Martin: When did you start drawing?

Blashko: I started drawing when I was about five, cartoons of cowboys and Indians, the neighbors, the usual things. Then, when I was about ten, I developed asthma which got progressively worse and I spent a lot of time home from school drawing. When I was in seventh grade we moved to the Madrona area. I didn't like my new school, so I quit. In the new house there was a special sun room that I used as a studio and I started working seriously. I would bring books home from the library and I devoted all my time and energy to drawing. As it turned out, the asthma was a blessing in disguise, and by the time I was twelve it had disappeared.

Bosché: Most parents wouldn't have supported the idea of their child becoming an artist during the depression. Was this true of your family?

Blashko: Ah, let me tell you about that. My parents were very encouraging and always believed in my talent. Especially supportive was my sister Beccy, who bought me art books and saved all of my drawings, literally every scrap! A funny thing happened that best illustrates my family's support. Shortly after I quit school, a teacher called to inquire as to the reason. My sister Sara answered the phone, and very directly informed the teacher that I was into drawing and wished to pursue it. Surprisingly, we never heard another thing from the school!

Martin: Most of your mature drawings, however, were observations taken from life. It appears that in 1935 you literally took to the streets, drawing everything you saw. Was this your best classroom?

Blashko: Right, in the streets.

Martin: Judging from your output from this period, you must have drawn obsessively.

Blashko: Yeah, all the time, like you say, studying street scenes and life on the docks, factories, and skid row. I was also fascinated by freaks and the circus. There was a side show I often visited at 12th and Jackson. I never drew on the spot, everything was from memory. I didn't even carry a notebook around with me.

Martin: So out of this prolific period came the work that was to appear in your 1938 show. I understand that the museum purchased some of these drawings.

Blashko: Yeah, for very little money I might add. When I walked into the museum with about ten drawings, Dr. Richard Fuller said he wanted to give me a show and that he was interested in buying some. One he was particularly interested in was *The Accordionist*. I went home and told my mother, who said to take $25 for it! Remember, this was in the depths of the depression. So when I went back to negotiate the sale with Fuller and he asked me what I wanted for it. I said, 'Well, can you offer me a figure?' He said $50. 'That's a good price,' I said, 'but you know I put a lot of work into it (two weeks) and I think it's worth more.' He then offered $100, so I agreed.

Martin: Were you happy with the price?

Blashko: No, (laughter) I didn't feel it was enough, but what could I do?

Martin: What did your mother say? Was she shocked?

Blashko: When I got home I casually told her that I had received $100, and she started crying! It was a lot of money in those days, but even then I didn't think it was sufficient.

Bosché: Did you come from a working class background?

Blashko: My father owned a truck and would go around the area buying hides, wool, and burlap sacks from farmers to sell, so, yeah, I would say it was a working class family.

Martin: Had it begun to sink in by this point that you couldn't support yourself through your art?

Blashko: Well, after I made the lithographs in 1939, I couldn't sell anything, so I began work as a warehouseman and longshoreman. There were few galleries in Seattle at that time and outlets for selling art were quite limited. Because of the depression, nobody was buying art.

Martin: So you were really dependent on continued support from Dr. Fuller at the museum?

Blashko: Yes, but I didn't get any. After the show was over and I had made the lithographs, I received no further support whatsoever. A recent article [*Reflex*, November, 1993] stated that due to continued patronage from Dr. Fuller, I was able to pursue my career. Well, this simply isn't true. He was basically responsible for the show, but only bought a few pieces. I had to be realistic, so I went to work.

Bosché: I'm curious. How did the content of your work differ from other work being shown at the time?

Blashko: I was very politically aware, my whole family was for that matter, and this influenced my point of view. That came out in my drawings.

David Martin: I might add, at that time in Seattle most of what you were seeing in visual arts was the influence of European Modernism, primarily through the teaching of Walter Isaacs and Ambrose Patterson at the University of Washington. There was also some Asian influence. To my knowledge, there was no one else working in a style similar to Abe's.

Martin: The names Mark Tobey, Morris Graves, Kenneth Callahan, and Guy Anderson seem to dominate any discussion of Northwest art from this period. Popular belief still maintains that these four are the only artists of merit from this time. Why is this?

David Martin: This is largely due to the fact that an artist's reputation rests on where his work is. Tobey, Graves, Callahan, and Anderson all worked at the Seattle Art Museum—Callahan, incidentally, was a curator there for many years—and consequently there is a large deposit of their work. And there was also a social thing happening that was a big factor.

Martin: Did having virtually no contact with other artists, or with a particular school, help or hinder you?

Blashko: I don't think it hindered me. Although I didn't have much personal contact with other artists, there were some great publications that kept me aware of work being done. The *New*

Masses, which politically was left wing, featured the work of many well known artists of the 1930s, like Joan Sloan, Stuart Davis, and George Bellow. I was also a contributor.

Martin: Around this time you applied to the Work Projects Administration, commonly known as the WPA. This would have expanded your contact with other artists. What happened?

Blashko: At the time I was too young. There was an age requirement of twenty or twenty-one, and I was only seventeen. Morris Graves had seen my work and I had his support, but I still couldn't get in.

Martin: Do you feel this was a significant factor in shaping your career?

Blashko: No, not really. It was a great disappointment. Nonetheless I continued with my drawing.

Martin: In 1941, you completed a rather controversial series of seven color drawings entitled *Rat Men.* In them, the realistically-drawn nude forms of women and children are shown being brutalized by their Nazi captors, who, in sharp contrast, are drawn in caricature, with rat-like teeth and tails. A powerful indictment of fascism, were these too controversial for Seattle?

Blashko: I never attempted to show *Rat Men* in Seattle simply because there were no outlets here at that time. I did send them around to different publications in New York, one was *American Artist,* which is still around. I got a letter from the associate editor who said he found them very powerful and would like to reproduce them in the next issue. I was then working in the shipyards and remember anxiously anticipating the issue. When I finally received it I found a reproduction of only one, which was significantly reduced. It was accompanied by a note from the editor: 'It is the inalienable right of an editor to change one's mind. Because these drawings are too shocking we're only reproducing one.'

Martin: Speaking of New York, you moved there in 1943. What was your initial impetus to move?

Blashko: After the 1938 exhibition and the printmaking in 1939, I couldn't sell anything and was supporting myself working on the docks. At this time my family was moving to another house and needed money for a down payment, so I approached Dr. Fuller with seven or eight drawings, hoping that he would buy them. He was very reluctant and acted as if he were doing me a great favor. He did, however, select several which he bought for very little money. These drawings, to the best of my knowledge, are in the museum's permanent collection. After this I saw no point in remaining in Seattle. I had saved enough money in the shipyard and eventually moved to New York, the 'Artist's Mecca.'

Martin: Is it true that you were initially offered a job there as a storyboard artist?

Blashko: No, not right away. In the beginning it was a murderous struggle. Eventually I found work in an animation studio owned by Paramount Pictures, called 'Famous Studios.'

Martin: Did you feel this thwarted your creativity?

Blashko: Well, it was good in that it provided a steady paycheck, and I liked the group of people I worked with. They were among the top animators of the period. Bill Tytla, to mention one, was like the Michelangelo of animation. He created Disney's *Night on Bald Mountain*, and the character Stromboli in *Pinocchio*.

David Martin: I'm curious, with the intensity in a city like New York, and its thriving street scenes, why didn't you continue drawing from what you saw around you.

Blashko: Because nobody would buy them there either! It was simple economics. Before I got work as an animator I considered going into advertising. Shortly after moving to New York I had the *Rat Men* drawings sent to me with the intention of showing them around to ad agencies. First I showed them to some of my left-wing artist friends who said, 'You're crazy to show these around. They'll kick you out!' I didn't know where to turn to so I started drawing from war-related photographs that I found in magazines. I got an agent who, as it turned out, was a real crook, and he showed them around with no results. He asked me if I had anything else, so I thought, 'What the hell, I'll show him my *Rat Men* drawings.' Upon seeing them he said, 'Why didn't you show me these before!' He took them to the biggest ad agencies and one wanted to utilize the style for a series. Nothing ever came of it, but the interesting thing was, contrary to what the progressive artists had told me, the agencies loved them!

Martin: I understand you've been working as a political cartoonist for a number of years. What else have you done while living in New York?

Blashko: I've worked for a variety of progressive publications. Unfortunately, a lot of the progressive newspapers are strapped financially and have curtailed using cartoons. I did some teaching at the Newark School of Fine and Industrial Art in New Jersey until their budget got cut. I'm currently working on a group of drawings of the East Village, which is where I live. I intend to publish them in book form.

Martin: Is the work you're doing now different from your earlier work?

Blashko: I'm now working with fine tip pens, pastels, color markers, etc., in a completely different style, but I'm still very much interested in what goes on around me and it's revealed in my present work.

Martin: Do you think the passion that inspired your early work is still there?

Blashko: The period that these early drawings came out of would be difficult to simulate today. However, I recently did make two lithographs in a similar style. And my work from the 1930s and 40s has now reached the attention of collectors. Three of my lithographs were purchased by the Library of Congress. I'm also represented by two galleries in New York. I derive a great deal of satisfaction knowing that my early work is getting positive response after lying dormant for so many years.

Martin: Recently I visited the Seattle Art Museum to view your work in permanent residence within the Northwest archives. Permanently buried is perhaps a more apt description, since this work hasn't been seen since your exhibition in 1938! Would you like to see more interest shown in your work by the Seattle Art Museum?

Blashko: Absolutely, along with other artists from this period. 📖

An exhibition in celebration of Abe Blashko's 90th birthday was held at the Susan Teller Gallery, New York City, in June, 2010. A collection of his drawings is in their permanent collection. Prints by Blashko are in the collections of the Library of Congress, Washington, D.C., the Columbus Museum of Art, the Nora Eccles Harrison Museum of Art at Utah State University, and Syracuse University.

The Equestrienne, 1938, Black Pencil, by Abe Blashko

The Allure of Us

Nico Vassilakis

the apex of a body of music.
meeting in a spiral within a gyre on fire.
the ends touch.
a language of high tones.

faster till trees bend.
great leaps more swift.
speed aware of nothing but itself.
a heaven of quick processes.

a measurement of truth.
ideas encased in certain types of space.
an ability to theorize.
absolutes perpetuate themselves.

design is mathematics.
the catalyst accelerates.
a nutrient toward off flux.
you can detain understanding.

the imprint of a temporary home.
the kiss of minutia.
the discharge is equal to the build-up.
this geometry is basic.

our mind conceives facts.
the findings are equal to nature.
the by product destroys the process which produced it.
information continues.

possibility is sense perception.
feeling through air with tongues on our hands.
utterance is what we are.
ecstatic crickets.

X

Volume 4, Number 1, Summer/Fall 1994

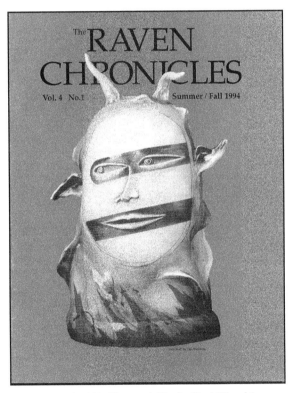

Hot Head, 1993, Glaze and Clay, by Patti Warashina

$4.50

POETRY

James Bertolino

Joseph Bruchac

Ryan Iwanaga

Lynn Martin

Richard Sanchez

Ann Spiers

David Lloyd Whited

FICTION

Gary Curtis

Gregory Hischak

Clifford Trafzer

ESSAY

Nora Martin

Tony Daniel

ART

SCULPTURE
Patti Warashina

PRINTS
Christel Kratohvil

PHOTOGRAPHY
Elaine Querry

DRAWINGS
David Hartz

Hear No Evil, Speak No Evil, See No Evil, 1993, Glaze and Clay, by Patti Warashina

The Business of Writing
An Interview with Sherman Alexie

E.K. Caldwell

P ullman, Washington, 1989: A young pre-med student at Washington State University was in serious trouble with his chosen major. He was plenty smart enough and had long considered himself a "science guy," but his equilibrium was giving him grief. He fainted three times in human anatomy class and, to fill credits while contemplating a career change, he took a writing class. Five poems later, his instructor Alex Kuo asked him what he was doing with the rest of his life. The young man replied he "was open to suggestions." Kuo had a suggestion. Writing. Fortunately for all of us, the young man said, "OK, I'll be a writer."

Five years later, 1994: Twenty-seven year old Sherman Alexie, from the Spokane Indian Reservation in Washington State, has published five books and has been called by *The New York Times* "one of the major lyric voices of our time." His first book, *The Business of Fancydancing* (Hanging Loose Press, 1992), was selected as *The New York Times Book Review* "1992 Notable Book of the Year." His second collection, *I Would Steal Horses* (March, 1992), claimed first place in Slipstream Press' fifth annual chapbook contest. That same year he was the recipient of a National Endowment for the Arts Poetry Fellowship; then *Old Shirts & New Skins* and *First Indian on the Moon* (recently nominated for the Poetry Society of America's William Carlos Williams Award) hit the presses. Next came the readings, securing an agent, and four rounds of bidding for his current book, *The Lone Ranger and Tonto Fistfight in Heaven* (recently nominated for the Pen/Hemingway Award). Now he has a contract for two more novels. His heart has palpitated hard on more than one occasion, but his equilibrium seems to be in good shape. He hasn't fainted once.

E.K. Caldwell: You have had amazing response to your work in a very short period of time. How are you dealing with that dramatic shift in rhythm?

Sherman Alexie: (laughing) A shift in reality is what it is. It's not real and it's not what matters. I think I knew that from the beginning. Certainly there's a lot of hype and fireworks going on, but once the fireworks are over, you go home. It's a game. I don't take it seriously because the important thing I'm doing is affecting people's lives and getting stories told that aren't always heard The rest of it is secondary.

Caldwell: How is all this travelling affecting your writing? How do you make time for new work?

Alexie: I'm a binge writer anyway. When I'm home I'll write ten or twelve hours a day for a couple of weeks and catch up. I do write a lot of poems on the road and most of what I write is fully written in my head before I ever put it on the page.

Caldwell: And the poems stay in your head without getting away from you?

Alexie: Yeah, they do. I don't know exactly how I do that. I've always had a very good memory and I can visualize the poems in my head and move things around. When it finally gets to the page it's usually pretty good and I don't have to do a lot of drafts. Sometimes not any drafts.

Caldwell: Reviewers say things like "Well, this is life on the reservation." Do you think that your work presents an accurate window of perception into life on the rez? Do you ever get concerned about people seeing it as perpetuating stereotypes?

Alexie: I think the problem is that when people like me get all this attention, well, then people think that I'm telling the *only* truth. They get this idea that I'm [presenting] the only image of life on a reservation and that what I'm saying is everything there is to say, but I'm just one set of eyes looking at my reservation and my own experience. I don't pretend to speak for all Indians. I don't pretend to speak for all the members of my own tribe or my tribe itself. To think that all Indian reservations are alike is not right at all. There are common cultural things, functional and dysfunctional. And I don't believe that everyone's experience is like mine. I don't believe that and I don't claim that.

Caldwell: How are the people from home responding to your work?

Alexie: (laughs) The people who didn't like me before still don't like me, and the people who liked me still do. I don't think it's really changed a lot. (laughing) Although, I used to be one of those weak little Indian boys who got the crap kicked out of him by other Indian boys on a daily basis. And a lot of those people seem to have forgotten that and now they're all friendly, and I'm like, "Well, don't you remember that time you broke my nose? I do. I've got a bump on my nose that I see in the mirror every day." People are kind of sycophantic, but generally I'm still "Junior" just like I've always been.

Caldwell: How are other established Native writers, who've been around and have still not gotten the attention you're getting, responding to your work?

Alexie: It's interesting, because the one I can think of who has been the most supportive has been writing longer than I have been alive. He has never gotten the kind of attention that his contemporaries have, and I'm not sure why because he's certainly as good a writer. That's Simon Ortiz. There is some sense of guilt at receiving this much attention because I know that a big reason for my success is because other writers have come before me and their stories have done well. Leslie Marmon Silko, James Welch,

Scott Momaday, Joy Harjo, and Simon are people who are my heroes. I've already been places they haven't been, and am getting closer to movie deals and levels they haven't been. I feel guilty in some sense but I know also that every generation is supposed to move forward a little bit beyond what has already happened. They were the trailblazers. I'm taking it a little farther. Joy and Adrian Louis and Simon and Leslie are really supportive, sending encouragement and correspondence and responding to my work. I have also become friends with others who are not as well known like Liz (Woody) and Vince (Wanassey) and Phil (Red Eagle). Having the support of other people out there telling the stories is important to me, and I'm hoping my success will help my contemporaries.

Caldwell: Would you speak to what you see as our responsibility as Native writers? Do you see that responsibility restricting/constricting certain avenues of creativity?

Alexie: We do have a cultural responsibility above and beyond what other people do, more than other ethnic groups, simply because we are so misrepresented and misunderstood and appropriated. We have a serious responsibility as writers to tell the truth. And to act as (and I hate to use the words because people put it on me and I don't like the responsibility) role models. We are more than just writers. We are storytellers. We are spokespeople. We are cultural ambassadors. We are politicians. We are activists. We are all of this simply by nature of what we do, without even wanting to be. So we're not like these other writers who can just pick and choose their expressions. They're chosen for us and we have to be aware of that. I also think we have a definite responsibility to live up to our words. As Native writers, we can talk the talk about the things that everybody should do and we should do, but if you're going to write about racism I don't think you should be racist. If you're going to write about sexism and exploitation, then I don't think you should be sleeping around. If you're going to write about violence and colonialism, then I don't think you should be doing it to your own family. I think we have a serious responsibility as Native writers to live traditionally in a contemporary world. And I don't think a lot of us do.

Caldwell: What do you think prevents us from doing that?

Alexie: A lot of it is our own dysfunction. While we may have more responsibilities because of what we do, that does not automatically make us healthy. Part of the danger in being any artist of whatever color is that you have to fall in love with your wrinkles. The danger is that if you fall in love with your wrinkles, then you don't want to get rid of them. You start to glorify them and perpetuate them. If you write about pain, you can end up inevitably searching for more pain to write about, that kind of thing. That self destructive route. We need to get away from that. We can write about pain and anger without having to let it consume us, and we have to learn how to do that in our lives as individuals before we can start doing it as writers.

Caldwell: What would you say to a young writer who is perhaps being drawn to write about something that is not typically perceived as "Indian"? Maybe some outrageous science fiction. They are feeling, perhaps, that they aren't "allowed" to write about that because it doesn't have anything to do with what is perceived as being Indian.

Alexie: I think that's great as long as they make their characters Indians. I'd love to see Indian science fiction that has Indians a hundred years from now, and they're riding in spaceships. I think that would be wonderful. As writers, though, I think whatever we do ends up being autobiography. If you start writing about things too far removed from yourself, it's not going to be good. Those young writers who want to write science fiction should put more of themselves into it. It doesn't mean they have to write about corn pollen and eagle feathers. I get tired of that, too. People expecting all this 'Indian wisdom' and four directions stuff. It doesn't need to be like that. But I would like to see their lives and their culture in their work, from their own perceptions and experiences and not so far removed that it's unrecognizable as being written by an Indian. There are a million science fiction writers out there. But being an Indian science fiction writer, well, that's something new and exciting.

Caldwell: What kinds of opportunities and avenues do you see opening up for Native writers?

Alexie: You know, I'm not sure. I know there's limited room for Native writers to be successful. There's usually only room at the top for one at a time. There will be one who sells all the copies and the rest of us are at various levels on the ladder. Eventually someone will come along and knock the one off the top and somebody else will be the million-seller Indian. I was happy getting my small press book of poems out, *The Business of Fancydancing.* I had no idea it would take off like it did. I didn't expect it to, but I certainly wanted it to—I dreamed about it, and I'm glad it did, but I would've been content to have a small press career. That would've been fine. I think writers have to be content and comfortable with the idea of that. I mean, we'd all love the huge audience. We haven't had as many opportunities to get it as other writers but you know as well as I do that we're gonna go out of fashion. I was right in the middle of it and it's going to start tailing off now. There are all these Indian books out, most of them written by non-Natives, but they're still classified as Indian books. They're going to glut the market with these bad books that nobody buys. Then the publishers aren't going to want to publish Indian books anymore because they don't sell. And they don't sell because they're awful. The good writing will be ignored again and it will have to go back to the small presses where good writing is always published the most. For ten or fifteen years it will go like that and then we'll resurface again because some book will come out of the woodwork and sell a lot of copies. It's like the stock market—be patient—it always ends up about the same anyway.

Caldwell: You sound like you're becoming schooled in the publishing experience. That must be trying after a point, dealing with the trappings of big business publishing.

Alexie: It's definitely big business. I sit down and write and it's art. The second it leaves my house it becomes commerce. And it's commerce with artistic intentions, rather than what I write now, which is artistic with commercial intentions. Yeah, it's frightneing. It's like "What am I? A pet rock?" You get the feeling that everything about you, you're selling. As a writer you're selling yourself. When I do readings and go on book tours I'm selling myself, which is dangerous. Because that can get very seductive. I've had the opportunity to sell my soul almost every day of the last couple of years to somebody or something.

Caldwell: How do you avoid that?

Alexie: You hear these stories about successful people who've become jerks. I think they were probably jerks to begin with and (laughs) success just provided an opportunity to magnify it. I wasn't a jerk to begin with and I'm not going to let this experience make me become a jerk. The best moments are not selling all the books, which is great. I like the money and I love the traveling and a lot of the people I've met. But the best things are times like when we were walking in a mall in Spokane and these tough little Indian boys, with all these problems of their own, came running up all excited to see me. Because I'm "Sherman, the Indian writer." Those are the moments that are most important. Or when I do young Indian writers' camps and workshops, the kids just flock and listen. And you walk from classroom to classroom and they're stopping me in the halls to read their poems and stories to me. That's the best part of it. Knowing that if somebody like that had been around earlier [for me], I might not have had to go through as many of the bad things that I did. Knowing that the Native writers who are spending time with younger writers are getting one of them, two of them, ten of them, a hundred of them, to start writing. And it doesn't matter if they publish or ever have a book. [What matters is] that they keep writing and realize that their thoughts and their stories and their emotions are valid and valuable. That's the most important thing we do. 📖

Indian Boy Love Song (#1)

Everyone I have lost
in the closing of a door
the click of the lock

is not forgotten, they
do not die but remain
within the soft edges
of the earth, the ash

of house fires and cancer
in sin and forgiveness
huddled under old blankets

dreaming their way into
my hands, my heart
closing tight like fists.

—Sherman Alexie

from *The Business of Fancydancing*

Climbing Together, Late Afternoon

Nancy Cherry

Behind your mother's house
an argument comes to an end.
At first we watch the sky.
This time of day clouds evaporate,
raptors hide in the eucalyptus
while the grass listens: foxtail,
cheat grass, brome. It rises
from your mother's hillside.
There is nothing else between us
but the mountain.
Anger brings us to this.
Flat on my back, I watch trees
bow to the mouth of October
and ants climb out of the grass
as the sun strikes
between my legs. So this
is how you pray.

Paris Dreams

Gary Curtis

[Letter 72]

Dear Paris:

Last I sent you seven fiery little poems, and fourteen dramatic new drawings, and still have not heard one word on publication dates! It would be very unwise to ignore me.

Sincerely, G.

[Diary excerpt]

Yesterday I told Roseman about being published in The Paris Review *and about the money and fame and so on. I also told her about going to New York City. She said, That's wonderful. How do you feel about that?*

I didn't know what to say. I didn't feel happy and I didn't feel sad. Finally I said, It just doesn't seem to matter that much anymore.

Then, for no reason, I became overwhelmed with emotion and I began to cry.

Roseman said, What are you feeling right now?

I covered my face with my hands and spoke thru my fingers. I said, I feel like I'm dead. I don't feel anything. I feel like I'm not really here anymore. That none of this is really happening.

Dear Paris:

I have composed several hypothetical letters that might give you a better idea of the kind of letters I need from you. Please make any corrections you think prudent.

Sincerely, G.

[Sample 1]

Dear Mr. Curtis:
    Thank you so much for taking the time to send the excellent drawings and wonderful poems. The work is very strong and I think fits nicely with the kind of work in this particular publication. Money and dates to follow.
    Paris

[Sample 2]

Dear Mr. Curtis:
    After your many submissions that so wonderfully demonstrate a gifted and uncompromising talent, we would be pleased to publish your work in the very near future, perhaps in our next issue.
    Respectfully, Paris

[Sample 3]

Dear Mr. Curtis:
    Hats off to you! Delicious wonderful work! You have obviously created a masterpiece and deserve to be published without further delay. We are now making plans for specific dates that would include a round trip ticket for you to New York City for further discussions of artistic details.
    Yours truly, Paris

[Another diary excerpt]

No more coffee breaks at the Greeks. Yesterday I got kicked out for wearing my work clothes. The owner actually told me not to come back. I said, I'm just having coffee. He said, Not in them pants you're not. I tried to explain, I'm an artist. I paint. I write. I do poems . . . He grabbed my arm and dragged me outside. Everybody in the place staring, and I hated it. I hated him. I hated all of them. He said, Get outa here. And I shouted back at him. I

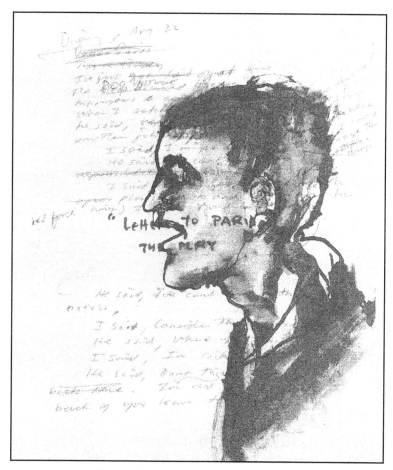

Letter to Paris, 1994, Drawing, by Gary Curtis

said, I am also presently resident manager of the St. Charles Hotel with a full set of master keys! He said, Bye, bye. Hypocritical little nobody! As soon as I'm published they'll be bragging about how I used to come into the place every day with my notebooks and write my famous poems and drink their lousy coffee. Bye, bye, yourself. Bastards!

Dear Paris:

   Since you have chosen to ignore me I have decided to give you one last chance. If I do not hear from you by this Friday noon, I will give my lawyer the green light.

   G.

Paris:

Your insistence on remaining silent will no longer work. If I do not hear from you by Friday at 7 p.m., I will make everything I know public and let the chips fall. At least I will still have my integrity if not having been published in your overrated pompous fucking rag!

Sincerely, G.

Dear Mr. Curtis:

You sound a little desperate. Do you really think your life is any more interesting than anyone else's? To be perfectly honest, your work is a bit on the sloppy side. You are not the only artist in the world with talent. I see thousands of manuscripts every week and most of them are no less worthy of being published than your work is. My god. It's just too distressing to even talk to somebody who doesn't see anyone else but himself.

Regrettably, Paris

Paris:

How dare you call me desperate! As for my being the only artist in the world with talent, I suppose you've never published anybody with a ego! And as for my being sloppy, what about that slob Kafka's filthy little room, or the way Vincent Van Gogh lived his entire life! I doubt very much if he worried about doing his laundry or picking up his dirty socks, and I doubt very much that you would have invited him to your lousy goddamn New York City!

G.

Dear G:

After reading your last letter it occurred to me that maybe you're a bit confused. I mean one minute you're saying one thing and the next minute you're saying something totally different. You seem to see everything in the extreme, either/or. I suspect that's why Roseman suggested the Lithium. Everything is not black or white. I think that's what Roseman is trying to get you to see.

 Paris

Dear Roseman:

 For personal reasons I am unable to continue my therapy until after I have been published in *Paris* as I am too busy with many details and may have to go to New York City very soon.

 Sincerely, Curtis

Dear Paris:

 Just a reminder that Mother's Day is coming up which would be the ideal time to publish the mother piece I sent you last July.

 Regards, Curtis

The Next Day

in a dingy room

somewhere downtown

the angry poet

spills his words

of rage and fury

across the silent page . . .

& dreams of *Paris*.

Dear Mr. Curtis,

Well I guess I should feel badly; it seems you've received some of our rejection slips in the past. But while I am glad that we ran the portfolio of your artwork, I offer no apology for the notices we send when we decide not to take unsolicited material.

I hope that it will not send you into paroxysms of hatred or self-loathing to hear that we have also chosen not to accept "Paris Dreams" for publication in the magazine. I did think they were funny, though, both funny and sad.

I wish you the very best, both as a poet/artist and with your therapy.

Sincerely,

Elizabeth Gaffney
Senior Editor

18 May, 1993

To: Elizabeth Gaffney
Senior Editor
The Paris Review

Dear Ms. Gaffney—

I loved the line in your letter, "paroxysms of hatred or self-loathing." Sounds like the perfect title for my movie, *Portrait of an Artist / Paroxysms of hatred or self-loathing*. Anyway, I hope you don't mind if I use it.

Sincerely,
Gary Curtis, 25 May 1993 📖

The Prodigal Sock Sits And Spins In The Big Picture

Gregory Hischak

I found this picture of you, waving from the front porch in your blue dress. Your mouth frozen in some seemingly eternal vowel. For the life of me I can't recall what it was you said pacing those worn porch boards on that last afternoon. Extinction means always having to say you're sorry.

I am thinking of your socks. Your favorite socks, lime green with red trim around the top. The ones that graced your feet that last afternoon. Those most favored socks moving from feet to hamper to washer to dryer to hamper; dumped across the bed, and only then the discovery made that one of those lime green socks had treacherously vanished. Somewhere within the confines of that warm rotating drum, the partnership was terminated. Now unmatched and ambling solo in places unknown. On some seemingly random agenda. Drifting from Kenmore to Kenmore across this blue green planet. Poor sock. Lime green with red trim, moving mysteriously. Moving with the perky cadence of a strolling continent. Poor sock.

Consider Australia. Australia drifting slowly away from his India. Stealing toward South America's inviting white breasts: Snow-covered tectonic uplifts beckoning across warm blue seas.

Consider India. Poor India. A jeweled tear rolls down her dusty brown cheek. Dancing her sad little Precambrian Jig along those newly-opened shores. "Write, Australia . . . write . . . won't you? Won't you?" If you love a continent let it go. If it loves you, the continent will come back. If it doesn't return, it was never your continent to begin with. Tectonics means always having to say where am I? Extinction means living in constant preparation of saying goodbye. The mouth in its constant readiness to ply through those elongated vowels and bitter consonants. While I am thinking about it: *goodbye.*

The final disappearance of the Horned Bolivian Terrier Moth. The demise of the Antiguan Bouillion Weal. The mastodon having disappeared only moments ago. Poor Weal. These passings in themselves regrettable and fill me with the desire to say I'm sorry, I'm sorry. Our own spin into oblivion and silence. The quiet yawning mouth of extinction ... I'm sorry. (Remember extinction means always having to say I'm sorry.) Inevitably, choices are made for me because I refuse to make them for myself ... for this, I am sorry, allow me to apologize. Out of that warm void of extinction my mouth frozen in some eternal apology.

You see first there is a crack. The crack fills with ocean and the ocean clouds with lint. The waters dry to salt, are pulled apart by mountains, ground down to scree and flooded again by ocean, again and again and again. Without even a brief question and answer period, when it is over it will begin again.

I am thinking of your socks. Poor socks. Lime green socks with red trim rolling past the windows of our dryer. Listen, we are all whirling past the portholes of our dryer. To be engaged and occasionally hugged as we tumble by ... If you have missed even one of us then you will have to wait. If you tire of standing then of course you may sit. Eventually we surface, on some future cycle, having completed our seemingly random agenda. We have come back.

One day India hears a scratch at her door. Opening it, she will find her Australia, curled and shivering. Skinny and prodigal, her Australia has returned. One night you may remove your blue dress. Pull back the quilt and the comforter and flannels and sheets, and there I will be. There. Your prodigal sock returned. Nothing is eternal, neither our vows of undying love nor the demise of that love. Nothing. Look, I have surfaced from graves of permia and gravel, of quilt and comforter, only to say, "*Hi. I have come back. Having experienced eternity for just a few minutes. I have come back and I have brought pictures. Pictures of me waving and telling you everything. Look here, pictures of me waving and telling you everything.*

Everything that I forgot to tell you the first time." 📖

Love Poem In Winter

Larry Laurence

—for L.R.

There's no moon in this poem.
If there were, it'd be full.
Trees bare. Lake frozen.

There's no peace in this poem.
If there were, it'd be borderless.
Sleep unguarded. A few lights
a kindness to late travelers.

There's no clitoris in this poem.
If there were, it'd be yours.
Shining and wet. A blue ocean,
far off, prepares itself.

There's no whiskey is this poem.
If there were, it'd be
to better times. Better times.

What there is, is this:
a pie tin frozen to the porch.
Suet. Stale bits of pumpernickel.
And the poor, lucky sparrows that have
entered this morning.

Prayer Flags On Barbed Wire

Nora Martin

"I had seen prayer flags all afternoon flying from houses, from bridges, from trees and from piles of stone. There were Hindu prayers written on them; and every flutter of the flags made the writer a beneficiary of their blessings."
—William O. Douglas, *Beyond the High Himalayas*

This is Montana. It is cold; it is brown. I am pinning palm-sized white pieces of paper to the barbed wire fence with hinged wooden clothespins. On each folded sheet is written a word, sometimes a sentence, one with what I call a complete poem.

At one time words flew around inside me and darted out everywhere like swallows in a huge barn. Right now my thoughts are few and labored, like my freezing breaths. They are tiny dried bird bones, which I arrange on the paper with tweezers. The papers flap and strain away from me, toward the south. Their movements give form to the wind rushing around me and down the flat valley, until it collides with the Spanish Peaks forty miles away.

> I want to inhale all
> this brittle wind,
> because my lungs
> never feel full.

My job is as a home educator with Headstart. I visit families once a week to help parents plan and present activities for their young children. Ten minutes ago, I left Lilly's kitchen. Lilly's husband is a ranch hand. Their old house, which sits on a bare knoll, comes with the job. So does the heating oil that pushes hot air up through vents under the table around my feet. It feels good.

Lilly has hot coffee on the stove when I come. We sit across the table from one another with her two brown-eyed, round-faced girls in between. They crawl over us to cut and glue the colored construction paper I've brought.

Lilly is old, I am young, but we are the same age. We are both thirty-six. Some of her children are grown; then came these two eager daughters. Lilly is heavy with aching bones and a hard face. Her hair is pulled back tight. She sometimes uses a cane to walk when her knees hurt. She smiles often and it is hard for me not to stare at the dark place where her teeth once were. Lilly loves the rambling old place with its stained walls and cozy bedrooms upstairs. She hasn't always had a house.

From where I am standing I can see the gray stone bluffs that are behind Lilly's barn in the distance. To the west the Tobacco Root Mountains are faint in windy haze. I believe the fence where I am leaving my writing is still part of the ranch where her husband works. But I never leave more than three papers and I never stop twice in the same place. There are endless miles of barbed wire fence in Montana on which I can leave my offerings.

Last winter, before her husband got the ranch job, Lilly's family was living in a small travel trailer. They could never get rid of the lice. The girls became reinfested several times. They often depended on the local food bank for donations. This winter they have two freezers full of deer and beef stored up. On the table in front of the kitchen window are stacks of vegetable seed packets. Lilly keeps them sitting out just for the pleasure of anticipation. She says, "Bud's going to till me a place to put in some flowers."

It is January, minus seven degrees, when we are discussing her garden. I feel her eagerness like a heavy smell in the air between us. She plans to bury all their struggles in the stony ground the moment it thaws. Lilly's prayer flags will be up and on their way by late June.

There is always a sense of relief when I can hook some of my thoughts on the fence. Each time I do, a space opens up inside me leaving room for the people in my life to enter and be digested. As I look back at the stark whiteness of my paper against the large empty space all around, I can almost see particles of myself break off the paper and blow away. It is like shedding dead skin cells leaving tiny bits of myself to mix with dirt and air.

Once Lilly and I sat and laughed as we compared hands. Unlike anything else about us, they are alike. Both of us have large square fingers and nails. Our hands, dry and callused, are never completely clean. Lilly's wear the work of the farm and mine are always ink and paint-stained.

In the evenings Lilly paints on little wooden animals which she uses to decorate straw wreaths. Last winter she painted ceramic owls and glued glitter onto tee-shirts for her girls. She told me, "When I do my crafts it takes a different way of thinking. I feel like I am in a deep place."

FOR LILLY
For years of warm air
on her feet.
For blue Bachelor Buttons
in brown grasses.
For time submerged in doing.

Lilly is always ready to start the project when I arrive. She takes the lead in working with her children. The things the girls make are tacked up all over the house. Whatever we are working on that day is carefully left out on the table for their father to see when he comes in for lunch.

I live three miles down a narrow dirt road. But between my road and town is Highway 191. Both my road and the highway are lined with barbed wire. Almost everything in Montana is contained within a barbed wire fence.

On Thursdays I visit Cassandra. She is twenty-two and has three children. Cassandra is smoothly round in her tight jeans and cropped-off shirt. She wears pink pumps that match her

Prayer Flags On Barbed Wire, 1994, Drawing, by Scott Martin

shirt. Her hair is blond and thin. The walls of her apartment are stark. There are never toys or books of any kind visible. She told me, "My kids woke me up three times yesterday. How can I keep them interested in watching television?" I have brought scissors, markers, and crayons for the children, which Cassandra keeps hidden. "It only makes a mess," she says. I have left silly putty and Play-Doh. I hear her tell the children, as soon as I have closed the door behind me, "Throw that stuff away."

On another Thursday at Cassandra's, I roll out large sheets of paper on the table. I let the children scoop their hands into mixing bowls of finger paint made from cornstarch and food coloring. Cassandra sits on the counter smoking. She tells me everything about her life. One week she says, "In high school, before I quit, I loved to oil paint." I say, "Join us." I hear no response. The next week she tells me, "I met a new man at the Black Swan Casino on Tuesday. We are going to Butte for the weekend with some of his friends." I want to ask her who will look after the children. But I know her alcoholic husband will. She will allow him to visit the children, if it suits her needs, despite his violence toward all of them.

I have found a secret place to leave my writings. It is at the remains of an old bridge that once crossed the Gallatin River. Here the water seeps out of the canyon and into the valley that meanders around the roots of the mountains. The barbed wire lies slack on the ground and only the river can read what I have written.

It doesn't matter where I leave my prayer tickets. In the past I have left them in imperfect quilt squares and crooked seams of embroidered pillows. The children I work with seem to have no difficulty producing gifts of themselves. If something is put into a child's hand they create with it. They leave their prayer tickets in blobs of glue and splats of paint.

Even Cassandra's son, Bobby, pounces on whatever it is I bring through the door. He often uses the materials in a destructive way. During one lesson, he took the scissors we were using to cut out life-sized paper dolls and grabbed my braid in one hand and starting cutting with the other. I said, pulling away, "Bobby, you need to cut paper only." Cassandra said from her place above us on the counter, "Oh Bobby." The boy does not like it that part of my job is to listen to his mother. When he needs my attention he climbs onto my lap and hits me in the face.

I know many more Cassandras than I do Lillys. The Cassandras sitting apart. The Cassandras wrapped so tightly in barbed wire they can't move. She tells me, "Those kids pulled all the food out of the refrigerator yesterday and spilled everything onto the floor while I was in bed. I kept them in their rooms all day." I listen. I give suggestions for child management. But I get no response.

CASSIE,
GET OUT THE WIRE CLIPPERS.

I move on. There are many fences down the road. I will do my job. I will write. If I no longer have anything to say, I will sew curtains. I will knit. I will dig in the dirt. Or I will crochet beer cans together into hats. And I will leave them on the fence posts that support the barbed wire. 📖

Refrigerator

Carter Revard

As winter snows
come sifting down,
white cold around
this kitchen's summer,
my small blue flame
with Freon blood
pulsing, expanding
around belly's ice,
my warm white body
freezes out famine,
swallows Provence and
provides Alaska's
food-filled winter
around belly's ice,
warmth for cats
curled at my feet
to lick their furred
forepaws clean,
pink-tonguing cream
from tipped whiskers,
between two winters
purring breaths out
warm as toast
curled at my feet.

Dressing the Salmon Queen, Olympic Peninsula

Ann Spiers

Knee deep in seaweed,
she slid with each step,
stuck in wrack so fresh
isopods still twitched
on the slippery surface.
Not even the sand fleas
had claimed it yet.

Amazed, she knelt,
gathered armfuls
from mounds so bright,
the seaweed glittered
flashes of brown, red, and green,
festoons of taffeta,
fit for a salmon queen.

Ribbon and eyelet, ravel and frill,
caught in wonder,
she selected sea lace and sea laurel,
draped red laver and fringe,
wound black tassel and blister wrack,
smoothed color changer and confetti,
hung whip and bladder,
picked sea rose and took red wing.

Robed in sargasso silks,
she turned seaward, saw the silver
break the sea surface.

The salmon came running,
groom for the bride,
caught in the wrack,
awed by the shreds,
dressed in the gown
raddled for eons
on the hoop
of the sea and the moon.

Heavenly Blue Holiday

Belle Randall

We're entering The Final Poem.
The foolsgold mouthpiece
is transformed

into the mouthpiece of a golden horn,
lifting the morning glories
to the sun,

while on the Morning Glory gramophone
a pair of golden lips
     brush a silver mike and sing

the dawn of Lady Day
and all things trumpet-shaped—
ear-horn with which you listen,

bell with which I ring.

XI

VOLUME 4, NUMBER 2, SPRING 1995

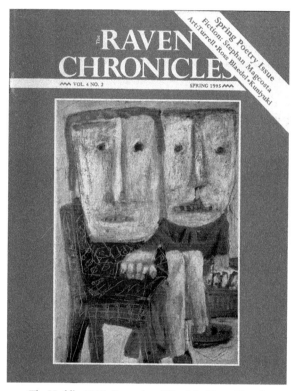

The Huddle, 1995, Enamel on Wood, by Terry Turrell

The Iceman

Alicia Hokanson

"....a man older than the pyramids
who walked the Alps before Buddha or Christ,
before Aristotle or Plato . . ."
        —PBS documentary

Taken by ice and given back,
he came to us whole and we broke him
looking for our past
stashed in his woven bags
and boots lined with grass,
etched in a bow of yew
or arrows of swift viburnum.

Another gone down on the dark journey
and returned with treasure:
sloeberries ripe with autumn sun,
news of places where earth gives up
its sharpest flint, or a meadow
of curative mushrooms far up the mountainside.

Did he pray to a goddess of snow or fire?
To some Vulcan of copper who blessed his axe?
As the storm overtook him
did he cry out for wife and daughter
weaving reeds for their roof by the lakeshore?

Unburied by his tribe, unburnt, unhallowed,
skin shriveled brown, his fingers curve
with blackened nails. The crust
around his hollowed eyes articulates
the centuries' slow speech
of glaciers, blue quiet of alpine skies.

Behind his knees, the skin's tattooed
with hexagrams for wildness and protection.

All Fall Down, 2018, Drawing, by Jon Strongbow

They Dance Alone

Stephan Magcosta

The pumpkin grinned in pale, misty moonlight from the top of a dumpster in Occidental Park. Halloween trash, strewn on wet cobblestones. Candy and gum wrappers, broken wine bottles, a florescent green condom, and cracked plastic skull. Strips of orange and black crepe paper hung from a maple and wound past a totem pole. Outlines in chalk of a woman and man lay on brick walkway, holding hands like lovers. The pumpkin rocked on the dumpster, grinning like he'd seen it all before.

Inside the pumpkin, a rat looked up from its holiday feast, furry cheeks bulging with stringy, gold flesh. Guarded and cautious, alert to a change in the cool evening mist. It peered through the lopsided eye of the pumpkin, jagged and carved like the smile. The rat sat and listened, nervous and twitching, rocking the pumpkin. A whisper of leaves and gossamer melody wove through the night.

The rat pulled back and stood on its hind legs to peer from the top of the pumpkin. Pointing its ears and flexing its toes, holding a mouthful of partly chewed pulp. The rat saw a woman at the edge of the park, dancing alone in the moonlight.

The woman sang softly and danced barefoot circles, turned pirouettes down the burnt-orange bricks. Her black skirt rustled and bracelets jangled as she held out her arms for an invisible partner. Silver streaks in black hair glistened in moonlight, framing the caramel sheen of her face. Hair down her shoulders, hanging in waves on an ivory sweater. As she turned, scarlet thread in her skirt swirled like ribbons of blood. Her eyes, dying fire, turning to coals.

The rat watched the woman, then looked beyond her, past her soft singing, watching the shadows congeal and draw near. The rat looked around and slid back in the pumpkin as the woman spun circles and danced.

Men were appearing alongside the park, masked in plumes of warm breath. Boots and bandannas, sweatshirts, straw hats. They wore what they'd carried from south of the border in bags bound together with tape and old string. In shapeless, frayed coats, they gathered at benches and leaned against trees. They all watched the woman and murmured in Spanish as she slowly spun circles and danced.

One popped a thermos and passed around swallows of *café con leche*. Steam from the lid that served as their cup. One offered smokes and lit them for neighbors, a cup of brown hands around bright orange flame.

They all watched her dance as the full moon was setting. They watched and saw faces, dreams lost in time. At the hour of dawn on the Day of the Dead, the woman danced on as pale morning light touched the mist.

Then she stumbled, arms folding, and spiraled to earth, a bird shot down from the sky. Someone stepped forward, another restrained him, as if lending help would show disrespect. They watched her rise slowly, up to her knees, clutching her skirt like it held all she owned. She knelt with her head bowed, still as a statue.

The one who stepped forward turned to his neighbor, an unspoken question lining his face.

Los desaparecidos was the reply. She dances with those who have now disappeared.

"*¿Quien?*" someone asked. "Who's disappeared?"

The answer arose from one who stood out, lighter in color and wearing a suit. Threadbare and old, a wide lapel style not seen in some years.

"Sometimes in my country," words falling soft as hourglass sand, "the women dance solo, with lost sons and husbands, taken from home in the middle of night or pulled off the street in plain light of day." He looked to one side, face cloaked in shadow.

"This one," he nodded, "steps with her son and also her long-vanished husband. She dances with both on the day of all saints. Their pictures are pinned to her sweater." He gestured toward black and white portraits next to her heart. One tinted sepia looked very old.

The woman stood slowly and held her arms open, embracing a partner that she alone saw. Resting her head on a shoulder unseen, in grief beyond measure, as if she were holding a cold, lifeless hand.

Murmurs arose from the men who were watching, a sighing from deep in the shadows. The woman said nothing and turned from their voices, her bracelets tinkling like bells.

"Why dance in this place?"

"How long have you been here?"

"My second week now. And people look at me as if I'm not there. Except for *la migra*. I was nearly caught twice by the border patrol. But why does she dance here? And wasn't she singing?"

"Look around for your answer."

Standing and seated in pale, misty light, the men looked like ghosts in a house with no walls.

"Her loved ones will visit wherever she dances. And no, she was crying, not singing a song."

The man in the suit then walked to a dumpster, measured and sure through the cobblestone park. He glanced at a pumpkin on one of the lids, opened the other and rummaged inside. Pulled out some blossoms now wilted and dry. Marigolds, coppered as dark, ancient suns.

He watched her spin slowly as mist burned away, her hands reaching out to the dawn. Shuffling over, he bowed as if offering gifts during mass, bouquet at her feet, now ashen and bloody. He whispered and slowly departed. Passing the dumpster, he nodded as if to a friend.

The rat stuck its head out the pumpkin's left eye and peered at the now vacant park. Morning light through tall trees, a few scattered leaves. A lone raven shrieked and flapped in slow circles, a band of grey pigeons picking at crumbs. As if by arrangement, they rose as one body, a wave curling into the sky. The rat watched the pigeons and leaped from the pumpkin, dragging its tail through the lopsided eye.

Rocking the pumpkin, grinning like he'd seen it all before. 📖

She Summons Ravens, Collage and Mixed Media, by Anita Endrezze

Before God

Kevin Miller

The woman in the pew in front of me
turns full face. She holds me with eyes
that ask nothing. She has no questions.
When she turns to face the altar, I am hers.
Her fingers follow the delicate bone of her cheek,
whisk at dust I cannot see, glide in a fine line
but do not touch the skin. I follow the curve
of flesh stretched to fine silk over ivory.
The air vanishes like the seconds before lightning.
One thousand one, one thousand two,
mea culpa, mea culpa, mea maxima culpa.
She tucks a sliver of hair behind an ear.
When she tilts her head, I lean to see her lips.
I read them slowly, each syllable I think I see,
I repeat. I watch the motion of her throat
as she swallows, and in my new prayer
she unfolds like the first iris of spring,
the soft curl of her tongue white into blue.

Pursuing The Run Away Hub Cap

Belle Randall

—a fractured villanelle

An Easter legend in reverse:
Washed ashore, the boy drowned.
What goes up must come down;

What goes around, comes around.
Getting her feet back on the ground,
Venus rubs her eyes and looks around.

"Like a Mardi Gras assassin clown,"
Our love began as our rebirth. Goodbye, goodbye:
Our little canoe disappearing around

A bend in the Tunnel of Love,
Where, Easter legend in reverse,
What goes around, comes around.

Later came the falling back to earth,
The getting our feet black on the ground.
I'll tell you an Easter legend in reverse,

Putting the cart before the hearse,
Of how a boy of only six can drown.
Our love began as our rebirth—

Tin cans tied to the car in mirth,
Long waits, with the radiator cooling down,
An Easter legend in reverse.

Momentary Comfort

Mira Chieko Shimabukuro

—for Ken

It might be about hot *O-cha*
just poured from a teapot.
Or transplanted tulips
that catch the morning sun
like a spotlight in the front yard.
Or maybe the beam
shining through the east window,
adding warmth to a carpet
inevitably it will cause to fade.

I wish I could explain
tea,
how later, it will get cold
so the stove needs to be reheated.
How, even as I let the hot liquid
slide down my throat, melt each knot
in my stomach, I am grateful
for this moment of pleasure and I know
it is just that. Later, I will need to move,
change the way I hold the kettle
so as to let tap water make music
against the stainless steel bottom.

On the burner, a steady whisper of water
will push into a scream
that I have learned to attend
so this signal for relief
will not overwhelm my senses
but rather remind me
of where I might stand.

When I carry the teapot to the sunlight,
beaming in the front room,
maybe I'll stretch down,
a cat in my own pleasure
rubbing against carpet that someday
will be torn up, possibly replaced,
from too many years
of what warms me
right now.

Raingem

Stephen Thomas

Raingems hang from rafter tails this morning,
as the working lake grows light at
seven: ten, March twelfth, nineteeneightynine.
A pool of silver, scaled with windwork, scored
by shipwakes and the seams of racing shells.
The light defines the masts at moorage,
bare limbs of the maples and the corner
of the neighbor's towering house. The smaller
details—twigs and rigging—have evaporated
in a silvery corona, not quite blinding.
When I close my eyes, a green ghost
with a purple halo, my hedged lake, remains,
where memory assists the ghost to stipulate faint
masts and limbs, which hover not quite there
and not quite not, abstract particulars.

I open eyes. The light has changed.
Crossmotions in the rippled scales appear. How,
driven north, they tend, it seems, southeast.
And now it is too bright to see and now,
a spill of diamonds spreads behind dark trees.
The masts, the hulks contract like twigs and rigging,
while the sun, as viewed through this, a
borrowed welder's mask, elongates at the land lip,
rises momently, momentously detaches, snaps
shut like a water droplet, dashing
earthward, bringing down upended in
its oscillating lens a minim moorage
and foreshortened spars.

Don Quixote In China

Qiu Xiaolong

Once more, you are going to mount
the bony horse, old, tired,
at the foot of the Great Wall
along the Yangtze River.
A cloud of dust rises, nothing
but the dust, and you
uphold your shield, as if
it were the setting sun
of an ancient empire.
In a bronze reflection
you discover a broken figure,
recognizable only in the shape
of a rusty suit of armor. You do not
dare lie down under the ash tree, or
doubts, like termites, will hollow
your trunk. Dear Sancho, dumb,
dutiful as ever, shoulders
a newly fixed lance, waiting
by a Ming post. He too has
to find himself something
to do, dragging his feet
along the unfamiliar road,
wondering.

Everything Repeated Many Times

Sean Brendan-Brown

I met a man on the bus in downtown Biloxi;
I'm sure he remembers me because everything he said he repeated many times,
his affliction I'm sure some doctor has a word
or phrase or explanation for—
everything repeated many times.

He told me about his house, he said his house
was yellow yellow yellow just like that and just
when I began to think his mind worked in threes
he said his favorite color was red red red red.

I'm sure many people felt sorry for him in his life
or were irritated with him repeating everything
but I wasn't sorry or irritated, I thought how nice
to have words stuck in your head over and over
robbed of the arrogance of eloquence, tripping
up fluidity, dynamics, sophistry, and oration
with the affliction of everything repeated
many times;
how difficult it would be to lie.

He told me his name name name was John,
just like that. I asked him again and he said
his name name name was John. How unimportant,
to be confirmed, to be called anything, to attach
the self to a leash of description. This is my
stop stop stop stop stop he said, by the casino
where the swordfish is red red red neon.
Someone laughed,
laughed at him, laughed behind their hand;

Western Movies, 1994-95, Oil, Enamel On Metal Panel, by Terry Turrell

I whispered it later,
when my txurn came, just
to see how it sounded: *stop stop stop stop stop*.

XII

VOLUME 5, NUMBER 1, SUMMER/FALL 1995, DOUBLE ISSUE

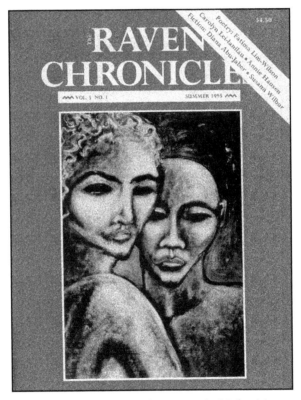

Observing, 1991, Hand-Painted Monotype, by Harlow Morgan

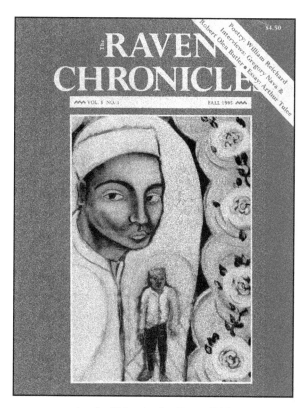

Another Voice, Another Room, 1995,
Acrylic With Ink, by Harlow Morgan

Irene

Diana Abu-Jaber

I

The summer that I was nineteen I thought that I might be pregnant. I came home for a visit, and one night, while we sat together, I asked my mother how she felt when she first learned that she was carrying me. She thought about this for a second and then turned toward me, into the hurricane lamp that sat on the porch.

"When I learned I was pregnant for the first time," she said, "well, I remember looking at my Aunt Gwen and my neighbor Mrs. Hillary and thinking they had felt this way. I was so young. I looked at all the women getting on and off the trolley cars, and the women walking in the streets, all the houses where I knew there were women living, and I wondered how many had felt this way or were feeling the same as me at that second." She looked at me. "Everything changed in my mind. I began to notice things, how the country grass looked corded, how the birds looked grey against the air. For a while, with practically every person I saw, I thought: there was a mother who felt this."

Gran, my mother's mother, was also visiting and she would walk to church every morning. Sometimes I would escort her and sit with her to watch the lazy, underwater gestures of a priest. I would forget to listen to the homily, my mind empty, or rather, distantly preoccupied with the difficulty of this pregnancy, the secret stuck in the back of my mind.

After I walked Gran back home I would, not without pangs of conscience, tell her and Mom I was going job hunting, and then walk to the Hotel Onondaga bar. There was something uplifting for me about this, moving from the chapel to the hotel's lobby, my hair still perfumed with frankincense, out of place in the bar's stale fragrance. At the upper end of the bar the darkness flared with the blue of a TV set. The businessmen inside would have been waiting, walking all morning in the streets until the bartender came to open up, and then they would sit at the bar and sometimes they would turn in the granular light, bearing the bluish grain of a missed shave.

"Buy you a drink?" someone would ask. The salesmen were the first to offer.

I came in all that June, and I would sit and watch the game shows with them and the soaps, too, with their tragic theme music that reminded us how we wasted time. I leaned into the bar counter and behind me the draperies leaked light and unraveling cigarette smoke. I stood near the draperies as evening pooled along the curb and working men and women came in, their faces marked with exhaustion. The bar would fill, a crib of heat, evening news playing over the television, the voices eroded each other, and people touched hands.

When I stayed in the bar that late I thought I might spot my grandfather in the lounge, just risen from the Onondaga River that ran below the banks of the hotel. He had jumped in on his thirty-eighth birthday, drunk and apparently in debt. But if he came back he would have been wrapped in weeds, blank-eyed from so many hours watching the bottoms of barges. Gran said he was a "Casanova." I couldn't help but look for some bit of his nature in myself, especially that impulse that pushed me toward strangers.

I drifted in and out of sleep and felt as if I were on a raft; the sheets like a hot breath. Then it was an ocean current that drove its winds up, and a cool climate of leaves and flowers splitting open. Something sucked my voice away.

The next morning, as my grandmother was knitting and my mother washed the windows, I told them about my dream. Mom put down her sponge and said, "That sounds like my dream about Chloe."

Gran put down her knitting. "Oh Iris."

I stared at my mother. "What?" I said. "Who's Chloe?"

"That was during my first marriage," she said. "I guess I never told you, it all happened so fast, it was so long ago. The first time

I was pregnant I went into labor two months early." She leaned back against the window, dwindling in the sun. "They began to deliver her right there in the ambulance. Somewhere between the house and the hospital we passed through a forest. I remember the trees blowing around us." Her hands turned slowly before her face. "It was so odd."

"Oh stop," Gran muttered.

"And there were birds! My God! I heard them out in the hospital parking lot and it felt like they were saying something to me, like the voice in your dream. And then suddenly Chloe was out there with them."

"Where?" I had never heard Mom talk like that.

She and Gran looked at each other then she turned back to her washing.

"This is ridiculous, it's just silly, careless talk, Irene," Gran said to me. "The baby died years before you were born."

"The body was all blue," Mom said, her back to us. "They tried to hide it from me in the hospital sheets. But I knew Chloe had left by then—she had changed, she had become—" Mom continued running her sponge over the window as she stopped speaking and we all stared at that spot. She lowered her sponge then, turned back to me and said, "Irene, when it is very early in the morning, before anyone is up, do you ever think you hear someone singing in the halls?" Her arms were white on her apron, the hair running down them wet with the washing water. She looked very pretty, almost young at that moment. "I'm serious," she said. "Sometimes I hear singing and laughter, sometimes footsteps. I wait for her to come to the bedroom door—"

"Well, I never have," Gran said.

I thought about it and it seemed to me that I had heard this soft laughter in the morning. In another part of the night, in another dream, I dreamed I heard my baby singing. But I was afraid to say this; I could only look at her.

"I've heard her many times in the morning," my mother said. "She was beautiful, she had blue eyes and such blonde hair."

My father was Jordanian. He taught international politics at the same college that I attended. He studied accounts of the world's violence from television and newspapers, and was possessed by this research, and tried to discuss it in the classroom. I remember his voice sifting into the halls through a shut door, my father's litany of the world's upheavals.

"What do you understand about 'home'?" he liked to ask his class. "Where is your place? Here? Where your parents are?" Each day he started out in a suit, his face gradually darkening; he wilted his shirt collars and his neck swelled beyond the top button and tie knot. At home in the evening my mother would kiss him and sit with her arms around him on the living room couch. Usually I stayed in the bedroom with Gran whenever she visited, knitting with her, refusing the upset of his daily return home; he was always too angry, with students or colleagues.

Every day the sound of the Onondaga River rose from its bed and moved over the fields into the main streets. In the evening my father walked over the bridges in town alone. I watched the bridge outside the Hotel Onondaga bar and sometimes saw him out there, detached from the rest of us with his bitterness. Dad often arranged to have the friends and sons of his brothers accepted into the university as they came of age. The unexpected spark of Arabic would edge around a door frame, the olive skin of my cousins suddenly there, graceful and surprising. Even in the town bars, filled with the local salesmen and their girls, there would be the pomaded heads of new relatives. They smelled of a French lemon perfume called #4119 that they used to wash their hands with. They turned up in platform shoes and heavy gold medallions, the essence of #4119 curling through the Hotel Onondaga. Amazingly to me, there were many young town women for whom my cousins seemed romantic and exotic. The guys never lacked for dates.

Sundays Dad would invite several of his nephews over for a midday dinner and Mom and Gran prepared the food. The men visiting would lapse into Arabic which neither of the women knew—I only slightly—and we looked into their world as if looking through a sheet.

I must have tried to tell Mom and Gran about my pregnancy a hundred times and then held back, almost in panic. I considered abortion, or perhaps going off for the remaining seven months and having it secretly then giving it up. But without anyone to talk to it lost some of its reality; it was easy to ignore the faint signs that my body gave me, so it seemed almost an idea, not a physical fact.

Then one of those August Sundays, Gran took me aside from the dinner table and said: "Never date foreign men. They're selfish and they'll make you miserable. I know, I married a selfish man!"

I watched my cousins at dinner and at the bars then, and I began to think that maybe I ought to at least try dating instead of hanging around all the live-long day, hoping for something to happen so I wouldn't have to decide for myself.

I watched the priest bending to his host and daydreamed about the Arabs dancing on the mirrored floor of the nightclub. My cousins had long black eyelashes webbing their eyes, prettier than girls. Dad said they were all children of war, and they did seem as though they were born out of it, like flowers that grew out of Hiroshima. They walked home from the bars at night, wandering over the fields, arms linked, their eyes and lips like blooms on their skin. After the raw air of the bar, the evening itself would surge up into one blue-edged blossom, a nightshade tipping its head. My cousins' bodies seemed to move, dancing and laughing through the air of the bright church. I sang, transported.

It was a night at the end of August, and I had left home with no particular intent. But on this night, instead of heading to the Hotel Onondaga, I ended up at the club where my cousins liked to go dancing. The air in the place was hot, flecked with red cigarette tips and flashing sweat. An Arab boy asked me to dance and we walked out on to the floor. He said his name was Amir, I didn't think he was a relative, I had never seen him before.

Later in the night, outside in the field beyond the parking lot, his fingers ran along my skin. Up on points of light the rain barely came down. We left our clothes behind us on the gravel. After, when we lay apart, the sweat drying away, he turned to look at me again and I could see he was angry.

"Why did you come with me?" he said.

I lay silently, I didn't know what he wanted me to say. He moved to separate himself from the dark stream that we made. A shadow passed over the moon and then swallows thronged the trees.

"What do you want with me?" His eyes were shining like tunnels and he sat up.

The birds scattered then, scrambling the air. I stood and quickly walked away from the boy, back into the rings of light around the parking lot. The trees and all the fields shook, rippling backwards.

The clothesline stood in a ruffle of grass. Mom raised her blue and white sheets so they floated parallel to the earth. I was in the garden below her, grinding the silky grass and seedlings in my fingers, wondering how to tell her. Finally I just went up the hill toward her. I stood slightly below on the incline.

She looked at me from among the flying sheets, the scrolls of her hair. "Irene?" she said, her voice blowing about the hill, around her paisley housecoat. She stepped toward me, her hair rising and falling.

I took a deep breath and said, "Mom, I'm pregnant."

The sheets unfurled on the line, showing off their white faces.

We stood, not speaking, by the hamper of clothes. Gran was sleeping in the house and my father was taking his riding mower around the nape of the lawn.

I stopped going to church and gave up on the bars. I began to walk in the streets, ignoring the looks of neighbors and passersby. I ignored my grandmother's face in the window.

I could not have possibly told Dad about my pregnancy. There was no telling what his reaction might have been—things were different between men and women in his country. Instead, I went for walks. The Onondaga streets were full of the ghosts of men; my grandfather climbed the spines of the houses, he stared down from the chimneys with his blue eyes. There were my cousins up in the bedrooms in the tall, turn-of-the-century houses, their backs to the windows as they held their American girls. They might have glanced through the curtains then turned back into their cigarette smoke.

Sometimes I walked all day and forgot to eat. I would go to bed and that was haunted with this idea of a husband. The fact was that I could not even begin to guess whose baby this was; I'd spent a silly, careless year in college. My dreams were invaded by hands, laughter, light eyes, nations of them swimming inside me.

I paused one evening on the front porch with my mother as I once used to before I began those walks. She hadn't said anything about the pregnancy at all. We watched our blowing trees, the leaves poised, before the last moment of warm air and the campaign into autumn.

She said, "It can be worth it to take chances, Irene, to try new things. Maybe you ought to try to understand your father better."

"What do you mean?" I asked, staring at her.

"Would you like to visit Jordan?"

She raised her face and seemed to bask in the evening light that spilled forward over her like steam. "He loves us—your father. When I was young, I felt like his love created whatever I was, I changed my shape to whatever his heart desired," she said, lifting her arms and laughing. "Sometimes that's what a person needs—a little push, a little help, to make things happen."

II

The night sky as the plane rolled into the Jordan airport was immense; it seemed deserted. Trees off the runways swayed. From the plane the passengers had to walk over the pavement to the air terminal and the air felt embedded with salt and oil. Crowds of men and women pushed against the chain link fences that lined the runway, watching us arrive and shaking the fences. I could not tell what they wanted, their Arabic rose in surges. I moved nervously along this gauntlet of voices, avoiding their eyes, and many of them turned to watch as I passed by.

My cousin Nasser, whom I had known from college, met me inside. He was smoking a Tiparillo and holding two bottles of Heineken. "Hey, Cos!" he cried out, handing me a bottle. "What's happening, man?"

"Nasser!" I was surprised. I hadn't written anyone there that I was coming, and then I thought, of course, my father did.

The glass bottle felt like it was melting in my hand and the hot air. I could still hear the echo of voices at the gates, then I realized it was the air conditioning roaring in the building around us.

"Those people out there—" I said, gesturing toward the door.

"Oh, never mind about them," he said. "They're ignorant, a bunch of peasants. They all go crazy when the planes from America and Amsterdam come in." He waved importantly to a customs officer, slipping us past the long line.

"But what do they want?"

"Oh, baby, please." He blew out a jet of brown smoke, waving his cigar around. "You don't understand. They are crazy, fucked up. I mean like fucked up peasants."

We claimed my luggage and went out to the lot where his car was waiting, a streak in the night. The trunk floated up and I could smell pine rising from its interior.

"I had to leave the States because, like, I had a nervous breakdown," he told me as we drove.

"I didn't know that."

"Yeah, it was too much for me, the scene, the money. I dropped out of college and sold the car my dad gave me, remember the Trans Am? I spent it all in Atlantic City, it was really a bad scene, man. But it's really a bad scene here too, you'll see, it's so fucked up, so boring." He leaned toward me from the steering wheel. Nasser's father, my Uncle Semia, owned much of the land that we drove through.

Later I lay on a mattress in my uncle's stone house and listened to the wind from the desert as it reached the shoulders of the city; in it I heard the accents in my cousin's voice. The substance of the day broke into fragments, turning like a plow from Arabic to English.

Nasser, who was twenty-six and engaged to be married, would rest with his head upon his mother's lap and she would stroke it, pressing it back upon the pillow of her belly. She worked for her men. The house was a totem around which the tribe gathered, women at its center. My female cousins, who were never sent to American schools, waited, working inside the homes, for their marriages to be arranged, and their skin softened to the colors of wheat, their voices to whispers.

There were no bars, no mosques, not even an open field beyond the parking lot for the women to hide in. In my aunt's and uncle's parlor currents of conversation passed among us, talk of small things, weather and family gossip. At night the moon that I had watched from the Hotel Onondaga stood in its penumbra, so near you could almost reach out the bedroom window and snatch it away. The eyes of women looked up at me in my dream, over the high city walls, the moon rolling over like a millstone.

I stood in front of my uncle's house, with its walkways and stone-anchored gardens, looking down the road, and asked my cousin Rima, "What's down there?"

"Oh we don't want to go there," she said, smiling, her English soft with its tutored accent. "Once you get outside the village it turns into desert."

"And in that direction?"

"Out there? That's where the border begins. Didn't they warn you? It's dangerous there, you know, you must never go there. They will stamp your passport if you cross and you will never be allowed back in again."

There were many parties to which I and my relatives were invited, and at these parties there were always steaming platters of lamb and bread and rice and buttermilk, all mounded up high. We didn't eat with forks but scooped the rice in cupped hands. Until my skin toughened the food sometimes burned. The black, heavily-lacquered doors to the kitchens swung open and women emerged as if from Victorian novels, consumed with work, the tide of a hundred chores: sewing, dusting, cooking—all building to this consummation at dinner.

"When your father and his brothers were children, all this area around their home was uncivilized and uncultivated," my aunt told me, her hand moving over the clusters of homes and the few gardens that shook in the breeze, thorns moving over the dirt. "The people here were very uneducated."

"Hicksville," Rima said, using a word she had often heard from Nasser.

"There were no schools for the children out here and your grandfather never wanted to go into the city, *Ya' Allah!*, explain to me the ways of men! So he brung the teachers here. But the women in this place were very spoiled, and the teachers usually were just graduated from high school and as ignorant as the children, so the women beat them day and night." My aunt clutched my arms laughing.

She stood about five feet tall and her face was seamed in makeup that might have dated from the pharaohs. She smelled of rice powder, kohl, and arsenic—used to liven up the color of the cheeks. Her body swathed in embroidered sheets moved with laughter and she held on to me, trembling and perfumed. "They bossed those teachers around! It was always 'Yasmine! My slippers!' or 'Nyla! Bring me sweets!' So the boys had at least eight or nine teachers go by. But finally there was an end. There was a war. For one whole year a terrible war."

"With Israel?"

"Between your grandmother and grandfather. She didn't want her children to be ignorant. She was a very educated woman in her time. She wanted her children to go to the school in the town and in the end she won. She saved those boys. Now your father is a doctor, a great man. And his brothers—all businessmen!" She smiled and among the gaps there was one tooth shining brilliantly, capped with gold. "What Mother could be happier?"

The camels off on the plains shone in the retreating sun. I walked to the far edge of my uncle's property and a valley opened up. There the animals took on their opalescence and they ran, stretching out their legs, things that I could never have even dreamed of. One camel, vaguely stirring, folded its legs, dropping to the earth.

Through the kitchen window I could hear my aunt singing I ez' zain, "beauty of the garden," the woman who waits for her love, though she waits twenty years. I touched my belly and with its slight distention under my fingers I remembered home, the Onondaga River with its inky surface. As a child, I was drawn to the water and would think of how people had thrown themselves in.

Nasser was driving us around Amman in great circles that wound up the hillsides of the city. He'd speed up and the air would come in hot, ragged blasts, then he'd slow down when girls or other drivers idled by the side of the road and shout at them through the opened windows.

"Hey Inglesee! Americanee!" he'd shout. "I got your number!"

"How'd you know they were American?" I asked.

"He doesn't know it," Rima said, leaning forward from the back seat. "He just wants to look cool."

"Hey give me a break, man. That girl was wearing shorts. What good Arab girl is going to be caught dead wearing shorts?"

Through the dashboard the car engine was bathing us in waves of heat. I had been in Jordan for three weeks and the sour-hot days were continuous. I gave up trying to sit straight, sliding along my seat as the car slid with its centripetal force.

"'I wish there were someplace to go," I said, talking into the rush of air. "Some excitement for once."

"We could go to the Dead Sea," Rima suggested. "Or we could go to Aqaba."

"Too far, too boring," Nasser sighed.

After our ride I sat alone in my aunt's parlor and watched the twilight move into the curtains. It was still, and the women were beginning preparations for dinner. Then Nasser came in by himself and bent toward me, his face blurred by the shade of the curtain mesh. "Hey Cos, I know a place to go."

Back in the car we headed out toward the desert into a sequence of plants that turned from green to gold and white.

The color rose up around us, over the unknown countryside. We brushed by the sides of mountains and traveled down between the valley and mountains.

We drove several miles out, then drew into the desert, a harbor of night flooding the desert floor, rippling with an underwater image. I felt depressed. I couldn't remember why I had ever agreed to come out in the first place.

At last we drove up to a huge sanded mound in the midst of the desert floor, a strange, simple place. We left the car and walked closer, and I could see that its surface was covered with minute, flickering marks.

"What is this?" I asked Nasser.

He smiled and rolled his eyes. "It's Uncle Adnan's house. Can you believe it?"

"What Uncle Adnan?" I thought my father had only four brothers.

"They don't really talk about Adnan. We're not supposed to know, I guess he's got water on the brain or something so they shipped him out here. I just found this place by accident one time when me and some of the dudes were out here driving around."

I looked closer at the mound. "Is he dangerous?"

Nasser shrugged. "Who knows? He's pretty intense, but he's a cool guy, he just never says anything."

We walked the circumference of the mound and found only one small mouth just large enough to crawl through. A hollow note quavered up from its lip in the breeze as if this were the instrument of the evening wind, a pipe of clay and sand.

"Hey Adnan!" Nasser shouted, chucking stones into the opening. "Come out so we can see you! *Ya haiwan*! Let us see you, *imshee!*"

"No, no, don't do that—" I started to say, then stopped as a spray of dust fell from the opening over the back of an emerging form. We watched a man crawl out on his hands and knees. When he stood he could not straighten up but held himself with a partial stoop. His face had the same milky shine as the sky, his hands, neck, and face glowed from moon light.

He smiled at me, gesturing toward his house and speaking Arabic.

"He says that this is his house," Nasser said.

"I thought you said that he doesn't talk."

Nasser shrugged. "So sometimes he does and sometimes he doesn't. Give me a break."

Adnan invited us inside and Nasser motioned for me to follow him in, rolling his eyes and saying, "Oh yeah, I know what he wants now."

Once we were inside Nasser handed him a tidy white joint that he fished from a cigarette pack in his shirt pocket. Adnan immediately put its tip to one of the wax tapers burning along the walls that lit the interior.

"Now he's happy. Do it up, Babe, go ahead," Nasser said. "If you ask me, he's got a totally shitty life."

The air inside was foul and stultifying, untouched by the wind stream that lifted its clear notes from the door. I tasted clay dust in the air that powdered down from the ceiling whenever I shifted position. I was taller than both Nasser and Adnan and, seated, I had to hunch forward in order to fit. There was no room to stand anywhere.

"My God," I said. I looked around. "How does he live? What does he eat?"

"Oh, people out in this direction leave him tons of garbage, leftover food, slop, sometimes I roll out with some weed. It's really a shitty life man, no kidding."

The smoke from the joint was filling the cave and my eyes began to water. Through the swimming light I could see bits of junk cluttering the floor like washed-up debris—an old calendar with a picture of a blonde in a bikini, a ball of tinfoil, a ballpoint pen, a plastic bic lighter. The shoulders of the wall were low; it felt like a burrow. The skin of Adnan's cranium was hairless, almost blue. I understood slowly that he was part of my father's unhappiness, this soul of dispossession, here, bleached white without the sun, tucked back into the womb of the earth.

We went back outside for air, and Adnan, tossing himself toward the wind, seemed to harness its life and it sang and whipped the sand around us like a wheel and we were at its center, turning, facing the moon. Then Adnan, gesturing for me to watch, picked up a pot that stood by the entrance, and, dipping in his fingers, began applying a muddy substance to the walls.

"Hey, what's he doing? What is that?" But Nasser only laughed, watching him.

Adnan stood like an artist. The earth mound before him, he applied his mud. He was laughing and he called something to me as the wind blew the hair around my head.

"He says he's making the walls thicker," Nasser told me, raising his voice above the thunder of wind. "Every day for twenty years he's come out to do this. Every day he makes the walls a little thicker."

The next day I walked back over the pavement to the plane. It had rained and fumes rose from oil smears. The crowds that had met me upon my arrival in Jordan had diffused with the bad weather. Later, when the plane circled over Kennedy, I thought of my father in his story of himself as a young man, just arriving in America, impressed not by the buildings but by the beautiful green of the earth, green everywhere, the trees and wide lawns that defied the city.

My mother picked me up at the airport. Gran had gone home, she told me, and Dad seemed happier. On the highway all the cars had their windshield wipers going and we rushed down a highway that was like a lane of water.

We rode in silence, each with our own thoughts. We were listening to the whispering of water, like a story of a river that dreams of being a woman, who bears babies from herself as water is born from water, open and always giving, giving life. 📖

Untitled, Drawing, by Jon Strongbow

The Dunes

D.L. Birchfield

"Tell us about the fire on the dunes, Grandfather," we had begged, as children. And Grandfather, obligingly, would tell us once more about that first summer in the valley, about how his father had come rushing into the half-built house shouting, "The dunes are on fire!"

And so they appeared to be, with blazing, leaping, bright orange tongues of flame, until the moon got full up behind them.

"Only in the summer," said Grandfather. "And only if the air is hot and dry just at moonrise."

We had to take his word for it because, while Father had seen them blaze, we had not yet been so fortunate.

The dunes were always there. You could see them on the horizon, looking taller than they actually were, looking smoother and more rounded than they actually were.

On a clear cold day you could count them. You could say that there is one dune and there is another. But let the season change, let the heat set the air to shimmering, where one dune ended and another began no one could say.

There was an awful truth about the dunes, a truth that each member of our family had known, a truth that each new member would come to know. And that truth was this: there was nothing there but dunes.

Just dunes, that's all they were, one dune being much like another. Great piles of sand that had somehow hardened in place; that's what they were, not quite sandstone and not quite sand; just dunes.

"Someday a geologist will stumble upon the dunes, then we'll find out what they are," my father once said.

"Why wait for a geologist to come here?" replied my grandfather.

"Of course! We can take pictures of the dunes and mail them to the university and they will send someone to find out what they are."

So off we went, to take photographs. And this not even two years after the whole weary lot of us had trudged back home saying we would never again make that trip, because—as we repeated to one another with the conviction of moral truth—"There is nothing there but dunes."

"We'll take pictures at regular intervals as we approach them," said my father.

And so we did. We took photographs from the house, from the top of the house, from the far end of the meadow, from the rise across the river, from the edge of the breaks, from measured distances all across the breaks, and from directly in front. We took photographs from every imaginable angle, from on top of one dune looking at another dune, from the bottom looking up, from the top looking down, and from so many angles among them that we were certain we had captured the very essence of the dunes.

Then we mailed the photographs to the university. If anyone ever took any notice of them, I imagine it was to ask, "What have you there?" And someone answered, "Dunes. That's all. Just dunes."

The dunes would have made a lot more sense if there had been rumors of buried treasure. A person could allow himself to feel foolish about digging for a thing like buried treasure. He could understand how the rumors might operate on his mind and not have to wonder what he was doing when the time came that he found himself digging up great piles of curiously hardened sand with a pick and shovel.

But not me, or my father, or Uncle Earl, or Aunt Alice—to this day we have never been able to figure out why we dug up the place, in deluxe fashion, making not just one trip, but three different trips, one of them in the dead of winter, looking for we knew not what, and finding only dunes.

"The dunes are on fire!" It had been my turn to shout, though I hardly needed to, with every other member of the family already crowded upon the front porch as was our long-standing custom at each moonrise in the summer.

"They really are, Grandfather!" my little sister had said, and Grandfather had never stood as tall as at that moment.

And indeed they were. They blazed gloriously, being a perfect match for the radiant glow on Grandfather's face, until the moon got full up behind them.

Now my son sits on the front porch more than he used to. It seems like only lately that he's begun to notice the dunes. You can see it in his eyes when he looks at them, that something ought to be there, that something couldn't help but be there, and if only a person would go there he would find something more than just dunes. 📖

Deer Stories

Alice Derry

White sky, white ground, and where they meet,
the slight brown of the plowed hills' curve

to distinguish earth from sky.
We come for all this space with nothing in it,

where we grew up, so many children
in our family there wasn't enough to go around.

Christmas Eve in this story you're telling me.
Deep snow. Something flashed

across your headlights as you came up the drive.
It was a deer, right?

Later you found her behind the shed.
Injured leg. But she could still hobble away.

Time after time. Nothing you could do.
There never is. In our childhood,

I was the older sister. My job, to watch you,
feed you. Once, Mom in the hospital,

and I with our baby brother, our aunt came for you.
You don't remember how you clung to me and wept.

Too young myself, I didn't fight to keep you.
Now it's between you and me. My giving in.

The summer you moved me across country,
we spent days together in the cab of a U-Haul.

We didn't agree on anything. "No sex
unless you're married," you said.

I was divorced, had had lovers. "What about me?"
"It's different. You need it more." Sullied.

She froze to death, didn't she? On Christmas Eve.
Next morning, you dragged her up the hill,

covered her head with rocks
to keep the coyotes out. You knew they'd get her.

Five of you—so I know something about brothers.
My second skin.

But I worry when we take my daughter to the zoo
that people will think I'm an older woman

with a young husband.
Too close or not close enough.

At the top of Rowena Grade once, my husband and I
stopped by two fawns on the side of the road.

Then we saw the doe, already through the fence.
Scared, because of us, she couldn't help them.

One found the opening, slipped through.
Mother and fawn took off, cutting their losses,

leaving the other bleating and running down the road.
We eased the car into motion. A story like that

won't ever get away. Both grown, we've come to agree
on most things, but I'll never be able to love you right.

Deer always seem to me like air itself.
Imperceptible, but we're breathing it.

A Barren Woman Puts On
Her Man Costume

Fatima Lim-Wilson

Let me tell myself:
It is not out of spite
Especially designed for me
But out of pride in our history
That the village, always,
Must celebrate crucial dates
On night of the full moon.
I put on my Man Costume.
Loose black shirt, looser
Trousers. That is all.
No need for thickened brows,
Added inches here and there,
Bush above my lips. No matter.
All know who I am.
After the solemn chants
And drumbeats, I know my cue.
The white chickens lying
Catatonic on the ground
Lose their heads to the silver
Ax. I scream and laughter begins.
Steaming rice and palm wine.
Clapping beat trying to keep up
With the frenzy of my feet
Churning dry dust. More laughter.
The girls-grown-to-women
Glance bold-eyed beneath their veils
At the boys-turned-to-men.
Little children, coaxed by the elders
First throw chicken bones, then larger

Stones. A bruise here, a cut there.
Not enough blood drawn to hurt.
I am driven to the edge
Of the firelit circle.
Now, it is their turn to dance.
First barely touching, merely mocking
Intimacy. With the heartbeat freed,
They play the ritual of newfangled lust.
All join in, and there, flickering
Near the center, my former husband's limbs
Tangle with the blooming branches
Of my younger sister.
Here, in my exile's hut,
I still feel the throb of drums,
The echo of my womb.
By my feet, ash heap
Of my tossed-off clothes.
This night's torment
Has just taken root.
The moon plants herself
By my window, showing off
Her beautiful emptiness.

The Girl Who Always Thought It Was Summer

Anna Odessa Linzer

It is winter.
I am five.
There is snow on the ground
and the white-washed
concrete garden wall where I sit
under bare branches of the oak tree,
in the low sun of this cold day,
legs crossed, young movie queen,
Miss America
wave, palm out, fan-like,
an already practiced gesture.

My mother's best friend, Mary, drives by,
zooming down the narrow tree-lined 57th Street,
going home in a shiny, new '55 Chevy wagon
filled with groceries, an ancient cocker spaniel,
a young collie, and more boys than I can count.
Home, she calls my mother, because
this is what she sees as she passes
our small white house:
A little girl in the snow
in a swim suit and a bathing cap,
small bare feet,
and from that winter on, it became story,
following me in my growing up like a title on my spine:
"The Girl Who Always Thought It Was Summer."

But what the story did not tell,
and what only I knew,
was the magic I slipped into when I found the pink

ruffled flowers of summer folded far in the back corner
of the smallest drawer of my painted chest,
behind lace slips and white cotton panties,
under wool sweaters,
in that secret place between memory and promise
that is always ripe with summer.

Yet, separated by days was another story,
told in other tongues,
a theatre piece, a performance:
It is still winter. I am still five,
but moving through the season so close now
to six. I am dancing
before the full-length hall mirror.
Same costume, but now in anklets, embroidered
with tiny rose buds, shuffle stepping
on the smooth, slippery surface
of the polished wood floor,
my eyes holding only myself in my reflection
as I dance, twirling too quickly into summer,
tumbling into the cold edge of black
wrought iron telephone table,
splitting lip, spilling blood, shedding tears.

And all these seasons later,
your lips find mine,
and they touch the numbed,
thin, jagged line
of the scar
and tiny stitch
marks that show only
in the clear light of summer.

Red Geranium in a Folger's Coffee Can

Kathleen Marie

The red geranium on her windowsill
lives in a Folger's coffee can

and bathes in aromas of
tortillas cooking on the comal,
onions frying in lard,
chopped garlic and green chile
waiting their turn.

Car fumes sneak through the open window.
She pauses between tortillas
gazes out her third floor tenant window
at the city that surrounds her
in this desert.

Her ancestors once owned 50 acres
of farming land in Sabinoso.
When their father,
her grandfather, died
her mother and uncle sold all of it.
Lured by neon promises,
they crushed the roots of
corn, green chile, and tomatoes
as they walked through the fields
on their way to the city.

Her mother bought beige make-up
to make her face lighter,

and red lipstick like the movie stars.
She shopped at the Piggly Wiggly for
canned corn, frozen green chiles, and canned tomatoes.

Now the daughter has a Folger's coffee can
that holds 50 acres of dirt, roots, and life
on her rented windowsill.
It took six months to go through
that three pound can of coffee.

It takes a lifetime
to recover roots.

*Comal is a round, cast iron lid from
  a wood-burning stove.*

Elena's Dance

Donna Miscolta

It has been stirring in Elena for months, pressing against her chest, pulsing at her throat, sending a hum through her head. Indigestion, she tells herself. But, really, she's not convinced. From downstairs the urgent buzz of the radio reaches her uncomprehending ears with the news of peasant revolts in Hungary and Yugoslavia, Gandhi-inspired outbreaks of civil disobedience on the Indian subcontinent, army mutinies in China, the spread of Bolshevik ideals to Africa.

But Elena knows little of Bolsheviks and all the rest. Even the Villista campaign, its promise diminished by the looting of haciendas and the sacking of towns from which she escaped, is removed from her memory—tucked away inside her like a letter, folded and forgotten inside a little-used pocket. Now, in this California city in a one-room apartment above the corner grocery, the limits of her world are fixed by newspapers that she does not read because the headlines in English baffle her, by street signs that are unfamiliar beyond a few blocks, and by conversations that rush past her undecoded in the aisles of the grocery—sounds that are bland and indifferent, like the bread she buys there. Perhaps it is indigestion, after all, this feeling that squeezes against her belly and throat, and makes it difficult to breathe.

The windows are open to the blue-black sky, but there is no breeze to move the heavy air inside the apartment. Across the street, the diner blinks its electric blue sign. EAT, it urges. Eat, she repeats to herself, only to practice her English vocabulary, knowing that the craving she feels is not for food. She sits rocking, the squeak of the chair chorusing with the sucking of the baby at her breast. She strokes Carmela's head as she turns to watch Rudy. He's in front of the bathroom mirror performing his ablutions. It's a Saturday night ritual, an act of devotion.

He's wearing just his underwear. His suit hangs smartly on the hook of the bathroom door, the stiff creases in the trousers giving them a look of alertness, as if wary of Rudy's muscular body. He leans over the bathroom sink and, intent upon his reflection, he stretches his upper lip down over his teeth, snips with precision at the hairs of his elegantly thin mustache, then retracts his lip approvingly in a smile. He rubs hair cream in his palms, sniffs at its glistening whiteness, and then massages it into his black hair one, two, three times—a calisthenic that works the muscles in the taut curve of his arms and shoulders. He swigs Listerine from the bottle, and, then, posed like a garden statue, he releases a stream of mouthwash to arc fountain-like into the sink. With rapid hands, he spanks his face and throat with cologne. Invigorated by the self-administered slaps, he draws himself into his fighter's stance, bounces on the balls of his feet toward his reflection and protects with his left while he delivers several mock blows with his right. Then he whirls to spar with his suit hanging on the door. Prevailing against both opponents, he leaps into the middle of the room, arms raised above his head in victory, and Elena, still watching, makes her mouth smile, while something clenches in her throat.

As he dresses, Rudy hums the popular songs of the day, inserting words here and there to display the progress of his American accent to Elena, who clings to her Spanish language as if it were a shawl cloaking her from the cold. Rudy wriggles into his jacket to the beat of the song he is humming, and then executes a few dance steps, again with his reflection, this time in the window, the neon blue of the diner sign flashing on his strutting figure.

On his way to the door, he stops to coo at Carmela. He is delighted as she throws her tiny fists at him and works her mouth in circles bubbly with saliva. "A fighter and a lover," Rudy laughs. "Just like me."

He drops a kiss on the braid wound in a knot at the back of Elena's head, and he leaves.

She listens as his footsteps fade down the stairs, hears the slam of the street door shut them out completely.

The smell of Rudy lingers on—a bouquet of hair creme, mouthwash and cologne. Elena disperses it momentarily with a sigh. Carmela's eyes flutter closed as her mouth slowly peels away from Elena's breast, releasing it with a tiny smack. Elena nudges the basket at her feet closer and lowers Carmela to nest inside the blanket her cousin Elvira sent. Elvira, ten years older than Elena and married to a silent and featureless gringo, had taken Elena in when she first arrived. And though Elvira had appointed herself chaperon to Elena, following her conduct with a severe eye, Elena had not left the dusty streets of San Blas to be smothered by her cousin's conventions. Within a few months she had met Rudy at a Saturday night dance, and in front of Elvira's reproving stare, Elena followed the lead of Rudy's smooth confident steps, responded to the press of his hand at the small of her back as he steered her left or right, answered the cue of his fingertips as they spun her away and then reeled her back in.

In between dances, Elena learned more about this dashing young man because Rudolfo Luis Borrego spoke as charmingly as he danced. First of all, he liked to be called Rudy, as in Rudy Vallee, and he crooned an imitation of the singer. He didn't mind being called Rudolph, though, as in Valentino, and he struck a swashbuckling pose. He said he was a painter and Elena imagined canvasses filled with passionate strokes of color until Rudy laughed and said no, he painted buildings—tall ones. But his real profession was boxing, and he bounced back and forth on the balls of his feet to demonstrate and then gracefully slid into a foxtrot because, he explained, dancing was an extension of his athletic training. Then he winked, adding that dancing was also romantic, especially with a partner as beautiful as Elena, and he took her in his arms and guided her effortlessly, in command of the music, in command of the other dancers who yielded the floor and the onlookers who watched with both envy and appreciation, and in command of Elena herself who surrendered to the fast-slow-fast-slow sway of Rudy's foxtrot.

This is what Elena contemplates as she sits in the rocking chair, alone with Carmela in the one-room apartment above the corner grocery. Carmela gurgles in her crib and Elena bends over her. She's still asleep, but Elena picks her up anyway. She begins to pace the room slowly, stopping now and then at the window to look beyond the blue sign of the diner to the community hall. All she can see is the roof, but she knows that the windows blaze yellow with light and inside sweating couples dance as if their lives depend on it. And she knows that Rudy is there, dancing with first one and then another of the partnerless women that line the wall near the punch table, fingering the glass beads on their necks, gazing with practiced nonchalance at the pairs of lilting bodies on the dance floor. As she paces the room, Elena hears Rudy's voice remind her that dancing is essential to his profession in the ring. It keeps his reflexes responsive, rehearses him for a fight.

She continues to walk the perimeter of the room and with each turn she quickens her pace, and as the room begins to shrink she remembers how she used to walk the plaza in San Blas until, finally, she resisted those boundaries, making her way north on a slow, crowded train to end up here in this apartment above the corner grocery. And the memory of why she came makes the disturbance she has felt in her stomach recede, leaving a purposeful calm.

Elena descends the stairs, lets the door slam shut behind her. She tucks the ends of her shawl around Carmela, though outside the night is warm and embracing. She crosses the street, passes under the cool blue wink of the diner sign and, as she turns the corner to the community hall, she can already hear the music. She enters the hall and pauses, lets her eyes take in the pair of potted palms that curve dreamily at each end of the stage where the band, its members dressed in matching powder blue jackets, delivers a tune brassy with jazz. She scans the dance floor, restless with the undulations of entwined pairs, and in the middle is Rudy, limbering his muscles, timing his reflexes for his next fight, swirling an orange-chiffoned brunette, and not yet seeing Elena, who approaches, poised and ready. 📖

Georgia Red Earth

Amy Pence

There's a precision. Then my wrists
itch. I drift through developments,

past the tangled mattresses, to the old
sharecropper's house. Joists and tin

roof suck off red earth. Confederate
jasmine pocks the wrecked windows.

My skin prickles with rash, finger
ready at the camera's shutter. Before

I know it, she's in my dreams: the sharecropper's daughter—the way we huddle

close under that tin roof, putting fingers
to our lips, waiting steadily, curiously

for the way our bodies—brown stains creeping
the mattress—will be emptied in the dark.

Plumes of White Rising
(Touching Hanford)

Arthur Tulee

—I don't need to touch my mortality, it touches me.

I am a Wishram Indian of the Yakama Indian Nation and this is my blood dripping into my eyes. I am talking quietly because I think you're close enough to hear me, because I've never been a loud talker, and because my head hurts. I gotta go, gotta move on, can't be stuck anymore. I fall on some sagebrush. I stand.

I leave red footprints, I leave the smell of gas, I leave the side of the road, I leave my wallet between the dashboard and some teeth. Can I climb barbed wire? I'm numb in my denim, I don't feel the points. I'm dizzy, it's dawn, I walk toward the sun's rising. I sing one of many morning songs; my breath is white, plumes of white rising. I tell myself I feel drums, I feel a heavy pulse in my ears. I fall on some sagebrush. I stand.

My foot is swollen in my cowboy boot. I touch stiff frozen fur and laugh. My eyes are slow, I see bones, more fur, my blood dripping on it all. I laugh. I fall on some sagebrush. I stand. My breath is white, plumes of white rising. I am thirsty. I hear Chewana, the Columbia River, miles away. I walk with 100-pound legs. I sing another morning song. I hear flies. I taste copper, salt, testosterone, thousands of generations of genetics, my redness. I still see stiff frozen fur and bones and my blood dripping on it all. I fall on some sagebrush. I stand. The sun is pale and I have no shade, no blanket, no more car. I am thirsty.

I sing with a dry throat of thankfulness, of the many gifts the Creator has given me to squander or ignore, like living. I cough thick, clotted clumps. I sing and I feel drums, I feel a heavy pulse in my ears. I fall on some sagebrush. I stand. I still see stiff frozen fur and bones and my blood dripping on it all. I'm numb in my denim. My breath is white, plumes of white rising. I walk with 150-pound legs. I touch my skull and part of my scalp is gone, one of my ears is gone. I'm dizzy, it's morning, I walk toward the risen sun. I'm sleepy and thirsty, stiff. I am a Wishram Indian and this is my blood dripping into my eyes. I fall on some sagebrush. I stand.

I hear Chewana, the Columbia River, miles away. I taste copper, salt, testosterone, thousands of generations of genetics, my redness. My blood is thawing the fur and the bones 'cuz my slow eyes see steam rising from the carcass, plumes of white rising. I laugh. I walk with 200-pound legs. My foot is swollen in my cowboy boot, I cut my tongue on broken, jagged teeth. I hear flies.

I hum a morning song because I've forgotten the words, can't remember. I hear drums, feel a heavy pulse in my ears. I sleep for two seconds and wake with a jerk, lying on top of some sagebrush. I stand. I see with my slow eyes that the carcass is thawed and is now breathing. I laugh. The sun is pale, I have no shade, no blanket, no more car.

I see with my slow eyes a giant concrete tipi miles away and so I walk with 250-pound legs toward this giant tipi. Coyote, now awake, runs to me. He licks my wounds, he licks me clean, he asks me to tell a story. And so I will, I will tell you all this story.

"Many years ago, one of the sleeping mountains exploded. Ash, fire, melting earth, melting snow, mud, all of the things threatened to kill all of the beautiful Yakama people and all their animal brothers and sisters. The sky grew dark, the earth shook, Chewana flowed backwards, and all the Yakama people and their animal brothers and sisters wondered what was happening, what to do, where to go. One of the Yakamas happened to be digging roots on Potato Hill near Pahto[1] and saw it all begin. He was a runner and so was able to keep just ahead of the angry mountain explosions. His hair caught on fire, his feet caught on fire, his backside caught on fire, and this helped him run faster. He sang in his pain, trying to think only of the beautiful Yakama people. When the people and their animal brothers and sisters saw this young man running toward them with his hair, feet, and backside on fire, they realized they had to flee south to their Warm Springs and Umatilla Cousins to avoid the ash, fire, melting earth, melting snow, and mud that would surely kill them all. To this day that young man still runs before the explosions, and we feel the tremors caused by his running feet."

When I finish the story, Coyote runs ahead barking to the giant concrete tipi because of course he is hungry. My slow eyes follow his trail. I walk with my 300-pound legs toward this giant concrete tipi. I fall on some sagebrush. I stand. I hear Chewana, the Columbia River, all around me and I am thirsty. With my slow eyes, I see stiff frozen fur and bones, the carcass touching the giant concrete tipi, the tipi that releases plumes of white rising, my blood dried on it all. I am a Wishram Indian of the Yakama Indian Nation and this is my blood dripping into my eyes, and these are my hands touching this giant concrete tipi. I fall on some sagebrush. I hear flies. 📖

1. Pahto: Mount Adams (12,307), the second highest peak in Washington state, stands in the southwestern part of the state. The Yakamas called it Pahto.

The Discovery of Amerika, II, 1993, Drawing, by Jon Strongbow

My Mother's Garden, June 1994

William Reichard

She hadn't planned on paradise,
what every tree knew as it grew
not against her will, but without it.

She shaped nothing but a rose bed
which wouldn't cooperate,
each red and yellow stem

falling brown in a blight
that took everyone's roses.
She got instead mulberry,

silver maple, sumacs
burning red at the edge of the yard
like the angel with the fiery sword

protecting one particular tree.
The animals all died,
even the bird when the furnace

went out, flooding the house with gas.
When each took its place
in a makeshift cemetery

at the back of the house,
a new tree grew,
some green compensation

for another lost life,
even a tree for the daughter
taken by disease,

the stand of red sumac
for the children killed in fire.
At seventy, everything achieves

some kind of balance,
even balance unsought,
credit in an illusive heaven

for every cultivated thing
which is planted, nurtured,
but does not take root.

The Twins From Tohoku

Susann Wilbur

My mother is wearing a deep blue robe embroidered with white chrysanthemums. The weightless silk billows in the morning breeze, and the spiky flowers seem to rise and fall on ocean waves. They are standing near the edge of the veranda that surrounds the teahouse. My father's face is in shadow, but his hair is beginning to fill with the pale light seeping through the trees behind him, and he reminds me of the golden-haired angels in my cousin Maria Serafina's Bible storybook.

I can't make out their words, but I hear the rumble of my father's voice, and I know when my mother is speaking because the rumbling stops and he bends his head down as if he is trying to catch her words with his eyes. I am standing by the open shoji drinking a glass of water, watching, silent. Suddenly a strange cry breaks from my father's lips and he sinks slowly out of my sight until I can see only the edges of his green robe and his hands on my mother's shoulders sliding down, down, until they circle her waist. I hear wet sounds, like those he makes when he kisses my cheeks and eyelids.

I want to leave. I want to be in my room, fast asleep beside my sister. I try to leave but my feet won't move, nor my eyes turn away.

My mother is making a circle of her arms, and even though I can't see it happening, I know she is folding them around my father, holding him against her because this is how she holds us, my sister and me, when we are hurt or troubled, pressing us against her breasts that smell of gardenias, whispering words or little songs in our ears that force us to stop crying because they ask questions we must answer.

My father is standing up tall again, cradling my mother's face in his hands. She looks very small and I don't know why, but I feel afraid. He slips a hand behind her head and the blue combs topple out, and when her hair drops to her waist, he wraps it around his hand like a bandage and clenches it in his fist. He says, I love you with my life Marichiko.

In a single moment of time I learn that love is dangerous, that it demands vitality, life, and that it can, if it wishes, command death. The glass drops from my hands and I watch the water darken my toes and the redwood planking of the veranda.

They move toward me as one. My father sweeps me into his big arms crooning, "Don't cry Plum Blossom. Hey, there's nothing for my big six-year-old girl to cry about." He brushes the hair from my wet cheeks and kisses me happy birthday, but it is my mother I want, her forgiveness, for knowing.

This is my earliest memory.

* * *

My father arrived in time for peace. He and an army friend were celebrating, he said, driving around the countryside, and somewhere in Kyoto they lost their way and stopped at the front gate of a large house to ask directions. In the courtyard they called out to anyone who might be home, and when there was no answer, my father knocked on the door. It was opened by a beautiful girl in a yellow and white kimono. She had pale luminous eyes and a smudge of apple green on her forehead. She was laughing, as if sharing a joke with someone inside the house.

* * *

It's my favorite time of day, when the sun is low and the trees become gigantic feathery creatures dancing against the rice paper walls. My mother says every one is a kami, a spirit, that they are kind and protective and sense our love for them. She takes the cover off the bath and slides open the shojis. The trees are so close I feel trembly, as though they are going to creep into the house and envelop us in their prickly arms.

We take turns, always in the same order. First my mother and I, and sometimes Catherine, wash my father. He sits on the little wood stool and we scrub him with sponges until he's covered with soap. After we rinse him off it's Catherine's turn, then mine, then my mother's.

My father and I are washing my mother while Catherine squats in front of the drain, laughing at the soapsuds sliding down through the slats. Lots of lather, my father says, Work it up into lots of bubbles. We sponge her back and arms and front until she begins to look like a ghost. She waves her arms and tries to scare us with spooky sounds, but we only laugh and hug and slide all over each other. I'm trying to wash her feet but she keeps wiggling her toes and finally I just squeeze a big blob of soap onto each foot and begin to scrub her legs.

I am more gentle as my hand moves toward her right hip, nearer the red-purple slash where a long time ago, before I was born, a monster tore open her flesh with his jagged green fangs, then jumped into the wound and sealed himself inside. I know it's a scar—I have one on my knee—but the monster is always in my head and sometimes I wake up crying because he is burying himself into her and I can't pull him out.

I touch it, run my finger up and down its length, up and down, again and again, feeling its shiny smoothness. It doesn't move with the true skin but clings to an inside part of her, as if it has a will of its own. I press my hand against the monster hiding in my mother's flesh; I want to love all of her so I must love the monster too. I kiss the teethmark stitches and the room is suddenly quiet. My father is crying. He embraces us, but he is still crying.

* * *

My father built the teahouse when he came back from the war. He built it on logs near the top of a hill where it was surrounded by redwoods and overlooked the ocean. We lived there in the summertime. By the time Catherine was born he had added two more rooms, and when Reuben was born we had six, but we still called it the teahouse.

The drive to Marin was only an hour or so, but walking into the teahouse was like stepping onto another planet. Once there, we became wildlife, running naked or nearly so among the cool ferns and towering trees of our hill, Mount della Robbia, or, as we more often called it, della Robbiyama. We spent summers exploring our green underworld minutely, prevailing upon its inhabitants to teach us the mysteries of nature. My father bought us a telescope and a microscope, and in time we became proficient with both.

* * *

One day I find a praying mantis. I have never seen one before, and intoxicated with my discovery, I run to show my mother who is sitting on the veranda painting translucent woodlands with preening cranes and willowy women on cream-colored silk. My mother is an artist and works from her imagination, or maybe her memory . . . I don't know. We place the creature in a large glass jar with holes punched in the metal lid for air. I slip in a fern tip and three rhododendron leaves dipped in water; I want the mantis to be happy. I also secretly hope it will die so I can examine it under the microscope.

Catherine clumps up the steps like an elephant. I shush her. We sit together, whispering and slurping fresh peaches, mesmerized by the slow, disjointed movements of the living green stick. My mother continues painting, and after a while the only sounds are the quiet trickle of the bamboo fountain and the purring of Yawarakai, our cat, whose name means "soft."

It is late in the afternoon when my mother rises from her chair, taking a moment to balance herself before collecting her paints and brushes. She says, Miranda, when you captured the mantis you interrupted its life's work. Now that you are going to set it free, you must remember to give thanks for the precious gift of its time. I cannot argue with my mother's ethics; there are no loopholes. I pout and unwillingly remove the lid, sliding the insect out of the jar onto the branch of a potted rhododendron where it quickly glides away into the plant's interior.

On my cushion at dinner that night I find a small scroll tied with a yellow ribbon. I untie the bow and unroll the silk. On it is painted a delicate green mantis poised prayerfully on a twig with two leaves and a flower bud.

* * *

My father liked to sing all the latest hits—from Chuck Berry and Elvis and Patti Page, Frank Sinatra and Tony Bennett—right along with *La Traviata* and *La Boheme*. My mother sang nursery rhymes and folk songs that she had learned as a child, and told us stories that no one else knew, about fox women and goblins and Okesa the dancer who was really a cat, and sometimes about ordinary people, like the fisherman's daughters.

* * *

There was a fisherman in Tohoku in northern Honshu who had twin daughters and a newborn son. One night a severe winter storm capsized his boat, and while trying to right it, he injured his back. The accident left him crippled and unable to earn enough money to feed or clothe his family. The two little girls tried hard not to be hungry, but sometimes their stomachs would give them away by grinding and groaning because of the emptiness, and when this happened they would go down to the edge of the water and sit on a rock, and cry quietly to each other.

One day a man who was traveling through the village saw the twins dancing with little stick dolls just outside their house, and though their clothes were rags and they wore no shoes, he was captivated by their play and their pretty songs and ordered his driver to stop. He told the girls' parents that he was a widower whose children were grown and married, and that he yearned to once again have little ones play in the rooms and gardens of his house in Kyoto, to enliven his lonely days with their exuberance and high-pitched voices and youthful energy. He promised to educate the two little girls and arrange excellent marriages for them as he had for his own four children.

The fisherman and his wife, who could never have even dreamed of such a life for their beloved daughters, considered the matter day and night, and at the end of one month, the adoption arrangement was concluded. The new father gave a large sum of money to the parents, to allay their sadness and also to enable them to buy food and clothing. When the day of parting came, the twins held their tears and clutched their stick dolls tightly against their chests as they climbed into the car with their new father and drove out of the village toward the beautiful city of Kyoto.

The new father kept his word. He loved the little girls very much. He called them My Flower Buds, and dressed them in the finest clothes and sent them to the very best schools. He brought special tutors to the house to teach them foreign languages and customs, musical instruments and painting.

Whenever they began to miss their parents, however, and ask to visit them, the new father would buy them gifts and tell them how much he loved them and assure them that they would pay them a visit next week or next month or during a holiday, the new father always had something planned—an excursion or a picnic—and as the years passed, the sisters, whose lives were very busy, asked less and less about their parents and eventually even forgot what they looked like. They tried to bring them into their minds and to paint them on paper, but the images faded until they were silvery and transparent as mountain mist. The sisters were very saddened by this, but they were also consoled, knowing that they had helped their family to live well and become prosperous.

* * *

My mother believes that the use of nicknames diminishes one's personal power and control of one's life. This is not a Japanese tradition but a personal opinion verging on the religious, and my father's family, rife with nicknames, has respectfully deferred to her where we are concerned. However, by a quirk of fate, my father escaped her rule.

The day she finally consented to speak to him—it was almost a year after the injury—he told her he was lucky, and by the time she discovered that the name of the young GI from California who had been trying for months to engage her in conversation and interest her in going for a walk perhaps, or to the reviving Kabuki, was Vincenzo della Robbia, it was too late. He refused to relinquish the name because he considered himself lucky from the moment they spoke, and somehow managed to convince her that a nickname like Lucky couldn't possibly be otherwise.

*   *   *

I am at the birthday party of a classmate. He is tall for his ten years, athletic, sandy-haired and loud. The festivities take place in the den, a room whose strange decorations he proudly displays to his captive audience. Souvenirs from Japan, he says. Right, Dad? Dad smiles and drinks his Coke. The birthday boy points out a Japanese sword, a dagger, buttons from a Japanese officer's uniform—I see Dad in the heat of battle snipping off buttons with a tiny silver scissors while ducking bullets—a ratty looking canteen, a rifle, and a glass jar in which are three ears. Dried. Like figs.

The Japs cut our guys' ears off, so my dad cut off theirs. Right, Dad?

Right, his dad says, raising the bottle in a toast.

I bet your father didn't bring home stuff as good as all this, says my classmate, spreading his arms expansively to include the whole exhibit. Did he? He is not speaking to the others, only to me.

I can't think of anything like this in my house. No, I answer, aware that many eyes are on me, a few waiting for me to rise to the challenge.

Well, he must've brought home something, he says. Every soldier brings home something when he goes to war. To remind him.

I wonder what it is that a soldier needs to be reminded of. I think furiously, my mind racing through my house and the objects in it, somehow understanding that credibility and reputation are involved here, my father's and mine, though I'm not sure why or how.

Immediately I become aware of a problem. My life has not been divided into ethnic partitions—it is simply my life, my home; the objects, words, foods, holidays. I am still thinking. My parents wear yukatas, or cotton kimonos, at home, but I don't know if they have anything to do with the war. My mother uses a pasta press to make noodles, but my grandmother does too, so I'm not sure if it's Japanese, and, anyway, I'm pretty certain it has nothing to do with the war. Quickly, quickly, I search through our rooms, closets, cupboards. I find ordinary things—clothes, toys, books, records, food, pots and pans and flower vases and teapots . . . aha! the teahouse I think—tatami, shakuhachi, Victrola, cushions, tub—but there is nothing, nothing from the war.

Jeez! What kind of soldier is your dad anyway? Didn't he bring home anything? demands the sandy-haired boy, smirking. His dad is smirking too.

Yes! Yes he did! I shout suddenly. He did! My mother!

*   *   *

When I walk down the street with my mother, people stare, and I smile to myself and pretend there is no one but the two of us. It isn't until I'm older that I realize not all of them stare because she is beautiful.

*   *   *

Even if you don't like 'em, you gotta admit it wouldn't be the worst thing in the world waking up and seeing Lucky's little Jap on the pillow next to yours.

*   *   *

I am happy for the sisters from Tohoku because they are no longer hungry and have a new father who loves them very much, a father who every afternoon listens to their stories about school, and after they finish their homework, bathes with them, and at bedtime takes them into his room, into his thick warm comfortable bed.

But I also feel very sad because they will never see their parents again. Just trying to imagine what it would be like never to see my mother and father again makes me cry. I tell my mother this is a terrible story and I wish she hadn't told it to me; I don't like the ending. If they had stayed together, she says, they all would have starved. Would that have been better? Neither ending is better I tell her. You're right, she says, neither one is better.

* * *

I wake up in the dark and hear singing, or chanting. It's my mother. A whispered argument and she is crying and then my father comes in and tells us not to worry, to go back to sleep, that my mother isn't feeling well. Reuben is frightened and crawls between Catherine and me.

Later, morning creeps through the shojis, wrapping the room in soft cottony light. Catherine is shaking me and pointing to the wall; there is something painted on it. I slide it open, walk into the hall and slide it shut again to get a better look. It's Kwannon, the Goddess of Mercy, I tell her. On the fusuma panel next to Kwannon are tall pine trees, symbols of long life. Reuben steps into the hall rubbing his eyes, smiling in amazement at first, saying, Wow and When did mommy do this? then plops his thumb into his mouth and sucks hard, as if it were the only thing keeping him connected to the earth. I take their hands and walk toward my parents' room. The hallway is like an art gallery; nearly every screen in the house has been painted.

My father is staring out the window into the trees. A branch from a potted rhododendron stretches itself like an arm across the opening, an arm with a huge burst of deep pink at its fingertips. He hears us and turns around, smiles and puts a finger to his lips. As he gets up, he waves us toward the door. My mother seems to be sleeping. She has her back to us and doesn't stir.

I ask about the paintings. You know how mommy is when she gets an idea, he says, leaving the thought unfinished. His laugh is not a happy one.

* * *

While he cooks a frittata for breakfast he tells us how one of his carpenters misread a set of blueprints and started building the bathroom in the middle of the living room. Catherine isn't so sure he's telling the truth, but Reuben thinks it's hilarious and laughs so hard he spills his orange juice. After we do the dishes my father sends us to scout for insects and plants to study—he has a project in mind. I go down to the beach instead.

It's drizzling, but nice. Sometimes my mother and I go for walks in the rain. I don't know exactly what I'm looking for, and it takes a long time, but as soon as I see it I know it's perfect. Black as midnight and with a white mark, like a splash or a starburst off to one side, it's smooth as glass, and I imagine it being polished by sand and waves and the bodies of sea creatures for millions and millions of years. I am certain it is a kami. I run all the way up the hill.

My father is with Catherine and Reuben on the veranda studying something under the microscope, a sloughed snakeskin, I think. My mother is sitting in the bedroom, staring out the window at the rhododendron's fingertips. I sit down and press myself against her so she'll know I'm there. We watch the drizzle and the pink flowers and the whitecaps that are scattered across the ocean like a hundred thousand seagulls, and after a time I open her hand and place the beautiful stone in it. She looks at it and smiles a smile that makes me want to cry, then takes me in her arms and pulls me back into the pillows, stroking my hair, and begins to tell me the story of the twins from Tohoku.

* * *

My father arrived in time for peace, and when the beautiful girl with luminous eyes opened the door, he forgot completely the words he had been practicing to ask for directions. He stood in the doorway, he said, staring, blushing a little, wishing he could say something clever, or even ridiculous. He wanted to wipe away the apple green smudge, or just touch it with a finger, and wondered if her hands were as soft as they looked. He wanted to determine the exact color of her eyes that reflected pale brown and green and gold, to remove his boots and pad softly into the house, feeling against the palm of his hand the smooth glide of a shoji as he opened it onto a garden where the tip of a willow branch dipped into a pool of clear water creating circles within circles, to take her hand and together peer into them, knowing that to do so would uncover the secret longings of his heart. He stared at the girl and smiled, aching to hear her laugh again, and it occurred to him that he might try to write a poem.

When he finally pulled his eyes from her in order to consult the dictionary in his trembling hand, she called out to someone in the courtyard, and following the direction of her voice and the tilt of her head, he turned to see his army friend, the farm-boy from Salinas who had drunk too much sake, speaking to a richly-dressed old man and a girl who looked just like the one at the door, who even had the same glittering eyes, the Ainu eyes of their mother who was from Hokkaido, he learned much later.

* * *

It is August and we are celebrating Obon. My mother is weaving little straw boats, five of them, and sends me to find something beautiful for each one. After some searching I return with a red pebble, a fragment of a speckled bird's egg, a grey feather with a black dot, and a yellow flower, and because I can't find anything else, I draw a picture of our cat Yawaraki. My mother likes the drawing best; it will be for my Aunt Miyoshi.

We place the objects in the boats along with bits of food and scented candles and carry them down the hill to the beach. We light the candles and clap our hands before setting the boats afloat on the Pacific Ocean, sending back to their graves the happy and contented spirits of my grandmother and grandfather, my uncle who died when he was a baby, Aunt Miyoshi, and someone called Mr. Ohama from Kyoto.

My mother lowers herself to the ground, shifting carefully onto her left hip. We kneel, surround her with our arms and mothlike kisses, and watch, still as ghosts in the moonlight, until the little boats disappear.

*   *   *

It's my sixteenth birthday and my mother gives me a tiny box wrapped in bright red paper. I hope it's a ring; all my friends are getting birthstone rings. It's not, though. It's an ivory ojime, slightly larger than my thumbnail, carved in the shape of a shojo, a mythical creature who sings and dances by the sea. She kisses me and laughs and hands me a small pouch of yellow silk. I collected them for you, she says, one for each year of your life. I loosen the drawstrings and pour them out on the table—an ivory monkey and Benten the Goddess of Good Luck, a jade cat, a rosette of carved turquoise, and glass beads brilliant with tiny flowers and stripes and zigzaggy lines. Happiness and luck—Japanese jewels, my father says.

*   *   *

I have just returned from a bead-buying trip to Asia. Meet me at the teahouse, I shout to my mother over the phone at the airport. She insists on picking me up, and we spend the long rush hour drive catching up on family happenings: Catherine will be teaching molecular biology at Berkeley in the fall, my father and Reuben lost the bid on a new suburban home development, and an unexpected project has fallen in my mother's lap—designing stage sets for a local theater company. I describe to her the less dangerous of my adventures in the mysterious world of Tibetan turquoise and Chinese jade.

We sit on the veranda beneath the overhang drinking hot tea. A light rain is falling and plinks softly on the rhododendron leaves and the redwood floor. I watch as my mother, a faint smile at the corners of her mouth, opens the small, intricately wrapped package I have given her. I bargained like a demon for it, but only when I told him it was for my mother and spoke a few words of Japanese did the dealer smile and drop the price another ten percent.

Age has merely flirted with her; an unlined hand lifts the Heavenly Being from its fuchsia and silver box. She exclaims, then admonishes; Asians have an instinct for jade, especially antique carvings, and through her tears she has managed to appraise it. Don't be silly, I tell her, you're my mother, and I lower the black silk ribbon down over her head. The two-inch Heavenly Being nestles celestially between her breasts.

This is not the first time we have come here, just the two of us. We are practiced. We link arms, sip our tea, and watch the rain. Later, easing ourselves into the bath, we sigh, pleased to be so civilized, so elegant, so fortunate to be able to let go of whatever cares plague us. My mother stretches her right leg, runs a hand over the pale silken cord on her hip. These things happen in war. They happen in peacetime too. Chest deep in water, I pour two glasses of wine—Verdicchio. *Lucia di Lammermoor* goes mad softly in the background, and we toast, as always, to long life. Not an atrocity, of course, like the Hiroshima Maidens, just a mishap.

The metal plate in my mother's body is grey and drab, screwed into solid bone as if the bone were a plank of wood. A broken piece of her is lying on a field somewhere, chewed on perhaps by a hungry animal, rained on, buried in the earth, disintegrating, becoming compost, dust. She is preceding herself to the grave. And in exchange for this piece of herself, in an unfair bit of East-West commerce, she has a souvenir that has become part of her, that through the years she prayed before the Butsudan with, painted waterfalls and nestling cranes with, cooked with, bathed giggling children with, made love with.

* * *

As he stood in the doorway consulting his dictionary he began thinking the unthinkable—that was how he put it—wondering if it might be at all possible to arrange, in some way, with an escort of course if that was how they did it, for her to accompany him to the Great Shrine of Amaterasu Omikami, the Heaven Shining Great August Spirit, or to the Kabuki, or on a picnic where the sunlight would play on the ocean behind her and draw wild dark rainbows on the sheen of her hair, and where she would teach him to eat yakitori and soba with chopsticks, the two of them laughing until he mastered the skill, and then he would pick a flower, a gardenia perhaps, and lean close to her while placing it behind her ear, very close, close enough to inhale it, close enough to press his face into her heavy black hair.

As he stood in the doorway paying little attention to the dictionary and much more to the fanciful imaginings flitting through his head, she ran past him into the courtyard to help her sister who cried out when the drunken farmboy from Salinas threw her to the ground.

Above there was a dazzling sun, and below, a flash of silver as the old man fell, and before anyone could stop him, the farmboy from Salinas bent over the girl on the ground and sliced her in half, from her pubis to her throat, and after a second stroke, like mighty Perseus, lifted his trophy with a victory cheer.

My mother called out to the gods who must have been very busy at that historical point in time and so did not hear her, and since there was nothing on heaven or earth to stop him, he lunged at her with his bayonet, but because she lost her balance and her body shifted, the blade only went through her hip and pinned her to the ground. My father shot him.

* * *

If I could, I would gently pry open the silken cord and remove the cold grey metal, the functional steel from which guns and tanks are fashioned. If I could, I would carve a clasp of golden topaz or emerald or lapis lazuli traced with the finest threads of gold that would hold her delicate bones together and spread its light and warmth throughout her body, would protect her when I cannot, and would allow her to dance above the ground instead of lower herself gingerly to it. 📖

Story

Diane Glancy

For Connie Hart, b. 1917, Lake Conda, who learned basket weaving by herself because her Koorie mother was not allowed to teach her in the mission. Connie's baskets now appear in the National Gallery of Victoria, Australia.

A woman makes a story because there's no shade, and you know how a story branches. A story's a tree unfolding. The leaves hide the beating sun. A story comes just like a tree where it stands after winter. The woman says the tree feels the sun through its bark. It feels the leaves pick-axing their way out. The tree moves all summer on those little plots called stems. You know some afternoons a story full of leaves and branching forks folds up and lifts. But there has to be leaves falling after the budding all summer. After the shade to stand between. Then rakes gather meaning. Not from a tree out of leaves, but from moving to story again. The woman says when it's cold, the bark looks like a column of hard, dark flames. In winter you can hold your hand to a tree.

XIII

VOLUME 5, NUMBER 2
WINTER 1995-96

Dialogue between Eve and the Serpent, No. 1, 1993,
Painting, by Elizabeth Sandvig

Kiko

Rane Arroyo

Where's my psychic paycheck?
Or love letter with condom enclosed?
I've stripped to my bones in
strangers' bedrooms, forced to be
my own demon lover. I shower.
It's all fucked up and down:
I hide in my house, reading Foucault,
dead of AIDS that he went outside of
his body to seek. How can my
pueblo not be postmodern?
Sí, see: my mailman is a woman!
Señor Andy García is *muy macho*,
but why "Andy" like in that Andy of
Mayberry, RFD? Or "Richard" Rodriguez
instead of Ricardo like Little Ricky's
last name in *I Love Lucy? Hola,*
head full of dreams. Old bills follow me
into a new century like stupid, faithful dogs.

Speedy Gonzalez, Jr.

Rane Arroyo

1.
So what? Who cares that Marilyn Monroe look-alikes o.d.?
Marilyn was a year of good wine. *Speedy*, a woman once called
me. I said, you're not Marilyn. I made her cry. I felt like a rich
man, a bastard, Columbus kicking pagan ass.

2.
My mother told me to iron my hair flat like some dumb blond
surfer, like a highway in California long after dark. "Imagine,
hijo," she said, "you speeding the hell out of yourself."

3.
I'm the best man. I try on a tuxedo, wrong size. I take it off. I'm
naked before the groom. I'm his best man but I'm the better
man. *Speedy*, he laughs, don't be afraid. Of what? Why not be
afraid? I ache when cartoon animals run, but their legs don't
carry them away.

8 Ball

Diane Glancy

Just look how this *outstanding*
has such an aura about it
where life and death and glories
and ignominies of *infintessitude* pass.
I lift my head above the roof
and look at the mystery and majesty
of the heavens.
The little smoking ball beneath it.
Polluted unfair suffering place.
God himself walked down to and was sent away
with bites in his hands and feet
from the mongrel earth.
Black arrogant ball.
Willful baby.
The speck
blot
hubcap
forgetful of the massive space it whines in
could squish it like a fly.
Little pike down the corridor of space.
This earth
this small fry.
We trust the little rolling marble.
This blue
this white streaked.
The long fall of it through space
more than an outpost yet not destination.
Heaven must be like
not tree
field
river

but attitude
feeling
shape of relationship
playing off one another
the corners of thought
in this little chickencoop.
Ancillary.
This something passing as a wagon train
to the other limits of charted territory
to the whatsoever where
all are bound.

Six of the Days of Love

Amy Halloran

We were halfway into Monday, I full-fancy willing to be skirting disbeliefs. I embraced them, sang to my subconscious, "Go to sleep. Show me what it is I know to be not true." He told me he lied to all his lovers. I could tell myself in a million ways his goodbye meant its opposite, meant another hello.

Halfway into Tuesday, I sailed through gusts of gutter-snipe. I still did not want to listen. Ghosts whispered, *Look out! He's telling the truth!* The rain, it was a waterfall I followed out my window, via screen. In the anxiety of the silence, I tried to find ways around the corner of indifference. Shut up, I told me, go to bed, fuckhead. Ease up. It's only another day. You're only another human. You're only alone.

The rain, it was a waterfall. I flew, cascading, watch-heard the company of bleating beads. The thunder broke my fall. I broke myself by listening: *this was the way it was.* I was not his though he was mine, in my imagination. The planes only intersected in my mind.

I was halfway into Wednesday, a million miles from when I'd said, "sure we can just be friends," thinking then with wine's fine fueling that any attachment would be good enough, would be more than, better than, nothing. I was halfway alone inside the week's middle, belly bloated, floating dead man in the pond when I truly backwards walked, dizzy, into Monday night, for the first time awake and hearing what he'd really said, what I really felt about this thing he called goodbye.

I was almost over Thursday when the energy of restlessness drove me finally to dial his number on the phone. He answered. He received.

"Hello?"

"I've finally figured out why it is you make me vomit when you touch my thigh."

"Oh yeah," he said, eyebrows leaning toward the ceiling. I could see it in the tone. It had been Thursday twice removed when he'd told me he liked cruelty, when he told me mean people were to be enjoyed. But it was just this day I could be cruel.

"I've finally decided why it is you make me sick. Touch me, tell me different things. Do you think that's the way to break my heart?"

Silence.

"Well, you know, it is."

No more would he receive. He said he could not handle my hostility. Hung up. I smiled a fuck you to the phone. It didn't ring.

Friday I was feasting full on fury at the turnaround, clock arms rolling. Guards changed. I carried high my anger, throttle open, leaking. My love had a pulse. It had. I severed. I watched the artery draining, dying, into Saturday. Cartoons colored my TV screen. Road Runner exploded his enemy, TNT, mine.

This week I shot the minotaur. Gasping, we lie dead. I rise. He slithers, sucking the stub of his tail, dragging his bloody butt on the scabby floor that rugged our forest of make-believes. Pine needles will heal into his wounds. My butt will shine in the mirror, a scarless full moon. I win. 📖

Manna in Gallup

Dawn Karima Pettigrew

I

My life is still there when I open my eyes. Smoke, sweat, and the sorrow of Seagram's Gin—left over since the night before the night before New Year's Eve—assault my sleepy lungs. When I realize that I am still alive and still me, it takes all the faith I have to swallow a sob.

Most mornings since my husband lost the little bit of job he did have, I have eaten my tears for breakfast. This morning is really afternoon, yet nobody in our pre-fab, peeling HUD house has made a motion. I will myself to sit up and almost fall again when I glance at the man who snores next to me. For ten of the rises and falls of his taut chest, I am made dizzy by a swell of hope. He stirs, I blink, and I realize that he is only my husband, and this is still my life. The hope I feel drowns like roaches who dive headfirst into slim glass bottles of Thunderbird.

II

When I had joy, when I was too young to have married anybody from anywhere, my mother made me a parrot from paint and papier-mâché. I hugged that parrot and loved it like nobody's business until my mother lynched it during my fifth birthday party. Other children pummeled it, beating it with broomsticks. Children and parents cheered when my parrot was decapitated and its blood ran thick with candy. My mother smiled at me like I ought to be happy.

For weeks after that, we found cut-paper confetti and caramel candy swirls in the laundry, in our coat pockets, in the folds of couch cushions—everywhere that had room for shards of tissue-thin paper and the sunshine mockery of butterscotch.

III

Today, Piñata-candy people are strewn across the flatness of the floor and all over the furniture. Ray Walks-Away, who fancy dances for not-so-much of a living, is intertwined with Carlos Tsosie from over at the Health Service who I think might just be dead until he coughs raggedly. When I got home from working at the End of the Trail Pancake House last night I must have just trampled right over the head of Sam Wayne who has temporarily replaced the welcome mat my Aunt Indiana gave us last Christmas. A woman lies passed out in front of the TV. She has no pants on, but she does have shoes, which I wish I had had the good sense to put on.

My vulnerable feet narrowly miss the land mines of busted bottles and loaded ashtrays. The better part of a deck of cards backed by the Budweiser logo lies, mid-hit, between gnawed frybread and a gaping can of Beer Nuts. I pick up what would have been the dealer's next card, the ace of hearts. The card is sticky with gin and juice. I lose. I remember why I prefer bingo.

My fingers find the scars left by unfiltered Camels and Marlboros in the table I used half a paycheck to buy. I must have had a spirit-world accident somewhere between community college and the rest of my life. I figure that's how I ended up here, sacrificing tables to make ashtrays, and playing morning-after blackjack with myself.

IV

When I turned six, we found that clay parrot's head. I glued its beak back on and buried it in the yard.

V

If I could trust my husband, I would invite him to eat with me. But ever since he found out where I hid the money I was saving for sturdy walking shoes and a dance shawl and spent it on Jack Daniels, Camels, and some fancy shawl dancer named Ina,

I don't trust him much farther than I can throw him. Seeing as he's six foot six inches and weighs around 270, that means I don't trust him with much of anything.

The mortification of wearing a neon feather in my hair while I greet people over at the End of the Trail Pancake House has paid off. Since my husband thinks I make half of what I do, I now own ten boxes of Wheaties, twelve cans of fruits and vegetables, four boxes of Ritz crackers in the stay-fresh packs, and ten cans of tuna and deviled ham—which I love. My stash is hidden in plain sight in the cupboard under the sink. Empty boxes of Tide, Best Yet Bleach, and Cascade conceal my secrets. Those boxes sit right on the shelf, big as day, and my husband, who wouldn't touch a cleaning product even if it was guaranteed to make him instant king of the entire world, has yet to suspect a thing.

So in these days full of nothing, when his food coupons and commodities start running thin, I eat—drink, really—a bowl of salt and potato soup with him and let our stomachs moan in harmony. The minute he collapses into a Coors coma, I open the cupboard door—which is on its last leg, last hinge, I should say. I feast like food is going out of style, which in a way, it is.

I am two Tide boxes from a fulfilling lunch of deviled ham and maybe an egg if I can find one. Rummaging through my hoard, I stop when a small shadow slips into the corner of my eye. Expecting spirits or the hung-over, I turn around slowly. A baby is standing in the doorway.

Not a baby, exactly. Just this side of a baby, though. She is standing on reasonably reliable legs that end in shocking red sneakers. Her hair has been cut by somebody who knew enough to know that it needed cutting, but not enough to know not to cut it themselves. From the steadiness of the step she takes, I decide she is probably just shy of three or four years old.

Her night-colored eyes dart from my face to my empty hands. From the twist of her tiny lips, I figure she must be hungry. My knees pop like clay cracking when I kneel to look her in her eyes. I have no earthly idea who she belongs to.

"Are you hungry, honey?" Stupid question. She is nodding at me like I offered her a slice of the moon with a drink of the sea to wash it down.

"What's your name?" She won't tell me. Perhaps a cracker will make her talk. I find a half of a stay-fresh package in the box meant for bleach and press a cracker in her tiny hand. By the time I make my body meet the floor again, she has made crumbs and the cracker is missing.

"You want another one? Then tell me your name."

Baby reasons for a moment and opts for the cracker.

"Nisa."

I should have been a child psychologist. Or at least somebody's mother. I have plenty of crackers and I try again. I feel the slightest bit guilty about bribing a baby.

"Who's your mama, sweetie pie?" The baby blinks back at me. "What about your daddy? Do you have a last name?"

Detective work is required here. "Do you know what tribe you are?"

The small person contemplates this like I just asked her all the names of God. She smiles for the first time, showing a surprising number of tiny teeth.

"Maybe," she says proudly, "maybe wanna-be."

My laughter aches from lack of use. I giggle until I taste my own tears. The crackers fall on the floor and the baby eats them all. 📖

Exorcism

Margaret Randall

Two dark wings, heartbeat of feathers.
Or will it be a breast this time,
surgically cornered
to block the known caress?

A puzzle of words crossed your silence.
Breathing becomes a code.
Of ease, only random numbers
remain.

You must fix anchor to this beating
of anticipated days.
Follow the blood
fresh beets deposit on the knife.

Stained fingers
lift them from the cooking pot,
steal them from heat, bathe them
so that touch is possible.

Finger the skins
that shear beneath a steady stream.
Clean and slice.
Discard remaining grit

until the memory of their plumpness calls.
Neither armored nor worn
but future in their perfect egos,
roots to be pared

as thin as the pages in this book of chance.
Add the translucence of onion,
white against the wine.
Balsamic vinegar, a bit of oil and salt.

Each minute brings its story.
Each new fear this adventure of wings.

Walking the Mysteries

Trisha Ready

"Lust is a natural human emotion," Father Tom began. "All passionate people lust after something. And we're talking about more than legs and behinds, brothers and sisters. Some people lust after beauty or music, money, even God. It isn't the lust that's bad, its what you do with the lust. And I say let yourself have it."

I could tell my dad wasn't really studying the hymnal like he pretended. He was listening to every damned word that priest said. His face looked sunburned with anger.

"Now if you decide to ignore your lust," Father Tom went on, "and you say to yourself, 'I've killed that wild dog. It doesn't trespass here,' you're lying. People who talk like that molest their own children. Molest—did you hear that? I'm talking incest, abuse. I'm talking about people who have no passions destroying people who have them. A repressed person who lusts can't let anyone else have intense feelings."

"Take the children home," my dad whispered to my mother. She was intent on listening and didn't budge until he stepped on her new black pumps. "Stop that," she said. "You take them yourself."

So he did, and we missed the rest of that sermon. But the following one was just as good. It was "Envy in the Closet." Father Renewal kind of eased into it, after a gospel that wasn't a gospel. He read from the newspaper. My dad started biting around the edges of his fingernails the moment we sat down.

The article Father Tom read was something about a man suing a neighborhood grocery for three million dollars because he'd spilled hot coffee on his penis. I sat up. The whole church was buzzing.

"Did that scare you?" the priest asked. "I'll bet every first grader in this building has heard that word. And the rest of you act like I just made it up. Well that's fine. I'm sure you're all listening now, and I hope you keep listening while I tell you about how envy gets twisted when we deny we even feel it.

"Envy. That's another of those natural things we all share. You're going on a trip to Europe this summer and I'm stuck visiting Barstow. Envy. You've got a front lawn as green as AstroTurf, and mine looks like a minefield for crabgrass.

"Now there's nothing wrong with saying to yourself or to your friend, 'I'm jealous of what you've got.' Maybe you even wish you had someone else's nose or thick head of hair. Just say it. That's what I'm asking. Because if you don't you start backstabbing anyone who comes within a ten foot radius of your bitter heart. You turn mean. Get to thinking the world owes you equal or better than the next man. See there, some of you are nodding. Envy that doesn't get spoken out directly turns ugly. That's why people love it when a movie star's life gets screwed up with drugs or bad marriages."

On that note, all of the collection basketmen, of whom my dad was the captain, stood up. Father Tom didn't seem to mind. Those six men in suits slid pool cue baskets down the aisles. Dollar bills and coins fell in.

Gluttony and sloth came on the same day that Father Tom shaved his head for the Lenten season. He was in a solemn mood; he kept pacing the altar and running one hand over his egg-smooth pate.

"Now gluttony and sloth are a little trickier," Father Tom began. "First thing is, you can't help but notice how repulsive the words sound." (People laughed.) "Gluttony makes you think about someone inhaling half a side of beef, with a pitcher of beer on the side. And sloth sounds like a heroin-induced sleep. Those are sleazy words, gluttony and sloth—loaded with darkness. If we're going to look at them at all, we have to change them a little. How about we call them indulgence and relaxation instead?

"Everybody indulges themselves. Some people do it constantly—like people who can't live without a drink, or men who have to have sex with every young woman who walks into their office. Some people just like a little ice cream, or an occasional cigarette or two. Even if people go to extremes with their indulgences they'll burn out quick enough. It's a neurosis, and I'll get to that in a second, brethren, which makes indulgences more complex.

"Same thing happens with relaxation. Who among you thinks relaxation is evil? Without it, we'd all be heart attack victims with chronic peptic ulcers and gray hair at twelve. What's the use of being alive if we can't have fun? Of course that has its extremes. Some people make a regular vocation out of taking it easy. And some people want everyone else to do the work for them, but there's two sides to that.

"I know a man back in San Francisco who can't stand the sight of people reading books. Says it's a waste of time. That people should be making things and working, not thinking so hard. There's a lot of people just like him scattered around. Maybe you're one of those people."

I swear Father Tom looked right at my dad who was balancing his checkbook and didn't seem to notice. I nodded my head, until my mom knocked with her fist on my shoulder.

"Well," Father Tom continued, "people who think readers are lazy are the sinners in my book. And you know why that is, brethren?" (I nodded my head again.) "Because we live in a completely neurotic society where contemplating ideas and feelings is a hateful thing.

"What we've all got to do is keep busy. That's right. Stuff things in your mouth; plan a diet; think about what you *didn't* eat and what that *didn't* make you. Fat for example. Or a flesh eater. And what's more, try to control everyone around you from doing the things you can't let yourself do. Don't let anyone smoke, God forbid! And if you've got a drinking problem, the rest of the world's gotta have one too."

I was leaning forward so far in my chair, my knees were resting on the bench in front of me. People were fidgeting. I looked over at Mrs. Applebaum who made her children eat raw vegetables and tofu for lunch. She was carving something in the wooden bench in front of her with a fingernail. It looked like she was holding her breath. He didn't spare a soul that Father Tom. He went for everybody's precious protected thing.

"Now laziness," he said. "Let's see what that becomes when it gets repressed. How many of you carry around little black books, and car phones, and beepers, and have your daily automated calendars memorized like digital Bibles?" (A few people raised their hands.) "Well, you're honest and I thank you for that. But you're not in the minority here. Nowadays, you'd think it was a virtue to run yourself ragged, wouldn't you?

"What's wrong with relaxing?" Father Tom asked. "It isn't a sin. But you've got all these busybodies who think people that aren't keeping up with them are either weak or inferior or dinosaurs. These neurotic-heads even squeeze in just enough spirituality and quality time with the family to give themselves a medal every week. Do you teach your children to act like this?"

My dad leaned over and whispered to my mom, "Did I tell you that we've started an investigation in the diocese about this clown?"

"Shhh," my mom snapped back. 📖

Shadow . . . Dreaming, 2001, Collage, by Carletta Carrington Wilson

Chewing the Sweetflag

Ron Welburn

Chewing the sweetflag kernel
sustains the high Lakota sound
around the drum, singing for
the Creator, and singing those 45s
about kissing your favorite woman
and passing her the root with your tongue.
Join me at the pond, they agree.
This root makes falsetto as strong as
Neville and Smokey and those yodeling pioneers
as we sing and drop our voices
to the Ojibwe level, and kiss and
roll around at the swamp of desire.
That Uncle Walt rhapsodized its effects
but there is no song long enough for lovers
in mists after the fire.

Recipe para Los Reyes y Las Reinas

Ken Gollersrud Ayala

Grow some corn
when ripe
pick it,
shuck it,
strip it,
save the husks
shave off those kernels

take a stone
beat,   thrash
sweat
and work that masa for five   hundred   years
or until you hear Tio José singing Mexican songs
strumming his guitar

Take a pig
boil till tender
add some tomatillos
spread it on the masa
wrap yourself inside the husks
steam until visions of Aztec Kings
tell you to return to your own time

Sprinkle with sugar and cinnamon

Eat at midnight

XIV

VOLUME 5, NUMBER 3
SPRING 1996

Raven, 1996, Cover Design and Illustration,
by Gayanna Magcosta

Spirits of the Ordinary
a play

Kathleen Alcalá

A man and a woman enter from either side of stage. They go upstage and pick up a small table, move it to center stage. On JULIO'S side of the table are a yarmulke and a prayer shawl, which he picks up and puts on. There are also a metal plate, a plume pen and an inkwell, some old books, and two or three glass vials of various sizes and colors. On SISTER LUCY'S side is a shawl, which she in turn puts on, revealing a crystal ball on her table. Two candles are at the middle of the table. They each light a candle. They do not know of each other's presence.

JULIO: [Speaking softly with a prayerful attitude] *Asufreme con las redomas de vino, afloshame con las mazana que dolorioza de amor yo* . . . Your children shall be like olive shoots around your table. From our forefathers before us, and unto our children's children.

LUCY: Oh, come on, what's the matter with this thing?

JULIO: Seventy times seventy times Thy name . . .

LUCY: Come on, it's so . . .

JULIO: We honor You with our prayers. We meditate on Thy mercies.

LUCY: [Polishes crystal ball with her shawl] Murky! There. That's better.

JULIO: [Sets down his book, holds his forehead, and picks up the plate before him, turning it as he looks at it] By clearing my mind of all else, by concentrating entirely on His will, I try, every day, to . . .

LUCY: Just show me if I'm gonna have a good day!

JULIO: Hasten the coming of the Messiah! [Sets down the plate]

LUCY: All I need is twenty-five bucks. Twenty-five more bucks and I can pay the lousy electric bill.

JULIO: [To audience] My father did this, and his father before him. We have studied the Kabbalah for generations, since my ancestors left Spain in the great Diaspora and came to the New World, to Mexico, in search of freedom. For you see [leans forward to whisper] we are Jews, although the neighbors don't know it. They think we are Catholic, like them. And on Sunday, we are. We attend Mass, and we make confession. But only for sins from the Old Testament! But on Friday we close our curtains, and light candles. Those who remember say the prayers. And those who don't remember anymore, well, they just light the candles and try to remember who we are. We have done this for hundreds of years. And we will continue to do this until He returns to establish His kingdom on earth. [Steps back]

LUCY: [To audience] You know, I used to dress like a nun—a long brown dress, a crucifix, the whole thing. I called myself Sister Lucy. I still do. I like that. It sounds . . . special. Holy. My grandmother was a real healer. She was Indian. And the desert was like, well, like her church. But people don't want that. Too much TV. They want their fortunes told by, you know, a gypsy! She had to dress the part. Bright clothes, jewelry, the whole thing. People want . . . romance!

JULIO: Devotion.

LUCY: Excitement!

JULIO: Humility.

LUCY: People need to believe in something. They need to have . . . faith. And faith is a living thing.

JULIO: Faith must be fed, like a river is fed by streams, every act of devotion adds to the whole.

LUCY: So I give them what they want. Fancy clothes and a crystal ball.

JULIO: Everything else is illusion. So I clear my thoughts, I clear my hearing, and I clear my sight . . .

LUCY: But my real interest is iridology. Do you know what that is? It's the science of reading someone's eyes.

JULIO: . . . for the eyes are the mirror to the soul.

LUCY: If I look in your eyes, I can see where you've been, and, more important, I can tell where you're going. Because *that's* what people pay for. And that's what Zacarías came in for. It was obvious where he'd been.

JULIO: My son was a good boy.

LUCY: A fast car, lots of cash.

JULIO: He helped me every day in the shop.

LUCY: He'd come straight from Vegas. And he was in a big hurry.

JULIO: And when he married, well, even though she wasn't Jewish, she was a fine woman, and he went with my blessing.

LUCY: He wasn't on his way to Sunday School.

JULIO: After all, who knows who's Jewish anymore? It's been a secret so long, we've all forgotten. Here we are, so far from [stops, points up], so close to the Americans, everything has become confused.

LUCY: He was in a big hurry. But he stopped to see me.

JULIO: But something happened to my son.

LUCY: Now why would someone with lots a cash, a fast car, and coke all over his nose stop to see a fortune teller in the middle of the desert?

JULIO: A terrible thing. He started to spend time with people who offered him . . . easy answers.

LUCY: Only one reason. *He wanted to see his own future.*

JULIO: And it took him far from all of us—his home, his family, and yes, even his faith.

LUCY: He knew he was in trouble, and he wanted to know if he would escape. He said his name was Zacarías.

JULIO: Yes, I know I had been hard on him. But I had such great expectations! My only son! And his future looked so bright [gestures toward the distance] so bright! So naturally I had hopes . . . as we all have had hopes for generations, that maybe, maybe HE was the one, the one who was sent to deliver us.

LUCY: Well, I looked in his eyes. And what I saw wasn't good. For one thing, he hadn't slept in days. For another, he had this, this LOOK in his eyes, as though he had seen something—something—from out of this world.

JULIO: So, when he went away, I thought, "sometimes they must go away for awhile, and find themselves." I returned to my studies and tried to see what would happen to him.

LUCY: So I concentrated on his persona, on clues that I could get from his clothes, his looks, but especially his eyes. At first, all I could see was white. But then it began to get clearer.

JULIO: Sometimes, if I clear my mind, if I repeat a certain passage of the Psalms until all impure thoughts have been driven from my head, I can see . . . as though through a cloud, or into a dream . . .

LUCY: Not a snowstorm . . .

JULIO: I could see . . .

LUCY: Not drugs . . .

JULIO: . . . my son!

LUCY: But a mountain. I don't know where . . .

JULIO: And oh! It was terrible! There he was, clinging to the side of a mountain!

LUCY: But definitely a mountain. And he was on it.

JULIO: What a terrible place to be!

LUCY: It was cold, so cold, I could feel it in my bones.

JULIO: But what was just as strange . . .

LUCY: So, naturally, I wanted my money up front. Twenty-five dollars, the usual for a simple reading. After all, I have to make a living, whether people like their futures or not.

JULIO: . . . was that he appeared to be happy! He *wanted* to be there, in this strange and alien place!

LUCY: So when I told him the truth, well, he got mad. He was hoping for something good, as we all are. But the feeling I got was very . . . cold. Other than that, I don't know what it meant. I was trying to figure out a way to put a good spin on it, but he could see it in my face. That's well, that's when he tried to hit me.

JULIO: Was he meeting someone? Had he received a sign? That's when I could no longer bear to watch.

LUCY: So I ran to the neighbor's and used her phone.

JULIO: I know that the Lord works in mysterious ways, and that perhaps my son's adventures are part of a greater plan.

LUCY: So then the police came. It's not my fault. It was his fate.

JULIO: And I pray every day for his safe return.

LUCY: That was yesterday. And I have this terrible feeling that he might return at any time. I can't get his image out of my head.

[Each looks into plate / ball]

JULIO: Who is that woman?

LUCY: But who is *that* guy?

[LUCY and JULIO move back and forth, mirroring each other]

JULIO: She looks like a, a . . .

LUCY: Some kind of religious guy! He's wearing some kind of a funny little hat, you know, like those guys with the hair . . . [She makes a gesture of curly sidelocks]

JULIO: *Como una gitana.* A gypsy. But I've never had a vision like this before . . . She looks so . . .

LUCY: And he's wearing a, a, shawl. [Looks at her own shawl] Kind of nice. Different. He looks so, so . . .

BOTH: . . . foreign.

LUCY: Like someone from the past.

JULIO: Like someone from the future.

LUCY: My past?

JULIO: My future? Or a future, one among many?

LUCY: Does this have something to do with Zacarías?

JULIO: What is the meaning of this vision?

LUCY: I don't know if I've ever actually seen anything so, so *clearly* in this thing before. [Checks behind the crystal ball]

JULIO: Could this be a sign to *me*?

LUCY: But what does it mean?

JULIO: Am I supposed to do something? Is my son in danger?

LUCY: Is he coming back? Am I in danger?

BOTH: [Shouting, faces close to the plate / ball] TELL ME!

[Bright flash—both pull back in wonder]

JULIO: I wonder if she can hear me.

LUCY: Maybe . . . Hello-*o-o* . . .

JULIO: She's starting to fade—if you see my son—

LUCY: Oh, it's getting dimmer, cloudy . . . *Wha-a-t?*

JULIO: Tell him, tell him that I—

LUCY: All but gone now, just a mist—

JULIO: Tell him that I love him!

LUCY and JULIO stand, looking into their instruments. They remove the shawl, yamulke and prayer shawl, fold them carefully on the table. They blow out the candles, pick up the table and move it upstage before exiting the way they came in. 📖

Family Grooming, Seattle, Photograph, by Irene H. Kuniyuki

Slouching Toward Aztlán

Stephan Magcosta

Please allow me to introduce myself,
I'm a man of wealth and taste.

No—not the devil. Though some feel my growing presence signals the end of life as we know it. I'm not here for sympathy either, so don't look at me like that as I stand on the curb, hoping someone stops to offer a day job.

Unless you claim indigenous blood, I was here before your ancestors. The Spanish originally charted this area from a settlement on Vancouver Island, and from the decks of the *Sutíl* and the *Mexicana*, sailing north from San Blas in 1792. A generation later Spain withdrew, leaving echoes on road signs and maps. Guemes and López, Pasco, Puerto de Nuestra Señora de Los Ángeles, now Port Angeles, y las Cascadas, the Cascades.

But some of us never left. We've been here more than two hundred years, strangers in a strange land. And more of us are coming back. Back to Aztlán.

The Aztecs called themselves the Mexica and traced their origins to the north, a mythical homeland called Aztlán, a place of reeds and white cranes. When they saw an eagle with a snake in its claw perched on a cactus, they built Tenochtitlán, now Mexico City. This is the stuff of pre-Columbian history and Chicano Studies.

Many of our homeless don't fit the traditional stereotype of the poor campesino. In an era when one out of ten Mexicans journeys al Norte through the tortilla curtain, we now have homeless brown people with training and a higher education, searching for minimum wage jobs. It seems the phenomenon of homeless who are highly educated former professionals draws media attention only when manifest in the Anglo community. Go figure otra vez.

So Feliz Cinco de Mayo. One hundred years before flower power was the rage of youth against the war in Vietnam, we took out Maximilian and Carlota, forever ending French rule south of the border. Bien cool—I don't live in the past. I'm as at home on the range in cyberspace as my vaquero ancestors who fearlessly rode the hills of Guerrero. And Tori Amos appeals as much as Tish Hinojosa.

This isn't because I've become more American. It's because America is becoming more me. I could say that bastardizing my culture with Happy Hour shooters and Taco Time specials lacks respect. But the truth runs deeper than convenient cliché. To paraphrase a dying conquistador addressing his indigenous captors, more of us will come, marry your children, and their sons will kill you.

America isn't a nation. It's a continent. So go ahead, put up a two-thousand-mile fence from TJ to Tejas. We'll eat mescalito, get down like Carlos Castaneda, and fly over your pinche fence.

Check it out. My father wasn't Mexicano, he was from another country colonized by the Spanish. But he lived in Mexico before emigrating to gringolandia. I asked him once how he got here. He told me he walked.

"No, Papa," I said. "I mean, how did you get to Washington?"

Me dice, "Oye, mijo. I just kept walking. One day, I was in Califas. After awhile el estado de Washington."

"Wasn't it dangerous," I asked, "because of the Border Patrol?"

My father smiled. "La Migra? No, mijo. I had help. The Cisco Kid was a friend of mine."

So yeah. We're coming back to where we've been for over two hundred years. It's what's hot. As for what's not—well, you don't see people driving in droves from Dover or Dublin. The growing influence is from the South and East, looking toward Asia.

We're coming back despite growing legislation to keep us out or give us la vida dura once we get here. In the meantime, late at night, on occasions like Cinco de Mayo, we curl up in sleeping bags where the ragged people go and listen to you cry out from cantinas the last words of Maximilian. Viva Mexico! As our parents tell us, *you don't become American, America becomes you.* 📖

Ryder's Light, 1989, Photograph, by Mary Randlett

Where the Quinault Runs into the Pacific: A Conversation with an Elder

Armando Martínez

Every star with no soul has died.
The poet sees saving the world, us,
the sea. Quick action and a full heart
make revolution. You write to see love.

I am poor with wood feet.
I am of you and those brown hands
cool as clay. Two worlds
different as above and beneath
water. I love love and struggle.

We search for a world where we can speak.
House lights shine into the sea and stop.
Turtles living full of squares. Ocean scars
salty chains. Here, green earth leaves
long hair in rain. Hands that rise
say, "change," and we begin.
Big, dark hats. I want to believe
the world is one line. Ocean floor
rebuilding homes poets live in.

Where did life begin?

Began in the holes
that form in the mind and mud.

Water running through. Grandfather. Eyes full.
Walking thick brush on the river's bank
with his cane, yelling at his dog,
or began
just the way
all rivers begin
in clouds
telling air
of wild women.

The Culture of Poetry, Survival in the 21st Century: Does Poetry Matter?

John Olson

[Editor's Note: This is the written introduction for a panel *Raven* produced in our forum series "Cultural Geography." It was supported by a grant from the King County Arts Commission/Hotel Motel Tax Funds. John Olson moderated and the panelists were Ted Joans, Colleen J. McElroy, Bart Baxter, Duane Niatum, and Sharon Hashimoto.]

This is a huge topic. I should say two topics. Concerning the latter, the "subtext" of today's discussion, I can only say yes, profoundly. "We are creatures of language and invent in turn with the sounds of our mouths," wrote Robert Duncan in *Fictive Certainties: Essays,* "or hands beating surfaces, or with marks upon a stone or arrangements of sticks, and other speech, a speech 'for its own sake' in answer to the World Order which was a language before ours." Poetry promotes a heightened awareness of particularity, of a reality larger than our own personalities, or history, or family, or city, or nation, or species. Poetry means different things to different people, but "for those of us whose sense of our common humanity has been outraged, the poem seems primarily political in its meaning: to arouse the conscience of the people against the existing order of dominion."

Concerning the head topic, the survival of poetry in the 21st century, I'm not so sure. It's a very confusing and heavily conflicted picture.

Discussions over the legitimacy of poetry are old; in European culture, they go back to the days of Plato, who felt doubtful about including poets and poetry in his utopian republic. "At all events we are well aware that poetry being such as we have described is not to be regarded seriously as attaining to the truth," said Socrates, "and he who listens to her, fearing for the safety of the city which is within him, should be on his guard against her seductions." In his *An Apology for Poetry*, Sir Philip Sidney, at the close of the sixteenth century in 1595 (which, incidentally, is the year Shakespeare quite probably composed *Richard II*, *Romeo and Juliet*, and *Midsummer Night's Dream*), lamented the state of poetry in England: "Poesy, thus embraced in all other places, should only find in our time a hard welcome in England, I think the very earth lamenteth it, and therefore decketh our soil with fewer laurels than it was accustomed . . . and now that an over-faint quietness should seem to strew the house for poets, they are almost in as good reputation as the mountebanks at Venice . . . so serves it for a piece of a reason why they are less grateful to idle England, which now can scarce endure the pain of a pen."

In the last decade or so here in the United States there has been a plethora of articles and books about the demise of poetry. "Who Killed Poetry," by Joseph Epstein, a particularly virulent statement about the snobbishness and obscurity of modern poetry, first appeared in *Commentary* in 1988, and was reprinted in an "extravagantly acrimonious symposium" in *The Writer's Chronicle*, the journal of the Association of Writers & Writing Programs (AWP). "Can Poetry Matter," by Dana Gioia, appeared in *The Atlantic Monthly* in May 1991. He, too, characterized modern American poetry as a cloistered, exclusive cult, made up of impotent sectarians more serious about making careers in institutions than producing a vital and quality art. "American poetry now belongs to a subculture," Gioia proclaims. "No longer part of the mainstream of artistic and intellectual life, it has become the specialized occupation of a relatively small and isolated group. As a class, poets are not without cultural status. Like priests in a town of agnostics, they still command a certain residual prestige. But as individual artists they are almost invisible." And in "Dead or Alive? Poetry at Risk," an article by Stephen Goode that appeared in the August 23rd issue of *Insight Magazine* in 1993, the author describes a befuddling perplexity: "Is poetry in America a lost cause? Widely popular in the nineteenth century, has it now been overwhelmed by the proliferation of other media—TV, films—that offer more instant gratification and more accessible entertainment? Or is poetry a dozing giant, gathering its strength, ready to rise from the backseat it has taken for so long and become, once again, a potent force in American life and culture? Plenty of convincing evidence can be mustered on both sides, revealing the state of confusion poetry is in these days. It's a long-simmering— and often volatile—debate about what audience poets should be reaching, what their goals should be and whether poetry has any purpose at all in late twentieth century American culture."

When I told a friend I was going to be moderating this discussion, and the topic of the discussion, he was extremely surprised. He thought poetry was all the rage right now. What with two TV shows, *The United States of Poetry* and *The Language of Life*, hosted by Bill Moyers, and gazillions of magazine and newspaper stories about the popularity of rap, poetry slams, poetry readings, poetry awards, poetry contests, poetry kings, poetry queens, poetry junkies, poetry janitors, and poetry plumbers, one might well assume that the entire North American continent was nourishing itself on a steady diet of poetry every day. But hey, this is the media, and we all know how much the media wants to please us and entertain us. The media has a bottomless facility for distortion. Remember the windstorm of last November? The media made it sound like the entire Northwest was about to be crushed by a wall of raging wind. They closed down the University of Washington. People rushed home in a panic. It was Orson Welles's radio production of *War of the Worlds* all over again.

Nevertheless, there is some truth to the popularity of poetry. Dana Gioia remarks that "there have never before been so many new books of poetry published, so many anthologies or literary magazines. Never has it been so easy to earn a living as a poet. There are now several thousand college-level jobs in teaching creative writing, and many more at the primary and secondary levels. Congress has even instituted the position of poet laureate, as have twenty-five states. One also finds a complex network of public subvention for poets, funded by federal, state, and local agencies, augmented by private support in the form of foundation fellowships, prizes, and subsidized retreats. There has also never before been so much published criticism about contemporary poetry; it fills dozens of literary newsletters and scholarly journals. The proliferation of new poetry and poetry programs is astounding by any historical measure."

On the surface, this is a very encouraging picture. But it's also a very false picture. Because at the same time as this explosion of publications and readings and creative writing programs, the audience continues to diminish. The same person who expresses astonishment over the alleged demise of poetry might be asked what poet they read: the answer would probably be "none." And if you asked that same person who Robert Creeley, or John Ashbery, or Joy Harjo, or Lyn Hejinian was, chances are they wouldn't have a clue. Allen Ginsberg is the only poet to emerge as a readily identifiable public figure in this country. But much of his fame rests on being a larger-than-life cult figure, a colorful and articulate spokesperson for America's subculture.

I've been attending poetry readings vigorously over the last several years and the more I attend them the more I begin to feel like I'm living on an asteroid. I keep seeing the same faces, time and time again. Now don't get me wrong. I like these faces; they're the faces of people I like. But they're the same faces. *Poetry Northwest* considers 40,000 poems a year," writes Charles Molesworth in *The Fierce Embrace*, "though the magazine has fewer than one thousand subscribers. Grim quip that it is, it is true: more people write poetry than read it."

The poets I've talked to about this forum and its topic react very differently, and have very different things to say, but the general consensus seems to be that it's a silly and boring topic. Who cares if poetry is marginalized? Of course it's marginalized. That's precisely where it should be. Poetry does just fine in the margins, thank you. And in fact there's a quote by the French surrealist poet André Breton which happens to be among my favorite quotes, the kind of quote I wouldn't mind having done in needlepoint and hanging on the wall, right above my desk: "Public approval is to be avoided above all. It is absolutely necessary to forbid the public entry if one wants to avoid confusion. I further emphasize that it is vital to keep the public exasperated at the door by a system of defiance and provocation."

Now why do I feel this way? I feel this way because it's vital to keep poetry free. Free of bias, free of assumption, free of preconception, free of certainty, free of dogma, free of adulteration and dilution and compromise.

In the preface to his collection of essays, *Prisms* (1955), Theodor W. Adorno wrote, "to write poetry after Auschwitz is barbaric. And this corrodes even the knowledge of why it has become impossible to write poetry today." So pervasive is the trend toward cleansing the world of difference and particularity, toward placing a marketable value on everything that exists, that even the attempt to resist it in art and poetry becomes a commodity, a product with a value and a market. I hope Adorno's assessment proves as wrong as it is bleak, but we live in a time that is so relentless in its push toward a homogenized world, so invincible in its economic grip, planet earth is going to end up as one big ball of concrete bristling with banks and parking meters. My feeling is we need fewer parking meters, fewer parking lots, and more sonnets and haikus exchanged on the daily market. 📖

New Colossus

JT Stewart

I came to the city
and slept in phone booths
when it rained.
—Ed Elmo
(Native American Poet)

Respect this phone booth
here on Broadway
Forget AT&T MCI Sprint
all their glossy seductions

Regard this phone booth
opening its glass bifold door
"to the tired
the poor
the
huddled masses yearning to breath
free
The wretched refuse
of our teeming streets"

Tonight
a man
who still speaks Lushootseed
braids and all
beds down here
what he dreams of no one knows

Tonight
as the millennium comes
he will carve a glass poem
that only ravens understand

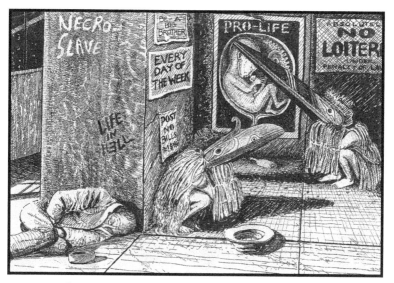

The Long Arm of The Law, 1993, Drawing, by Jon Strongbow

kiss/her. that/she. don't/know/*howwww.*

Carletta Carrington Wilson

in powdery blue dark   she is *dream/dancin'*   night/so/long
    with him

               breath   breath
                   beneath
                        they nod   *into the nape*

                               of/a/melodious/song
                    nal
                 tur
involutions . . . currings . . . a   noc
                    pulse   *and/him*

intricate incantation of gourd   marimba   sax-o-phone

               wrapped/in   the/rhythm   of/hymns
be/there/them
      dreaming prayers
          in vernal mouths
            violet/black blooms
               blossom up a room
                 transfigured sweet toil
                   full of nectar & soil

            inside each cry
        a pink pulsing heart
      radiantly rooted
      night-dressed in nocturnes
    herbivorous with hue of momentous blues
blowin' one velvety crush onto a sunset's blush

sun & moon
    do croon
      to the dizzyin' abyss
        of a lunar-tailed kiss
          dancin'   romancin'
            their silvery
             night. lighted. hair

XV

VOLUME 6, NUMBER 1
FALL 1996

Closed Book, 1995, Painting, by Barbara Earl Thomas

Love's Labor Lost: Equality

Omar S. Castañeda

I. Illicit Hues

She thought she might become a terrier, her toenails clicking in his kitchen, her head cocked expectantly at his door, her tongue flicking up. She thought she would circle his mountain goat rug until curling comfortably at his feet. She might accept a woman wanting him in front of the fire—their drinking of blood-red wines, their laughter, the woman's smooth delicious throat. She'd content herself with his fingers under her muzzle, scratching, his large hand stroking the arch of her back. All because someday he would make room for her on his bed, say in his husky, sonorous voice, "That's my good girl," or "Yeah-ess: Princess, Bay-bee, Sweet-ums." And there in his sheets, she would ascend into metamorphic dreams. It was uncertain.

On Tuesdays, with the regularity of ash, she waited in the alcove beside his office. She always imagined him coming out of his room, asking her for a piece of paper to write a quick note for another student. "Oh," she'd hear him say, "you got, maybe, a piece of scrap paper or something," his eyes not really looking, not really stopping, but scurrying over the flat surfaces of the alcove.

In that dream, she pulls out a Bic pen, blue, and places the thin blade in her hands. The ink bleeds through her skin and is siphoned up by his fingertips. She is perspiring, nibbling her inner lip, until she can't take it anymore and flees. "Hey!" he shouts. "I just wanted a goddamned scrap from you." His voice is very high; his forearms are veined with ink, his mouth dribbles blue. "Just something! Just a little bit of nothing!" But his voice is far away, trailing, diminishing, like a tail of comet dust.

On Wednesdays, she watched him from a campus park bench and found something of a dromedary in him: his long neck and reflective pose; his woolly chin-chin.

On Thursdays, she cracked pistachios between her knees and waited for him to appear and for her breath to disappear. Always, it was the secretive dip of his fingers into his inner coat pocket that sent her writhing, salty red spots dappling her knees.

On weekends, she imagined two hundred phone calls.

Courting? This?

When she finally sleeps with him it is his back that grows curly black hair. Yes. He growls into her ear. His face lengthens. His nose grows cold. He laps affectionately at her throat. He, ha-ha, he!

"Sit!" she says. "Heel!"

She falls impatiently back into his pillow and lights a Camel Filter.

He whimpers away.

Blue smoke rises to the ceiling. She can hear him lapping his red thing and wonders how she ever thought he was so?

He crouches in the corner.

Handsome? Dangerous?

One of his legs paddle-wheels at a flea and scratches against the blue shag rug.

"God, Frank. It's not like we promised each other anything."

"Yip."

"I was honest with you from the start."

"Woof."

Her hand droops to the edge of the bed. She feels exhausted. "God. OK."

He comes trailing an ecstatic spray of pee. Yellow.

"I'm sorry," she says.

His tail slices the air.

There is power yet in his beagle eyes: Her heart unfrowns. "Was it anything I did?"

"No," he whispers, feeling the bones of his teeth shrink back. "No."

"Sure?"

"It was me."

"Hmm?" She watches his ears shorten; lobes begin to appear.

"I mean it was me."

"M-hmmm?" But she is remembering the smell of a Baskin-Robins, long ago. When? Where? One we went to?

"I mean, why—" he says, "that is when—I asked for, you know, to lie down . . ."

"Yes-ums?"

"Down, lie down, I said. With the begonia over your ear. And the butter dribbled—"

"Better?"

"Butter! Are you deaf?"

"But you wanted it melted."

The word brings back his erection.

She giggles. "It was too hot."

His tongue flicks up against her earlobe.

"You're my professor!" she whines with exaggeration, her fingers curled lightly around him.

Frank shudders. He leans his head back to better feel her intimate caress. But something else takes hold of him and he crumples into her lap.

"What?" she asks.

His fur reappears. His paws grow hard curved nails. "I'm afraid," he confesses.

Marcelina nods. And softer, her voice bruised, her voice filling with something genuine: "Me too, Frank."

Another man stands atop a brown building facing his Victorian literature professor's colonial house. "Aargh!" we hear. Or perhaps, "It's me! Why can't you see this?" Or, "Oh! Oh! Oh!" It is a voice. Heard atop a brown building. Only that is certain.

II. Original Sin

7 Parrot noticed yellow flecks shifting in the river bottom. He tried, rather naively, to pinch out the gold with his fingers, but failed. Instead, he scooped out a handful of sand and placed it into his cupped shirt. The water drained away, leaving a pile of gold-streaked sand. He again tried to pick

away the minute flecks, but it was really a hopeless task. The flecks he did manage to pull out were not enough to cover a fingernail. 7 Parrot saved the gold between his gums and front teeth. It was painless and efficacious.

Later, in a playful mood, 7 Parrot merely smiled to show off his find. Shield Bearer was impressed. She took her husband's arm, wiggled a fingernail up to his elbow and pulled him close. "Palomita!" she said with teeth set on edge.

7 Parrot kissed her and pulled back to be marveled at again. Shield Bearer, however, had marveled enough in this passive way. She slowly undid his binding clothes. She ran her fingernail across his nipples, along the muscles of his belly till they twitched beneath the skin. She kissed his hip bone, softly, suckingly, her admiration full of tongue.

7 Parrot smiled goldenly into Shield Bearer's desire. She stroked his brightly colored beak and whispered, "Macaw. Lord. Christ!" She rubbed the red and yellow feathers of his cheek back toward his neck. "God, I want you," she said, removing his trousers from around his scrawny ankles.

Wrapped in each other's arms, they could not comprehend anything of the world outside their love. So, it was with difficulty that they separated the next morning. They argued viciously with their touches and tongues—both of them arguing against working that day—but shadowing those same arguments was the argument that won: that their reunion would be even more ardent once ripened with anticipation.

In the field, 7 Parrot stared into the air and allowed his desire for Shield Bearer to consume him, to build in him a series of images that entwined with such speed that their connections seemed mystical, magical, beyond any guiding frame. He saw egg dripping from the bottom of a nest. He climbed the golden tree and found two whole eggs and the scattered shell of a third. He re-imagined the fluid as it had protruded like a translucent twig, became globular, then dropped under its own weight. This image brought back, first, the previous night's passion, then his gold-flecked teeth reflected in Shield Bearer's eyes. Then he imagined the lump of sand by the river with its tiny gold flecks. Instantly, 7 Parrot envisioned the viscous and loving gaze of his wife pouring through the nest.

He suddenly grasped the knowledge emerging from that infinite sea of images, and plucked the nest from the tree as if it were an apple. Back at the river, he scooped the gold speckled sand into the nest. In time, he managed to pan a nugget of gold the size of his littlest tooth.

Ah. The lovers' passionate cries sprang from their throats as birds do, sharply, from vermilion hills, and the air burst with their vespertine fervor as the sky shocks in storm.

"It is from that moment on," 7 Parrot recounted to Shield Bearer as they lay in bed, "that I gave up farming. There is nothing but the ordinary in it. I have come home with gold in my teeth! I have stood before my wife with the sun a parturition of my mouth. You have turned my life from one of drabness to one of passion."

"I love you," she replied.

"I love you, my apple. Oh, I love you." 7 Parrot kissed the curve of her shoulder. "Together, there's nothing we can't feel, nothing of passion we will not have as our own."

Shield Bearer blushed with his excitement. "As for me," Shield Bearer said finally, solemnly, still breathless from their intimate struggle, "I've decided to shadow you. Where you thrive, so will I. Where you breathe, my happiness abounds."

7 Parrot stroked her moon face. "Follow me."

"I am your shadow," she said.

The following day, 7 Parrot took the bird nest and a pot and prepared to experiment. He put a particularly glittery pile of sand into his pot and resolved to go through it later, fleck by fleck. When 7 Parrot thought to look in the pot, the sand was dried. He stared dumbly at the pile and harrumphed through his nose. The air whisked away the minute grains. The flecks of gold remained still. He harrumphed again and the soft grains of sand blew to the side of the pot. In this way—humphing and harrumphing—7 Parrot cleared enough sand so that he could lift out the gold. But he grew impatient—and not a little hyperventilated.

7 Parrot recalled how volcanoes made a pudding of rocks, trees and not just a few animals. From that moment on, he knew fire was the route to glory. He proved the correct stacking of stones and earth to funnel heat. With that furnace, he discovered the various melting points of matter. It wasn't long before he created a metal pot and attempted his first smelting of gold. His first attempts taught him the problems of separating gold from iron, gold from bronze, gold from limestone. He wasted precious gold as quickly as he extracted it, with nothing more to show for it but curiously gilded pots and pans and long handled tongs. It wasn't until he had smelted enough worthless items to fill an ark that he discovered very little heat was needed to smith his fleck and gold nuggets into fine gold sheets. He looked back on the piles from his Stone Age, Iron Age, Bronze Age and giggled with pride.

After weeks and months, 7 parrot and Shield Bearer stepped into the dull wine light of the world and lit up the sky. Everywhere the first people begat and disseminated so that among their multiplicity there would be some who recognized the true Sun and Moon, and others who were chattel.

Dressed in quetzal feathers, leg trappings, ear pins, nose plugs and gold-threaded clothes, 7 Parrot exclaimed: "I am great and shall rule over all people. I am the sun and light, you are the moon and shadow. Great is our brightness. We are the track and the path for the world. Our eyes are silver, our faces green jade, blue turquoise. When we walk, people will say that the sun has arisen. They will say that the moon is soon to follow. They will cry out that they have no fear in the valley of the sun and the moon."

Shield Bearer smiled her gold covered teeth. Gold dots hung beneath her eyes, in her ears were long pieces of green jade, interlaced with gold. Her fingernails were rounded in jewels.

"We are the creators," 7 Parrot said, "we parure of the earth."

Shield Bearer stroked her husband's arm. She ran two fingers from his beak, down his feathered chest and to the warm bunch behind a golden brooch. "Make love to me," she said.

III. A Bird In Hand

"I am Destroyer of Mountains," he says. 2 Leg flattens seedlings and flowers with as much joy as he swats down insolent trees and stony crags. With bitter tears streaming down his face, he stamps down the mountains, so that, to others, he seems a mere monster bent on destruction, but truly he is filled with a dream of fairness.

"Goddamn you!" he roars at whatever rises up. When he stamps his feet, the mountain tops crumble. Birds fly up from the roiling dust.

He chases a blue cloud of birds northward. He screams at them, his arms flailing, but they fly on. Lumbering northward, he sees the earth turn colors beneath his feet. Above, the sky swirls vermilion, blue-black, suddenly turquoise. He walks.

Leagues out, 2 Leg surprises a covey of quail. The birds erupt, skimming beside the weed entangled arms of 2 Leg, snipping the air with their small beaks, screaming at him in terror. He captures one. The tiny head rubs from side to side over his fingers. Even with rough hands, 2 Leg can feel the nervous muscles and the rapid beating of its heart. 2 Leg strokes the feathers against his coarse cheeks. He holds the creature under his nose. He smells the sky tucked there among the wings and sees the slowly rolling clouds move across the bird's eyes.

"It isn't fair," he says.

A sorrow moves across his throat and belly like the flush of blood after breaking fast. He draws his fingers across the animal's face, stroking backward from the beak. He rubs downward over the frail neck, the trembling wings. He caresses the rubbery belly, then fingers the twig legs to their knotty knees.

"We should all be alike," 2 Leg whispers.

He pinches the skull. Fluids spill over his knuckles. He tears a wing from the body and rubs it over his chest. He rips free the other wing and rubs it up and down his bare legs. He pinches off the crushed head and lays it beside the wings, then he carefully snips down the torso with the tips of his teeth.

The bird's body opens. Fluids trickle down his forearms as he scoops the bird over his nose, eyes and mouth. He breathes the inside of the bird. He licks deep the red cavity. He shudders. He licks against the wet and fleshy insides and shudders. He swallows the small organs tongued loose like pearls and cannot control his shuddering. He slides the bird mask down to his neck and rubs the warm blood around his throat. "Ungh," he groans.

2 Leg places the remains over the wings and head, and rolls face down over the dissected bird. He stands erect.

There in the north, where the earth turns white against the sky, 2 Leg discovers how to capture birds. He fills bushes with salt, places lime on branches and sets tar across feeders. Once captured, they fall to his cruel investigations. Boiling the live bodies, he discovers their methods of screaming. He sees how their bones move to carry their plump weight; how a finger has extended to give them flight; how hair coarsens into feathers; how the beak of a lowly lizard hides inside each soaring bird. He sees this and breaks his finger by trying to extend it. He coats his head with mud and allows the stinking entanglement of hair to harden. He eats the birds' raw bones. He eats their twitching wings. He pushes their mangled bodies into his mouth and jumps from trees to fly.

When all this causes not one bit of change, 2 Leg grabs the birds and fills their stomachs with stones. He pulls out their feathers and covers them with grass. He removes their legs and lets them roll in the wind like tumbleweeds. But they multiply faster than he can kill them.

One day, 2 Leg catches the smell of roasting flesh. He smells grease sizzling in fire and sees birds cooking to a golden brown. There is no one around. 2 Leg approaches and lets the smoke rise up into his face. "This is wonderful," he says. He closes his eyes to enjoy the precious odor of roasting flesh. He revels in the charred flesh spit over an orange-red fire.

2 Leg shudders.

"This is fine," he says huskily. "Oh, this is very fine." He lifts out one of the birds. He holds the stick in both hands like a lover's token, holding it close to his chest, his elbows pressing into his sides, his face mooning over the charred birds.

2 Leg rubs the side of his face against the cooked bird. He enjoys the slipperiness of his face as he runs a finger through the smudge of grease. "Very good," he says.

He inserts the entire stick and bird into his mouth. He chews open-mouthed so the flavors permeate his throat, his nasal passages and rise up to his eyes. Bits and pieces fall from his lips. Bits of the wood, pieces, stick to his teeth. He shudders and drools.

Women appear by the clearing.

2 Leg swallows what remains in his mouth and eyes them. He feels the freshly eaten bird roaring like poison in his stomach.

They say nothing. They do not move.

"I am Destroyer of Mountains," he says, but falls to the ground in pain.

The women move to stand over him. His body convulses.

"There was a mountain inside you," they say. 📖

For The Lummi Girl Who Found Her Magic In Horses

Tiffany Midge

Every other word she spoke was *horse this, horse that,*
with an other-worldly grin conjuring long salty afternoons
pony riding beneath the falling sun.
She could have been a silhouette traveling along the crimson
body of Arizona rock or circling the spiny backbones
of desert cliffs, she'd only visited in picture books.

If she told me her horse had wings and took her on nightly flights
through the shimmering stars straight to the moon,
I would have believed her.

If she told me her horse was a blazing ribbon of flame galloping
across the Pacific Ocean like a Jesus pony trotting on water,
running forever to save us, I would have believed her.

I could see she found her magic in horses.
I could see each time the word *horse* escaped from her throat,
an eruption of stretched sinew and bones of an animal too holy
to appear in daylight reached out to capture a fringe
of this world's curtain.

She attempted to keep their tossing heads in the corral of her heart,
their unrestrained tricks secured beneath the fence of her ribcage,
only they continued to fly out like the laughing wild spirit they were.

Horse spirit and horse magic ignited by the dreaming
of a Lummi girl
who sang their names in the shadow of sundown.

Who offered them the sweets of her voice in ragged meadows,
who called them her own in the pale blue mornings across the
land she calls home.

One by one they leapt into the classroom air,
and she pulled hard on their reins,
led them back in.

Blue Funnel Line, 1991, Photograph, by Dean Wong

Bitch

Kristin Naca

—for Carolyn Kizer

I

I slap your face
  say your name & hold
    you—insides flailing
till you slip, turn, & shake
  me down with your knuckles
    to the groove below
my eye, clinching
  skin between your teeth.
    My limbs lose to the cuffed
control, tight straight-
  lace tying me down, my clit
    an exposed slip-knot. They
have arms, legs, & muscles ache
  with spark, with burn. I remember
    days like gasoline
& bystanders jeering with
  flames of *dyke* & *bitch*
    ripping through to
hold lips to my lips, your
  thigh against mine & fingernails
    to my naked belly—this,
& the way you clamp
  your vagina tightening
    its grip around my fist.

II

The cold burn of snow,
Your white fingers slap
Against my dark skin.
Red imprint stings with
Blood & the quick pull/release
Of my pulse pleading
Yes & no & again.
& I say this color don't
Rub off & baby I know
When a beating's
A beating. This is something
Daddy don't
Talk about—his white
Skin against mine,
The sweat from his hand,
The smell that stays
On my skin for a week/
The one that doesn't smell,
The pleading that don't
Say no—just
No more. Marked my skin
With Blood & Emptiness.
But your white against
My yellowness, traces
Of vapor coming off
Your breath, oil from
Touches painting my body,
My gritty and colorless
Scars fill with you,
Blood & the quick pull/release
Of my own pulse pleading
Yes & no & again.

III

Bitch, my skin is
Twisting in your hands, my face pressed
  against the gridiron sky,
My eyes fill with tears
My ears laughing. And when I say
I love you, it is with
Everything I am and everything you are
And so my bitch I love you
  and bitch you.
Bitch this world.

Glimpses

Robert Shimabukuro

Childhood (Before Go Mainland)

1. Re-Creation

Slowly, wen' climb up the mango tree, and sit down where plenty branches and leaves come together. Make one perfect seat fo' watch ball game. From there, could see the whole field. Our jalopy house, look like ready to fall down, was the bleachers, where Mickey Mantle, Willie Mays, Hank Aaron, Ted Williams, Stan Musial, Jackie Robinson, all kind folks wen' hit some monstrous home runs. Sometimes wen' bust our window and land in the kitchen. Some even wen' way over the roof, bashing the banana plants in back of the house.

Infield and outfield grass, kinda tall, 'cause we no mo' lawn mower and had to cut all the grass with sickle. Balls going deep right field wen' wind through banana plants, one avocado tree, mountain apple tree, guava tree, torch ginger plants, and the mango tree I stay in. Left field, not much. Short poke to the bleachers.

"Ed Lopat, on the mound," I go, try copy Carlos Rivas, sportscaster in Hawaii. They recreate baseball all the time. My other favorite Frank Valenti. But this time I copy Carlos. "Toes the rubber. Starts his windup. Rocks, kicks, and fires. Low. Outside. Ball one."

Sam then wen' come out of the house. He nevah see me 'cause was partly hidden by the leaves. I crouch down, make sure he no see me. He pick up the ball. Funny looking, but okay. Mom wen' cover some futon stuffing with denim she got from old pair jeans. She stitch 'em up real good, so look like one ball.

Sam pick up one of the bats. No matter which one. They all the same. Broken bats we wen' scavenge from somewhere, glue, nail, tape 'em together. Good enough for our denim ball. He throw up the ball and swing. Miss.

"Swung on and missed. Strike one," I say softly. "Good curve ball. Williams steps out of the batter's box. Takes a good look at Lopat. Now steps back in. Cocks his bat as Lopat goes into his motion, winds, and fires."

Sam connect this time. Thud. He watch as the ball land on the roof.

"It's going, going, gone! Williams has just tagged Lopat for number thirty-four on the season!" I excited now.

Sam look up as he circle the bases. You could tell, he feel shame. He stop, and both of us watch the ball roll back into the yard.

Just then wen' hear a loud snap. I look back and see the broadcast booth broke from the main limb. "Ohhhhh!" I yell. First, I try jump off, then just ride the branch down. Wham! I hit the ground, but was real good luck because the leaves and the tall grass wen' break my fall.

Sam rush up. "You all right?"

"Yeah. A little shaky. Think I'm okay."

"How long were you up there, anyway? And what were you doing?"

"Broadcasting a Yankees–Red Sox game. Got a little lost. Thought you were Ted Williams."

Sam look at me, then at the leaves and branches. "Dumb. I was Yogi Berra," he say, then both of us laugh. Laughs of relief. Good thing too. Take away the shock of falling off the tree.

I look up the tree. About twenty feet off the ground was another similar spot. Ideal for broadcasting. But at twice the height of the old broadcasting seat. "Look, get another spot, up there. Higher. Can see better from over there, I think."

"Less leaves. You'll be able to see what's happening better. Be able to tell the difference between Ted Williams and Yogi Berra now. They're built totally different, you know." And he walk off.

He was right. Sam look like neither, but fo' sure was closer to Berra than Williams.

2. Asthma attack

I sit up on the futon Sam and I wen' put next to the sofa fo' sleep. I slowly roll over to the sofa, put my arm on the seat, lay my head on my arm. Slowly, I wen' breathe in, breathe out.

"You okay?" Sam asked, waking up.

Thought about asking him fo' turn on the light so I could read. Decided not to. When I have asthma attack, lotta times I sit cross-legged on the floor, j'like all the ol' folks, 'cept I go rest my head on the low table or sofa, and read till I fall asleep.

But no can read now, and get three-four hours before sunrise. Mo' bettah I get some sleep right away. But hard. Third time already I get asthma attack this school year and only November. Going miss another math quiz. Teacher already wen' ask how come I get sick on quiz day. Geez. J'like I getting sick on purpose. No fair. Nothing fo' do but wait. I wonder how long goin' take fo' get over this time.

"You okay?" Sam ask again.

"Some more asthma. Go back sleep. Wake you if need help."

"Sure?"

"Yeah," I tell him. Really not sure, but no like bother him. Think about school for little while, then wen' fall asleep. When I wake up, all sweaty. Was really hot. I like go *shiko*, but hardly can move, was so hard fo' breathe.

"Eh, Sam, wake up," I say, just loud enough so he hear me. Talk soft because otherwise use up too much air fo' talk. Better save air. "Gotta go *shiko*," I tell him when he wake up.

"Okay," he said, got up and grabbed my arm. He always so cheery and willing fo' help. Me, always so grumpy, especially when no can breathe.

He pull me up. I lean on his shoulder. We go down the hall to the toilet. He broad. Lots of shoulder fo' lean on. Strong back. He walk slowly fo' me. We walk like this: Gasp, wheeze. Take one step. Gasp, wheeze. Take another. All the way to the toilet.

When asthma not so bad, lean over, rest my hand on the toilet tank, go *shiko*. When real bad, gotta sit down on the toilet seat, leave the toilet door open and lean my head on the door knob. This time was real bad.

Sam wen' sit down on the stairs and wait. Funny kind house. Get three steps to one store room. Store room because nobody like one bedroom you gotta go through the toilet to get to.

"You going to school tomorrow?" Sam asked after a slight wait, a little sleepy.

"Don't know. See how I feel in the morning. *Pau* already. Help me back."

And we go back: Gasp, wheeze. Take one step. Gasp, wheeze, take another.

3. Sissy

"Sam, like play football?"

"Tackle or touch?"

"Tackle, maybe flag."

"Where?"

"Manoa Field."

"With who?"

"My friends. Rodney. Harvey. Gordon. Whoever else we can get."

"Oh."

"Why you ask all these questions? You like play or not?"

"No."

"Why not?"

"Just don't."

"Geez, Sam. Sometimes you so sissy."

He looked at me, hurt, then turned and walked back into the house just as Toki-nesan sauntered out to the porch.

"What did you call him?" she demanded, daring me to repeat.

"Uh, nothing," I replied.

"WHAT DID YOU CALL HIM?" she yelled.

"Uh, a sissy," I answered very softly.

"How dare you call him a sissy!"

I didn't know what to answer. I knew that I had hurt him, since he had turned and left, and Toki had heard me before I had a chance to follow Sam and apologize and repair the damage. It had happened so fast. Besides, I rationalized, however unfairly, the fact that Toki was fighting this battle for him right now seemed to prove my point.

But I had said it. There was nothing I could do now but weather this lecture from Toki. "He's your brother. He's your older brother. I don't want to hear you call him that again. Ever. You understand?"

"Yes," I answered contritely.

"Now go apologize to him."

I went into the house and looked for him. He was in the can. I sat outside and waited. Seemed like a long time.

"Sorry, Sam," I told him when he finally came out. "Was just a little frustrated."

"It's okay," he said softly. "You aren't the first to call me that." Those words, said softly and matter-of-factly, hit me like a fire-cracker. My head. My heart. My stomach. My neck. Everywhere hurt. Simultaneously.

I didn't feel like playing football any more. I moped around the house the rest of the day.

4. Monopoly

"Mom, can you play with us?" Sam asked after dinner.

"No, I've got too much work to do," she answered.

"Like what?"

"Oh, like washing the dishes, folding and hanging up the clothes."

"Well, if we help you will you play with us?"

Mom, not wanting to turn down an opportunity at a little volunteerism on our part (or at least Sam's part), but still wanting to see what Sam was negotiating, teasingly asked, "Play what?"

"Monopoly," Sam answered quickly. It was not one of Mom's favorite games because it was a long game, and Mom always felt that she had more work to do. It was not one of my favorites either, because I always tired of it after one or two hours. But Sam was

Canton Alley 1991, Photograph, by Dean Wong

negotiating. And after all, if we were going to help Mom, we had to get something out of it.

So there we were. Eleven-year-old Sam and me, just about to turn ten, washing dishes, while eight-year-old Ann was helping Mom with the clothes. Tom, home after one year at Columbia University, was lying on our couch in the "parlor," reading the *Honolulu Star Bulletin* after a day in the pineapple fields.

Dad was sitting on the floor at our dining table, reading the *Hawaii Times*, the Japanese language newspaper. His reading glasses, purchased from Kress store, were perched low on his nose.

Sam was happy and singing loudly. Mom had not played much with us lately. She seemed extremely busy and preoccupied, although she was happy that Tom had returned for the summer. "When you left, I thought, this could be the last time I might see you," she had told him.

New York was a long ways away. She was fully aware that after Dad had left Okinawa at age seventeen to come to Hawaii, he never saw his mother again. And when Tom left for New York City in 1952, it had been a seventeen-hour flight and cost more than our family could afford. I never did find out how my parents put together the funds for Tom to go to New York.

Our family went through some hard times while Tom was away. Cabbage and rice. If lucky, canned corned beef cabbage and rice. Or maybe cabbage soup and rice. I just remember a lot of cabbage. It seemed the worrying had taken its toll on Mom. But Sam was oblivious to all that now. Mom had agreed to play with us and all was right with the world.

Sam broke into my thoughts. "Get the hot water from the stove."

"Okay, here," I said, handing the kettle to him.

I watched him pour the water and some dish soap into a large bowl which we used as a dishpan. And he began to wash the dishes, while I rinsed. If I got ahead of him, I would dry some of the dishes. If he got ahead of me he would tend to the kerosene stove to heat some more water. It seemed to go on and on. Nine in our family, I had repeated to people often. "We' got enough for a baseball team." I was noting how many dishes nine folks used for one meal.

Sam had always been more optimistic than me. He just kept going through the dishes, repeating, "Mom's going to play Monopoly with us."

"If we ever get through these dishes," I answered, wondering where Roy was at, thinking we sure could use his help now. Six-year-old Ned was going back and forth between Ann and Mom with the clothes, and Sam and I with the dishes.

"They're almost done. You almost done?" he asked.

"Yes," said Sam.

"Especially if you help us," I piped in.

"Okay, but I'm helping Mom and Ann right now."

"Good. But first take these dishes and put them on the table," I said, handing him a couple of plates I had just dried.

As he reluctantly did as he was told (after all, he was younger than me), Sam's spirit brightened. "Ned, go get the monopoly set. We can start soon."

He scampered out of the kitchen, got out the monopoly set, and began setting up the monopoly board.

Sam was excitedly cleaning the sink and I was putting away the last few dishes, thinking that I would just bag the Monopoly and go to sleep, when I heard Tom say, "Oh, Mom's going to play? Great! Then I want to play too."

Dad perked up immediately. "What? Mom's going to play? Count me in." And he got up from his spot and went into the parlor.

Everyone wanted to play. Mom was a big attraction. A treat. I felt a sinking sensation. Ominous. I could see the pecking order coming in to play. Monopoly only had six tokens, or "kinis" as we used to call them. Six kinis. That's Dad, Mom, Tom, Toki, Roy, Sam. Stops there. No Bob, Ann or Ned. I was getting upset at this turn of events. I no longer felt like going to bed.

Sam saw it coming too. He was getting agitated. We quickly finished up and ran into the parlor. Not even a sixth kini for Sam. Ann and Ned had decided they would combine for one.

Sam exploded, and went into one of his fits. "This game is for us!" he yelled at Tom, Roy, and Dad. "Mom said she would play with us," with a big emphasis on "us," I might add.

"I tell you what," Toki offered. "Ann can play with me, and Ned can play with Mom, and you and Bob can play together. That way everybody plays. How's that?"

It seemed fair to me. It was late. I was going to drop off soon, and Ann and Ned would probably drop off after the first two or three rounds.

But Sam was not to be appeased so easily.

"NO," he screamed, as tears began streaming down his face. "It's not fair. This was for Mom and us younger kids!" And he didn't stop, continuing to challenge the established pecking order, and gathering steam as he continued. "You ALways have YOUR way! YOU NEVER let ME HAVE MINE! WE WORKED FOR THIS!" He was now screaming at the top of his voice.

I was in shock. All of us were in shock. It had been a while since Sam had gone off like this. But after spending all that time washing the dishes, I had to admit, he had a real gripe. But he was getting "onreal." And I also knew that any minute, Dad was going to blow his cool, and we would have a royal scene on our hands.

"Hey, Sam," I said, trying to get his attention. "Look, I'm tired. You don't have to share with me. I'll just go to sleep."

"NO!" he screamed at me, still crying. "YOU`RE GOING TO PLAY! WE'RE GOING TO PLAY WITH MOM! JUST US!"

That just about did it for Dad. "YOU GO TO BED! RIGHT NOW! ... NOW, I SAID!"

A sudden quiet came upon Sam. Deathly quiet. It scared me, when he got that way. He started to withdraw. He was there physically, but in no other sense. He knew he was not going to win. And he retreated to somewhere safe. He stared at Dad, looking through him, then walked away. I followed him. We got our futon, found a place to lay it out and got our toothbrushes. Sam didn't say another word the rest of the night.

"I'm going to put Ann and Ned to bed," Mom said quietly. "You folks can play."

"I don't feel like playing, if you aren't," Tom answered.

Dad simply walked away. Roy and Toki decided to forget the whole episode. Nobody played Monopoly that night.

After Go Mainland

1. Coming Out

Sam seemed to have something on his mind the whole weekend. But now he seemed ready to go home to Seattle. "Well, thanks for the hospitality," he said. "I gotta get going home."

"You want to get something to eat first?" I offered. "I got to go over to Cathie's a little later."

"You know I was going to ask you about that," he answered, then proceeded to pepper me with questions about my love life. Cathie and I had been separated for a few years, but we still did things together now and then. Sam was curious about that. And about the other women he had been introduced to when he had visited. I soon gathered that he was really trying to draw me into asking him about his love life.

"How about you? Any women out there for you?"

"You know, Bob, it's funny that you asked, but I've wanted to tell you something. It's been about two weeks; I decided to come out of the closet. Remember when you were up in Seattle with Mira last week?" His rapid-fire speech sounded very rehearsed. "And Mira wanted to know why I had those hospital slippers around the house? Well, I just didn't feel like telling her then. But the reason was I had some anal warts removed. I just couldn't tell Mira that. So I thought I'd just tell you the next time we were alone."

"Sounds awful," I commented, also realizing what he was really telling me. "How do you get something like that?"

"Gay sex," he said quickly, then paused waiting for a reaction.

"So . . . that's a hell of a way to tell me you're gay. You break the news to everyone by telling them about anal warts?" I asked, then burst out laughing. So did he, sounding relieved at my reaction.

"Well, as a matter of fact, others have made the same point. That I use the surgery as an opener. 'Weird,' they said."

"So, you're gonna tell the rest of the family?"

"Don't know. If anyone asks, I won't deny it. But I don't know when I'll tell the others."

"You want any help in this?"

"No. But likewise, if anyone asks, just tell them. I'll have to deal with it sooner or later."

"And Mom? You want me to tell her? Or you're gonna tell her yourself?"

"That's something I'll have to do myself."

"Well, I've got a suggestion. Don't tell her the same way you told me."

Sam and I cracked up again.

He then proceeded to recount his whole coming out process excitedly (and you had to know Sam to understand how exhilarated he was by it), his therapy, counseling, our early childhood together, the possible effects it would have on the rest of our family. Sometimes Sam would get worked up about stuff, and I just zoned out into my own world while he went on. A defense mechanism I had developed to deal with these moods of Sam.

When he was on to something it was best to just let him finish what he had to say. Sometimes, he would talk for ten, fifteen minutes straight, going over every itsy-bitsy insignificant detail. Often, his monologue, or tirade, or running commentary, would try my patience. But I knew that I could not interrupt him, nor could I change the subject. That would be tempting his emotional stability.

I instead thought about a scene twenty years earlier when I had called him a sissy. My stomach hurt once again. How cruel I had been. And I had missed the whole point of Toki's lecture.

I was brought back when I heard Sam say, "And I wrote this letter to Dad." Sam and Dad had gone through some rough times together. In addition to his moods of extremely charged verbal diarrhea, Sam was stubborn and tenacious. I mean, real stubborn. If he couldn't get his way, he went out of control. During those times, Dad had paid a lot of attention, some of it cruel, to Sam's emotional outbursts until he mellowed out some by the time he was seven or eight. But there was a price. Sam was socially paralyzed for years. Pacified and imprisoned. By Dad. By friends. Perhaps by a younger brother. By name-calling. Only when Dad died did Sam feel a little freer to express himself.

"What did you tell him?" I asked.

"Oh, it was a reconciliation letter. That I was doing fine. That I could accept him for what he was. And he could accept me for what I was. That I could go on with my life. I also told him I was gay, and it should be all right with him."

"What do you think he'd say?"

"Don't know," Sam answered, shrugging his shoulders.

2. Diagnosis

One day after Memorial Day, 1987, trying to put the pieces together. Sam has been trying to shake a cough for more than six months. And now, driving south to my sister Ann's home in Gilroy, California, a phone conversation with Sam and his partner Bruce, the night before, weighs heavily on my mind.

"Sam's very ill," Bruce said. "He's got pneumonia. Had a fever of 105 degrees in Northampton. The doctor there wanted to do more tests, but Sam wanted to come back to Seattle for the testing. We'll hear the results tomorrow." He sounded serious.

Sam, a little more optimistic as usual, said he was fine, much better than a week ago.

All three of us had refused to mention what we all suspected. We didn't dare. Perhaps we had feared compromising the test results.

Sam's cough had been puzzling. Then forty-three, he had always been so healthy. He generally shook off colds and other viruses quickly. He had gone entire school years without missing a day. I found his school attendance records somewhat miraculous, since I had spent so much of my childhood ill at home.

My mind had been racing during the fifteen hours on the

road. Ann greeted me and said quietly, "Sam called. Wants you to call him. Said he tested positive for AIDS."

Feeling very tired, beaten and resigned, I called him. "I've got pneumocystis," he says, "the pneumonia that confirms AIDS."

3. Prognosis

Octber 18, 1988. A cold, foggy, drizzly day in Seattle. Dr. Dreis broke the news gently to Sam, Bruce, Lesli, and me: his life could be measured "in terms of days and weeks rather than months. Also I wouldn't want to pound on your chest and break your ribs and cause you more pain just on the chance you could live a few more hours," he told Sam softly, his voice slightly wavering.

It apparently came as a surprise to Sam. He still looked upon his death as an event in the "distant" future. Dreis' words hit him hard. "Well," he said, in his inimitable definitive manner, "I'll still have hope," just daring anyone to take that away from him.

"Great!" answered everyone in the room.

"Well, miracles do happen," offered the Doctor. "Are you afraid?" continued Dreis.

"No," answered Sam.

"Are you surprised, Sam?"

"Yes, a little. In Northampton, I figured out that I was going to die before I was forty-five. But I still looked at it as the distant future."

"Are you sad?"

"Yes, but even more for Bruce. I'll be gone. But Bruce will be alone."

I was surprised that Bruce and Leslie maintained their composure. But everyone was crying. I felt like mush. I was standing, and I felt like I was watching a movie, distanced from the scene. I felt the tears rolling, but I also saw some stardust. My legs started to buckle. I leaned against the shower door until I felt better, and moved to a chair. It was quiet in the room. Deathly quiet. I don't know how long. . . .

Although Sam still talks about his life in terms of months, he is dealing with the brevity. "My only regret is that I won't live long enough to see the day Reagan leaves office," he told us. And later, he added with a resigned sigh, "I guess I'll never see the Mariners in a World Series."

Commented Leslie, "Neither will we, Sam."

4. Sam and the Bank Manager

There is a lot of flurry one morning as Sam decides to get up off his deathbed and pay a visit to a bank manager who has been "hassling" Sam over some unpaid bills of "his" now-defunct Brass Ring Theater.

Esti, who is caring for Sam that day, and Bruce (by phone) try to convince Sam that it is not in his best interests, health-wise, to argue with the bank, or even go out. Of course, Sam wins the argument, as he simply threatens to drive up to the bank himself. Esti falls into line. Upon arrival at the bank, Sam orders Esti, "You sit in the car. I want to do this alone."

A worried Esti sits in the car, waiting, as a shriveled, unshaven, disheveled Sam, dressed in clothes now five sizes too large and barely able to walk, dukes it out with the neat and proper bank manager. Who knows what transpired? Sam wouldn't say. "Well," he tells Esti as he slowly pulls himself back into the car, "I guess he won't be bothering me again."

He was right about that. Nobody's bothering him now. 📖

En La Casa Museo de Augustin Lara, Veracruz

Gail E. Tremblay

—for Lidia Huante

I wandered around looking at pictures,
photos that measured a lifetime spent
writing the music beautiful women loved
and sang, women that teased lyrics alive
with their tongues, making notes caress
like kisses 'til a whole generation swooned
over this man's words, rhythms, his harmonies
that vibrated so gracefully against the skin.
And the women in the photos were not just
beautiful, they sang insouciantly, the spice
of their spirits lit their voices, they gave
more light than candles—they were the saints
every sinner wished to pray to. The house sat
on a corner, a pristine white and full of wind
blowing in over a shimmering sea. Everything
felt fresh and full of whispering energy.
The piano was placed near a window
overlooking the waves, home of conches
and luminous fish, a place where palm trees
couldn't help but get a little drunk on the sun.
I sat on the white divan, and a charming
older man played every song I named.
Twice I cried, longing for you, my friend,
whose mother, a cook for farm workers,
died much too young when you were only
seventeen. We who grew up on different
coasts, on rock and roll, years later
would celebrate your mother's memory

cooking mole for Thanksgiving and playing
Toña La Negra singing with that weighty
woman's voice all these marvelous
compositions that keep memory alive—
Oh how I miss your presence in this room.

Black Tulip, Photograph, by Theodore C. Van Alst, Jr.

Casa de Cortez, Antigua, Veracruz

Gail E. Tremblay

Light sifts through leaves of trees
that perch atop the walls of this ruin
and send adventitious roots scaling down
to finger dirt beneath red tiled floors
and round stones that pave the patio
of this old house, the first skeletal remains
of a colonial floor plan laid out
to make foreigners feel at home
in someone else's country. One wonders
at Cortés' luck, given as a gift Malinalli.
At first, he tried to give her away
to one of his lieutenants, but realized,
it didn't matter whether or not
he found her pretty—she was his fate;
she had the tongue he would use
to reshape a continent, to make allies
he would later betray as he did her.
But at this point in the story,
it was her skill with languages
that amazed him—in a mere month,
she could whisper in his ear words
he learned from his mother; she could
answer his million questions, name
the unnamable things he had never seen.
He was her passage out of slavery;
she, a Mexican noblewoman, angry
at being tossed away by her own people.
In this house, she became mistress,
gave orders, advised the conqueror.
It was here that she learned
about a god whose death would end

the need to sacrifice to the sun,
and in whose name millions
would be sacrificed to foreign greed.
One wonders what she understood
of her role in history as she learned
to eat his bread. As she was baptized
Doña Marina, did she ever guess
how much suffering she would help
initiate? The people re-christened her
Malinche, she whose spirit haunts
these shadows trapped by her ancient
desires to have things the world refused,
getting instead an endless notoriety—
who by aiding the abuser became also abused.

Iconography of the Slain

Carletta Carrington Wilson

Sunday, 23rd, May 1751

All traces of shore have disappeared. The wind blows from the east. A dampness has settled into my clothes. Today, I insisted that I keep her in my cabin. Captain Davenport stared incredulously, protested heartily, then, abruptly, took leave.

Ever since I went down among them I fail to sleep. Air thicker than that which engulfed me on the coast burned within the hold. They stretched like the shadow of some putrid black river from end to end. Twisting towards me, straining against the irons, with barely enough strength to breathe, they raised themselves and glared, as we removed the dead. Every liquid contained within the bounds of human flesh comes coursing out. We are helpless to stop it. Some deliver their own final blow by willing themselves dead.

So the spirit lifted me up, and took me away, and I went in bitterness, in the heat of my spirit; but the hand of the Lord was strong upon me. Ezekiel 3:14

Let me start, again, from the beginning. Each time I begin again I discover something new. One small gem illuminates my memory. Who else can I speak to of this, but you? Remember, when I spoke to you that fated night? We were walking through a tunnel of fog. The air was chandeliered with a chill that even you noticed. With unaccustomed fervor I announced, no confessed, that I felt I was being called. Remember how the stones echoed my words? We were just returning from the meeting of the Society. It was our third meeting, was it not? But this night it was pressed upon me to go to visit my uncle in South Carolina to view the negroes firsthand. Your voice, raised in counterpoint against the passing din of a horse and carriage reassured me of your devotion.

With your blessings, with the support of the Society, I embarked, hopeful, reassured in the righteousness of my mission.

> *When I say unto the wicked, thou shalt surely die; and thou givest him not warning nor speakest to warn the wicked from his wicked way, to save his life; the same wicked man shall die in his iniquity; but his blood will I require at thy hand. Ezekiel 4:18*

My uncle, Robert B. Davis, received me cautiously. After so many years in America, I found him changed. He was unlike the man my mother spoke so fondly of on so many Liverpool nights. My uncle would not give me license to preach among his negroes. In every manner was I thwarted. Uncle, as well as the other planters, said they saw no need for the word of God to be spread among their slaves. "How can brutes without souls be in need of redemption?" they countered.

Each night, when the plantation was draped in a curtain of stars and clouds, I heard night creatures calling to the earth. From beneath its plowed flesh the earth sighed an answer.

It was placed upon my heart to journey to Africa. What a perfect solution! If we could ship slaves across the sea why not leave their heathenism in Africa and ship Christians, disembark souls bathed in the baptism of Christ from sea to sea?

> *Thou shalt know also that thy seed shall be great, and thy offspring as the grass of the earth. Job 5:25*

When I arrived at Cape Coast they had been without the benefit of a Man of God for some time. Africa overflows with infidels, white and black. Barbarous heathens, professors of Mohammed, and those who have no feeling for the church, abound. Therefore, I set humbly about my Father's work.

All I asked was that they grant me the opportunity to speak of the redemption of Christ. If possible, perhaps, I may perform the baptism for those who are called. The Governor said he would not stand in my way, but that the traders would not tolerate any interference in their business. They are not at cross purposes with me, I informed him. They must come to the fort, do they not? And are held here, yes? With the aid of an interpreter I could begin to go among them. Besides, there are gromettos, traders, mulattos, sailors, factors, and captains who, also, can benefit from the Lord's work.

When I lie down, I say, when shall I arise, and the night be gone? And I am full of tossing to and fro unto the dawning of the day. Job 9:4

I will purge myself of every ounce of memory of them. They, who are stacked, in irons, on shelves like so many pieces of meat. They, who came stumbling into town, wide-eyed, cringing, weak from fear. And me, praying for them, imploring them to pray for their idolatrous sins. Imploring them to accept God, a God whose faith is deeper than the inland roads, wet and dry, that reach into the interior and pull them out and across the sea.

24ᵗʰ, May 1751

The rains came last night. My dear, sweet Lucinda, I am most impatient to gaze, once more, upon your precious face to drink in every melodious word. You must know that I have not, once, betrayed you in all these lonely years. I do not betray you now, but I cannot bear to let happen to Solemn what has befallen so many of her kind.

26ᵗʰ, May 1751

I had drunk so much since I went down among them. When they refuse to eat, I force them. When their injuries are too much to bear I assist the surgeon in their care.

I did not know they captured her. She was standing near the women and children staring into the sea. When I caught her eye she turned away from me. Immediately, I raced to cover her nakedness with my shirt. She is young and delicate as a rose before bloom, this child in whom I see a becoming woman. I named her. Named her Solemn.

28ᵗʰ May

I first saw her during an evening when I was visiting the mulatto merchant, Jacob Moore, a man of much repute among natives and our men in the trade. I had just finished saying that I would, if necessary, present my case to the Governor if we could not come to some agreement alone. Weary of me he lapsed into a stubborn silence. I took the opportunity to examine his room, my eye becoming accustomed to the dimness. He had fashioned his abode in the manner of an Englishman. That he had once traveled to England was clear. There were relics of his visit, a small painting, some fine cloth strewn across a chair, two pewter goblets set awkwardly among wooden bowls. It is then I noticed someone standing in the shadows by the door. The setting sun fringed and framed the figure. Even so, I could not take my eyes off of her flesh, it being nearly the blue-black of the prized indigo cloth.

They were children of fools, yea, children of base men; they were viler than the earth. Job 30:8

10ᵗʰ June

Yesterday, cutting the water, I spied five or six sharks. The sun was working its way above the ship in air enraged with heat. Not one bird flew in the sky. I spied a black shouting at the men, "Me favorite fellah!" "Favorite fellah!"

Swearing, the men told him to shove off, but he seemed determined to make his point. Finally, Captain Davenport, carrying irons, came among them. The man hurried off. Strangely, he is the only black the Captain permits to move about freely. Every other man must endure irons laced about their ankles, choking them at the neck, piercing, pinching and tearing their skin. It is no wonder he refuses to be bound by them.

Sunday, 13ᵗʰ June

I counseled the Captain, I told him of my suspicion regarding the African. Earlier today, I saw him, curiously, demanding food

Last Book: Sing, Bird, Hope, 1995, Painting,
by Barbara Earl Thomas, Photograph by Richard Nicol

for *his* slaves. His torso was covered in gris-gris. How surprising to find them upon his person. Usually, the natives strip or are stripped of everything. Sometimes, as they board the ships, you can see them or the men throwing their beaded necklaces into the sea. Still, their chiseled teeth and flesh engraved with rude designs will ever remind them and us of the torrid land that birthed them.

Scarcely had the man begun his tirade when he spied the Captain coming towards us. He quickly moved on. I believe he was in league with Jacob Moore. Still, I haven't figured out the relationship between the Captain and the African. Why, of all the men slaves, is he allowed to move about like he is free?

The men call Captain Davenport "Deadeye" behind his back. The man has transported many, slave and free, across this treacherous sea. Accord to the men he lost sight in one eye to a disease which afflicts the negroes. It is an eye in which the whitened pupil is surrounded by a milky grayish blue. It remains in the same position no matter what the other eye may do. I imagine that it is fixed upon some unseen face or object. In fact, the eye reminds me of the eyes of one of our men who died on the coast. Revulsion and defiance are words that come to mind, but even they are not sufficient. I do not wish to see what that poor man saw upon his death. Half the cargo of this harvester of death barely rest among the living, the other half, clearly, already belong to the dead. The men say that the Captain's sightlessness gives him the uncanny ability to pluck the dead, the near dead, from among the living.

So it is, also, with us. The men and I move about the ship performing tasks of the living. But, when we rest our heads, we fall back upon cold, hard beds not confident we shall wake. Forgive me, my dear, my black mood. Days weigh upon me. I am uneasy, restless, and unsure. Nights are endless trials of fitful sleeping. I've taken to tying Solemn in the corner of my cabin with a thick rope. I know, but trust me my dear, it is for the best that I do so. Still, I sleep, dreamless, feeling as if someone is standing over me . . . watching.

I am poured out like water, and all my bones are out of joint; my heart is like wax, it is melted in the midst of my bowels. My strength is dried up like a potsherd; and my tongue cleaveth to my jaws; and thou hast brought me into the dust of death. Psalms 22:14-15

Soon after my arrival on the coast, I was beset with fever. For weeks I labored against illness until I had to, finally, take to my bed. Solemn was bought to care for me. She came in the company of an old wizen woman who had been teaching her the use of herbs and other potions. The Governor, I learned, intervened on my behalf. He paid Jacob Moore to come to my aid. Hampered by the cloak of fever my memory is vague. Yet, I know I traveled to the gates of that great kingdom and was about to cross the threshold when the touch of a cool hand upon my brow awakened me. Upon opening my eyes, questioning silent eyes gazed into mine.

Wednesday, 16th June

Today, the girls and women were made to dance on the deck. The men were made to drum. Our men pursued the females mercilessly. I spoke to Captain Davenport to no avail. Arguments erupted over them. The men conducted themselves shamelessly. Fights broke out. I checked to make sure Solemn was secure. I found her huddled in her corner clutching her shirt.

Friday, June 18th

The worst began last night. The men delighted in displays of drunkenness. Uproarious singing could be heard throughout the ship. In this state they went among the women and girls. Dared me to speak against them. For my silence, I keep Solemn safe.

I found out something about that African. He is a Mandingo diviner. How could I fail to see? He is known on the coast and in the interior for his knowledge of the natives who are sold into the trade. Certain tribes, it seems, are better suited to be slaves because of their temperament and capacity for work. Oddly, they struck a deal. The diviner's here to travel to America to see the town where the Captain unloads the slaves and, then, on to Liverpool and back to the coast. The Captain, in return, is curious to see if the man's powers of prophecy, so impressive in his land, extend across the sea. How absurd!

20th June

Morning came. The sun made a sluggish journey across the sky. I got up early as it is so difficult to sleep. The sky seemed as if it was burning. Every rolling cloud was white as smoke. I felt, not for the first time, a terrible uneasiness. Something has bewitched the men. The Captain does nothing to curb their advances towards the women.

> *And in that day it shall come to pass, that the glory of Jacob shall be made thin, and the fatness of his flesh shall wax lean. Isaiah 17:4*

22nd June

Jacob Moore's compound was raided then burned to the ground. He dealt in an unsavory manner with one Chief too many. Coincidentally, I was on my way to confront him about his interference in my business. Jacob, I came to learn, also, did business with the Mandingo seer. The place was still burning when I arrived. After a frantic search, I discovered her hiding deep in the garden near the fence. On subsequent visits, Jacob and I would argue, heatedly, long into the night. Sometimes I wonder, but I am most positive, that it was her, Solemn, who stayed by my side, who served me in my most needed hour. Even though she did not communicate with me in words, I was aware that she had been listening to my every word. Did she understand English? I was determined to discover if this was so. Had she been listening, listening to us all along? Many nights I observed how she attended to Jacob with a subtle grace. She is not a dumb creature like the rest of them. Can't you see, I could not leave her, abandon her now that Jacob was gone. At first, I sought to place her with someone who would use her well. But then, after I brought her to my place she began to cook and care for me.

Before I left the coast, I sold her to a man who promised that she would not leave those shores. Dearest, it is to her credit, by the will of the Lord, that I live.

I recall one particular instance when I came upon Solemn in Jacob Moore's garden. Not knowing I was there she moved about freely. A bright cloth draping her body moved like undulating water. Birds sang and trilled their melodies through tree-fringed air. The sun, though strong, in those moments did not burn me. If there was such a being as a black Eve, I thought, I Charles Patterson Edwards, beheld her in her garden tending the fecund earth.

Of course, many a white man, out of loneliness, has taken up with these creatures. Their children parade shamelessly through the streets. In this strange land there are these odd creatures called chameleons. In an attempt to save themselves from their predators, they can change color at will and, seemingly, disappear against the bark of trees or in a stretch of grass. They do not have one color that belongs, exclusively, to themselves. These white and black children share a similar fate. They are neither one color nor the other. They are neither wholly free nor only slave. They can be master, trader, factor, or slave. They are neither loved nor accepted by the natives or whites and so exist in a kind of purgatory between the two worlds. This circumstance impels them to acts of duplicity. They use or will be used as the circumstance prevails.

Jacob Moore is such a man and thusly so cannot be trusted. He had been keeping Solemn out of the sight of white men and the traders. Why he let her come into my presence, I'll never know but I believe, in his own odd way, the man came to trust me.

Often, I found myself staring at his skin. You could trace the two lines of his parentage in the features of his person. The range of skin colors, hair, and features about the face of this kind of person is astounding. Sometimes, their color is indistinguishable from that of a white, but when they speak their tongues burn black.

30ᵗʰ June

This afternoon, I caught sight of that Mandingo near my cabin door. I admonished him, sternly, not to return or I will see to it that he is fastened, permanently, in irons. Frustratingly, I can only get a few of the men to pray each evening with me. The cook is the exception. I try to spend time with him each day.

> *He hath said in his heart, I shall not be moved; for I shall never be in adversity.*
> *His mouth is full of cursing and deceit and fraud; under his tongue is mischief and vanity. Psalm 10:6-7*

3ʳᵈ July 1751

I glimpsed a thin moon dancing among the clouds when Jacob Moore came to speak, face to face, with me. Surely, he had been avoiding me as I had only received word once since our last meeting. So often a quarrel which erupts between two men in the fort penetrates everyone's mood. It was like this that evening. There are men, like him, who hunger to exchange blows. I felt a seething anger. He accused me of lying. Said I was trying to destroy him and, therefore, the trade he had built up after much effort. His arm swept, in a full arc, inland. All this venom this man was spewing because I spoke, freely, to the Governor, yes, behind his back. A filthy fetish was thrust before my eyes. He accused me of having someone plant such rubbish in his house. The fetish, a confused conglomerate of objects, reeking an offensive odor, was dangled before my face. Someone had wrapped an ancient snakeskin around a crudely rendered cross. Splatters of dried blood covered the thing. Yanking it from his hands, I denied every accusation accordingly. As white as he is on the outside, he is as black as the barbarians in this wretched land. Suddenly, the courtyard echoed with the sound of our blows. We fought. Oh, yes, all of my pent-up passion erupted. Every hatred I possessed for this godforsaken outpost one meter from the gates of hell, was expended on that man. Cursed him, I did. Cursed the blood that courses through his veins. Cursed the man and woman responsible for his despicable birth. "You are a worthless man!" "Damn you, damn you to hell, damn you!" Freeing the cross, I ripped the snakeskin to shreds.

This is how I came to strip myself of every implement of the cloth save the cross you gave me, save the inclination to kneel each day for forgiveness and plead for mercy in prayer.

And it was revealed in mine ears by the Lord of hosts. Surely this iniquity shall not be purged from you til ye die, saith the Lord God of hosts. Isaiah 22:14

5th *July*

The mad roar of waves fills me. Surely, we will be crushed beneath the mighty paws of the sea. Keep this in your heart, Lucinda. By the grace of the spirit, I did not by my hand kill that man, though, in my heart, I sought to do so.

Tonight, Captain Davenport, having drunk too much over dinner let it slip that Solemn is Jacob Moore's sister. How could that be? He said they are the children of a slave woman. Jacob, as I've said, being the offspring of some unknown white man paid to free his black mother and Solemn, his half-sister, before the man left the coast. Herein lies the rub. How did the Captain, then, come into the possession of Jacob's mother? I tell you. Every deal is a deal with a devil.

The fifteenth day

We rise to fog. Smoke-gray air curls about the ship Marie. Men appear and disappear, going about their tasks, as if characters in a play. Usually, the sea answers the munificent Marie as she plows and plunders through its waves. But, today, the sea is silent. My eye begins, so early, its worrisome twitch.

I am about to search for Captain Davenport when I hear the first cry of alarm. More shouts soon follow after. The Marie is engulfed in a forest of fog. The masts stand like so many ancient trees. Ropes sway like branches. From within its far reaches strange and fabulous beasts, in the shape of men, women, and children, emerge.

Wheeling, dashing back and forth, I am surprised by their dexterity. They come at us, swerve and disappear. Particularly, given the chains, even the near-dead show their worth. Both sexes carry children. At every opening, they force them through the net, throw them into the sea. Shadows ... shadows ... I grab two little ones and hold them fast until a man tears them from my arms. I reach for another, find myself entangled in a web of clawing, biting women. I try for more but they are shadows ... shadows. They climb the net, the poop rail, any climbable surface and escape into the sea. They fly from the ship. Climb so high, leap, then soar into the water. They are like rats against the wood, desperate to escape, finding every possible means to flee.

Harsh cries rend the air. Suddenly, we are beset by sea birds diving, swooping, swerving. They come as if called. A whump, whump, whoosh of wings clamors about our faces. Bare feet slap the deck; hands across the face of drums. Birds call. Drums answer.

Captain Deadeye comes tearing into the havoc capturing every shadow he can claim. Lashing out, his voice is acrid with the stench of madness.

She weepeth sore in the night, and her tears are on her cheeks;
among all her lovers she hath none to comfort her; all her friends
have dealt treacherously with her, they are become her enemies.
Lamentations 1:2

I race to my cabin. To my astonishment he is here! Both of them are struggling to wrench her free. Her face is no longer the expressionless mask I observe everyday. It is twisted, contorted into a face possessing a strange despair. *Aiiiii . . . aiiiii . . . aiiiii. Whose voice do I hear? Who is that sorely weeping? Who whispers? Who speaks! Who is speaking? Who? Who?*

I stare at the blood-caked rope, realizing that this is the first time I have heard her voice. She is begging him to leave, frantically pushing him away, but the man refuses and insists on struggling with the knot. The knot knows its work. I made it so that it would be impossible to cut or undo without me. She belongs to me. Who are you to cry to her? What unintelligible litany of words do you think will strengthen your hands and arms? *Leave her be!* He stands, defeated. She has, finally, convinced him to flee. All this I am witness to, the mangled ankle, the twisted leg and blood painting her limbs. Nearly hysterical, she kicks the man away.

First, I find it hard to understand the word. His voice is weary but drenched with this sorrowful word. Wumbu . . . Wumbu . . . How could it be that I did not know it until now. The sound of his voice pulls away from her face a name that has fit her like a mask. "Solemn!" I scream while punching and pushing him away.

Within seconds, Deadeye and his men race in before I am able to deliver another blow. They tear into the Mandingo with viciousness and he returns the same. Spit, blood, and sweat fly into my face until I, too, join in the fray.

And I heard a loud voice saying in heaven. Now is come
salvation, and strength, and the kingdom of our God, and
the power of his Christ; for the accuser of our brethren is cast
down, which accused them before our God day and night.
And they overcame him by the blood of the Lamb, and by the
word of their testimony; and they loved not their lives unto
the death. Revelation 12:10-11

We take turns lashing his body. Our arms can barely lift the whip but we command our bodies to obey. Every surviving slave is made to watch. Solemn must stand directly before him. Their eyes were locked until he could no longer see. She mouths soundless invocations; shakes in small tremors but does not cry.

Deadeye accuses me of conspiring mutiny among the slaves. "How so?" I say. "I warned *you* about the Mandingo." Even the cook refuses to speak favorably on my behalf. He says I took the slave as my concubine, kept her away from him and the other men. This prompts Deadeye to accuse me of fomenting the uprising, then of aiding and abetting their escape.

I swear I never touched her. Each man stares at me with a sick grin. "You are a god-damn liar!" Deadeye counters, kicking me to the cabin floor. I follow the eye, the dead one. A glistening marble stares at me. "Surely, you have cost me more than half my cargo." The lips twitch and turn every word. "You fool, why make me pay for your mistake?" "You knew the Mandingo could not be trusted! You heard what they said of him. That he could see beyond the eyes of men. Surely, you were witness to his bewitching gift of prophecy. Even I found his predictions uncanny, but true. Why not you? Why would you let such a creature on board this ship? Why would you bargain with the devil? If God prevails from sea to sea, what stops the devil then? What stops the devil, then? You lie! You lied!! You were going to sell him! Yes, you were going to sell him, too!"

A raspy whisper escapes his lips. Rum, salt air, and rancid breath envelop me. Nevertheless, I stare down the murderous tongue chilled by this beast of a man whose cruelty is, now, reserved for no one but me.

8ᵗʰ? or 13ᵗʰ? July

I have been thrown in with common men, sailors scraped from the scourge of the earth and pressed into service. I am fairly tortured by them any moment of the day or night. They are exceedingly happy that, now, I am the only one to go down among the negroes. My duty is to clean up behind them and to save as many as I can. Who will save me? Who can save me except my Lord? When I carry up the dead I feel the weight of a lifetime sink from their body into mine. With the weight of the dead, I descend again into a hold from which, I fear, I shall never emerge, again.

Forgive me . . . forgive me . . . my dear Lucinda Marie. No longer am I the man who left you with tears in your eyes. I have become someone, even I, do not recognize. As long as I thought I might see you again, I was reluctant to confess. Off I went to Africa with the hopes and dreams of an innocent, foolish man. How naïve to believe I could convert any one of them. When Reverend Glenn first visited my family he touched my heart with the word of his work among the benighted. He spoke, strongly, about how much we must persist in bringing the word of God to them. I began to find things, however, almost daily that disturbed me. Soon after my arrival, I learned that the church had been built on land sacred to the natives. First, I discovered a fetish, then a fowl that had, clearly, been sacrificed. Implements and vessels of worship were smashed or stolen, one by one.

When I spoke to Jacob Moore he denied any knowledge of these occurrences. You see, several of his people were assigned to service the church. They had to know what was happening. They were responsible for much of the cleaning and repairs. They are called gromettos, simply negroes in employ, the employ of whom? They are not, generally, sold away. I implored him to look into this disturbing matter, to search their quarters, to punish what I suspected in my heart. The man refused. He would have no part in it. Gods, white or black, had done not a thing for him, he'd say, so why should he for they?

Forgive me, Lucinda Marie. I beg you. Forgive me, for I have lied. My lies, like thorns, pierce me. I fear, as I confess to you, I shall never again anticipate your embrace. That evening, when I came in after drinking long into the night, I found her sleeping. Usually, she was awake and staring, wide-eyed, at me across the darkened room. But this night, she lay nearly naked, sprawled upon her back. A full moon fell upon every part of her. Her skin is night-black. Where, I wondered, did the night end and her skin begin? Yes, by the luster, the velvet luster I had long longed to touch. So much a child, and yet, I felt my pulse racing and my body eager for the woman I saw sleeping within that girl. I flew into the night. Night spread her dark stain inside me.

It is sometime near the end of July, I believe. It really does not, any longer, matter.

I dreamt, last night, of the rolling hills beyond your parent's home and of the green ribbon of trees that skirt them. We were sitting outside. You, gently rocking in your grandmother's favorite chair, and I, staring at the silken bouquet of your hair as the wind gently played it undone. Every part of me wanted to touch you, to be touched by you, and so I stood and walked towards the chair. A passing cloud blocked out the rays of the sun. As shadows fell upon your face your skin darkened and darkened and darkened until the smiling girl rocking in the chair was Solemn. She was staring at me in that expressionless manner by which I came to know her. Her naked skin was engraved with those crudely drawn designs. I could not move, only watch as her body began to swell. The designs changed shape and moved, fleetingly, across her flesh as if some invisible hand were drawing them. I had the odd sense that they possessed some meaning and just as I thought it, so it was. I began to read her flesh. A flesh flushed with words. They were names. Immediately, it came to me that they were the names of the dead; the dead who freed themselves by willing themselves dead; the dead who flew into the sea. Some strange whispering commenced from her flesh as she moved about the chair, her breasts growing fuller, heavier beneath moaning, trembling breaths. Every moving line brought forth sound, brought forth another name for me read and I read as if my life depended upon me knowing every one.

The chair creaks and tilts beneath the expanding weight as her body grows ever so large. Solemn eyes never leave my face. Neither do my eyes leave hers. Spreading her legs she heaves. Trembles. I tremble. What I feared has come true. Clear liquid runs down from between her thighs and pools beneath the chair. Wide, wider she spreads her legs, leaning back, giving herself fully to pain or pleasure, of which how can I tell? Finally, the moist crown of a head appears.

As if pulled by invisible hands, the baby turns this way and that until tiny arms wave. Gaining control, the infant hoists itself round to stare, fully alert, at me. The grey-blue eyes of my mum capture me. The lips part, but do not speak. Searching that face, I find Solemn's mouth on a canvas of skin that drinks in the pure black of her, the ruddy white of me. "Where, in God's name, do you think you'll ever be free of me? Jacob Patterson Edwards claims you. I claim you with my golden veins!"

I was cast upon thee from the womb; thou art my God from my mother's belly.
Be not far from me; for trouble is near; for there is none to help.
Psalms 22: 9-10

The sky is conquered by huge black birds; it was their cry that I heard. I am standing at the door of Jacob Moore's trading place. The Mandingo seer is adorning Solemn's breast with beads. An unseen hand is forcing me to my knees as bars pass from Jacob to the Mandingo's hand. The gold, then, passes from the Mandingo to Captain Davenport. Deadeye makes a cross out of the gold bars striking them as they ring melodiously. Suddenly, fetishes cover every wall. Upon each fetish the serpent of Eve drapes across a cross; a golden bleeding cross. Elephant tusks, glass beads, lengths of indigo-dyed cloth rise, pile upon pile, in a maddening array. Beneath them I see the bones. Every which-a-way bones, bones from a body like mine.

Jacob grabs onto Solemn, pulls then pushes her towards the door. Deadeye latches onto Jacob and tries to reach her, pulling both of them back. At least that is what I believe until I see the flash. Deadeye slices into Jacob. A wounded Jacob draws his knife and just as swift begins to stab at the Captain.

The diviner, the Captain, Jacob Moore and me scream as if from the same throat. We tear into one another slicing, thrusting, jabbing. . . . No one falls. No one dies.

In the blue beginnings of night Solemn flings the door open. I feel myself being pushed against the wall by waves. As the sea rushes in, every object moves according to its mass. There begins a mournful clanking like metal against a shoe.

Through the rising sea I see Solemn flee. For an instant, I follow her frantic dash across the shore. The ships are waiting. There beyond the beach, traders will spy an item of trade and begin their pursuit.

Myself, I find in irons. Yet, I am not in irons alone. Deadeye Davenport, Jacob Moore, and the Mandingo are linked to me as I to them. A churning sea the purple of our furious blood, twists, lifts, and pulls. A long, twisting chain is pulling, pulling us deeper, deeper down into God's endless sea until the hot salty water grows as cool, then cold and colder in that black deep. We fall into sleep; a sleep which we fight as strenuously as we fight one another. But, they are rising, rising up to meet us from unfounded depths. Luminous, skeletal broken bodies, they're offering themselves, offering the jewelry of the dead, a countless bounty of bodiless bones.

Never shall I see you, again, Lucinda. My Lucinda. What a fool to ask you to wait, to trust I would return the same man you set free with so much love and faith. Pray. Pray for my soul. Pray that I go to that eternal rest for this night though I die, eternally, shall I live.

He that leadeth into captivity shall go into captivity; he that killeth with the sword must be killed with the sword. Here is the patience and the faith of the saints. Revelation 13:10 📖

A Man Cleaning His Fish, 1987, Painting, by Barbara Earl Thomas,
Photograph by Richard Nicol

Some Fly

Barbara Earl Thomas

It was mornings. Whenever the girl thought of fishing it was always mornings and very early ones wrapped in the sounds of people rising before the sun—before the day had a chance to warm and dry itself. These were dark mornings filled with the hushed tones of parents' voices drifting in from the kitchen along with the smell of coffee cooked in tin percolators. It was her ritual on these mornings to raise one eyelid cautiously to spy the light filtering in from the kitchen outlining her closed bedroom door. Lying quietly and perfectly still she could glimpse a shadowy movement. This was further evidence that it was happening. And no matter how many times it had happened before, this moment always caught her off guard, coming like some unexpected fluttering wave of excitement raising up from somewhere deep in her stomach to wash over her anew.

There was something about these mornings that made her bed seem warmer and more precious, like some dark safe cave warmed by the heat she had generated and stored all night. She held onto each moment in an effort to make time stop so she might possess it forever—that place and the comfort of those voices whose words she could not quite make out through the space and mysterious light between them. Perhaps it was because she knew they would soon find her that she made no move to make her presence known. She imagined that somewhere between the loading of the boxes of food, fishing poles, and the distant muffled whooshing of the opening and closing of the heavy car doors on that '55 Buick—that it occurred to one of them that she wasn't there. And it was this that triggered the moment of their beckoning. And then these voices that she had only seconds before imagined to be from some distant other world would call out, addressing her personally. With this thought she was already imagining the first loss of the morning—it was her feet slipping down from between the sheets losing heat as they went. It was her swift entry into morning accompanied by the gentle brutality of waking, focusing eyes, feet hitting cool floors, taking her down away from the bed and toward the bathroom to wash away what little comfort was left from only moments before.

When the call came it was always the same. It was her name spoken from the hushed quiet of morning in tones of gentle urgency. *"Bobby, Bobby—get up girl get yourself ready. Ain't no time for draggin' now."* And carried along with the sounds of their voices were the scenes from the prior evening's preparation. Her anticipation made real. She always stayed up late the night before a fishing trip while her parents prepared; for the smells, the sounds, the excitement of schedules suspended which signaled the possibility that something really special was about to happen. On these evenings the house was filled with a sense of gaiety, friends dropping by and sometimes music, especially if one of the several roomers who lived in their big old house was around. If it was Clarence he would put "Kansas City" on the record player and they would dance. He'd say, *"Com' on Mickey let's dance."* He always called her Mickey, this was his special name for her. He'd swing her in and out with his Tennessee bopping style, all the while rhythmically keeping time with the metronome of his snapping fingers to the chant of *"I'm goin' to Kansas City, Kansas City here I come. They got some crazy little women there and I'm gonna get me one."* As she danced her body gave way to the urgent desire in the singer's voice, the wanting to go with no way to really imagine a place other than the one she was in. Sometimes her mother would come out of the kitchen from where she had been frying chicken or making one of her many tons of potato salad she always fixed for the trip, to join in. If she did Bobby would dance with them both. Slipping easily back and forth between them, reading their movements, she followed their leads on the swings and the turns. Even at eight she knew that this was the danger and the art of the dance, what it was all about. It was having your body keep rhythm and time in memory when you were swung out, or risk losing your step, or worse, be lost until the end of the dance.

It was this anticipation of going that she loved and that carried with it the prospect of having some unimaginable adventure. It was her Kansas City. There might be kids at the lake and maybe they would talk, play, and make up rules for the universe in which they found themselves briefly without parents. This was anticipation that rose up in her like faith offering a promise that always existed just out of reach but for which there were always enough signs on which to hang any hope.

During these morning hours her mind could easily skip over how strongly she had protested, only days before, having to go out into the yard to dig worms with her father after a full day's watering. She could even forget that she didn't really like fish much once they were caught or being out in the boat too long when her parents made her go out with them. At this point she had only recently convinced her parents that she was old enough to stay onshore alone in the car while they spent the morning fishing. And she was both thrilled and terrified at the prospect of this independence. She did make them promise, however, that they wouldn't row out too far so that when the sun came up she could run to the edge of the bank and find them, so she could wave. If she couldn't find them right away her eight-year-old bravery would dissolve and she would become frantic until she could finally pick them out from among the two or three other rented rowboats floating quietly on the stillness of the lake. When they finally saw her jumping up and down and madly waving, they would always wave back just like it was some great surprise for them to see someone they knew on shore waving out to them.

In preparation for these trips her father would count the worms and gather the fishing poles. And he might spend hours re-dressing his rigs as he fondly referred to them. These were his fishing poles and all the bright bobbles, bobbers, and the heavy weights and sinkers that went with them. But it was his reel that he loved most and he always saved its preparation for last. He'd tinker with it using pipe cleaners and some kind of oil to service its many crevices and moving parts. When finally it was shiny and perfectly clean he would attach it to his pole, looking at it intently for a moment or two. Then taking a stance he would go through the motions of casting out and reeling in his line. Bringing his arm and pole back as if they were one, he would make one smooth gliding motion and then at just the right moment he would snap his wrist and in his eyes you could see his imaginary line as it sailed across the living room landing in exactly the right place. When this was done he would place his hand gently on his fishing reel turning it one revolution after the other rhythmically moving it through its paces and all the time it would be making these smooth clicking noises in easy steady motions. At the end of it all a slight smile would appear just at the corner of his lips, one that she believed he thought no one else could see. It was an inside, self-satisfied smile that relayed shades of a secret. The girl believed that fishermen had secrets mined from the power of concentration and the ability to sit long hours without moving, that had to do with luck, timing, skill, and just the right bait. With that look she knew he was planning to catch a hundred of something—could be crappie, perch, bass or catfish. Whatever it was destined to be, he would bring it up from the bottom of the lake flipping and flapping big fat gray and shiny.

He gathered worms, jars of shammy skins, and pale pink fish eggs. This was the bait for bottom fishing. And her family—every last one of them from aunts and uncles to grandparents—were bottom fishermen. They'd cast out their lines deep down onto the lake's floor where the fish swam in the shadows while grazing off the underwater murky plains. Of the fish they caught, catfish were her least favorite. They were ugly, thick-skinned, wide-mouthed fish with whiskers and spiky sharp fins that you could barely see. After being caught catfish hardly ever died right away. Most times they would swim around in the bucket trying to fight with the other fish or anyone who was foolish enough to plunge a hand in without paying attention. But, whenever Bobby maligned the catfish, her grandfather, who would often accompany them on these trips, would never fail to remind her that she'd be ugly too, if she had to be down there swimming around on the bottom of the lake all day. Raising an eyebrow he'd say wryly, "*And Missy, there ain't a damn thing wrong with being ugly. And besides, a catfish is the only thing a Negro ain't never had to fight nobody for, so I'm obligated to catch as many as I can.*"

Lakes were always their destination, big deep green lakes, like Camel Lake, where they were going this time. She remembered her grandfather saying that Camel Lake was so deep that it didn't even have a bottom, it just went on and on. Story had it, he'd say, "*when anyone fell in, all that deep cold water just held the bodies down so you'd never see 'em again. And, they wouldn't even drag for 'em, there just wasn't no need.*"

Each time her grandfather repeated this story, and invariably he did, she'd be filled with a mixture of fascination and dread. And, it was this sense of mystery that followed her out into the boat on the lake. Leaning carefully over the side she'd stare as hard as she could down into the depths of the lake, down through slated green aqueous sheets to see if she could figure out the nature of this bottomlessness. She'd peer down into the water as if waiting for a sign or until she felt like she was going to lose consciousness. Curiously enough this was the same feeling she got whenever she thought about God and forever, which was something she did fairly often, especially when she found herself sitting quietly on her front porch alone. Fixing on a point in her mind she'd move out slowly through her imaginings from the porch to the sky, from the sky to the stars, from the stars to the galaxy, pausing briefly at each point to carefully picture her next destination. Finally she would arrive at this place that was like this nothingness, which seemed to be wrapped in a dome of silence. And God and forever, she supposed, was behind all of this. On these occasions she sensed that she was just this side of understanding something crucial if only she could hold on and not get lost in her thinking. It was like dancing, trying to keep step in time and memory. These states of near revelation could leave her breathless, which was exactly how she felt whenever she was out in the boat pondering that bottomless lake.

It was precisely at these moments of mysterious impasse when she thought her family ought to seriously consider giving up bottom fishing and take up fly fishing like her father was always promising. Far as she could tell from his stories and the pictures she saw in his sportsman's magazines it had all the advantages associated with a fishing trip and none of the perils. She could recall evenings when her father would sit for hours in front of the television silently tying flies, like he was just practicing for some undetermined future fly fishing time. If he was in the mood, he would talk to her. And she loved nothing better than to catch him in a place where he would allow her to cajole him, to pull him out from that dark recess where he so often seemed to go. Best of all, if the mood was just right and he was willing he would tell stories for hours or let her quiz him on whatever curious topic she was caught on at the time.

She would start in, "*What you doin' Daddy?*" Or, "*What are those?*" He'd say, "*These is flies Bobby, use these for fly fishin', don't need no worms. One of these days,*" he'd say, "*me and your mother goin' to go fly fishin'. Yes sir, we're goin' to get all geared up and go down to one of them rivers and catch us some steelhead.*" She knew he meant as soon as he could afford to get all geared up. He'd say, "*This rich people fishin' Bobby, and you got to have the right gear.*" And sure enough she'd seen pictures in her father's sportsman magazines of these tall fisherman casting out into clear running streams which ran bubbling over rocks and the sun was always out. These were fishermen dressed from head to toe in rubber suits sporting fancy hip boots. And while she had personally never seen a steelhead this was proof enough for her that someone had found a way around bottomless lakes.

In many ways she imagined fly fishing to be the flip side of bottom fishing. In fly fishing she imagined fishermen without boats, who were never cold, catching fish without worms, as they leaped and swam through light-filled rivers and streams of crystal clear water—and all with visible bottoms. These were fish that lived by the light who swam up stream and only ate colorful flies. She imagined that they didn't even have guts like the fish her family caught.

A few seconds later she'd query, "*Well if fly fishing is rich people fishing, is what we do poor people fishing?*" He'd look at her with mock impatience. Shaking his head he would lean forward to peer into the other room to see if her mother was listening. When he was sure she was within earshot he would answer with a long drawn out "*Nooo . . . Bobby we fish like we do because of your mother and all them other crazy Louisiana country people that goes with us* (meaning her grandparents Doc and Ethel Lee). *It's cause I'm a Florida boy* (said "Farida") *that I got some sense, and that I got other ideas about fishin'.*" Her mother, taking the bait, would call back from the kitchen, "*Your father don't know no more about a fly fish than he does about the Man in the Moon.*" With her mother's retort in place the pace was set. And she could feel them slip down into that space where they would go sometime if humor and life allowed and when it did, it was life made into perfect theater.

She'd say to her father, "*So Doc and Ethel Lee the reason we have to go lake fishin' and can't go fly fishin'?*" "*Well, Bobby as far as I can tell Doc loves a catfish about as good as does Ethel Lee. And believe you me—you ain't goin' to convince that Negro that fishin' is anything different from catchin' a catfish. Anyway,*" he'd say, "*you can't teach nobody from Louisiana nothin'. Just look here, I been with your mother all these years and I ain't taught her nothin' yet.*" At this point, he would set his lips and shake his head as if he had happened upon some truth that no one in the world could possibly deny. She could hear her mother laughing from the kitchen saying, "*Now, Wright* (she always called him by his surname), *you ought to be ashamed of yourself talkin' about daddy like that. I'm goin' tell him.*" To this her father shot back over his shoulder, "*Lula Mae, dear heart, I want you to tell that old daddy of yours exactly what I said, which is that he is a catfishin' son-of-a-bitch—and believe you me that old man ain't goin' to have no trouble with the truth.*"

Worrying out loud Bobby took the next step. Narrowing her eyes down until her brows nearly touched the top of her eyelashes, she said, "*So daddy, don't you think mommy's too short to fly fish?*" Considering her mother's short round frame she worried that her mother might be too small and low to the ground to stand up firmly in any river. She had visions of her mother in a head-to-toe rubber suit being upended by the river, with it just floating off with her like she was some little rubber bobber. For certainly, she had never seen anyone in her father's magazines who seemed so likely as her mother to have such a problem. When she said this to her father he let out a low bemused chortle that gently shook his whole body. Because he could see it too. He said, "*Bobby you ain't wrong about that—but don't worry none about your mother. You know we'll just tie a rope around her and attach it to a tree. That way, she won't go too far and when we're ready to go we'll just pull her back in and throw her in the back of the truck with the rest of the fish.*" With that resolved Bobby added, "*Well I think we better do it to Ethel Lee too 'cause she ain't no bigger than mommy.*" Thinking about it for a second or two, he said, "*You right about that 'cause with the mood that old woman's gonna be in when we put out in the middle of some river talkin' about some fly fishin'—well, she's gonna be so mad she gonna need to be tied to somethin'.*"

With that said, they would all hit the floor laughing long and hard, until they were overtaken by the physical demands of laughter and the irony of their own predicament. Words played out like dancing, and it was rapture to catch each other's dreams filtered and transformed through the common lens this fishing place engendered. This was good time and if times were good, they could go on like this for hours weaving one tale into the other with each one more fantastic than the last.

Fishing became a country, a place to go in the head and heart, an instrument for dreaming together. She knew this. And thus, she employed herself to listen, to watch, to catch their rhythm and match it by interjecting or underscoring just the right word and phrase to punctuate their play, to hold them in this country, as long as she could, where their energy seemed weightless, and the stresses of their daily lives evaporated.

When they were in that place, there was always enough of everything; food, gas, heating oil, and furniture payments. It was a place where together they knew exactly how to prepare and what to plan for. And they were in charge of the mystery and all its possible fruit. If only they could dwell there. It would be like an endless preparation for the best trip, away from bottomless lakes up toward a perfect state of light and breathlessness which she was certain had to feel something like finding God and forever. 📖

Cultural Geography:
A Raven Forum Series

T he following essays were written as oral presentations, as part of a forum series Raven hosted and produced. The series was funded by a grant from the King County Arts Commission/Hotel-Motel Tax Funds. They were presented during National Poetry Month (April 1996), and held at two locations, the downtown Seattle Public Library and the Douglass-Truth Library in Central Seattle.

The forum topic, "Lunatic or Lover, Madman or Shaman: The Role of the Poet in Contemporary Culture(s)," was discussed on April 20, 1996, at the Douglass-Truth Library. Moderator: Michael Hureaux; Panelists: Jody Aliesan, Paul r. Harding, Roy D. Wilson, and Deborah A. Miranda

Deborah A. Miranda:

I 've given the title of this panel a lot of thought, "Lunatic or Lover, Madman or Shaman: The Role of the Poet in Con-temporary Culture(s)." One of the reasons I've only been THINKING about it is because it's kind of hard to write my brilliant insights down while cleaning houses, and that's what I do for a living: I'm a housecleaner. I'm also a poet. This gives you some idea of where I fit into this culture!

Here are some of the things I remembered while mopping floors, cleaning toilets, and folding clothes.

First, the role of the poet is all tied up in the definition of what a poet is. Kurt Vonnegut has this nifty thing he calls his "Canary in the Coal Mine Theory." Canaries, as you might already know, were used in the bad old days to test the air quality in coal mines. If the air got bad, contaminated with gases, their convenient little early warning devices—canaries—would keel over before the air was toxic enough to affect the humans, and give the humans that extra edge of time to get out of the mine.

Panel, 1996: Roy D. Wilson, Deborah A. Miranda, Jody Aliesan,
Paul r. Harding, Michael Hureaux

Graphic, but maybe accurate. Vonnegut proposed that poets and artists fill the same role in society: when writers start getting censored, persecuted, jailed, or blocked from earning a living because of what they produce, our society has reached a level of crisis that demands some kind of immediate action to save not only the artistic segment of culture, but every one else too.

Then there's what Adrienne Rich says in *What is Found There: Notebooks on Poetry and Politics.* She says that a poet's job is to "name the nameless," and she muses on the power of names and the incredible chutzpah of naming—the act of naming itself. No one gives us this power, she says: we are driven to name, to define, and to reveal—poetry is almost an entity that won't stop harassing the poet! Rich warns, however, that "much of what you need has been lost"—our cultural inheritance gouged out by genocide, massacre, intellectual blacklisting. We have to accept that loss as an integral part of what we can use to create with.

At a workshop last summer, Grace Paley told me that every writer is obsessed. They have one or two focal points in their lives to which all of their work refers over and over again. I was having a rough time producing any work at this workshop, struggling with personal demons that said, "You're never going to move on to new ground, you are going to bore everyone to death with the details of your loss!" But a good writer, Grace said, is one who finds that obsession and milks it for all it's worth, in as many ways as she can. And the way to find your obsession? "Tell the story you are most afraid to tell," she said. "Not the one you don't want to tell, but do. Not the one you think you are afraid of telling. The REAL story, the one that scares the shit out of you." I went on to produce a piece of writing that not only told my story honestly and well, but which brought a response from my listeners.

People told me that this was their story too, that I had said things the way they had felt them. I realized that Grace was right: by addressing my deepest fears, I could best reach other people. It could have been selfish or gratuitous, but because I was honest, it wasn't.

I also like what the poet Chrystos says: "Poets are slow motion Mad Max movies . . . making poems is about walking into the firing range . . . that loss is not loss if we write about it. You may be gone but I have these words I've strung together like beadwork and you, yourself, have been captured . . . ." She's telling us that poets can use their craft as a way to not only define loss, but alleviate it as well.

Then there's Frederick. Frederick is a little gray mouse in the children's book of that name, written and illustrated by Leo Lionni. While all the other mice gather seeds and grasses, Frederick lolls about breathing in the rich air, watching dragonflies' rainbow wings, listening to birds. Then, in the winter, each mouse contributes food for all to survive. They have enough. But winter goes on and on, and the little mouse society becomes bored and depressed. That's when they remember what Frederick gathered, and they ask him, Frederick, what about YOUR supplies?? And he tells them what he gathered: colors, warmth, red poppies in yellow wheat—words. When he's done, the mice are transformed. They have found a sustenance beyond that which their bodies demand. "Why Frederick," they say, "you're a poet!"

Is he? What IS a poet's role? Why do we do what we do, and for what cause?

Are we canaries whose role is to keel over when society becomes too rigid and conservative? Are we keepers of the names, creating and defining by the power of language? Are we responsible for brute truthfulness, for facing fear without shirking? Are we a form of container, a basket, the material on which we write that which cannot be forgotten? Are we, as Frederick tells us, an anti-depressant in the form of memory?

Poetry, maybe, is the process of survival. In order to survive we need those who can do all of these things: warn, name, tell the truth, preserve, and inspire. As a poet, I can tell you that I have revealed myself to be both lunatic AND lover, definitely a madwoman, and possibly some mutant form of Shaman as well. I don't know. I'm still evolving.

Perhaps there's a clue to be had in the significance of dreams. Poet Joy Harjo says the work she's accomplished through dreams is some of the most powerful and important work she's ever done. I'll leave you with two dreams I've had that have given me direction as a poet.

The first dream came about when I was wrestling with the concept of being, or not being, a witness to the destruction of California Indian tribes. As a fifth generation survivor of the mission system, what am I "allowed" to be witness to? What can I contribute? In the dream, I have volunteered to be part of a memory experiment in which scientists lock up a bunch of Indians in a mission and record our responses. As soon as the huge mission doors slammed shut, each of the people present—from many tribes, all ages, men and women—simultaneously and without volition, opened their mouths and began to scream. I myself felt my throat open, and a scream came up from the deepest parts of me—and yet, it wasn't my voice. It wasn't my scream.

It was somebody else's scream. What this dream did for me was open me up to the possibility of being a voice for others, of accepting that my own pain was at once personal and universal, and that yes, I had a right to be a survivor, to be a witness.

The second dream was very simple. I was in my car, driving down a highway fresh and green, just after a rain. I was following a small pickup truck very closely, because the driver of this truck knew our destination, and I didn't. So I took care to follow every turn and weave of the truck.

This was my entire dream, except for one detail: across the back of the truck, on the tailgate, was the usual logo: TOYOTA. But the first letter had been changed to C, and the last letter to E. I was following COYOTE.

Jody Aliesan:

These days, especially in a city, our definition of culture/ community is often something other than geographic: it's a matter of affinity, experience, solidarity, common purpose, and struggle. For example, I consider myself a member of:

—the women's community, ever since the second wave of feminism in the late 1960s–early 1970s when I had the first experience of my words being useful to others, the function of the "cultural worker;"

—what I will call, in order to be most inclusive, the queer community: gay, lesbian, bisexual, and transgendered people;

—the "counter-culture" or "alternative community, although I might not choose those labels;

—and other communities, such as those who have suffered rape or clinical depression.

But my sense of the place of the poet in a culture has come most (consciously or unconsciously) from what's leaked into me out of my Irish ancestry.

> "Gaelic bards were perceived as a particular obstacle by the colonizers, not just because they epitomized a cultural tradition which the occupiers hope to destroy, but more practically, because they were figures of political influence in their own right, second only to the chieftains, to whom they sat next to in council," Declan Kiberd, "Irish Literature and Irish History," *The Oxford Illustrated History of Ireland.*

"The resident officials in Ireland gave considerable thought to the wiping-out of the two significant and overlapping elements in Irish society: the traveling craftsmen, messengers, and entertainers, and the learned class of brehons [jurists] and poets ... This would have torn asunder significant parts of the structure of Irish society, more particularly by eliminating the jurists—the poets were more difficult to silence," D.B. Quinn, *The Elizabethans and the Irish.*

In ancient Irish/Gaelic culture, the people, led by their chieftains, were married to the land. But there was an itinerant learned class who moved with safe conduct around the country, uniting the nation:

—*the druids* (a word I hesitate to use because of what's been invented about them by New Age writers. If you read anything that claims to know what the druids believed or what rituals they used, it's creative writing. Everything was oral, and it was all lost). They were priests, healers, and philosophers:

—*the brehons*, who were judges, legal counselors, and scholars of the law;

—*the bhards*, who kept the genealogies, and recited the eulogies and elegies; and

—*the filii*, the poets, who were the seers, historians, and keepers of the myths and sagas. They looked forward and backward and spoke of what they saw.

All this was orally produced and transmitted, and the filii studied twenty-one years before they were considered poets— they were walking libraries among the clans and members of scholarly communities.

Most important to me is their twofold function: *telling the truth* and *speaking for those who cannot speak for themselves.* Giving them words. The poets were called to sit beside chieftains because they could be counted on to do this. And they were protected from the consequences.

After this ancient culture was finally crushed, the poets became dispossessed outcasts sheltered by the people; itinerant teachers and custodians of literacy during the Penal Years of the seventeenth century when the native Irish were forbidden education. They were hunted down, because they raised the spirit of the people and reminded them of their history, of who they were. Their power of critique and satire was feared.

So what does this mean for me, personally? What does it have to do with the present? During the reign of the English King Henry VIII, ancient Irish manuscripts on animal skin were cut into strips and used to stiffen the spines of English books. Now these books are being taken apart and the strips recovered. One of them includes a fragment that reads: "The poet is the wick in the lamp of the community. Not the oil, and not the flame; but the simple piece of cloth that unites the two so that the people can see their own light."

I am a member of communities. I feel a responsibility to them. Being a poet is a job, a calling, a way of life (also a doom, a fate, and a curse). It's a function among other human beings, an absurd assignment—but somebody has to do it.

So I contribute to my communities as a poet by doing things like organizing benefit readings for Hands Off Washington, or providing an invocation at Tilth's 20th Anniversary conference; dedicating royalties (such as they are), or donating books and performances to auctions. Most of all I believe I contribute by living my life, writing about what moves me, from my community-influenced point of view, and telling the truth: pursuing it down through the mazes of my own self-delusion and denial.

But here's the central paradox: I can do this best if I'm separate, detached, standing one step away, independent and spiritually itinerant. If I don't belong to anyone, no one owns me. Then I can speak the truth, even if I'm not protected from the consequences.

It's a matter of binocular vision: one eye is the personal "I," the ego, the personality; the other is the mythic eye, that sees my life as representative of human experience. So my community, my culture, is our common humanity. I aspire to speak for that.

Roy D. Wilson:

Poetry is power. Making poetry means making power, empowering. In the words of June Jordan, poetry means taking control of the language of your life.

Dr. King says power is the ability to achieve purpose. The poet achieves purpose by the use of the word, and because poets deal with purpose and power, they must also be responsible.

Everyone is or can be a poet, because everyone can tell the truth. The role of the poet is to be honest. There is little distinction between a poet and a leader since both roles demand truth. A duty to say how it really is as well as a responsibility to say how it ought to be. Power is not flat, nor does it exist only in the physical realm. There is personal power. Political power. Economic power. Cultural and spiritual power. There is group power, nation state power. Of course, there is also lack of power. A poet lives so that life, love, and lofty noble relations gain power.

In the words of [student poet] Armando Martinez, "a poet must always be willing to speak up because a word or a line can save a life." June Jordan affirms Armando's statement by saying "good poems can interdict a suicide, rescue a love affair, and build a revolution."

While poetry requires the poet to express herself, the primary role of the poet remains not self-expression but representational expression. The poet amplifies the voice of others. When the poet tells the truth, she speaks the lines which others recognize as their own.

The poet cannot hide from reality—from his or her being of a specific nation, born at a specific historical moment, and being of a particular race, class, gender, and personality.

Two hundred years ago the written word was used exclusively by the economic and ecclesiastical elite in their battles for dominion over peoples and places. Popular use of writing is still very new. Today's poets have the privilege of writing the word in the battles for equality and justice.

Today, people around the planet live confronted by violence, fragmentation, scarcity of jobs, livable wages, housing, and health care. The poet plays an important role in helping to confront this condition. The poet can lift up and comfort.

Our sister (poet) Michelle T. Clinton claims that "the power of the word opens a door that can embrace and heal fragmentation. The power of the poem is the power capable of transforming the individual and communities." The role of the poet," says Michelle, "is to transform despair into care, and to change communities of caring into collective groups for survival, wholeness, and political action. In a deeply spiritual way, language cares, the word can change us, poems can connect us to our truest selves and our most essential community of humanity."

To represent the feelings of another, instead of just saying what you feel, takes discipline and love. The role of the poet is not an easy role, which is perhaps another reason poetry frightens some people. Many of us make a career of avoiding pain and running from decisions. We use entertainment. Mind melting. Spectatorism. The role of the poet is to struggle so that each of us is prepared to confront problems and difficulties. The poet performs the role of healer and problem-solver. The Costa Rican poet Mayra Jimenez says the role of the poet is to "take responsibility for each other." To do this, the poet in each of us must not only be unselfish, but must also pursue excellence in order to take care of others with the word. A poet "must stand out, taking on the leadership role in every task you accomplish." One can and ought to be a poet and a good student. A poet and an exemplary worker. There is no contradiction between the role of a poet and the role of a community servant.

Poets also perfect the role of being good listeners. The poet in you hungers for kindred voices which articulate ideas and experiences different from your own voice. The ideal poet seeks out and promotes diverse voices for the beauty and devotion to the acts of speaking and listening, which ought to be the first and last purpose to every social encounter. 📖

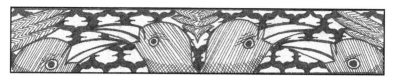

Ravens, Drawing, by Kree Arvanitas

XVI

Raven Notes

NOTES, PERMISSIONS, AND
PUBLICATION CREDITS

Daniel F. Aga: "Between Ocean and Sky"—the original title in *Raven Chronicles, Vol. 1, No. 2, Winter 1991-92* was "Tala, 1987."

Rane Ramón Arroyo: The two poems included in this anthology, "Kiko" and "Speedy Gonzalez, Jr.," were included in *The Singing Shark* (Bilingual Press, 1996), which won the 1997 Carl Sandburg Poetry Prize.

Kathleen de Azevedo: The story, "Rosea Socorro Katz, Coconut," appears in a slightly different form, in her novel *Samba Dreamers*, University of Arizona Press, Tucson, 2006.

Anna Bálint: "Bus Terminal" appeared in her poetry collection, *spread them crimsonsleeves like wings*, Poetry Around Press, Seattle, 1993.

Bart Baxter: "Peace For The Arsonist" was included in his book *Peace for the Arsonist*, Bacchae Press, Bristolville, Ohio, 1995.

Steven Jesse Bernstein: "Pictures of the War" is reprinted from the anthology *In Our Hearts and Minds, The Northwest and Central America*, Empty Bowl Press, Port Townsend, Washington, 1986.

Abe Blashko: *The Blind Violinist*, 1938, lithographic crayon, Eugene Fuller Memorial Collection, Seattle Art Museum. Used with permission of Abe Blashko and Seattle Art Museum.

Abe Blashko: *The Equestrienne*, 1938, black pencil, Gift of Abe Blashko, Seattle Art Museum. Used with permission of Abe Blashko and Seattle Art Museum.

Phoebe Bosché: "Me and The Other," an interview with Charles Johnson, was reprinted in *Passing The Three Gates, Interviews with Charles Johnson*, edited by Jim McWilliams, University of Washington Press, 2004.

Sean Brendan-Brown: "Everything Repeated Many Times," was reprinted in *No Stopping Any Time*, Tri-Color Press, 2014.

Omar S. Castaneda: "Love's Labor Lost: Equality"—every effort was made to gain permission for reprinting this work from his heirs and the executors of his estate.

Lise Erdrich: A version of "Red-Eyed Helldiver" was published in her fiction collection *Night Train*, Coffee House Press, 2008.

Diane Glancy: "Story" appears in *The Shadow's Horse*, University of Arizona Press, 2003, and *Rooms: New and Selected Poems*, Salt Publishing, Cambridge, England, 2005. "8 Ball" is the last poem in *Primer Of the Obsolete*, Juniper Prize, University of Massachusetts Press, 2004.

Sharon Hashimoto: "Okasan: From The Journal She Keeps In Her Head," reprinted from *Reparations: Poems*, Brooding Heron Press, 1992.

Tiffany Midge: "Written in Blood" appeared in *Poesía Indígena Estadounidense Contemporánea*, Eds. Hedeen, McAdams, Nunez, La Cabra Ediciones, 2011, and in her collection *Outlaws, Renegades, and Saints: Diary of a Mixed-up Halfbreed*, Greenfield Review Press, 1996. "Cowboys & Indians" also appeared in *Outlaws, Renegades, and Saints*. "For The Lummi Girl Who Found Her Magic In Horses," appeared in *A Shade of Spring: An Anthology of New Native Writers*, Ed. Michael Paul Martin, Toronto:7th Generation Books, 1998, and in *The Woman Who Married a Bear*, University of New Mexico Press, 2016.

Kevin Miller :"Before God" appeared in *Light That Whispers Morning*, Blue Begonia Press,1994.

Bill Ransom: "The Liberation of Father Free" subsequently appeared in his hybrid collection, *Learning the Ropes: A Creative Autobiography*, Utah State University Press, 1995.

Ann Spiers: "Dressing The Salmon Queen, Olympic Penninsula"— the poem's algae list is from *Seaweeds At Ebb Tide*, by Muriel Lewin Guberlet, University of Washington Press, 1956.

Marilyn Stablein: "Sacred Waters" was reprinted in *Sleeping in Caves: A Sixties Himalayan Memoir*, Monkfish Publishers, Rhinebeck, New York, 2003; reprinted by Pilgrim's Publishing, Varanasi, India, 2006.

Terry Turrell: *Western Movies, 1994-95*, oil, enamel on metal panel, photo by Rod Slemmons, courtesy of Mia Gallery, .

Ron Welburn: "Chewing the Sweetflag" is in a manuscript collection, "Carnelian Star," which is looking for a publisher.

David Lloyd Whited: "The Killdeer" and "Four Views of the Desert: Our Ennui, Her Ennui, His Ennui, Their Ennui," reprinted in *City of Destiny*, arranged by dan raphael, nine muses books, Winston, Oregon, 2017.

Elizabeth Woody: "The last salmon . . ." is an excerpt from the poem "The English in the Daughter of a Wasco/Sahaptin Woman, Spoken in the Absence of Her Mother's True Language," included in *Luminaries of the Humble*, University of Arizona Press, 1994.

Janet Yoder: "River Talk with Vi Hilbert" was included in the anthology, *Writings About Vi Hilbert by her Friends*, Lushootseed Research,1992, edited by Janet Yoder. "River Talk" will also be included in a collection of personal essays by Janet Yoder inspired by thirty years of friendship with Hilbert. The working title of the collection is "Where the Language Lives: Sharing Indian Time with Vi Hilbert."

BIOGRAPHICAL NOTES
Artists/Illustrators

Seattle-based artist **Alfredo Arreguín** has exhibited his work internationally, recently at the Museo de Cadiz in Spain (2015). He has exhibited solo shows at Linda Hodges Gallery since 2001. In 1980, he received a fellowship from the National Endowment for the Arts. In 1988, Arreguin won the commission to design the poster for the Centennial Celebration of the State of Washington (the image was his painting *Washingtonia*); that same year he was invited to design the White House Easter Egg. Perhaps the climatic moment of his success came in 1994, when the Smithsonian Institution acquired his triptych, *Sueño (Dream: Eve Before Adam)*, for inclusion in the collection of the National Museum of American Art. Arreguín's work is now in the permanent collections of two Smithsonian Museums: The National Museum of American Art and the National Portrait Gallery.

Kree Arvanitas is a mixed-media artist based in Seattle, with cultural roots in Greece and Western Europe (Netherlands). An autodidact, she has been illustrating or drawing since childhood. Currently she is focusing on acrylic, altered photos, mixed-media, and collage as her "weapons of choice" under the name RebelDog Studio. She co-curated the exhibit *Artful Henna* in 2010 (with artist Jeanie Lewis), which featured henna-inspired art on and off the human body from internationally acclaimed body artists; she curated *Tesseract: 4 Artists, 4 Dimensions* in 2015, featuring three other artists (Matthew Potter, Lesley Rialto, and Jeanie Lewis). Kree is Art Director for a new online magazine, *Enzyme Arts Magazine* (*https://www.facebook.com/enzymemag/*), and is a member of CoCA Seattle (Center On Contemporary Art) and A/NT Gallery in Seattle, Washington.

Rick Bartow (December 16, 1946-April 2, 2016) was a Vietnam Veteran, a life-long musician and songwriter, a widower, an enrolled member of the Mad River Band of Wiyot Indians, and is considered one of the most important leaders in contemporary Native American art. Froelick Gallery in Portland, Oregon, has represented Rick since 1995, and continues to represent his estate. Bartow's honors and exhibitions include over one hundred solo exhibitions at museums and galleries, including the traveling retrospective *Things You Know But Cannot Explain*, organized by the Jordan Schnitzer Museum of Art at the University of Oregon; *We Were Always Here*, a large-scale sculpture commissioned by The Smithsonian/National Museum of the American Indian, which sits on the National Mall in Washington, D.C.; *Dog's Journey: A 20 Year Survey*, at The A.D. Gallery, University of North Carolina, Pembroke, and Missoula Art Museum (2011-2012); a bronze sculpture purchased by TriMet, located on Portland's transit mall; a mid-career perspective and monograph *My Eye*, organized by the Hallie Ford Museum (2002-04); *Continuum*, at The Smithsonian/ NMAI (2003); and The Eiteljorg Museum Fellowship for Native American Fine Art, Indianapolis (2001). His carving *The Cedar Mill Pole* was displayed in the Jacqueline Kennedy Garden at the White House in 1997.

Abe Blashko (1920-January 13, 2011) was an artist and political satirist. Among his large body of work were important contributions to progressive publications, including the *New Masses* and *People's World*. Born in Seattle, Blashko was self-taught and started his professional career in 1938 with a solo show of twenty-five drawings at the Seattle Art Museum. Reviewer Kenneth Callahan noted in the *Seattle Post-Intelligencer* that his drawings were remarkably fully developed for a young man of just eighteen. During the Great Depression he was a warehouse worker/longshoreman on the docks in Seattle while continuing his development as an artist. In 1943, Blashko moved to New York City, where he worked for Paramount Studios as an animator, and later did commercial artwork. In a letter written a few years before his death, Blashko told Patricia Junker, a curator at the Seattle Art Museum, what inspired his work. "The turbulent social and political events of the 1930s were major contributors to my early development of a point of view. I was able to feel the pulse of that period and was fascinated with the faces and activities of the people around me, a fascination with their work, play, determination, strength, greed, and evil." Blashko was affiliated with a number of galleries, including the Susan Teller Gallery that hosted a seventy-five-year retrospective of his work in 2010. His work is in many permanent museum collections, including the Library of Congress and the National Gallery of Art in Washington D.C., the Portland, Oregon Art Museum, and University College, London.

Gary Curtis: (see page 477 for bio).

Anita Endrezze is an author and artist. Her short story collection, *Butterfly Moon*, was published in 2012 by the University of Arizona Press. Anita's Red Bird Press Chapbooks include *Breaking Edges* (2012), and *A Thousand Branches* (2014). Her work has been translated into ten languages and taught around the world. She won the Bumbershoot/ Weyerhaeuser Award, a Washington State Governor's Writing Award, and a GAP Award for her poetry. She collaborates on art projects with a small group of women. An altered book project on the value of art in Latin America is archived at the Smithsonian. She has also worked on an altered book about Don Quixote. She is half-European (Slovenian, German, and Italian), and half Yaqui (a nation native to Mexico). She has MS and is housebound.

Frank S. Fujii (January 14, 1930-October 3, 2016): Beloved Seattle artist and teacher, Fujii, a Nisei, was born in Seattle's Central District. He was the youngest of nine siblings. He attended Maryknoll School and Garfield High School before enrolling at the University of Washington, where he earned an M.F.A. Fujii was a popular teacher at Franklin and Cleveland High Schools, and later worked in the graphic arts department at Seattle Central Community College for seventeen years before retiring in 1989. In the 1990s he had a major show of his work at the Wing Luke Museum in Seattle.

Irene H. Kuniyuki's photography before art school was mostly landscapes, birds, plants, dogs, cats, urbanscapes. She then expanded to photographing dancers and performing artists, and graffiti—documenting the changing urban areas of Seattle. "The challenge for me has been re-examining nature photography with my particular vision that I used for art photos. Photographing fast moving birds such as osprey, bald eagles, crows, and seagulls became my primary objective between 2007 and 2010." To see more of her work and products, visit *www.zazzle.com/kuniyuki.*

Scott Martin: (see page 487 for bio).

Harlow Morgan was awarded an Artist Trust GAP Grant in 1995. Her work was included in Vita Gallery, Portland, Oregon, and Seattle Art Museum's Rental Sales Gallery. Selections of her paintings were included in *Images of American Immigration, 1991-1993*, a two-year nationwide touring exhibit. Her solo exhibition, *A Removable Feast*, was held at the Art Works Gallery in Seattle in 1995. **Morgan:** "The women in my family introduced me to different cultures. They were the storytellers, the ones who prepared food, using a mix of exotic and peasant recipes. My mother grew up in Germany during the rise and fall of the Third Reich. In her late teens she came to America, and attended chef school in New York City. My grandma was a seamstress at MGM Studios."

Fran Murphy has exhibited his work nationally since the late 1960s. He was educated at Clark University and the School of the Worcester Art Museum in Worcester, Massachusetts. He's been represented by galleries in Seattle, Los Angles, New Orleans, and Houston.

Tonya Namura (Anthology Cover Designer) has spent her entire life giving physical form to stories. As a kid, she copied out poems from books in the library, falling in love with the shapes of letters and the arrangement of words on the page. She moved on to design the yearbook in high school, and the newspaper and literary magazine in college, discovering how covers and fonts and even paper choice could influence how stories are received. Her professional gigs have included everything from catalogs and mathematical texts to national magazines and nonprofit marketing materials. Most recently, she's been designing books for MoonPath Press, Concrete Wolf Poetry Series, World Enough Writers, and Empty Bowl Press. To Tonya, every project has a story just waiting for its best possible form.

Caroline Orr has tribal affiliations with the Confederated Tribes of the Colville Reservation, Washington State, and the Lillooet Okanagan and Lakes Bands, British Columbia, Canada. She has a B.A. (Art) and a B.F.A. (Painting) from the University of Washington. Her work has been exhibited in Seattle, San Francisco, Hood River, Oregon, and the Burke Museum, Seattle. She has worked in oils, glass, and printmaking—pulling monoprints from paintings on plexiglass.

Mary Randlett is considered one of the major figures in Northwest art and her photographs are held in at least forty permanent collections, including the Metropolitan Museum of Art and the Smithsonian Institution. Born in 1924, Mary's career in photography has spanned a period of sixty-five years. "Mary Randlett's photographic vision of the Northwest is big-hearted, intricate, tender, and fully inhabited by the animals, tides, forests, mountains, and spirits that dwell there. What others may take for granted, Randlett sees as quintessential: overcast days with endless and often exquisite variations of gray clouds, raindrops on puddles, dripping branches, and distant shafts of sunlight breaking through the cloud cover. She is steeped in the history of the Northwest and its many art forms." (*Mary Randlett: Landscapes*, University of Washington Press, 2007.) In 2010, Randlett collaborated with poet/writer Frances McCue on *The Car That Brought You Here Still Runs*, and, in 2014, on *Mary Randlett Portraits* (both from the University of Washington Press).

Elizabeth Sandvig is a distinguished artist and longtime contributor over many decades to the civic and cultural life of Washington State. She earned a B.A. at Pomona College, Claremont, California, and an M.A. at Harvard University. In 1966, she had her first exhibition at the Francine Seders Gallery in Seattle. As Peggy Weiss, Art Program Director at Harborview Medical Center, states: "Elizabeth Sandvig has created an outstanding, curiosity-driven body of work that reflects her sense of adventure. . . . Frequently inspired by dreams and forays of the imagination, and imbued with the celebratory spirit the artist absorbed as a young girl living in Mexico, her work is bold, sometimes humorous, and often delivered in color that is explosive and joyous. . . . A pioneer in the advent of public art legislation and a leader on behalf of women, Sandvig is recognized as a central creative figure in Washington State, and an inspiration among working artists at all stages of their careers."

Marilyn Stablein (see page 501 for bio).

Jon Strongbow "In 1984 I moved to Queen Anne Hill from my little house in Olympia, Washington, where I was living with my French wife and writing . In '85 or '86 I got involved with Red Sky Poetry Theater, falling in love with all the wonderful characters: Phoebe, Roberto, Marion, Michael, Bruce Goose, Stephen, and so on. I mostly did my poems in a song form, and continued writing and performing until around '92, when I switched to instrumental music and began drawing what I referred to as the *Secret City Series*. I gave out free black and white prints at the door when people bought a ticket to my floating cabaret, the Secret City Cabaret, which moved about town, starting at the OK Hotel, then the Eastlake Cafe, then Puss Puss, then Black Citroen. I joined the Pike Place Market in 1999, and continued working on that series of drawings, which I now call the *Secret Seattle Series*." See more of Strongbow's work at *jonstrongbow.com*

Barbara Earl Thomas (see page 502 for bio).

Terry Turrell was born in Spokane, Washington, and grew up in Idaho and Washington State. He first gained local fame at the Pike Place Market in Seattle, selling his silk-screened and hand-painted T-shirts, which he did for nearly twenty years. Since 1986, he has devoted himself to painting and sculpture, gaining national recognition. Self-taught, Turrell incorporates wood, tin cans, tar, metal, and other found materials to create strikingly original work, both enigmatic and whimsical, with a beautiful edginess indicative of his Northwest roots. Creating imagery that is most often figurative in nature, Turrell favors both painting and sculpting equally, often working within the two mediums simultaneously.

Theodore C. Van Alst, Jr. lives in Portland, Oregon. His linked story collection about growing up in Chicago, *Sacred Smokes*, was published in 2018, by the University of New Mexico Press. His writing and photography have been published in *The Rumpus, Entropy, Electric Literature, The Raven Chronicles, High Desert Journal, Indian Country Today, Literary Orphans*, and *Yellow Medicine Review*, among others. "The West and Northwest present a tapestry so visually rich it can be difficult some days to decide where to rest your eye. But whether walking, driving, or flying, I'm always ready for that light that's just about to become magic, that self-composing vista, that relative from the woods or the sky who I only have to ask for a picture. I hope I've shown at least a little of the inspiration I'm blessed to see daily."

Patti Warashina: born in Spokane, Washington, is an American artist known for her imaginative ceramic sculptures. She received her B.F.A. in 1962, and M.F.A. in 1964, from the University of Washington, Seattle, where she studied with sculptors Robert Sperry, Harold Myers, Rudy Autio, Shōji Hamada, Shinsaku Hamada, and Ruth Penington. She began teaching in 1964, and has taught at Wisconsin State University, Eastern Michigan University, the Cornish School of Allied Arts, and the University of Washington. During the 1970s and 1980s, Warashina, Sperry, and Howard Kottler ran the ceramics program at the University of Washington's School of Art, growing it into one of the best-known in the United States. In 2012, the American Museum of Ceramic Art held a retrospective exhibition, *Patti Warashina: Wit and Wisdom*, in Pomona, California. In 1994, she was elected to the American Craft Council's College of Fellows. She received the Twining Humber Lifetime Achievement/Woman of the Year Award (2001) from Seattle's Artist Trust, the University of Washington Division of the Arts Distinguished Alumna Award (2003), and was interviewed for Smithsonian's Archives of American Art (2005). Her works are in the collection of the Museum of Arts and Design, New York, National Museum of Modern Art, Kyoto, and the Smithsonian American Art Museum.

Gloria White-Calico: born in Browning, Montana, in 1960, White-Calico lived with her mother and grandmother in Great Falls, Montana, and Sacramento, California, before settling in Seattle, Washington. Although she calls herself an "Urban Indian," she maintains strong ties to both the Blackfeet culture of her grandfather, and the Alaskan heritage of her grandmother, an Athabaskan Indian whose tribe fished along the Yukon River. Her grandparents met while attending the Chemawa Boarding School, and later moved to her grandfather's home on the Blackfeet Reservation in northwestern Montana. She began study at the University of Washington in 1979, graduating in 1990, with a B.F.A. in Painting and a B.A. in Native American Studies. White-Calico's dual heritage is reflected in her rich variety of subject matter and has influenced her love of bright colors and her experiments of adding media such as buttons, beads, and feathers to her paintings. "Color and texture," she says, "are strong sensory and tactile media, and my interpretations of life revolve around them. As an only child who frequently moved, sometimes to a new school every year, art became a source of escape into a world of imagination. Painting and drawing became my means of survival."

Carletta Carrington Wilson (see page 506 for bio).

Dean Wong is a Seattle-based, award-winning photojournalist, photographer, and writer, who has documented the Chinatowns of the West Coast and Asian Pacific America for forty years. Wong was born and raised in Seattle's Chinatown-International District, and continues to photograph his neighborhood each time he visits. His book, *Seeing the Light: Four Decades in Chinatown* (Chin Music Press, Inc., 2016), received positive reviews in *The New York Times* and *South China Morning Post*. He has been featured in *The Stranger*, *The International Examiner*, on KUOW Radio, and in the *Ballard News Tribune*. Wong is documenting Portland, Oregon's shrinking Chinatown. His words and pictures were on exhibit in 2017, at the Portland Chinatown History Museum, and he photographed Seattle's Jack Straw Cultural Center's artist and education programs from 1995 to 2008.

BIOGRAPHICAL NOTES
WRITERS

Daniel F. Aga lives in American Samoa with his wife and youngest of three children. Dan retired after thirty-five years of teaching high school, community college, and at the Universities of Hawaii, Golden Gate, and Argosy. His essay, "The Individual and the Fa'a Samoa" (1987), became the basis for his presentation series, "The Search for Common Values" (1998-2018). He is the writer and director of the two-hour documentary, *A History of American Samoa* (2009). He dedicates his story, "Between Ocean and Sky" to his father—Mageo Tamatane Aga (1921-1995).

Diana Abu-Jaber is the author of two memoirs: *Life Without A Recipe*—an Indie Next title—and *The Language of Baklava*, as well as four novels, including *Birds of Paradise*; *Origin*; *Crescent*; and *Arabian Jazz*. Her YA fantasy novel, *Silver World*, is forthcoming from Random House. Diana teaches writing and literature at Portland State University and lives with her husband and daughter in Fort Lauderdale. **Abu-Jaber:** " 'Irene' was an early story for me, part of my doctoral dissertation, which was made up of linked stories that followed the same group of characters."

Jody Aliesan (April 22, 1943-January 14, 2012) was a poet, writer, activist, and feminist. She died in Vancouver, Canada (having received her citizenship in 2011), where she emigrated after the onset of the 2003 Iraq War. The most recent of her eleven books, *True North/Nord Vrai*, was published in 2007 by Blue Begonia Press. Her poems, stories, articles, essays, reviews, and songs are found in international periodicals, anthologies, and recordings, and have earned grants and awards including a literary fellowship from the NEA. She served for many years as contributing poetry editor for *The Raven Chronicles*. Jody earned her B.A. from Occidental College and her M.A. from Brandeis University. She moved to Seattle in 1970, where she worked until 2005 for PCC. In 1999 she co-founded and directed the PCC Farmland Trust, a nonprofit group that works to save threatened Washington farmland. Deeply involved in the second wave of feminism, she worked against war and for social justice all her life. Her papers are collected at the University of Washington library (http://archiveswest.orbiscascade. org/ark:/80444/xv69784/).

Rane Ramón Arroyo (November 15, 1954-May 7, 2010) was an American poet, playwright, and scholar of Puerto Rican descent. He was a professor of English and Creative Writing at the University of Toledo in Ohio. His work deals extensively with issues of immigration, Latino culture, and homosexuality. He won the 2004–05 John Ciardi Poetry Prize for *The Portable Famine*; the 1997 Carl Sandburg Poetry Prize for his book, *The Singing Shark*; and a 1997 Pushcart Prize for the poem "Breathing Lessons," as published in *Ploughshares*. Other awards include: Stonewall Books Chapbook Prize, The Sonora Review Chapbook Prize, the Hart Crane Memorial Poetry Prize, and a 2007 Ohio Arts Council Excellence Award in Poetry. His last public poetry reading was at SUNY/Brockport on March 31, 2010. His last three words to the public at that reading were: "Live. Then Write." Those three words were words he not only lived by but demanded of his creative writing students. He died in the early morning of May 7, 2010, due to a cerebral hemorrhage.

Ken Gollersrud Ayala is a native of Southern California and has lived in Washington State for thirty years. He is of Mexican American descent, third generation, and Scandinavian descent. He has a B.A. in Sociology from Cal State University at Long Beach, and a M.L.S. from the University of Washington. Ken has worked for the Seattle Public Library for twenty-six years and he is currently a librarian at the High Point Branch in West Seattle, serving teens and adults. **Ayala:** "The inspiration for 'Recipe para Los Reyes y Las Reinas' was my Tía Agnes and Tío José. Agnes was an incredible grandmother, mother, daughter, sister, and aunt. Both were born in the state of Guanajuato. She was a wonderful cook. They were both very proud of their Mexican Ancestry and culture. This poem is a small tribute to their beautiful lives they shared with family and friends."

Kathleen de Azevedo's work has appeared in *The Los Angeles Times*, *Américas, Boston Review, Greensboro Review, Hayden's Ferry Review,*

Green Mountains Review, Michigan Quarterly Review, Gettysburg Review, Gulf Coast, Cimarron Review, and *TriQuarterly,* among others. Her novel, *Samba Dreamers* (University of Arizona Press, 2006), about Brazilians in the U.S., was nominated for the Northern California Book Award and won the 2007 Pen Oakland Josephine Miles Award, given to books which address human rights issues. She was born in Rio de Janeiro, Brazil, and currently lives in the San Francisco Bay Area. **Azevedo:** "I wrote 'Rosea Socorro Katz Coconut' while in the University of Washington's M.F.A. program. As I was eating breakfast, NPR radio did a bit on Carmen Miranda. So much reminded me of my mother (who, like Carmen Miranda, was a displaced Brazilian) that I was moved to write. Years later, this short story became the inspiration for my novel *Samba Dreamers.*"

Anna Bálint edited *Words From the Café,* Raven Chronicles Press, 2016, an anthology of writing from people in recovery. She is also the author of *Horse Thief,* a collection of short fiction spanning cultures and continents, and two earlier books of poetry. Anna has taught creative writing for many years and in many places, including in prisons, Writers in the Schools, Antioch University, and Richard Hugo House. Currently, she teaches adults in recovery from the traumas of homelessness, addiction, and mental illness with Seattle's Path With Art, and at the Safe Place Writing Circle at Recovery Café in Seattle. **Bálint:** "Years ago, I went through a period of writing poems rooted in the experience of being stuck someplace, for example, my car was broken down, or I was stuck in traffic, or waiting on someone who had yet to show. 'Bus Terminal' was one of these poems. In this case, I was stuck in a Greyhound Bus Station, waiting for a bus back to Seattle."

Bart Baxter retired as a pilot from Alaska Airlines in 2009. During the last decade he has lived and worked in Mumbai, India, London, England, and Addis Ababa, Ethiopia. He is now back in the Pacific Northwest. Baxter, award-winning poet and master of poetic form, and Seattle Poet Populist in 2001, was born in Sherman, Texas. After graduating (B.A. with honors) from the University of Texas, he did postgraduate studies at Boise State University and the University of Washington. His work has appeared in the *Formalist, The Ohio Poetry Review,* and

Poetry, among others. His poetry collections include: *A Man, Ostensibly*, Egress Studio Press, Bellingham, 2004; *The Man with St. Vitus' Dance*, Floating Bridge Press, Seattle, 2000 (includes CD); *Sonnets from the Mare Imbrium*, Floating Bridge Press, Seattle, 1999; *Peace for the Arsonist*, Bacchae Press, Bristolville, Ohio, 1995; *Driving Wrong*, Poetry Around Press, Seattle, 1992.

Dina Ben-Lev taught English at Cornish College of the Arts, University of Washington, University of Cincinnati, and Bethune-Cookman College. Her work appeared in *The Sun, Field, Poetry East, The Raven Chronicles*, and *The Gettysburg Review*. Her poetry books include *Sober on a Small Plane*, Wind Pub, 1995; *Broken Heliz: Poems, First Series: Poetry*, Mid List Press, 1997; and *Note for a Missing Friend (The Hudson Valley Writers' Center Poetry Series)*, Slapering Hol Press, 1991.

Steven J. (Jesse) Bernstein (December 4, 1950-October 22, 1991) was a Jewish American underground writer and performance artist, famous for his recordings with Sub Pop records and close relationship with William S. Burroughs. Bernstein's substance abuse issues and mental illness contributed to his provocative local celebrity in Seattle, though they ultimately culminated in his suicide. His substance abuse issues began as the aftermath of his stay in the Camarillo State Hospital in Camarillo, California, as an adolescent. He moved to Seattle, Washington, in January 1967, where he adopted the moniker, Jesse, and began performing and self-publishing chapbooks of his poetry (the first chapbook was *Choking On Sixth*, Outlaw Press #1, 1979). Bernstein would become something of an icon to many in Seattle's underground music scene. Notable fans included Kurt Cobain and Oliver Stone. Though often noted for his connection to grunge and punk rock, Bernstein saw himself primarily as a poet and his live performances in Seattle, such as his regular readings at the Dogtown Poetry Theater and Red Sky Poetry Theatre, were influential in Seattle, and he is credited as a major influence by many local poets from his era. He died by his on hand in 1991; the 2010 documentary film, *I Am Secretly an Important Man*, by filmmaker Peter Sillen, chronicles Jesse's life and art.

James Bertolino taught literature and creative writing for thirty-six years, and retired from a position as Writer-in-Residence at Willamette

University in 2006. Bertolino's poetry has been appearing internationally in books, magazines, and anthologies for well over forty years. His first book was published in 1968, and his most recent of twenty-seven titles appeared in 2014—*Ravenous Bliss: New and Selected Love Poems* from MoonPath Press. Bertolino's poetry has been recognized nationally by the Book-of-the-Month Club Poetry Fellowship, the Discovery Award, a Hart Crane publication award, a National Endowment for the Arts fellowship, two Quarterly Review of Literature book publication awards, and the Jeanne Lohmann Poetry Prize for Washington State Poets. Twelve volumes and fifteen chapbooks of his poetry and prose have been published by such publishers as Copper Canyon Press, Carnegie Mellon University Press, New Rivers Press, Ithaca House (associated with Cornell University), Bonewhistle Press (associated with Brown University), Quarterly Review of Literature Award Series (Princeton University), Cherry Grove Collections, and World Enough Writers. Two of his out-of-print books have been reprinted by the Connecticut College Contemporary American Poetry Archive. He lives with his wife Anita K. Boyle—herself a poet, poetry publisher, and graphic designer—as well as a dog and two cats on five rural acres near Bellingham, Washington.

Don L. Birchfield (July 10, 1948-September 7, 2012), Choctaw/Chickasaw/Welsh, and member of the Choctaw Nation of Oklahoma, passed into the spirit world in Lethbridge, Alberta, Canada. Born in Atoka County, Oklahoma, he graduated from the University of Oklahoma College of Law in 1975. Don was an award-winning author and a tenured professor of Native American Studies at the University of Lethbridge, where he was a champion of, and mentor to, numerous students. Birchfield's most recent book, *How Choctaws Invented Civilization and Why Choctaws Will Conquer the World* (University of New Mexico Press, 2007), examines academe, American history, and American policy relations with American Indians in the author's characteristic humor and irreverence. He was coeditor of *Durable Breath: Contemporary Native American Poetry* (Salmon Run Press, Anchorage, Alaska, 1994), and author of *The Oklahoma Basic Intelligence Test: New and Collected Elementary, Epistolary, Autobiographical, and Oratorical Choctologies* (Greenfield Review Press, New York, 1998), and *Field of Honor: A Novel* (University of Oklahoma Press, 2004).

Sean Brendan-Brown is a two-time NEA grant recipient, 1997 poetry and 2010 fiction, as well as a graduate of the Iowa Writer's Workshop (M.F.A. Poetry). A medically-retired Marine, he holds a B.B.A. from Pacific Lutheran University. His work has been published (as himself and as Fernand Roqueplan) in the *Notre Dame Review, Wisconsin Review, Indiana Review, Texas Review, Poetry East, Southampton Review, The Coil Magazine* (online), and elsewhere. He has books from a variety of independent presses including LitSum, Puddinghouse Press, and Snark Publishing. Sean's collection of short stories, *Beat It To Fit, Paint It To Match: The Collected Short Stories: 2000-2015*, was published by Tri-Color Press in 2015, and his poetry chapbook, *No Stopping Any Time*, was published by Tri-Color Press in 2014.

Estelle Kimberly (E.K.) Conner Caldwell (February 3, 1954-August 11, 1997) was a respected Native poet, musician, writer, and interviewer. Her interviews included writers Sherman Alexie and James Welch, singer-songwriter and educator Buffy Sainte-Marie, poet Elizabeth Woody, activist and AIM member Dino Butler, musician and activist John Trudell, writer and activist Winona LaDuke, actor and musician Litefoot, the late AIDS activist Bonnie Blackwolf, and visual artists Rick Bartow, Jesse Hummingbird, and Norman Guardipee. Her poetry and stories have been published in a variety of anthologies and journals including: *For She is the Tree of Life; Grandmothers Through the Eyes of Women Writers, Blue Dawn, Red Earth, Gatherings VII*, and *Reinventing the Enemy's Language*. In addition to her writing and musical endeavors, Kim was active in a variety of organizations including Wordcraft Circle of Native Writers and Storytellers, Oregon Native Youth Council, the Native American AIDS Prevention Center, and Native American Journalism Association (NAJA).

Omar Sigfrido Castañeda (September 6, 1954-January 11, 1997) was born in Guatemala City, Guatemala, but grew up in Michigan and Indiana after his family moved to the United States. Although he became an American citizen in 1986, he returned to Guatemala on numerous occasions to study Mayan life and culture for his novels, short stories, and picture book. Before becoming a respected novelist and English professor, Castañeda joined the U.S. military, where he served for four years in avionics (electronics used in airplanes) communications maintenance. After his service in the military, he attended Indiana University in Bloomington, where he earned a B.A. in 1980, and an M.F.A. in 1983. Castañeda was an award-winning writer, earning such prestigious honors as an Ernest Hemingway fellowship, a Critchfield Research Award, a Fulbright Central American Research Grant (during which he wrote *Among the Volcanoes*), and a Pulitzer Prize nomination. His primary literary influences were Gabriel García Márquez and Miguel Ángel Asturias. Castañeda was a professor of writing at Western Washington University at the time of his death. Books include *Naranjo the Muse: A collection of Stories* (1997), *Abuela's Weave* (1995), *Imagining Isabel* (1994), and *Among the Volcanoes* (1991).

Nancy Cherry: "Time is the great leveler. Looking back to see the small and petty stand beside warmth and affection brings me around to agree with the man who told George Bailey (*It's a Wonderful Life*, 1946) 'Youth is wasted on the young.'" Most recently, her book of poems, *El Verano Burning*, was published in June, 2014, by Radiolarian Press of Astoria, Oregon. Her work has appeared in *West Marin Review, Abstract Magazine, Spillway, Mid-American Review, Nimrod, Cimarron Review, Comstock,* and *Calyx*.

Gary Curtis is a writer, artist, and playwright. He grew up in Montana, worked as a mechanical engineer in Chicago, where he received six patents working for ITW Company, then moved to Seattle in the 1980s where he wrote plays and fiction, then began painting and studying bronze casting. His paintings, sculptures, and verbo-visual installations have appeared irregularly in the Seattle area, many times at Davidson Galleries. His most recent artwork is in a mixture of cast glass and fired clay figures. His favorite artists are Chaim Soutine and Anselm Kiefer. **Curtis:** "The artistic impulse changes your world view, in my opinion. My current project is how to build my next art studio/ living space. A very exciting prospect."

Alice Derry was educated in Washington, Montana, Washington, D.C., and Germany. She received her M.F.A. from Goddard College, and taught English and German for many years at Peninsula College in Port Angeles, Washington. Her collections of poetry include *Tremolo* (Red Hen Press, 2011), *Strangers to Their Courage* (Louisiana State

University Press, 2001), *Clearwater* (Blue Begonia Press, 1997), and *Stages of Twilight* (Breitenbush Books, 1986, chosen by Raymond Carver as King County Arts Publication Award winner). **Derry**: "I see 'Deer Stories' as beginning a technique which has interested me a lot: letting many, somewhat unlike things, collide in a poem until they do make a meaning. Poems usually come to me when two unlike things coalesce to become something else. I've always loved dahlias, and in my poem, 'The Woman Who Loved Dahlias,' I reached back to why I persisted in trying to grow them. I never knew my grandmother Alma, and in the poem I was trying to reach for some connection with her, to her. My poems are still trying to make connections with family and family history, to understand why family members can be so close but so distant."

John Enright was born in Buffalo, New York, in 1945. He completed a masters degree in folklore at U.C. Berkeley, before devoting the 1970s to the publishing industry in New York, San Francisco, and Hong Kong. In 1981, he left the United States to teach at the American Samoa Community College, and spent the next twenty-six years living on the islands of the South Pacific, working for cultural, historical, and natural resource preservation. His collection of poems from Samoa, *14 Degrees South*, won the University of the South Pacific Press's inaugural International Literature Competition. He is the author of the acclaimed Det. Apelu Soifua *Jungle Beat Mystery Series* (Thomas & Mercer), which is set in Samoa, and a new novel series, *The Dominick Chronicles* (Yucca Publishing), about an American wanderer. **Enright**: On writing "Teaching Thoreau": "It was my first year in the English Department at ASCC. One of my courses was American Lit. For all my students English was their second language and America a foreign culture. Most of them had never been off their island. Before teaching Frost I took the class on a visit to the walk-in freezer in the cafeteria. If you've never been cold, Frost doesn't make much sense. Rugged individualism is not a virtue but a vice in Samoan culture. Teaching Thoreau was an especially difficult task. We all lived on an edge between the ocean and the bush. What's his point? I was living out toward the end of the island, a ways from campus. The roadside cemetery was on the way home. The horse was real. I loved teaching those students. They taught me a lot."

Heid Ellen Erdrich is an Ojibwe writer of poetry, short stories, and nonfiction. She comes from a family of seven siblings, including sisters Louise Erdrich (who ranks among the most renowned contemporary Native American writers) and Lise Erdrich. Erdrich graduated from Dartmouth College in 1986 with a B.A. in Literature and Creative Writing. She earned two master's degrees from Johns Hopkins University, one in poetry (1989) and another in fiction (1990). Much of her career has been devoted to the teaching of writing; in 2003, she was named Mentor of the Year for her work with the Wordcraft Circle of Native Writers and Storytellers—an organization whose mission is to "ensure the voices of Native American and Indigenous writers and storytellers— past, present, and future—are heard throughout the world." Erdrich has taught at Johns Hopkins, Augsburg University, and the University of St. Thomas. She published four volumes of poetry: *Fishing for Myth* (1997); *The Mother's Tongue* (2005); *National Monuments* (2008), which won the Minnesota Book Award; and *Cell Traffic* (2012).

Lise Erdrich retired after three decades in Indian health and education. She has had children's books, fiction, and essays published. Honors and awards include the International Reading Association Children's Choice and Teachers' Choice Awards, the Carter G. Woodson Award from the National Council on Social Studies, and the National Festival for the Book "50 States 50 Books" pick for North Dakota. Her two picture books were illustrated by Native artists: *Sacagawea*, illustrated by Julie Buffalohead (Lerner, 2003), and *Bears Make Rock Soup*, illustrated by Lisa Fifield (re-issued in paperback by Lee & Low, 2014). Her book of stories, *Night Train*, was published by Coffee House Press in 2008. **Erdrich:** "I recall writing these stories just to keep them around in some form or other. I loved to hang out with elders when I was young, and they are gone now."

Tess Gallagher was born in Port Angeles, Washington, and is an American poet, essayist, and short story writer. She attended the University of Washington, where she studied creative writing with Theodore Roethke, and, later, Nelson Bentley, as well as David Wagoner and Mark Strand. Her honors include a fellowship from the Guggenheim Foundation, two National Endowment for the Arts awards, The Maxine Cushing Gray Endowed Libraries Visiting Writers Fellowship (University of Washington), and the Elliston Award for "best book of poetry published by a small press" for the collection *Instructions to the Double* (1976). Her late husband, Raymond Carver, encouraged her to write short stories, some of which were collected in *The Lover of Horses* (1987) and *At the Owl Woman Saloon* (1996). Her book, *Moon Crossing Bridge*, is a collection of love poems written for Carver after his death from cancer in 1988. *Moon Crossing Bridge* was followed in 2002 by the collection *Dear Ghosts. Distant Rain*, published in 2006, is a conversation between Tess and Jakuchō Setouchi, a Buddhist nun from Kyoto, which took place after Carver's death.

Diane Glancy is professor emerita at Macalester College in St. Paul, Minnesota, where she taught Native American literature and creative writing. Glancy received the 2014 Lifetime Achievement Award from the Wordcraft Circle of Native Writers, and the 2016 Arrell Gibson Lifetime Achievement Award from the Oklahoma Center for the Book. Among her other awards are two National Endowment for the Arts Fellowships, a Minnesota Book Award, an Oklahoma Book Award, an American Book Award from the Before Columbus Foundation, and a Sundance Screenwriting Fellowship. Her books of fiction, poetry, and non-fiction include, among the dozens she has written, *Report to the Department of the Interior: Poems* (2015), and *Fort Marion Prisoners and the Trauma of Native Education* (2014). She co-edited the anthology, *The World Is One Place: Native American Poets Visit the Middle East* (2017). Glancy: "'Story'—I was in Australia in the early 1990s where I visited the National Gallery in Victoria. I was glad to see the museum recognizing the aboriginal basket makers. Somehow I felt the oneness of that world. The basket weaver weaving the story of her basket. The structure of language working as a tree. '8 Ball'—I don't play pool. Except once when I was at a native residency school in Rowe, New Mexico. There was a balcony on the porch that overlooked a valley. There was a broad sky above it. Largeness also comes sometimes in new surroundings. I had Christ in mind. The loneliness also sometimes of new places. It's what he must have felt during his tenure on earth."

Leonard Goodman was the author of dozens of short stories. His fiction was published in *The Worcester Review*, *Portland Review*, *Playgirl*, *Outerbridge*, and *Hawaii Review*, among others. He received an Individual Artist Grant, in 1990, from the Seattle Arts Commission towards travel to the Soviet Union to research his novel in progress, "Stone Crossing," an excerpt of which is published in this anthology. Battered by circumstances, plagued by drugs, alcoholism, and violence, his characters were nevertheless blessed with humor and the grace of forgiveness that guaranteed their survival. Lenny never let us forget that each of us is only a step away from the abyss, and his response was laughter. An active member in the Touchstone Writers Group until his death, Leonard passed away in December, 1995. "Stone Crossing" remains unpublished.

Amy Halloran lives in Troy, New York, a worn-out industrial city that's finding a new future. She ran the Troy Waterfront Farmers Market for many years, and started writing about agriculture when she left that job to raise kids. "I felt compelled to tell the stories of food—not in mouthwatering words, but in the details that most of us can't imagine. We live removed from the realities of farming. I want to illustrate the work it takes to eat." She now runs a community meals program and food pantry at Unity House, a human services agency. They collect and redistribute groceries from America's over-productive food system, and make meals to share. "While my writing and cooking may seem very different, I think they share the problem that we don't value food and feeding, farming and the environment. I want to change that, through conversations and stories." She is author of *The New Bread Basket: How the New Crop of Grain Growers, Plant Breeders, Millers, Maltsters, Bakers, Brewers, and Local Food Activists Are Redefining Our Daily Loaf* (2015).

Paul r. Harding's published work includes a full-length book of poetry, *Hot Mustard & Lay Me Down* (En Theos Press, 2003), a chapbook, *Excerpts of Lamentation & Evidence of Starlite* (Aurius Unlimited, 1993), and collections of verse in magazines *Konch, Transition, Coon Bidness, Berkeley Poetry Review, Raven Chronicles, Earshot Jazz,* and various anthologies. His unpublished manuscripts of early poetry are housed in both the Gwendolyn Brooks Papers at the Bancroft Library, University of California, and the Derek Walcott Collection at the Alma Jordan Library, University of West Indies. He was awarded a Philip Whalen Memorial Grant for Poetry, and an Edith K. Draham Scholarship for fiction. Harding's Spoken Music has been performed with legendary

Charles Gayle, Gary Bartz, Ravi Coltrane, Michael Bisio, Burnt Sugar Arkestra Chamber, and other renowned musicians. He is a former Earshot Jazz Board of Directors President, former Urban League of Metropolitan Seattle Education Director, and founder of ULMS Children's University. He currently tutors literacy for Highbridge Voices in the Bronx, New York. **Harding:** "'Florida, Miami' came from watching a pitch-black woman standing under an umbrella on a corner in Miami. 'Sweetest' is some riff from a soul ballad."

Sharon Hashimoto teaches writing at Highline College in Des Moines, Washington. Her book of poetry, *The Crane Wife* (Story Line Press, 2003), was co-winner of the Nicholas Roerich Prize. She is a recipient of a National Endowment for the Arts Fellowship in Poetry, and she has recent fiction and poetry in or is forthcoming in *Shenandoah, Moss, River Styx, North American Review* and *Footbridge Above the Falls* (Rose Alley Press, forthcoming in 2019). She is currently at work on a novel.

Gregory Hischak is a poet, playwright, and Curator of the Edward Gorey House in Yarmouth Port, Massachusetts. His writings have appeared in *Atlanta Review, Bellingham Review, Ebettson Street, Exquisite Corpse, Green Mountain Review, Mid-America Poetry Review, Third Coast, Vincent Brothers Review,* and *Zymbol,* among others. His plays have been staged by Boston Playwrights Theatre, Portland Stage Company, the Humana Festival of New American Plays, Salem Theatre Company, and the Source Festival, among others. His collection, *Parts & Labor,* was published in 2013 by Pond Road Press, and he is the recipient of a 2015 fellowship in dramatic writing from the Massachusetts Cultural Council. **Hischak:** "The piece in this anthology, 'Prodigal Sock,' is a very early stab at writing, and given the chance to edit it (which I graciously was) I still opted to let it remain an artifact. It would be like drawing pants on a cave painting otherwise. It is a snapshot of something long ago."

Alicia Hokanson is a lifelong resident of the Pacific Northwest. She received her B.A. and M.A. from the University of Washington. She recently retired from a forty-year career teaching English, writing, and drama, mostly to middle school students; twenty-seven years were spent at Lakeside School in Seattle. In 2003, she was named the River of Words Poetry Teacher of the Year. She now devotes her time to writing, reading, tutoring, and political activism in Seattle and on Waldron Island. Her first book, *Mapping the Distance*, was selected by Carolyn Kizer for the King County Arts Commission Publication Prize in 1988. Two chapbooks, *Phosphorous* and *Insistent in the Skin*, were published by Brooding Heron Press, Waldron Island. **Hokanson:** "'The Iceman' was inspired by the PBS film which I watched with my teaching colleagues and students. The questions surrounding the mystery of who the Iceman might have been, and the miracle of his remains being unveiled by a melting glacier thousands of years after his death, prompted the poem."

Donnell W. Hunter (June 5, 1930-February 4, 2013) was educated at Ricks College, Utah State University, University of Montana, and earned an M.A. in English, Literature, and Fine Arts. He taught at Madison High School, Ricks College, Church College of Hawaii, and Brigham Young University. Donnell was an active member of The Church of Jesus Christ of Latter-day Saints. He enjoyed writing poetry and was published in forty-seven states; he also authored the hymn, "The Lord Gave Me a Temple," found in the *LDS Children's Primary Song Book*. His many hobbies included woodworking of fine furniture, even making his own coffin, painting with watercolors and oils, sculpture, operating his own printing press and printing his own chapbooks and the chapbooks of William Stafford and others. He was a bird expert, he made homemade bread since 1977, and he loved to play chess and scrabble.

Arthur J. Johnson was a Washington, D.C.-based writer/editor whose work appeared in *Catalyst, Lady, Chocolate Singles, Nommo 2 Anthology, The Guide, Peer Point*, and others. His play, *Shades of Grey*, was produced in 1989 at the Takoma Theatre in Washington, D.C.

Lauren Kaushansky currently teaches at Stony Brook University in New York. She received her B.A. from UCLA and her M.A. in Education from Antioch University, Seattle, Washington. Along with being recognized as one of four finalists for "Educator of the Year" (San Diego, 2010), Kaushansky received The Faculty Award for Mentoring which allowed her to travel and write poetry in Australia (2005–2006). Kaushansky has published poems in *The Seattle Review* and *California State Poetry Quarterly*, and essays in *The English Journal* and *The Journal* *of Museum Education.* **Kaushansky:** "I was raised on romantic westerns and I was sure that after obtaining a pair of shiny bright handcuffs the possibility of being a sheriff with a posse would not be far behind. This poem, 'After Reading Raven Stories,' describes my one and only shoplifting incident. Having neither Raven's skill nor swiftness, Mom caught me and forced me back into the store to return the loot, apologize, and repeat over and over how it was wrong. Certainly I learned my lesson, though in truth, every time I hear a Raven story, I can't help but cheer for the trickster!"

Marion Kimes (March 28, 1930-March 31, 2014) Poet Belle Randall: "In the Northwest where she has been a vital presence for thirty-plus years, friends and admirers of the poet Marion Kimes know her to possess a cheek as hollow and a beauty as severe as Samuel Beckett's, coupled with a voice as clanging as the pots and pans one bangs on New Year's Eve—a metallic voice, like the one that caused Katherine Hepburn to lose two roles on Broadway before it was recognized for the distinctive and subtle instrument it was. 'Words must churn . . . to keep us from flying out the window on an updraft,' says Kimes—a danger that would seem merely whimsical coming from another poet, yet seems a distinct possibility for Kimes—who, in her physical presence, possesses the steely fragility of a sparrow coupled with a voice that recalls the admonishment of thirteenth century poet Yang Tsai: 'You should have the sound of stone and metal in your use of words.' On the page, as in her person, Marion Kimes is a very convincing poet. Like Whitman, she projects an authenticity which certifies her claim to poetry more convincingly than résumés or blurbs could ever do. . . ." Kimes had many chapbooks and books published, the last was *Last Year's Horse, The Unpublished Poems,* nine muses books, Oregon, 2009.

Dorothy Robinson Schenck Kneubuhl (March 24, 1921-2004) was born in Honolulu, Hawaii, to Congregationalist Missionary parents Norman and Dorothy, who had settled there to spread the gospel primarily to the Chinese sugar cane field workers. "Dotsy," as she was known, attended the elite Punahou School, and then Wellesley College. She married part-Samoan writer John Alexander Kneubuhl, in New Haven, Connecticut, at Yale University, in 1942. They settled in Los Angeles, initially in Laurel Canyon, and left to return to live at John's family estate in American Samoa in 1968, when he became disillusioned with the entertainment industry. Dotsy became an accomplished painter towards the end of her life, inspired by the power and strength of the themes and characters of Polynesian myth, and by her natural surroundings. An avid chronicler, she wrote daily of her life in the South Pacific. Widowed in 1992, she remained in Samoa until she died of Alzheimer's Disease in 2004, and is buried there next to John.

Larry Laurence's books are a full-length volume of poems, *Life Of The Bones To Come*, Black Heron Press, Seattle, chosen as a National Poetry Month selection by the National Association Of College Stores; a chapbook, *Scenes Beginning With The Footbridge At The Lake*, Brooding Heron Press, Waldron Island, Washington; and an e-chapbook, *Successions Of Words Are So*, E-Ratio Editions, New York. His poems have appeared in the anthologies *How Much Earth: The Fresno Poets*, Roundhouse Press, Berkeley, and *Jack Straw Writers*, Jack Straw Productions, Seattle; and in journals including *CutBank, Floating Bridge Review, Poetry Northwest, POOL, Raven Chronicles*, and *Southern Poetry Review*. Larry earned an M.A., English, at California State University, Fresno, studying poetry under Philip Levine.

Stacey Levine is the author of four books of fiction. Her story collection, *The Girl With Brown Fur*, which was longlisted for The Story Prize, was also shortlisted for the Washington State Book Award in 2012. Her novel, *Frances Johnson*, was shortlisted for the Washington State Book Award in 2005, and her collection, *My Horse And Other Stories*, won a PEN/West Fiction Award. *My Horse* and Levine's novel *Dra-* were published by the much-lauded Sun & Moon Press in the 1990s. A Puschcart Prize nominee, her fiction has appeared in the *Denver Quarterly, Fence, Tin House, The Fairy Tale Review, The Iowa Review, The Notre Dame Review, Yeti*, and other venues. Levine received a Stranger Genius Award for Literature in 2009, and her fiction has been translated for Japanese and Danish publications.

Fatima Lim-Wilson has written two award-winning collections of poetry, *Wandering Roots, 1978-1988/From the Hothouse, 1989-1990* (Anvil, 1991) and *Crossing the Snow Bridge* (Ohio State University Press, 1995). She has won a Pushcart Prize, the Philippine National

Book Award, the Colorado Book Authors Award (for *Wandering Roots/ From the Hothouse*), and the Ohio State University Press Award. She obtained her Ph.D. from the University of Denver, her M.A. from the State University of New York at Buffalo, and her B.A. from Ateneo de Manila University. For two years, she worked as the Confidential Assistant to the Spokesperson of former Philippine President Corazon Aquino. Currently based in Seattle, Washington, she teaches online courses at American Military University, DeVry University, and St. Leo University. In 2008, she received an AMU grant which funded her month-long research in the Philippines. Her poems have been published in *The Santa Clara Review, Taos Review, Philadelphia Poets, Black Mountain College II Review, Paris Atlantic,* and *Gems of Philippine Literature.*

Anna Odessa Linzer is the author of the award-winning novels *Ghost Dancing* and *A River Story*, that was adapted into a two-person performance piece. Anna's home waters are the Salish Sea. Her childhood summers were spent along the beaches and her life since has been lived along these same beaches. The beaches have washed up bits of stories, and like the people she has known, they have entered into her work. *Home Waters*—a trilogy of three novels, *Blind Virgil, Dancing On Waters,* and *A River Story*—was published as a limited edition by Marquand Editions, Seattle, publisher of handmade art books. Her stories, poems, and essays have been published in anthologies and literary magazines. She has been the Chair of a PEN awards panel and of a Northwest Native American conference.

Stephan Magcosta has worked as staff writer for *The Stranger*, film editor for *seattlesquare.com* (RIP), and guest film curator at the University of Washington's Henry Art Gallery for the series, "The Good, the Bad, and the Mariachi." He's read on NPR and—as he often writes for food—his work has popped up all over the place, including ad copy for a bridal bootcamp. Newer stuff includes *Straightened Out*, a feature-length screenplay (story by Mark Mueller), and a new draft of his first novel, *Quetzalcoatl in Love*. **Magcosta:** " 'Slouching Toward Aztlan'—The title derives from 'The Second Coming' by W.B. Yeats ('And what rough beast, its hour come round at last, / Slouches towards Bethlehem to be born?'). Wordplay aside, I was drawn to the poet's sense of apocalypse and cyclical time. It was written to be read aloud before an audience of unsuspecting innocents. 'They Dance Alone'—At the time, fiction writing was so new, I often held my breath at the beginning of a sentence, as if stepping across the line on the bottom of the pool into deep water. It was inspired by a song of the same name, Sting's 1987 protest of Pinochet's cruelty. Women in mourning dancing with photographs of their loved ones speaks its own truth. The park is Occidental Park in Seattle's Pioneer Square. At a certain hour, rats stream across the cobblestones for nightly forage."

Kathleen Marie is a New Mexican single mother of three children. Her work appeared in *The Single Parent* and *Vista*.

Nora Martin earned a teaching degree at the University of Alaska, and taught in several rural schools, including one in the Tlingit village of Klukwan. She now lives, teaches, and works as a public school librarian in Bozeman, Montana. She is author of the YA novel, *The Eagle's Shadow* (Scholastic Press, 1997), the picture book, *The Stone Dancers* (illustrated by Jill Kastner, Atheneum Books for Young Readers, 1995), and the YA novels *Flight of the Fisherbird* (Bloomsbury USA Children's Books, 2003) and *A Perfect Snow* (Bloomsbury USA Children's Books, 2002). **Martin:** "It is easy to only write about the outside part—But when I really think about it, the real life is my inside life. It is built on layers of tiny flashes of memory: A particular moment on the beach. The color of the sky on that day in June. Seeing an ermine in the snow. Sillouettes of winter trees and summer birds. My son once said that he thought the world is full of miracles, but that they are minute—almost invisible. He is right and I love looking for those tiny miracles, but that place can be shut up in the dark for long periods of time; kept locked out by the necessities of lesson planning and oil changes in the car. That is the world that this essay, 'Prayer Flags On Barbed Wire,' came from, and I am so gladdened by this opportunity to revisit it."

Scott Martin grew up in Normandy Park, in the Pacific Northwest. He is an artist and illustrator, and proprietor of Tin Hat Novelties, the originators and makers of National Waffle Association products (which can be found from Tulsa to Timbuktu) and a host of other original novelty items. A former sign painter, he now works as a designer and project manager for Davis Sign Company, near Georgetown, Seattle.

He has been *Raven Chronicles'* art director for many years, wrote and produced a *Raven* online column, "Art Is Where You Find It," and interviewed many Seattle-area artists, including Terry Turrell, Patti Warashina, and Abe Blashko, for Raven. His paintings and drawings have been exhibited at the Globe Cafe, House, and Free Mars Cafe.

Armando Martínez was thirteen years old when he wrote his poem, "Where the Quinault Runs Into the Pacific: A Conversation with an Elder." He participated, in the mid-1990s, in El Centro de la Raza's Leadership Poetry Workshop (located in Seattle), a forum for young poets to develop community leadership qualities along with their art.

Valerie J. Matsumoto is a professor in the Department of History and the Department of Asian American Studies at UCLA. In addition to her book, *City Girls: The Nisei Social World in Los Angeles, 1920-1950* (Oxford University Press, 2014), she is the author of *Farming the Home Place: A Japanese American Community in California, 1919-1982* (Cornell University, 1993), and she co-edited the essay collection, *Over the Edge: Remapping the American West* (University of California Press, 1999). She was the first recipient of the Toshio and Doris Hoshide Distinguished Teaching Award, received the UCLA Distinguished Teaching Award, and has twice received the Award for Excellence in Graduate Mentoring and Teaching from the UCLA Asian American Studies Graduate Student Association.

Tiffany Midge is a contributor/writer at *McSweeney's*, and a humor columnist for *Indian Country Today Media Network*. Her poetry collection, *The Woman Who Married a Bear* (University of New Mexico Press, 2016), won the Kenyon Review Earthworks Indigenous Poetry Prize and a 2017 Western Heritage Award. Her book of comic essays, "Bury My Heart at Chuck E. Cheese's" is forthcoming from University of Nebraska Press. Recent work appears in *McSweeney's, Okey-Pankey, The Butter, Waxwing, The Offing, World Literature Today,* and *Moss.* Midge served as the first poet laureate in Moscow, Idaho (2015-2018), and aspires to be the distinguished writer-in-residence in Seattle's Space Needle. She is an enrolled member of the Standing Rock Sioux Reservation, and is Hunkpapa Lakota, and allergic to horses. **Midge:** "'Written In Blood' was the result of finding *Apache* and *redskin* as synonyms for *murderer* in an old thesaurus I often used. To compound the irony, I happened to have been trying to write a poem about Wounded Knee. 'Cowboys & Indians' was a riff on growing up in a mixed race environment, and my father's romantic ideas about Montana and old westerns. 'For The Lummi Girl Who Found Her Magic In Horses' came about when I was a guest teacher for a student writing conference at Lummi Tribal College. There's always that one student who knocks you out."

Kevin Miller lives in Tacoma, Washington. In June, 2018, he completed his fortieth year of teaching as a volunteer at St. Patrick's School in Tacoma. Pleasure Boat Studio published his third collection of poems, *Home & Away: The Old Town Poems*, in 2009. Blue Begonia Press published his first two collections, *Everywhere Was Far* and *Light That Whispers Morning*. **Miller:** " 'Before God' supports the belief that heavenly bodies are the most important thing about church."

Deborah A. Miranda is an enrolled member of the Ohlone-Costanoan Esselen Nation of California. Born in Los Angeles, she grew up in Washington State, earning a B.S. (teaching moderate special-needs children) from Wheelock College in 1983, and an M.A. and Ph.D. in English from the University of Washington. Miranda's collections of poetry include *Raised by Humans* (2015); *Indian Cartography: Poems* (1999), winner of the Diane Decorah Memorial First Book Award from the Native Writers' Circle of the Americas; and *The Zen of La Llorona* (2005), nominated for a Lambda Literary Award. Miranda also received the 2000 Writer of the Year Award for Poetry from the Wordcraft Circle of Native Writers and Storytellers. Her mixed-genre collection, *Bad Indians: A Tribal Memoir* (2013), won a Gold Medal from the Independent Publisher's Association and the PEN Oakland Josephine Miles Literary Award, and was shortlisted for the William Saroyan Award. She is an Associate Professor at Washington and Lee University in Lexington, Virginia.

Donna Miscolta is the author of the novel *When the de la Cruz Family Danced* (Signal 8 Press, 2011). Her short story manuscript, *Hola and Goodbye: Una Familia in Stories*, won the Doris Bakwin Award for Writing by a Woman and was published by Carolina Wren Press in 2017. Her story, "Ana's Dance," won the 2013 Lascaux Prize for Short

Fiction. Other stories have appeared in *The Adirondack Review, Blue-stem, Crate, Hawaii Pacific Review, Waxwing,* and *Spartan.* A two-time recipient of an Artist Trust Fellowship, she has also received awards from 4Culture, the Bread Loaf/Rona Jaffe Foundation, and the City of Seattle. **Miscolta:** "'Elena's Dance' was one of the earliest stories I wrote. It was based on a story about my grandparents that I'd heard often from my mother and aunts. Years later, when I had a collection of stories for a book, I developed this story further. I also changed the name of the character to Ana, because an editor told me I had too many names that started with an *E* in the story collection. So, Elena became Ana. The revised story, twice as long and with a renamed protagonist, won the Lascaux Prize for Short Fiction, and appeared in the *Lascaux Review* in April 2014. It is part of my story collection, *Hola and Goodbye: Una Familia in Stories.*"

Joycelyn Moody is the Sue E. Denman Distinguished Chair in American Literature and Professor of English at the University of Texas at San Antonio, where she teaches Black autobiography, Black feminist theories, and nineteenth-century African American literature. She is Founding Director of the UTSA African American Literatures and Cultures Institute. Her scholarship includes book chapters, books, and scholarly articles. In 2015, she co-edited special issues of the journals, *MELUS: Multi-Ethnic Literatures of the United States* and *American Periodicals,* both on the topic of black print cultures. **Moody:** "My essay about the awarding of the Nobel Prize for Literature to Toni Morrison grew out of my enthusiasm about the then-unprecedented level of praise for African American women as cultural producers. I had been transfixed—and grief-struck—by the disparagement of Black women during my first few weeks at the University of Washington in Seattle, which overlapped with media coverage of Anita Hill's brave outing of Clarence Thomas as a sexual predator. I felt hurt and stunned by all the Black people who resented Hill's testimony and by extension resented all Black women. Hill seemed to me the kind of southern Black woman filling Morrison's novels for better and for worse. Morrison's brilliance at portraying complex and credible Black women characters never ceases to move me. In 1993, Morrison's Nobel Prize healed me."

Kristin Naca is a poet, non-fiction writer, and screenwriter whose passions include Latina/o/x, bilingual, Asian American, and queer/feminist subjects. Her first collection of poetry, *Bird Eating Bird*, was selected by Pulitzer Prize-winning poet, Yusef Komunyakaa, for the National Poetry Series mtvU prize, and published by Harper Perennial (2009). Her writing has appeared in *Prairie Schooner, Indiana Review, Bloom, ART PAPERS*, and *Poetry*, to name a few. The latter she published under her former name in Santería, Iyawó, as a newly-initiated priest in the religion. She has led poetry workshops at Macondo, last co-teaching with inaugural poet Richard Blanco. She has served as a mentor, in the Loft Mentor Program. She is the recipient of a Minnesota State Arts Board grant, an Astraea Lesbian writers fellowship, and was awarded the McKnight Fellowship in Poetry in 2016. Naca debuted new poems at AWP, in 2016, on a panel with Beth Bachmann, Nick Flynn, and Saeed Jones, reflecting on the musical influences of the Los Angeles rock scene.

Duane Niatum: Poet, fiction writer, playwright, and editor, he has been writing poems, stories and essays for over fifty years. As a child and youth, he studied S'Klallam tribal ways with his maternal grandfather. He earned a B.A. from the University of Washington, where he studied with Theodore Roethke and Elizabeth Bishop, an M.A. from Johns Hopkins University, and a Ph.D. in American culture from the University of Michigan. He has published numerous collections of poetry, including *Ascending Red Moon Cedar* (1974); *Song for the Harvester of Dreams* (1980), which won the Before Columbus Foundation's American Book Award; *Drawings of the Song Animals: New and Selected Poems* (1991); *Agate Songs on the Path of Red Cedar* (2011) and *Earth Vowels* (2017). A former editor for Harper & Row's Native American Authors series, Niatum also edited the Native American literature anthologies, *Carriers of the Dream Wheel* (1975) and *Harper's Anthology of Twentieth Century American Poetry* (1988). His own poetry has been widely anthologized and translated into more than a dozen languages.

John Olson is the author of numerous books of poetry and prose poetry, including *Echo Regime, Free Stream Velocity, Backscatter: New and Selected Poems, Larynx Galaxy* and *Dada Budapest*. He was the recipient of the *The Stranger's* 2004 Literature Genius Award, and in

2012 was one of eight finalists for the Washington State Arts Innovator Award. He has also published four novels, including *Souls of Wind* (shortlisted for The Believer Book Award, 2008), *The Nothing That Is*, *The Seeing Machine*, and *In Advance of the Broken Justy*. **Olson:** "It's been twenty years since I wrote 'The Culture of Poetry . . . Does Poetry Matter?' Sadly, the medium—like the health of our air and water and funding of public education—appears even more threatened now. That the intellectual life of our culture has been steadily deteriorating is also sadly evident. Forty-two percent of all college graduates will never read another book after graduation. I'm sure that percentage is much higher when it comes to reading a book of poetry. Poetry is not what people turn to after a hard day of work and want to unwind and regenerate. 'The Sweat': I was invited to my first sweat lodge ceremony in the early 90s. This was a time of great personal change for me. I'd quit drinking, quit smoking, and begun submitting my creative writing in earnest. I felt like I'd crawled out of my dark ages of substance abuse and entered a renaissance of running and sweat. I'd gotten sober, but I hadn't relinquished my old hippie ways. I won't say I wanted to get high, but I did want a transcendent experience, an altered state of consciousness. The sweat lodge provided that, but it also provided a great deal of friendship, good food, and a deepened respect for the planet on which we ride."

Amy Pence authored the poetry collections, *Armor, Amour* (Ninebark Press, 2012) and *The Decadent Lovely* (Main Street Rag, 2010), and the chapbook *Skin's Dark Night* (2River Press, 2003). Winner of the Claire Keyes Poetry Award from Soundings East, Pence has published in *The Antioch Review*, *The Oxford American*, and *Juked*, among others. She's also published short fiction, interviews, reviews, and essays in a variety of journals, including *WSQ*, *The Rumpus*, *The Conversant*, *Colorado Review*, *Poets & Writers*, and *The Writer's Chronicle*. Her hybrid, genre-bending book on Emily Dickinson, *[It] Incandescent*, was published by Ninebark Press in 2018. She was Guest Poetry Editor for Volume 20 of *The Raven Chronicles*, and lives in Atlanta, Georgia. **Pence:** "I wrote 'Georgia Red Earth' shortly after my move from the West to a semi-rural town in Georgia. Many aspects of the South surprised me then. New developments were cropping up and earth movers carelessly tore down cabins on farms that I could tell held a complicated history. I photographed some of these dwellings, imagining my way into those sites of power. This poem has not appeared in any of my collections; oddly enough, I just went searching for it in my copy of *The Raven Chronicles* because over twenty years later, the poem may find her home in a chapbook I'm working on now, titled 'How to Build a Vivarium.'"

Dawn Karima Pettigrew is a Native American Music Award Winner for her CD, *The Desire of Nations*. She is the author of two novels: *The Way We Make Sense*, a Finalist for the Native American First Book Award, and *The Marriage of Saints*, a volume in University of Oklahoma's American Indian Studies Series and a Finalist for the New Mexico Book Award. She is the co-author of *Children Learn What They Read*, a book about multiculturalism in children's literature. Pettigrew, a Creek/Cherokee Shellshaker, Women's Traditional Southern Cloth Powwow Dancer, Jingle Dress Dancer, Indigenous Theologian, Filmmaker, and Journalist, is a graduate of Harvard University, and holds an M.F.A. in Creative Writing from Ohio State University, and a Ph.D. conducted at University of Kentucky/Trinity Seminary. Her home is the Qualla Boundary Reservation in Cherokee, North Carolina.

Richard Ploetz studied playwriting at the Yale School of Drama and received an M.F.A. in Fiction from Columbia University. Richard teaches composition and playwriting at NYU and is a member of the faculty at Lehman College in the adult degree program. He is a member of Emerging Artists Theater, NYC, and the Dramatists Guild. His stories have been published in *Crazy Quilt, XBI, American Literary Review, Raven Chronicles, A Loving Voice, Timbuktu, Hayden's Ferry Review, Outerbridge, Amaranth Review, The Quarterly, Passages North*, and *The Portable Lower East Side*. **Ploetz:** "In 1967-1968 my wife and I taught in Unalaska, Alaska, in a one room schoolhouse. We were fortunate to be befriended by a Native Aleut grandmother, Anfesha Shapsnikoff, wise and practiced in the old ways. She took us salmon seining, berry picking, and taught us to weave the watertight baskets from native grasses. I was impressed by her respect and closeness to nature—kill only what you eat. She influenced me to write this story, 'Hunter.'"

Freda Quenneville (1937-July 10, 1996) was an award-winning poet whose works appeared in over forty magazines, including *The New Yorker, The Nation, The Chicago Tribune, The Seattle Review, Poetry*

Northwest, and *Prairie Schooner.* Born in Georgia, she attended the University of Washington and lived most of her life near Seattle. Her lyrics were commissioned and performed by the Sacred Earth Singers, the Seattle Women's Ensemble, and the Vancouver Women's Chorus. *Child of the Ocmulgee: The Selected Poems of Freda Quenneville* (Michigan State University Press, 2002) is a selection of Freda Quenneville's nature poetry. Garrick Davis, editor of *Contemporary Poetry Review,* said: "The myriad small details of the physical world formed the symbolic landscape from which she created a lyrical and affirmative body of work over three decades. The poems are presented in roughly chronological order and provide an ideal introduction to one of the most neglected poets of the Northwest. Quenneville said of her vocation, 'It may take years of experience to distil the drop that fuels one line of a poem, years of observation to know one real thing about oneself and thus, the world.'"

Belle Randall was born in Ellensburg, Washington, earned a B.A. at the University of California Berkeley, an M.A. at Stanford University, and a second M.A. at the University of Washington. Her precise use of form and meter often shapes portraits of both observed life and interior states. She is the author of the poetry collections, *101 Different Ways of Playing Solitaire and Other Poems* (1973), and *The Coast Starlight* (2010). She coedited *Exploding Flowers: Selected Poems of Luis Garcia* (2004) with Richard Denner. Her honors include a Wallace Stegner Fellowship at Stanford University, Poetry's Inez Boulton Award, Waywiser Press' Anthony Hecht Prize, and a fellowship from the National Endowment for the Arts. Founding poetry editor of the interdisciplinary journal *Common Knowledge,* Randall lives in Seattle, where she has taught at Cornish College of the Arts and in the University of Washington's extension program. **Randall:** "On writing the poem 'Pursuing The Run Away Hub Cap': Poets often assume that conventional forms like the villanelle will frustrate their attempts at expression, but this poem was written as an exercise, to see if the form could help me get going at a time when I was feeling otherwise stifled."

Margaret Randall is a poet, essayist, oral historian, translator, photographer, and social activist. She lived in Latin America for twenty-three years (in Mexico, Cuba, and Nicaragua). From 1962 to 1969 she and Mexican poet Sergio Mondragón co-edited *El Corno Emplumado / The*

Plumed Horn, a bilingual literary quarterly that published some of the best new work of the sixties. When she came home in 1984, the U.S. government ordered her deported because it found some of her writing to be "against the good order and happiness of the United States." With the support of many writers and others, she won her case in 1989. Randall's recent poetry titles include *As If The Empty Chair / Como Si La Silla Vacia*, *The Rhizome As A Field Of Broken Bones*, *About Little Charlie Lindbergh*, *She Becomes Time*, and *The Morning After: Poetry & Prose In A Post-Truth World* (all from Wings Press). *Exporting Revolution: Cuba's Global Solidarity* was published by Duke University Press in 2017. Red Mountain Press in Santa Fe and The Operating System in Brooklyn have published her translations of individual Cuban poets. In 2017, Randall received the Medalla al Mérito Literario, awarded by Literatura en el Bravo in Ciudad Juárez, Mexico. *Time's Language: Selected Poems 1959-2018* was published by Wings Press in September, 2018. Randall lives in Albuquerque with her partner (now wife) of more than thirty years, the painter Barbara Byers, and travels extensively to read, lecture, and teach.

Bill Ransom's first short story publication was in *Gamut Magazine* at Washington State University in 1965. His name was spelled "Sansom", a suitably karmic beginning. His first book was poetry from Copper Canyon Press, in 1974: *Finding True North & Critter*. He received two NEA fellowships, one in poetry and one in fiction. His short stories were a three-time selection of the PEN/NEA Syndicated Fiction Project that placed short fiction into the Sunday magazine sections of ten of the country's top newspapers: "What Elena Said," "Learning the Ropes," and "Uncle Hungry." "Uncle Hungry" turned into his first solo novel, *Jaguar*, in 1995. Short stories, along with novel excerpts, poetry, and articles, appear in his collections *Learning the Ropes* (Utah State University, 1995) and *The Woman and the War Baby* (Blue Begonia Press, 2008). **Ransom:** "I wrote 'The Liberation of Father Free' while working on the Putnam novel, *The Lazarus Effect*, at Frank Herbert's place in Hana, Hawaii. I'd worked construction some years before in Port Townsend with the guy who was building Frank's house, and he invited me to the crew's weekly Friday luau. Though haole, I had a Hawaiian daughter whom they met, so I became privy to local gossip. Usually the local priest came, as well. A priest whom I admired from my misspent youth, Father Free SJ, had the perfect name for this young fictional priest, so I used it. The real Father Free had passed away, a wise and thoughtful counselor. I watched this new young haole priest for nine months as he learned many a precious, human lesson that didn't come in the seminary."

dan raphael: For over three decades, dan has been active in the Northwest as poet, performer, editor, and reading host. *The Closer You Get to Nowhere*, his twentieth book, will be published in late 2018 by Last Word Press, which published his *Everyone in this MOVIE gets paid* (2016). Raphael is known for the energy of his performances of his highly imaginative and driven poetry in places like Bumbershoot, Cascadia Poetry Festival, Powell's Books, Wordstock, Red Sky Poetry Theatre, Reed College, and Portland Jazz Festival. He is prose editor of *Unlikely Stories*, and every Wednesday writes and records a news poem for KBOO Evening News, a listener-sponsored radio station in Portland, Oregon.

Trisha Ready is a writer, musician, and psychologist who manages a Seattle-based Psychotherapy Practice working with small groups. Her book, *Music in Therapeutic Practice: Using Rhythm to Bridge Communication Barriers*, was published by Rowman & Littlefield in 2016. The book focuses on listening to music with patients experiencing psychosis and other mental health issues. Trisha has published in a variety of media, including *The Raven Chronicles* and *The Stranger*. Her *Stranger* essay—"How listening to Music and Fighting with Susan Sontag Helped Me Cope with Chemo"—was chosen by Longreads as one of the best essays of 2015. **Ready:** "I did not remember having written this story, 'Walking The Mysterics,' when I first re-read it. The second time I read it I recognized a light and playful tone that seemed both familiar and evasive. At the time I wrote this story I was watching hours of TV evangelists as my main form of entertainment and escape. Father Tom's kind of cadence and pacing had become more innate. Re-reading this story made me miss writing fiction. I seldom attempt invented stories these days. I'm really grateful to *The Raven Chronicles* for printing my essays and stories over the years, and for offering a welcoming place for so many voices."

Philip Harold Red Eagle is of Dakota and Puget Sound Salish heritage. Philip was born in Tacoma, Washington, and raised in the Northwest, including Sitka, Alaska. He holds two degrees from the University of Washington, a B.F.A. in Metal Design from the School of Art (1983) and a B.A. in Editorial Journalism from the School of Communications (1987). Philip's poetry, fiction, essays and reviews have been included in *Art Access, Encyclopedia of North American Indians, Humanities Today, Nobody's Orphan Child* (Anthology, Red Sky Poetry Theatre, 1996), *Northwest Ethnic News, The Raven Chronicles,* and *Red Ink.* His novel (actually two novellas), *Red Earth: A Vietnam Warrior's Journey* (Holy Cow Press, 1997), is in a second printing. Philip is originator and co-founder of *The Raven Chronicles* and is currently working in the area of cultural resurgence. He is part of the Canoe Nations Program which is bringing back the Traditional Carved Canoe to the Northwest. He is primarily concerned with using the canoe as a mechanism in which to bring about cultural change among the tribes, to bring the notion of traditional ideas about healing and pride among Native youth. The focus of the use of these canoes has been in canoe journeys which encourage group cooperation, discipline, and cultural pride.

William Reichard is a writer, editor, and educator, and he lives in Saint Paul, Minnesota. He has published five collections of poetry, including *Two Men Rowing Madly Toward Infinity* (Broadstone Books, 2016); *Sin Eater* (Mid-List Press, 2010); and *This Brightness* (Mid-List Press, 2007). Reichard is the editor of *American Tensions: Literature of Identity and the Search for Social Justice* (New Village Press, 2011), an anthology of contemporary fiction, poetry, and creative nonfiction focusing on social justice issues. He has a Ph.D. in American Literature and an M.A. in Creative Writing from the University of Minnesota. **Reichard:** "I wrote 'My Mother's Garden, June 1994' at a time of transition in my family. I was the last of ten children, and grew up in a small rural village in south-central Minnesota, in the house that my family had lived in for almost fifty years. My father had died several years earlier, and after I went to college, my mother lived alone in an aging house that needed constant upkeep. After a series of deaths in the family, a lifetime of factory work, and increasing health issues, my mother wasn't up to the task of caring for the house. She loved the house, and had always had a beautiful garden, but she couldn't afford to repair it, and so sold it and moved to a much smaller house in a neighboring town. She didn't want to move, but felt she had no choice. The poem was a way for me to record years of memories of my mother's garden, sometimes the only refuge she had in the world, and something she has always regretted having to leave. The poem is an homage to an independent woman who has always had a deep love for the natural world."

Carter Revard, Osage on his father's side, was born in 1931 and grew up on the Osage Reservation in Oklahoma. In 1952 his grandmother gave him the Osage name Nompehwahteh (meaning "fear-inspiring"). He graduated from the University of Tulsa, won a Rhodes Scholarship to Oxford University (one of the first Native Americans to do so), earned a Ph.D. in English literature from Yale University, and from 1956 until retiring in 1996 taught Medieval and American Indian literature at Amherst College, Washington University in St. Louis, and elsewhere. Since 1961 he has lived in St. Louis. His collections of poems, memoirs, and essays include *Ponca War Dancers* (1980); *Cowboys and Indians Christmas Shopping* (1992); *An Eagle Nation* (1993, winner of the Oklahoma Book Award for Poetry); *Family Matters, Tribal Affairs* (1998); and his memoir in prose and poetry, *Winning the Dust Bowl* (2001). His poems have been translated into French, Spanish, German, Italian, and Hungarian. "Refrigerator" has not been published anywhere since it appeared in *Raven Chronicles*.

Lawrence Revard published his first poem in *Raven Chronicles*, and has since published poems in *Pleiades, New Orleans Review, Prairie Schooner, New Letters*, and elsewhere. His translations of John Milton's Latin and Italian poems were published in *John Milton Complete Shorter Poems*, Wiley-Blackwell, 2009. Revard holds a B.A. in Ancient Greek from Carleton College, an M.F.A. in Poetry from the University of Iowa's Writers' Workshop, and a Ph.D. in English and American literature at Washington University in St. Louis. He taught composition, speech, business writing, and literature classes at the University of Iowa, Webster University, Lindenwood University, Moberly Area Community College, and the University of Missouri in Columbia. He lives and works in his birth city of St. Louis, Missouri. **Revard:** " 'Crow Speaks to Wolf' was written while I was still living in Minnesota, refusing to admit that it was too cold a state for me."

David Romtvedt's most recent books are the poetry collection *Dilemmas of the Angels* (LSU Press, 2017) and the novel *Zelestina Urza in Outer Space* (University of Nevada Center for Basque Studies, 2015). He is the recipient of the National Poetry Series Award, two NEA fellowships, and the Wyoming Governor's Arts Award. He served as poet laureate of Wyoming from 2005-2012. He lives in Buffalo, Wyoming, and works as a writer and musician. He serves as an Emeritus Professor at the University of Wyoming where he taught creative writing and a variety of courses in cultural studies focused on the role of food and music in community maintenance. With the band, the Fireants, he plays dance music of the Americas, and with the band, Ospa, Basque traditional music in new and old arrangements.

Mira Shimabukuro is a poet, writer, and Senior Lecturer at the University of Washington, Bothell. A Northwest native, Mira grew up in Portland, Oregon, attended The Evergreen State College for her B.A. and the University of Washington for her M.F.A. After a long hiatus from academia, Mira also completed a Ph.D. in Composition and Rhetoric at the University of Wisconsin-Madison. Focusing on cultural rhetorics and literacy history, Mira studied the ways Japanese Americans used writing in the so-called "internment" camps during World War II, scholarship that resulted in her book, *Relocating Authority: Japanese Americans Writing to Redress Mass Incarceration* (University Press of Colorado, 2016). Her older work, mainly poetry, can be found in such journals as *CALYX, Bamboo Ridge Quarterly, Seattle Review* and *Raven Chronicles*. In the mid-1990s, she served on CALYX Press' Young Women's Editorial Collective, with whom she co-edited *Present Tense: Writing and Art by Young Women*. She lives in Seattle, Washington. Shimabukuro: "'Momentary Comfort' was written when I was twenty years old, after an argument with a housemate."

Robert (Bob) Shimabukuro has been a writer/columnist/editor for the *Pacific Citizen, International Examiner* (Seattle's pan-Asian American newspaper), and *The Retiree Advocate Newsletter* (for Puget Sound Advocates for Retirement Action—PSARA). He was the (founding) executive director of Asian Pacific AIDS Council, and was a researcher and builder for the celebrated, 1992 exhibit, *E.O. 9066: Fifty Years Before and Fifty Years After* at the Wing Luke Asian Museum. He is the author of *Born in Seattle: The Campaign for Japanese American Redress* (University of Washington Press, 2001). He has been a volunteer in social justice work, including farm worker rights, anti-apartheid work, and Asian/Pacific Islander issues wherever he has resided, in Portland, Los Angeles, and Seattle. **Shimabukuro:** "'Glimpses' was written as part of a larger project, a mémoire of myself as a reflection of the relationships that were formed within my family. I was in my thirties when I decided on this structure. I wanted to focus on my dad who had an indelible impact on my mom and six siblings. But when my brother Sam told me he had AIDs, I immediately started writing and turned my attention to the relationship that Sam and I had built up over the years. I wanted to tell him how I felt about him, and to help me work through his dying so young. Sam was forty-four when he died."

Eddie Silva was born on a dairy farm in Sandpoint, Idaho. He studied at the University of Montana and University of Massachusetts-Amherst, where he studied with poets Richard Hugo, Patricia Goedicke, Dara Wier, and James Tate. He taught writing and literature at colleges and universities in Baltimore and St. Louis, was a poet-in-the-schools in Maryland, and, after more than a decade of itinerancy, settled in St. Louis more than twenty years ago. He was arts editor for the local alternative weekly, and for many years has been manager of publications, blogger, and video producer for the St. Louis Symphony. **Silva:** "One day someone asked, What would you most like to give your father? My father had a tough life, yet nevertheless managed to live decently and raise three kids and love our mother through sixty-two years of marriage. I thought of all the cowboy paraphernalia he kept around him and of how fondly he recalled summers herding cattle with his brother when they were teenagers in the Bears Paw Mountains of Montana. That old cowboy needed a horse. So I wrote him one in my poem, 'A Horse For My Father.'"

Ann Spiers is Vashon Island's inaugural poet laureate and current president of Vashon Audubon. She earned her M.A. in Literature and Creative Writing from the University of Washington. Her poems appear widely, including anthologies such as *Weathered Pages, New Poets of the American West, 500 Handmade Books,* and online in *Fire on her Tongue, A Sense of Place: NW Geospatial Poetry.* Her chapbooks include

Tide Turn, Volcano Blue, and *A Wild Taste* (May Day); *Long Climb into Grace* (FootHills); *The Herodotus Poems* (Brooding Heron); *What Rain Does* (Egress Studio); *Bunker Trail* (Finishing Line). **Spiers:** "The experience to create the poem, 'Dressing the Salmon Queen'—At Cape Alava, in November, winter winds detach and push its fulsome, annual seaweed growth to the beach. The seaweed has been shredded, and the billions of bits in red, brown, and green, form mounds three feet deep and six feet wide, stretching continuously from south of Cannonball Island (Tskawahyah) to the seastack at the trail head. The aroma of organics disintegrating and the mad dance of myriad isopods feeding are combined to sanctify the hike to the longhouse to leave an offering."

Marilyn Stablein is an award-winning poet, essayist, fiction writer, and mixed media artist whose sculptural artist's books, altered books, and performance art concern visual narrative, travelog, and memoir. She is author of fifteen books, including *Vermin: A Traveler's Bestiary; Houseboat on the Ganges & A Room in Kathmandu; Night Travels to Tibet; Sleeping in Caves: A Sixties Himalayan Memoir;* a collection of eco-essays set in the Northwest, *Climate of Extremes: Landscape and Imagination;* and *Splitting Hard Ground: Poems* (New Mexico Book Award). A former book critic for *The Seattle Times* and founding board member of Seattle Arts and Lectures, she received writing degrees from the University of Washington and the University of Houston. Her limited edition artist books are exhibited internationally and are in private and public collections. She is based in Portland, Oregon. **Stablein:** "In my twenties, two experiences in India shaped my awareness of the sanctity of water. When I lived on a houseboat docked at a popular bathing ghat on the Ganges, a constant stream of pilgrims bathed, washed clothes, and chanted just outside my door. Their fervor and devotion made a deep impression on me. During a drought in the mountains I had to carry water to drink and cook with. If you have to carry the water you use daily, you learn fast not to waste a precious drop. Water is heavy!"

JT Stewart (poet, writer, playwright, public artist, editor, teacher) co-founded the Clarion West SF Writers' Workshop in 1984. As a public artist, JT considers the following as representative of her work: poetry broadsides placed at the Seattle Art Museum, the Washington State Convention Center Galleries, and the Allen Library (University of Washington). She was Poetry Editor for *Seattle Poets and Photographers: A Millennium Reflection* (Seattle Arts Commission, 1999). JT has gotten grants from Artist Trust, 4Culture, and the NEH. Viewers can see her poetry broadsides in the permanent installation *Raven Brings Light To This House Of Stories* (Allen Library). She currently serves as a juror (one of eighty from five countries) for the yearly SOVAS Awards (Society of Voice Arts & Sciences). Stewart: "I got the inspiration for writing 'New Collossus' while teaching at the Fishtrap Writers Workshop in Walawa Lake, Oregon, where I taught a playwriting workshop and met Ed Edmo—the subject of my poem.

Barbara Earl Thomas is a Seattle-based, award-winning writer and visual artist with a career that spans more than thirty years. She is a graduate of the School of Art, University of Washington, where she received her Master of Arts in 1977. She counts herself most fortunate to have had mentorships with Michael Spafford and Jacob Lawrence who have both influenced her work. In 2013, Thomas received the Seattle Mayor's Arts Award and in 2016, the Washington State Governor's Arts Award, the Artist Trust Irving and Yvonne Twining Humber Award, and the Seattle Stranger Genius Award for excellence in the arts. She was nationally noted for her exhibition, *Heaven On Fire*, a major career survey with The Bainbridge Island Art Museum. In 2017, Thomas joined the Claire Oliver Gallery in New York with her solo exhibit, *Blood Letting and Other Stories*. As of 2018 she is working on Seattle Sound Transit's I-90 station commission and preparing for the September 2018 Expo Chicago. Through her art administrative work in agencies such as the Seattle Arts Commission and Bumbershoot, she has given time and energy in support of individual artists in all genres. She was the first executive director of the Northwest African American Museum, from 2008 to 2012, where she was instrumental in creating the agency and the broad-based support that it now sustains.

Stephen Thomas played his role in Seattle's poetry scene of the 80s, 90s and early 00s. He performed often at Red Sky Poetry Theater, at Bumbershoot, and many other regional venues, as well as farther afield. In 1984, he founded and built The Cabaret Hegel, where now an off-ramp leads I-5 traffic into the Industrial Flats. There Stephen presented and performed with many other Northwest writers and musicians, including Jesse Bernstein. He has published his work in many ephemeral magazines, as well as in *Exquisite Corpse, Poetry Northwest, The Malahat Review, Windfall, Malpais Review,* and others. His book, *Journeyman,* was published by Charles Potts' Tsunami Inc. He currently lives, writes, and performs in Germany. He has two new collections, *Jones, as is,* and *Bonfire,* which are looking for publishers. **Thomas:** " 'A Man Walks Into A Bar'—I was sitting in front of the fireplace in my friend Eddie Bell's house, while Michael Johnson, an old drinking buddy, with a Camel in one hand and a glass of Jack Daniels in the other, berated me for the superabundance of Twelve-Step Programs. I was newly sober, and, for Michael, accountable for Overeaters Anonymous, Gamblers Anonymous, Shoppers Anonymous, and every other Blank A in the book. As a poet I ought to know and maintain, he insisted, a narrow, precise definition of addiction. Just before my reading at Elliott Bay Books, I learned from Charlie Burks, I think, that Jesse Bernstein had taken his own life. It seemed right to me, then, to dedicate the poem to him.'Raingem'—At the time I wrote this poem, I was living in a shack on the eastern slope of Queen Anne. I would wake up typically at six or seven, as soon as the grip of the alcohol in my bloodstream let go of my brain, to a view of Lake Union. Being self-absorbed and composed largely of water, with a sprinkling of starlight, I've always been interested in what water does with light and vice versa. As far as I know, I coined the term raingem, that morning, and the poem followed."

Joyce Thompson is the author of six novels, two collections of stories, and a memoir, *Sailing My Shoe to Timbuktu: A Woman's Adventurous Search for Family, Spirit, and Love* (HarperCollins, 2003). She's taught writing in public schools, extension and M.F.A. programs, had a play produced, and owns a tech marketing business. She lives in Oakland, California, where the barrio meets the 'hood.

Gail Tremblay is an Onondaga/Mi'Kmaq poet, writer, teacher, and artist born in Buffalo, New York. After graduating from the University of New Hampshire with a B.A. in drama, she earned an M.F.A. in Creative Writing from the University of Oregon. She has been a member of the faculty at The Evergreen State College in Washington State since 1980, where she has mentored students in the fields of visual arts, writing, Native American and cultural studies. Tremblay is the author of four books of poetry: *Night Gives Women the Word* (1979), *Talking to the Grandfathers* (1981), *Indian Singing in Twentieth Century America* (Calyx Books, 1990, revised 1998), and *Farther From and Too Close to Home* (Lone Willow Press, 2014). Blending modern and traditional styles in both her writing and her artwork, Tremblay juxtaposes the modern Native American experience with tradition, placing emphasis on the encounters between past and present. Her poetry explores the isolation that accompanies cultural misunderstanding and centuries of oppression, and has been widely anthologized and translated into French, German, Spanish, and Japanese.

Arthur Tulee is a member of the Yakama Indian Nation. He has had his work published in Bumbershoot's literary anthology *ERGO!*, the *Artist Trust Newsletter*, *Northwest Ethnic News*, *Raven Chronicles*, and *upstream*. **Tulee:** "My family has been my biggest influence. We would always tell stories and stretch the truth. I wrote 'Plumes of White Rising' because I wanted to share with readers and listeners the visual of my homeland. The hills, valleys, vegetation, dust, cold nights, and strong sunshine that my people know well. I wanted to show the struggle we have moving forward, looking back, staying still. I wanted to put in the middle of all this, the Hanford Nuclear Reservation and its nuclear reactor cooling towers."

Nico Vassilakis wrestles letters to free them of their word scrum. Many of his results can be found online and on his website, *Staring Poetics: http://staringpoetics.weebly.com/*. His books include *Diesel Hand* (Chax Press, Letterpress, 2018), *In the Breast Pocket of a Fine Overcast Day* (CreateSpace, 2017), and *ALPHABET NOIR*, a book of texts about visual poetry (c_L Books, 2016). Nico is vispo editor for *COLDFRONT* online magazine: *http://coldfrontmag.com/category/vispo/*.

Ron Welburn is of Gingaskin Cherokee, Assateague, Lenape, and African American descent, and is the North American liaison for the Welburn-Gibbons Cherokees of Bermuda. He hold degrees from Lincoln University in Philadelphia and NYU's Program in American Civilization. He has taught at University of Massachusetts-Amherst for nearly thirty years, and served as director of the department's American

Studies Graduate Concentration, and co-founded and directed the Certificate Program in Native American Indian Studies (Anthropology). He has led teacher workshops and book discussions for the Five College Public School Partnership, state arts and humanities councils in New York, Connecticut, and Massachusetts, and for the Mashantucket Pequot Library and Research Center. His book reviews have appeared in *CHOICE*, *American Indian Culture and Research Journal*, and elsewhere. His seventh book of poems was *Council Decisions, Poems* (Revised and Expanded Edition, Bowman Books of the Greenfield Review Press, 2012).

David Lloyd Whited (January 28, 1951-November 30, 2014) was a storyteller and a Trickster. And a spellbinding interpreter/reader of his work to an audience. Whited was born and raised in Oregon's Umpqua Valley. He graduated from Bowling Green State University in 1976 with an M.F.A. in Poetry. First poet picked in the Distinguished Poets Series in Seattle's literary heyday, he authored numerous poetry books, including: *Three in One* (Red Sky Press); *Shadow Dance* and *Olde Man Coyote Goes to Towne* (nine muses books). Raven published several collaborations David created with artist Glenda Guilmet, for instance the "Shadow Dance Series," 1993. We also published numerous poems, including "Four Views of the Desert," "The Unemployment Line On Venus," and "Smart Bombs: A Euphemism For Lack Of Good Intelligence." David spent the bulk of his professional life as a planner for the Puyallup Tribe. He coauthored numerous ethnohistory articles and a monograph on the subject of health and mental health among the Puyallup Tribal community. David lived on Vashon Island with his wife Marian, four cats, eleven raccoons, and numerous other critters.

Susann Wilbur: "I'd been a writer and editor for most of my adult life when I stopped at a book fair in Seattle in the late nineties. A single, brightly lit room was tucked into one side of the cavernous space and filled with large display cases. As I circled them I was mesmerized, trying to understand what I was looking at. They were books—hand-cut, hand-folded, hand-painted, hand-printed on hand-made paper. 'Artist books' someone said. Some did look like books. Some looked more like sculptures. Some told stories or included poems, and some had just random words. I knew instantly that this was a most wonderful world to inhabit and I wanted very much to belong. Within months of my Seattle visit I found a door into this world, and with the help of my mentor, the late Gloria Helfgott, I learned how to tell a story with color and strokes and the movement of different papers made in Japan and India and Italy. The inspiration for writing 'The Twins From Tohoku'—Many years ago, I read a story translated from a Japanese newspaper about the confession of a man who had adopted young children in order to take advantage of them sexually. I was particularly haunted by the item, especially as we were living in the aftermath of the McMartin Preschool frenzy. The primary inspiration, however, was my need to examine hatred and celebrate 'otherness.' I grew up in an immigrant family with distinct cultural and linguistic differences. My children grew up in a very different multicultural and multilingual family, and it has made them perceptive, tolerant, curious, and extremely thoughtful people."

Carletta Carrington Wilson is a visual and literary artist. Her poems have been published in *Calyx Journal, Make It True: Poems from Cascadia, Cimarron Review, Obsidian III, The Seattle Review, Raven Chronicles, Beyond the Frontier: African American Poetry for the 21st Century, The Journal: Book Club of Washington, Pilgrimage, Uncommon Waters: Women Write About Fishing*, and *Seattle Poets and Photographers: A Millennium Reflection*, and online in *Rattapallax: Innovative Northwest Poets* and *Torch*. **Wilson:** "On creating 'Iconography of the Slain'—I persist in creating works in which I attempt to 'see through time.' In particular, I try to return to a historical moment in which a lived experience is revisited. It is astounding how individuals, somehow, survive catastrophic events. For a time, I would wonder how and why one person survived when so many around them succumbed to the tragic events of their time like war, famine, and disease. Enslavement is one such occurrence. Of the countless accounts describing the transatlantic slave trade, the voices describing people, places, and experiences are male, both African and European. I wanted to explore the forces that were at work in the captivity of a young woman in that luminal stage between childhood and womanhood. And she, alone in the world, will survive as death haunts every breath."

Roy D. Wilson is Executive Director of the Institute for Community Leadership, located in Kent, Washington. He holds an Ed.D. in Educational Leadership and Change from Fielding Graduate University, and an M.A. in Creative Writing and a B.A. in English both from the University of Washington. Wilson is a published author, scholar, and presenter on civil rights, nonviolence, and liberatory leadership practices. He has served as director of various non-governmental entities including Seattle Managua Sister City Association, International Relations Director for El Centro de la Raza, and founder of the Institute for Community Leadership and the Jack Hunter O'Dell Education Center. Roy has received international, state, and regional awards for his work in civil rights and confronting racial and socio-economic disparities. He is widely published and his work has been featured in *Life Magazine*, *The New York Times*, *The Washington Post*, *Miami Herald*, *The Seattle Times*, *Oakland Tribune*, in a national Public Radio TV Special, *The United States of Poetry*, and a National television feature on the Nickelodeon Network.

Don Wilsun (June 1, 1946-May 8, 2003) was born in New Orleans to a large Cajun family and died in Seattle, Washington. Wilsun attended McNeese State University in Lake Charles and served in the Peace Corps in Morocco; he arrived in Seattle in the 1960s as a VISTA volunteer. Wilsun, who previously co-founded Dogtown Poetry Theater with Joe Scozzy, was a driving force in the founding of Red Sky Poetry Theatre (RSPT). Along with Joe Keppler, Tom Parson (who also started the Bumbershoot Small Press Fair in 1977), and Judith Roche, whose home was used as a meeting place, Wilsun formed the core of what would become RSPT. Prior to forming RSPT, Wilsun held ad hoc readings which were simply called Poetry Theatre. He named his labor of love, "Red Sky," because one day he was putting up flyers in the Pike Place Market and, as he was doing so, saw an amazing red sunset; he wrote a poem called "Red Sky." The first reading was on May 24, 1981. Poetry books: *Orcas Island, Sing Sundancer, Love and Waste, Frog Legs, Sweet Skin*, and *Lynchings*. Audio Recording: *Fish Bones* (1989). Theatrical: *Tropic of Cedar*.

Elizabeth Woody is an enrolled member of the Confederate Tribes of Warm Springs in Oregon, and was born in Ganado, Arizona. She studied at the Institute of American Indian Arts in Santa Fe, New Mexico, and earned a B.A. in the humanities from The Evergreen State College in Olympia, Washington, and a M.A. in Public Administration from the Hatfield School of Government at Portland State University. Her collections of poetry include *Hand into Stone* (1988, reprinted as *Seven Hands, Seven Hearts: Prose and Poetry*, 1994), winner of the American Book Award from the Before Columbus Foundation, and *Luminaries of the Humble* (University of Arizona Press, 1994). A practicing artist, Woody also illustrated Sherman Alexie's poetry collection *Old Shirts and New Skins* (1993). Woody worked as a program coordinator for the National Science Foundation's Center for Coastal Margin Observation & Prediction; she is a founding member of the Northwest Native American Writers Association and a board member of Soapstone, a writing retreat for women. In 2017 she was named the eighth Poet Laureate of the state of Oregon.

Qiu Xiaolong was born in Shanghai, China. He published prize-winning poetry, translation, and criticism in Chinese in the 80s, and became a member of the Chinese Writers' Association. In 1988, he came to the United States as a Ford Foundation Fellow, started writing in English, and obtained a Ph.D. in comparative literature at Washington University. He is the author of *Death of a Red Heroine* (2000), *A Loyal Character Dancer* (2002), *When Red Is Black* (2004), *A Case of Two Cities* (2006), Red Mandarin Dress (2007), *The Mao Case* (2009), *Don't Cry, Tai Lake* (2012), *Shanghai Redemption* (2015), and *Becoming Inspector Chen* (in French and Italian, 2016 and 2017)—the critically acclaimed, award-winning Inspector Chen series. His own poetry collections include *Lines Around China* (2003) and *Poems of Inspector Chen* (2016). Qiu's books have sold over two million copies worldwide and have been published in twenty languages. He currently lives in St. Louis with his wife and daughter.

Janet Yoder lives with her husband on their Seattle houseboat, the floating nation of Tui Tui. Her writing has appeared in *Bayou, Porcupine, Passager, The MacGuffin, North Dakota Quarterly, The Evansville Review,*

The Massachusetts Review, Pilgrimage, River Teeth, and *Chautauqua.* She is currently at work on a collection of personal essays inspired by her friendship with Skagit tribal elder, the late Vi Hilbert. **Yoder:** "On writing 'River Talk with Vi Hilbert'—In the fall of 1978, I walked into a classroom on the second floor of Denny Hall at the University of Washington and met Vi Hilbert, elder of the Upper Skagit tribe. Vi was teaching her language—Lushootseed. Lushootseed is the language of Puget Sound. Lushootseed is the language Chief Seattle spoke here 150 years ago. Lushootseed is the language his ancestors spoke here for hundreds of years. Though people have spoken Lushootseed longer than people have spoken English, Lushootseed nearly died and was saved largely by the work of Vi Hilbert. Vi's wake-up call came when linguist Thom Hess asked for her help. He was working with an elder named Louise George who had told him Vi might remember Lushootseed, her childhood language. Vi told him she did not remember it, but he asked her to come to his work session anyway. Vi came, heard the old recordings of her relatives, and found she did, indeed, remember Lushootseed. She spent the rest of her life researching, preserving, and sharing the Lushootseed language, stories, and culture. So Vi found her right work, work that came down to her like a gift. Right now, writing about Vi is my right work."

BIOGRAPHICAL NOTES
Foreword

Claudia Castro Luna served as Seattle's first Civic Poet from 2015-2017, and has been appointed the fifth Washington State Poet Laureate. Luna's term will run from February 1, 2018 to January 31, 2020. As the first immigrant and woman of color to assume the role of State Poet Laureate, she will be advocating for poetry during a particularly fraught period for both the humanities (the current administration proposed eliminating the National Endowments for the Arts and Humanities last year) and immigrant populations, who are confronting uncertainty in the face of travel bans and heated rhetoric. Luna is the author of *This City* (Floating Bridge Press, 2016) and *Killing Marias* (Two Sylvias Press, 2017). She is a Hedgebrook and VONA alumna, the recipient of a King County 4Culture grant, and a Jack Straw Fellow. Born in El Salvador, she came to the United States in 1981. She has an M.F.A. in poetry, an M.A. in Urban Planning, and a K-12 teaching certificate. Her poems have appeared in *Poetry Northwest, La Bloga, City Arts, Taos Journal of International Poetry and Art,* among others. Her non-fiction work can be read in the anthologies *The Wandering Song: Central American Writing in the United States* (Tia Chucha Press, 2017); *Vanishing Points: Contemporary Salvadoran Narrative* (Kalina Eds); and in *This Is The Place: Women Writing About Home* (Seal Press, 2017). Living in English and Spanish, Luna writes and teaches in Seattle, where she gardens and keeps chickens with her husband and their three children.

BIOGRAPHICAL NOTES
EDITORS

Kathleen Alcalá is the author of a short story collection, three novels set in 19th century Mexico and the Southwest, and a collection of essays based on family history. Her work has received the Western States Book Award, the Governor's Writers Award, and a Pacific Northwest Booksellers Association Book Award. She received her second Artist Trust Fellowship in 2008, and was honored by the national Latino writers group, Con Tinta, at the Associated Writing Programs Conference in 2014. She has been designated an Island Treasure in the Arts. Kathleen's latest book is *The Deepest Roots: Finding Food and Community on a Pacific Northwest Island*, University of Washington Press, 2016.

Phoebe Bosché is a cultural activist, and has been managing editor of The Raven Chronicles literary organization/Raven Chronicles Press since 1991. Since 1984, she has organized literary events and readings in the Pacific Northwest. In 1985, she co-founded, along with poet Roberto Valenza, "Alternative To Loud Boats," a literary and musical festival which ran for ten years in various venues in Seattle. She was co-editor of *Swale Magazine* (with Valenza) and *Sky Views*, a monthly literary publication of Red Sky Poetry Theater, in the mid-1980s to early 1990s. Her spoken word poems appear in various publications, including the anthology *Durable Breath, Contemporary Native American Poetry*, Salmon Run Publishing Co., Anchorage, Alaska, and *Open Sky*. She is a full-time editor and book designer. Her favorite poet is Archy, the cockroach, whose muse is Mehitabel, the alley cat.

Paul Hunter has published fine letterpress poetry under the imprint of Wood Works Press since 1994: twenty-six books and over sixty broadsides. His poems have appeared in *Alaska Fisherman's Journal, Beloit Poetry Journal, Bloomsbury Review, Iowa Review, North American Review, Poetry, Poetry Northwest, Prairie Schooner, Raven Chronicles, The Small Farmer's Journal, The Southern Review, Spoon River Poetry Review*, and *Windfall*, as well as in seven full-length books and three chapbooks. His first collection of farming poems, *Breaking Ground*, Silverfish Review Press, 2004, was reviewed in *The New York Times*, and received the 2004 Washington State Book Award. A second volume of farming poems, *Ripening*, was published in 2007, a third, *Come the Harvest*, in 2008, and the fourth, *Stubble Field*, in 2012, all from Silverfish Review Press. He has been a featured poet on *The News Hour*, and has a prose book on small-scale, sustainable farming, *One Seed to Another: The New Small Farming*, published by the Small Farmer's Journal. His new book of prose poetry, *Clownery, In lieu of a life spent in harness*, was published in 2017 by Davila Art & Books, Sisters, Oregon.

Stephanie Lawyer grew up in Mexico and has lived and worked in the U.S., the UK, and Asia. She edited in-house for Secker & Warburg in London, and Little, Brown in Boston, and worked for more than a decade in Hong Kong as a freelance editor and literary agent. Since moving to the West Coast in 1995, she has judged fiction for the Kiriyama Book Prize, edited the prize's online magazine, the *WaterBridge Review*, and worked with *Raven Chronicles* as an editor and a board member. Stephanie is currently an independent editor based in Albuquerque, New Mexico, with an interest in literary fiction, nonfiction, and translation. She is developing an online project, *http://per-e-gren.org*, a collaboration of emerging immigrant writers and literary translators working in Spanish and English.

ACKNOWLEDGMENTS

Raven is indebted to our 2018 co-sponsors for partial funding of our programs: the Seattle Office of Arts & Culture (Civic Partners); 4Culture/King County Lodging Tax (Arts Sustained Support Program). Special thanks to the Washington State Arts Commission/ArtsWA, with National Endowment (NEA) funding for project support for this anthology. And to all Raven subscribers and donors over the past twenty-seven years. Special thanks to Jack Straw Cultural Center, and Joan Rabinowitz, for support of our Raven reading series, from 1997-2017. And thanks to the generosity of Anonymous, Alfredo Arrequín, Minnie A. Collins, Carl Chew, Larry Eickstaedt, Robert Flor, Larry Laurence, Lawrence Matsuda, John Mifsud, Kevin Miller, and Pamela Mills, for their generous donations in support of Raven publications and programs in 2018.

Founded in 1991

PUBLISHER
Raven Chronicles Press,
501(c)(3) Organization

MANAGING DIRECTOR
PHOEBE BOSCHÉ, SEATTLE

FOUNDERS
KATHLEEN ALCALÁ
PHOEBE BOSCHÉ
PHILIP RED EAGLE

ANTHOLOGY EDITORS
KATHLEEN ALCALÁ
PHOEBE BOSCHÉ
PAUL HUNTER
STEPHANIE LAWYER
WITH
MATT BRIGGS
TIFFANY MIDGE

COPY EDITORS
KATHLEEN ALCALÁ, PHOEBE BOSCHÉ,
PAUL HUNTER, LARRY LAURENCE, ANNA MOCKLER,
STEPHANIE LAWYER, ANN SPIERS

CPSIA information can be obtained
at www.ICGtesting.com
Printed in the USA
FSHW022356021118
53512FS

9 780997 946857